STUDIES IN EARLY MODERN CULTURAL,
POLITICAL AND SOCIAL HISTORY

Volume 24

DOMESTIC CULTURE IN EARLY MODERN ENGLAND

Studies in Early Modern Cultural, Political and Social History

ISSN: 1476-9107

Series editors

Tim Harris – Brown University
Stephen Taylor – Durham University
Andy Wood – Durham University

Previously published titles in the series
are listed at the back of this volume

DOMESTIC CULTURE
IN EARLY MODERN ENGLAND

Antony Buxton

THE BOYDELL PRESS

First published 2015
The Boydell Press, Woodbridge

ISBN 978-1-78327-041-5

The Boydell Press is an imprint of Boydell & Brewer Ltd
PO Box 9, Woodbridge, Suffolk IP12 3DF, UK
and of Boydell & Brewer Inc.
668 Mt Hope Avenue, Rochester, NY 14620-2731, USA
website: www.boydellandbrewer.com

A catalogue record for this book is available
from the British Library

The publisher has no responsibility for the continued existence or accuracy of
URLs for external or third-party internet websites referred to in this book, and
does not guarantee that any content on such websites is, or will remain, accurate
or appropriate

This publication is printed on acid-free paper

Printed and bound in Great Britain by
TJ International Ltd, Padstow, Cornwall

FSC
www.fsc.org
MIX
Paper from
responsible sources
FSC® C013056

In fond memory of my parents, Edmund and Katherine

Contents

CONTENTS

Illustrations

Figures

FIGURES

The images from Johann Amos Commenius, *Orbis Sensualium Pictus* (London, 1672) are reproduced from the 1967 facsimile edition published by Sydney University Press.

If not otherwise stated, images are by the author

The author and publishers are grateful to all the institutions and individuals listed for permission to reproduce the materials in which they hold copyright. Every effort has been made to trace the copyright holders; apologies are offered for any omission, and the publishers will be pleased to add any necessary acknowledgement in subsequent editions

Tables

Additional tables referred to in the footnotes can be found at http://
boybrew.co/9781783270415. The online appendices consist of:

Abbreviations

Bodleian Library Collections, University of Oxford	Bod
Oxfordshire History Centre Archives (Oxfordshire County Council)	OHCA
Oxford English Dictionary	*OED*
Mary Lobel, ed., *A History of the County of Oxford: Volume 7, Dorchester and Thame Hundreds*, Victoria County History (London, Institute for Historical Research, 1962)	VCH

Note on Currency

Values given in the probate inventories and wills were in pounds (£), shillings (s) and pence (d). (12 pence constitute 1 shilling, 20 shillings 1 pound). In this study the £ s d denomination was converted into a decimal value for the sake of calculation and appears as such in the text. Where values are derived directly from the original document they are expressed in £ s d.

Preface

This study is based on doctoral research carried out at the Department for Continuing Education at the University of Oxford. A career prior to academia in the conservation and restoration of historic furniture had already generated my interest in the relationship between people and the objects with which they enact their lives and social relationships, especially in the domestic context. Significant in the development of my knowledge in this area were conversations with authorities of the British vernacular furniture tradition, Bernard Cotton, and of early modern oak furniture, Victor Chinnery, whose work has been drawn on substantially for this study. Victor's early death has been a great loss to that area of study. I have been immensely fortunate to deliver courses for the Department for Continuing Education on both domestic and international programmes, initially in furniture history, but latterly focussed on all aspects of domestic life in Britain in the modern period. I am grateful to the many students who have enthusiastically shared in the exploration of these themes over the past fifteen years, and the stimulating exchanges with departmental colleagues.

It was out of one such class that the suggestion arose of the possibilities of probate inventories as a rich source of information on the mainly non-elite material culture of the early modern period. The inventories from the peculiar archdeaconry court of Thame presented a highly suitable body of data for a microstudy, rich in material and contextual detail and consistent in compilation, spanning the seventeenth century and located in an Oxfordshire community which experienced on a local scale many of the major economic and social developments of the early modern period. Mary Hodges was a valued and supportive guide to the data, having led a group of local historians transcribing inventories, wills and other court records, and whose work has proved of great value to this study. Initial researches resulted in an article in the journal *Oxoniensia* (2002) exploring the social use of space through the distribution of furniture in the early part of the seventeenth century. As editor of the journal, Adrienne Rosen provided invaluable assistance in the production of that piece, and when Malcolm Airs had suggested doctoral research as a way of progressing and broadening the inquiry Adrienne generously also agreed to supervise the study. I am extremely grateful for her attempts to instil historical perspectives and methodology. I have drawn on the expertise of David Clark and Paul Barnwell for advice on vernacular building. Under the enthusiastic direction of Jeffrey Thomas, the Department for Continuing Education provided friendly support throughout, and Kellogg College not only a place to share the experience with other doctoral students but also generous financial assistance. Special thanks are due to Ian Miller and David Baker at Oxford University IT (Computing) Services, without whose patient advice and assistance in the effective construction of the Access database this study would simply not have been possible. Within the university the staff of the libraries that I have used – the faculty libraries for history, and social and cultural anthropology, and the Rewley House and Bodleian libraries – have all been unfailingly helpful, and staff at the Oxfordshire History Centre have also always provided great assistance.

During the course of the study it became evident that effective interpretative perspectives might be those developed in the archaeological and anthropological study of material culture. Chris Gosden provided crucial interest in the potential of applying archaeological methodology to textual assemblages of objects associated in place and through time, and I owe great gratitude to Dan Hicks for generously agreeing to oversee the study, doing his best to introduce a sound theoretical base and crucially insisting that the study could be most effective on a localised scale. The theoretical journey was also greatly enriched by discussions at the Institute of Archaeology's Materiality Discussion Group, organised by Linda Hulin and Zena Kamash. Gary Lock meticulously guided the final stages of the doctoral research with great generosity and enthusiasm.

I am extremely grateful to Michael Middeke and to Boydell and Brewer for their assessment of the worth of this study, and especially to Megan Milan for patiently guiding a sometimes intractable author. Jessica Cuthbert-Smith has provided a meticulous final revision of the text. Lastly I owe a great debt of gratitude to Annie for her unfailing support during the preparation of this volume. Without those mentioned here, and many others who through chance conversations or the suggestion of fruitful approaches enriched the research, this study would not have reached a conclusion. To them belongs much of the credit for any worth it may have; any shortcomings are entirely mine.

Introduction

This book is a study of domestic life in early modern England. More specifically, its chief focus is a detailed account of the daily life of largely non-elite households of the market town of Thame in Oxfordshire through the seventeenth century, drawn from the evidence of probate inventories. But in addition the work examines the manner in which domestic life operated within and was influenced by the wider local and national culture, and also seeks to address the wider consideration of the significance of domestic life in the historical narrative and the manner in which the totality of domestic culture might best be theorised, interpreted and analysed.

The Historiography of Domesticity

The home place is central to the experience and identity of the individual and of the domestic group, and thus arguably should enjoy a significant place within historical inquiry. As Fernand Braudel has argued, the discernible developments of the past were constructed on the myriad of events which constituted daily life, an understanding of which becomes essential to a true reading of the historical totality.[1] The larger historical narrative is thus significantly founded on the mundane events of everyday life, and everyday life itself influenced by external events and circumstances. This being so, it might be assumed that the home has featured significantly in historical inquiry and literature. Whilst this is the case for some elements of domestic life (and this is especially true of the early modern period, when the household was seen as the fundamental building block of civil society),[2] the non-elite home itself and the operation of domestic life have not until recently featured as significant foci of the historical narrative. This may well be because domestic life consists of such a wide range of manifestations

[1] F. Braudel, *Civilization and Capitalism 15th to 18th Century: Volume 1, The Structures of Everyday Life: The Limits of the Possible* (London: Collins, 1979/1981), p. 29
[2] See, for example, Keith Wrightson, *Earthly Necessities: Economic Lives in Early Modern Britain 1470–1750* (London: Penguin Books, 2000/2002) especially chapters 1 and 2

– as physical structure of the dwelling and its furnishings and ornamentation, as a social group and the setting for social discourse, and as a place of production and consumption – that as a totality it does not lend itself to neat accommodation within any one strand of historical inquiry. The use of a particular form of evidence – documentary and textual, pictorial, architectural or artefactual – demands a distinct methodology and thus has a tendency to prescribe the extent of an inquiry. The initial emphasis of historical inquiry towards large movements and elite cultures was inimical to an interest in the minutiae of the mundane.[3] The use of evidence drawn from the domestic domain has therefore tended to be selective and serving the purposes of an inquiry focussed elsewhere rather than on the domestic unit per se. This discussion of the historiographical context of domesticity focusses on the early modern period, but arguably similar observations could be made of earlier and later periods.

Historical inquiry thus has tended towards specialisms of period and evidential focus – political, social and economic – and more evidentially defined aspects such as architecture and art, and recent additions such as histories of gender and of race. Of these, social history has had particular recourse to the evidence provided by domestic life. Studies of elite culture have often incorporated the elite home as the context of the display of status and social and political negotiation, corresponding with Levi-Strauss's identification of the physical structure of the house with biological entity.[4] The focus on elite culture has also been expressed in studies of domestic architecture and interior decoration,[5] and Mark Girouard's *Life in the English Country House* (1987) stands as a masterly account of the relationship of architecture space and social conduct.[6] Historical biographies and studies of the elite have also employed genealogy to describe the importance of consanguineal and marital domestic relationships in the establishment

---

[3] J. H. Plumb argues that Western historiography grew out of a desire to comprehend the influence and circumstances of conflicting ideologies. J. H. Plumb *The Death of the Past* (London: Macmillan, 1969), pp. 102–45. However, during the early twentieth century the influence of psychology and sociology created a greater awareness of the operation of symbolism and ritual in social life (Johan Huizinga, *The Waning of the Middle Ages*, 1924). The foundation in 1929 by Lucien Lefebvre and Marc Bloch of *Annales d'Histoire Economique et Sociale* provided an impetus for a greater emphasis on the interrelationship between economic circumstance and social relationships, especially in the work of Fernand Braudel.
[4] C. Lévi-Strauss, *Anthropology and Myth: Lectures, 1951–1982*, trans. R. Willis (Oxford: Basil Blackwell, 1987), p. 151. See, for example, D. N. Durant, *Bess of Hardwick: Portrait of an Elizabethan Dynast*, rev. edn (London: Peter Owen, 1999) and M. Girouard, *Hardwick Hall* (London: National Trust, 1989). The many National Trust guidebooks dedicated to specific historical country houses also provide scholarly accounts of both house and inhabitants.
[5] For example Jeremy Musson, Roy Strong and Paul Barker, *English Country House Interiors* (New Haven and London: Yale University Press, 1978)
[6] Mark Girouard, *Life in the English Country House* (New Haven and London: Yale University Press, 1978)

and maintenance of social status.[7] At a non-elite level, studies of marital strategies and kinship have drawn on parish records of baptisms, marriages and funerals, testamentary evidence and contemporary written accounts. For example, Ralph Houlbrooke's *The English Family 1450–1700* (1984) and *English Family Life 1576–1716* (1988) provide a detailed survey of the experience of early modern relationships in the home (albeit often from elite sources), Jeremy Boulton's *Neighbourhood and Society* (1987) a rich portrait of neighbourhood society in seventeenth-century Southwark, within which the households were situated, Naomi Tadmoor has explored the complex dynamic of the early modern 'household family' (1996), and Keith Wrightson's *Earthly Necessities* (2000) and *English Society 1580–1680* (1982) the role of the household in the wider early modern social and economic narrative.[8] Historical demography has drawn on parish records in wider studies of population dynamics which reveal the composition of the early modern household.[9]

This growth of interest in non-elite domesticity has also been manifested in studies of vernacular architecture, with an emphasis on materials, techniques and regional variations and traditions; for example Maurice Barley's *The English Farmhouse and Cottage* (1961) explored regional variations in domestic vernacular forms, a study developed in Brunskill's *Houses and Cottages of Britain* (1997).[10] An exploration of the material fabric has also resulted in a greater understanding of the social dynamics giving rise to architectural expression and change, particularly W. G. Hoskins's concept of a 'Great Rebuilding' of vernacular homes in the early modern period – resulting from a changing economic context – and the debate it engendered.[11] The development of local historiography has further engaged the

[7] Lawrence Stone and Jeanne C. Fawtier, *An Open Elite? England, 1540–1880* (Oxford: Clarendon Press, 1995)
[8] Ralph A. Houlbrooke, *The English Family 1450–1700* (London: Longman, 1984); Ralph A. Houlbrooke, *English Family Life, 1576–1716: An Anthology from Diaries* (Oxford: Basil Blackwell, 1988); J. Boulton, *Neighbourhood and Society: A London Suburb in the Seventeenth Century* (Cambridge and New York: Cambridge University Press, 1987); N. Tadmoor, 'The Concept of Household-Family in Eighteenth Century England', *Past and Present* 151 (May 1996), 111–40; Wrightson, *Earthly Necessities*, especially chapters 1 and 2; Keith Wrightson, *English Society 1580–1680* (Abingdon: Routledge, 2003). Further examples are: Lawrence Stone, *Family, Sex and Marriage in England 1500–1800* (London: Weidenfeld and Nicolson, 1977); Richard Wall, Peter Laslett and Jean Robin, *Family Forms in Historic Europe* (Cambridge: Cambridge University Press, 1983); Mary Abbott, *Family Ties: English Families 1540–1920* (London: Routledge, 1993)
[9] Peter Laslett and Richard Wall, eds, *Household and Family in Past Time* (Cambridge: Cambridge University Press, 1972)
[10] M. W. Barley, *The English Farmhouse and Cottage* (London: Routledge & Kegan Paul, 1961); R. W. Brunskill, *Houses and Cottages of Britain: Origins and Development of Traditional Domestic Design* (London: Victor Gollancz, 1997)
[11] W. G. Hoskins, 'The Rebuilding of Rural England, 1570–1640', *Past and Present* 4 (1953), 44–59; R. Machin, 'The Great Rebuilding: A Reassessment', *Past and Present* 77 (November 1977), 33–56; C. R. J. Currie, 'Time and Chance: Modelling the Attrition of Old Houses',

household as a key component of communities, both social and economic, of which Wrightson and Levine's *Poverty and Piety in an English Village: Terling 1525–1700* (1979) is a good example.[12] Accounts can often be descriptive rather than analytical – on a large scale the Victoria County History publications are the most notable cases – and tend to focus on the structure and dynamic of the community rather than that of the household.[13] An exception is Alcock's comprehensive survey which, thanks to a rich range of evidence, brings together both the built structures and the social culture of the village of Stoneleigh in Warwickshire in the early modern period.[14] Non-elite households have featured particularly in economic histories, identifying them as key locations of early modern economic production and consumption. Overton, Whittle, Dean and Hann's study *Production and Consumption in English Households, 1600–1750* (2004) examines the household as the locus of early modern production and consumption in Kent and Cornwall, whilst Jane Whittle's 'The House as a Place of Work in Early Modern Rural England' (2011) focusses on its economically productive role.[15] Lorna Weatherill's extensive survey *Consumer Behaviour and Material Culture in Britain 1660–1760* (1988) and Carol Shammas's *The Industrial Pre-consumer in England and America* (1990) both engage with the home as the place of consumption,[16] whilst Craig Muldrew's *The Economy of Obligation* (1988) explores the reinforcement of household economic interests through peer social relationships in this period.[17] And this developing focus on non-elite domestic material culture is explored in its social and affective context in Richardson and Hamling's *Everyday Objects: Medieval and Early Modern Material Culture and its Meanings* (2010) and Amanda Vickery's *Early Modern Things: Objects and Their Histories, 1500–1800* (2012).[18]

Vernacular Architecture 19 (1988), 1–9; C. King, '"Closure" and the Urban Great Rebuilding in Early Modern Norwich', *Post-Medieval Archaeology* 44:1 (2010), 54–80; M. Johnson, 'Rethinking the Great Rebuilding', *Oxford Journal of Archaeology* 12:1 (1993), 117–25

[12] K. Wrightson, and D. Levine, *Poverty and Piety in an English Village: Terling 1525–1700* (New York: Academic Press, 1979)

[13] J. M. Bestall, *History of Chesterfield* (Chesterfield: Borough of Chesterfield, 1974) is but one example of very many local histories which have made a meticulous record of the local past. The Victoria County Histories (VCH) project has made accessible a vast amount of detailed evidence of the local past, on which this study has drawn.

[14] N. W. Alcock, *People at Home: Living in a Warwickshire Village 1500–1800* (Chichester: Phillimore, 1993)

[15] M. Overton, J. Whittle, D. Dean and A. Hann, *Production and Consumption in English Households, 1600–1750* (London: Routledge, 2004); Jane Whittle, 'The House as a Place of Work in Early Modern Rural England', *Home Cultures* 8:2 (July 2011), 133–50

[16] L. Weatherill, *Consumer Behaviour and Material Culture in Britain 1660–1760* (London: Routledge, 1988); C, Shammas, *The Industrial Pre-Consumer in England and America* (Oxford: Clarendon Press, 1990)

[17] Craig Muldrew, *The Economy of Obligation : The Culture of Credit and Social Relations in Early Modern England* (Basingstoke: Macmillan, 1998)

[18] C. Richardson and T. Hamling, eds, *Everyday Objects: Medieval and Early Modern Material*

Economic histories make considerable use of the goods listed in probate inventories, and this source of evidence – by one reckoning consisting of approximately one million inventories in archives across the country[19] – has proved a rich source of evidence for early modern local historians; Havinden's *Household and Farm Inventories in Oxfordshire 1550–90* (1965), Steer's *Farm and Cottage Inventories of Mid-Essex 1635–1749* (1969), Alcock's *People at Home: Living in a Warwickshire Village 1500–1800* (1993), Priestly, Corfield and Sutermeister's 'Rooms and Room Use in Norwich Housing, 1580–1730' (1982), Brown's 'Continuity and Change in the Urban House: Developments in Domestic Space Organisation in 17th-Century London' (1986) and Earle's *The Making of the English Middle Class: Business, Society and Family Life in London, 1660–1730* (1989), amongst many others.[20] The value of probate inventories as historical evidence and their analysis will be examined further below.

Early modern historiography therefore tends to focus selectively on the domestic domain as the seat of elite social culture, as an architectural expression, as the key unit in biological and social reproduction, and as the locus of economic production and consumption. This evidence and such studies greatly enhance understanding of historical processes of the period, but provide a limited comprehension of the total and multifaceted domestic context from which such evidence is derived. Studies of domestic life set within the interpretive framework of historical geography do place greater emphasis on the role of the physical, economic and cultural environment, for example Blunt and Dowling's *Home* (2006).[21] The interlinked nature of the various components of domestic culture – material and spatial, social and conceptual – is, however, embraced within ethnographic or anthropological and by extension historical archaeology studies, focussing on the material evidence significantly enhanced by testamentary and documentary records, thus drawing together various strands of complementary evidence. The association made by Levi-Strauss between the physical domicile and the

---

Culture and its Meanings (Aldershot: Ashgate, 2010); Amanda Vickery, *Early Modern Things: Objects and their Histories, 1500–1800* (London: Routledge, 2012)

[19] T. Arkell, 'Interpreting Probate Inventories', *When Death Do Us Part: Understanding and Interpreting the Probate Records of Early Modern England*, ed. T. Arkell, N. Evans and N. Goose (Oxford: Leopard's Head Press, 2000), p. 72

[20] M. A. Havinden, *Household and Farm Inventories in Oxfordshire 1550–90* (London: HMSO, 1965); F. W. Steer, *Farm and Cottage Inventories of Mid-Essex 1635–1749* (London and Chichester: Phillimore, 1969); Alcock, *People at Home*; U. Priestly, P. J. Corfield and H. Sutermeister, 'Rooms and Room Use in Norwich Housing, 1580–1730', *Post-Medieval Archaeology* 16 (1982), 93–123; F. E. Brown, 'Continuity and Change in the Urban House: Developments in Domestic Space Organisation in 17th-Century London', *Comparative Studies in Society and History* 28 (1986), 558–90; P. Earle, *The Making of the English Middle Class: Business, Society and Family Life in London, 1660–1730* (London: Methuen, 1989)

[21] A. Blunt and R. Dowling, *Home* (London: Routledge, 2006). See also J. Stobart and A. Owens, eds, *Urban Fortunes: Property and Inheritance in the Town, 1700–1900* (Aldershot: Ashgate, 2000); Brown, 'Continuity and Change'

biological unit has already been mentioned, and Carsten and Hugh Jones's *About the House: Levi-Strauss and Beyond* (1995) furthers this association of the physical, social and conceptual within the home, whilst Ian Hodder's *The Domestication of Europe* (1990) theorises the conceptual basis of domesticity from the archaeological record.[22] The exploration of domestic life from archaeological and anthropological perspectives is further demonstrated by the collected volumes *The Archaeology of Household Activities* (edited by Penelope Allison, 1999) and *At Home: An Anthropology of Domestic Space* (edited by Irene Cieraad, 1999).[23]

Historical Ethnography

Whilst suggesting that anthropological and archaeological perspectives might be of value to historical inquiry, it should be emphasised that such a dialogue is not new. In the mid-twentieth century a rapprochement was sought between disciplines which, it was argued, were distinct in technique and scale rather than aim. Anthropology, argued Keith Thomas, does not, as in much historical inquiry segregate human activity into distinct spheres but seeks to explain social phenomena by reference to their wider context, and in so doing also touches on intimate and conceptual areas of daily life then largely neglected by the historian.[24] Thomas himself employed functionalist anthropological perspectives on belief in his seminal study, *Religion and the Decline of Magic* (1971),[25] and the breadth of anthropological contextualisation has latterly been employed in some local histories.[26] For historians, documentary evidence is the primary window into the past,

---

[22] Lévi-Strauss, *Anthropology and Myth*; J. Carsten and S. Hugh-Jones, eds, *About the House: Levi-Strauss and Beyond* (Cambridge: Cambridge University Press, 1995); I. Hodder, *The Domestication of Europe* (Oxford: Blackwell, 1990)

[23] Penelope M. Allison, ed., *The Archaeology of Household Activities* (New York: Routledge, 1999); Irene Cieraad, ed., *At Home: An Anthropology of Domestic Space* (Syracuse: Syracuse University Press, 1999)

[24] Keith Thomas, 'History and Anthropology', *Past and Present* 24 (1963), 3–24, B. Axel 'Introduction: Historical Anthropology and its Vicissitudes', *From the Margins: Historical Anthropology and its Futures*, ed. B. Axel (Durham and London: Duke University Press, 2002). The interrelation between history and anthropology was debated in the early 1960s, both historians and anthropologists proposing and opposing a convergence of methodologies. E. E. Evans-Pritchard, *Anthropology and History* (Manchester: Manchester University Press, 1961); Isaac Schapera, 'Should Anthropologists be Historians?', *Journal of the Royal Anthropological Institute of Great Britain and Ireland* 92 (1962), 143–56

[25] Keith Thomas, *Religion and the Decline of Magic* (London: Weidenfeld and Nicolson, 1971). Arguably this work benefits from both the then current anthropological functionalist understanding of beliefs systems and the tendency to see them as 'primitive' superstition

[26] David Gentilcore, 'The Ethnography of Everyday Life', *Early Modern Italy, 1550–1796* ed. John Marino (Oxford: Oxford University Press, 2002); David Gentilcore, 'Anthropological Approaches', *Writing Early Modern History*, ed. Garthine Walker (London: Hodder Education, 2005)

and the developing field of historical archaeology has engaged with the document as both artefact and as source of evidence; indeed, artefacts and documents are seen as complementary facets of the same material culture.[27] In recognising that a reconstruction of the multifaceted experience of life involves diverse strands of evidence, historical archaeology embraces an interdisciplinary approach to the study of materiality, in effect employing anthropological perspectives to create historical ethnographies.[28] The impetus for this approach came from investigation of the colonial period in North America, where documentary sources existed which could inform the material record. The interpretation of the early American household has followed historiographical currents, initially focussing on the functional and adaptive nature of the household, then as a site of conflict of class, ethnicity or gender, and latterly as a place of practice with an ongoing construction of meaning. Examples of this integrated approach, fusing the material record with documentary evidence, are Anne Yentsch's *A Chesapeake Family and their Slaves: A Study in Historical Archaeology* (1994), a comprehensive survey of the lives of a colonial household, and Mark Leone's *The Archaeology of Liberty in an American Capital* (2005), a study of urban culture in Annapolis, Maryland.[29] Perhaps the most influential and significant of all studies are those of James Deetz of the Plymouth colony, in *In Small Things Forgotten* (1977) and his and Patricia Deetz's *The Time of their Lives* (2000), which combine the archaeological record of house traces and artefacts with the contents of probate inventories (which constitute some of the earliest documentary evidence of colonial life) to weave a sensitive narrative of the intimate relationship between early Americans and their domestic material environment.[30] A strong motivation for these studies was the desire to use the material record to access the lives of ordinary people in the past; for Glassie it promises 'authentic history' rescuing from anonymity 'the average people of the past'.[31] To quote Comaroff and Comaroff, the

[27] L. A. Wilkie, 'Documentary Archaeology, *The Cambridge Companion to Historical Archaeology*, ed. D. Hicks and M. C. Beaudry (Cambridge: Cambridge University Press, 2006), pp. 13–14

[28] R. Joyce, 'Writing Historical Archaeology', *The Cambridge Companion to Historical Archaeology*, ed. Hicks and Beaudry, p. 49; M. D. Cochran and M. C. Beaudry, 'Material Culture Studies and Historical Archaeology', *The Cambridge Companion to Historical Archaeology*, ed. Hicks and Beaudry, pp. 192–5; Wilkie, 'Documentary Archaeology', pp. 14–15

[29] A. E. Yentsch, *A Chesapeake Family and their Slaves: A Study in Historical Archaeology* (Cambridge: Cambridge University Press, 1994); M. Leone, *The Archaeology of Liberty in an American Capital: Excavations in Annapolis* (Berkeley: University of California Press, 2005)

[30] J. Deetz, *In Small Things Forgotten: An Archaeology of Early American Life* (New York: Doubleday, 1977); J. Deetz and P. S. Deetz, *The Times of their Lives* (New York: Freeman, 2000). A similar weaving together of the material and documentary record has been achieved by Amanda Vickery in her study *Behind Closed Doors: At Home in Georgian England* (London: Yale University Press, 2009)

[31] H. H. Glassie, *Folk Housing in Middle Virginia: A Structural Analysis of Historic Artifacts* (Tennessee: University of Tennessee Press, 1975); J. King, 'Historical Archaeology, Identities

'poetics of history [are found] in the mute meanings transacted thorough goods and practices…in the landscape of the everyday'.[32] Glassie and Deetz both identified a shift in colonial domestic life from collective values to a 'Georgian' emphasis on consumption, segregation and privacy. Deetz's analysis was heavily influenced by the theoretical approach evolved in studies of material culture, demonstrating that social dynamics can be understood through the meanings which are attached to objects. Data from inventories is thus informed by ethno-archaeology, and vice versa. In Britain historical archaeology has focussed on the role of objects in contemporary contexts, and relational approaches using objects to understand social life.[33] One of the most significant British studies employing probate inventories as supplementary evidence to the social significance of architectural forms, Matthew Johnson's study of vernacular housing in Suffolk employs a structuralist interpretation of space, inspired by the work of Henry Glassie.[34] For Glassie and Johnson early modern house builders developed an 'artefactual grammar' to translate changing social conceptions of domestic space into new forms of building.[35] In his study Johnson was able to employ, as Alcock did, the extant evidence of the vernacular architecture of the period and information from a limited number of inventories to suggest the way in which the social dynamic of the early modern household altered, with relative access to hall and chamber changing in line with a greater desire for privacy and more discreet socialising: a shift from an 'open' to a 'closed' household.[36] Material evidence is thus employed in conjunction with documentary sources to build a picture of changing modes of behaviour in the home.

One of the advantages of historical archaeology in the modern period is the availability of contemporary written and pictorial sources to help to indicate conceptual values. The probate inventories employed as the primary source of this study were composed by contemporaries and in their description and association of objects, monetary valuation and the affective significance of bequests in wills suggest the contemporary associations of these objects and therefore their perceived values. Conduct literature, letters and diaries, and pictorial sources, such as engravings on ballad sheets, point

and Biographies', *The Cambridge Companion to Historical Archaeology*, ed. Hicks and Beaudry, p. 296

[32] J. Comaroff and J. Comaroff, *Ethnicity and the Historical Imagination* (Boulder and Oxford: Westview, 1992), p. 35

[33] S. Tarlow and S. West, *The Familiar Past: Archaeologies of Later Historical Britain* (London and New York: Routledge, 1999); D. Miller, *Material Cultures: Why Some Things Matter* (London: UCL Press, 1988);

[D.] Miller, *Home Possessions: Material Culture Behind Closed Doors* (Oxford: Berg, 2001)

[34] M. Johnson, *Housing Culture: Traditional Architecture in an English Landscape* (London: UCL Press, 1993)

[35] Glassie, *Folk Housing in Middle Virginia*; Johnson, *Housing Culture*, p. 38

[36] *Ibid.*, pp. 122–8

to the ideologies which lay behind actions but may also contain agendas which, whilst interesting, mean that they must be interpreted with caution. The variety of sources employed by historical archaeologists makes them aware of the potential contradictions between words and things, and that no single story can give a full account for the phenomena that they study.[37] But whilst artefacts provide an awareness of the materiality of the past that is missing in a textual record, the textual record can give voice to the personalities of the past. This diversity empowers the historical archaeologist to narrate from multiple positions – the *heteroglossia* of Mikhail Bakhtin – celebrating diversity rather than taking a reductive approach to the evidence.[38] To quote Hicks, 'our "inclusive" search for answers has distracted us from the strengths of historical archaeology: the diversity, the complexity, that its many methods and materials bring', 'historical archaeology's strengths do not lie in priming material ... to answer big questions, short-circuit complexity, or tidy up messiness and contradiction'.[39] Rather than shying away from the complexity of their material, historical archaeologists and ethnologists can celebrate the polyphony, the 'multiplicity of voices' of their narratives, a contested space between the present and past, a place where time, space and multiple voices overlap and comingle.

This empowering diversity of perspectives offered by historical ethnology is the interpretive perspective adopted by this study. Probate inventories are treated as historical artefacts, and the objects listed within as assemblages of deposited objects, their different locations as sites dated according to the probate process. Whilst the objects listed themselves are not present, their material properties can to a large extent be deduced from the evidence of textual descriptions and of other extant examples. The objects thus can be associated and contextualised spatially and temporally according the documentary source, and their meanings enriched by other contemporary sources, textual and pictorial. From this combination of evidence it is hoped to illuminate the domestic life of the period and the ordering of domestic culture.

A Theoretical and Interpretive Framework for Domestic Culture

Given that domestic life consists of a number of interrelated expressions – material, social and conceptual – the interrogation of such complexity requires theoretical perspectives and interpretive frameworks. But, as the domestic domain consists of different forms of evidence, such theoretical

---

[37] Joyce, 'Writing Historical Archaeology', pp. 48–9
[38] M. M. Bakhtin, *The Dialogic Imagination: Four Essays*, (Austin: University of Texas Press, 1981), pp. 288–93; Joyce, 'Writing Historical Archaeology', pp. 49, 55
[39] D. Hicks, 'From "Questions that Count" to Stories that "Matter" in Historical Archaeology' *Antiquity* 78 (2004), 934–9

positions may derive from different disciplinary perspectives. It is argued here that by bringing together theoretical elements which illuminate parts of the domestic complex, it is possible to create a better theoretical comprehension of the whole, and thus avenues by which the evidence can be interrogated.

The interpretation of domesticity should be founded in an understanding of the nature of domesticity. At root human life consists of a physical engagement with the environment the better to survive and to replicate. The very process of domestication and its structures – physical, social and institutional – has moved this engagement beyond survival derived from nature to the negotiation of an artificial environment. However, the *primary* form of engagement with the environment remains one which is physical, engendering sensory and cognitive responses. This engagement corresponds with Edmund Husserl's assertion that the elemental knowledge of the world and sense of personal identity is created through the encounter with the phenomena of the world, and the sensory responses that they engender.[40] Domestic life at an elemental level, therefore, is one of the experiences of being in place and responses to that engagement as a sensory and cognitive being. Even where the historical evidence for domesticity is, as often, epistemological – for example, social discourse and ideology – it is important to recognise as its context this primary ontological level of engagement on which all other domestic expressions rest, elegantly expressed by Maslow in his hierarchy of needs.[41] Humans may preoccupy themselves with matters of social engagement and agency but the degree to which physical needs are met has a significant subconscious impact on their emotions and conduct.

Following Husserl, Martin Heidegger further developed the phenomenological perspective, viewing human life as inextricably enmeshed in its physical environment, with no division between the material and the conceptual. For Heidegger the human being, *Dasein*, is part of the material world and its conceptual universe is drawn from its experiences in that world, from the objects and people around it.[42] The internal consciousness of *Dasein* is founded on experiences in the world, the context of which constitute its conceptualisation of the world. Heidegger thus sees all encounters with the world set in the context of associations, which are themselves the

---

[40] According to Husserl, the phenomena encountered in engagement with the environment can be viewed as 'the essences immanent to pure consciousness': 'These essences are maintained by Husserl to structure not only all cognitive acts ... but also the pre-conceptual and pre-philosophical meanings that shape the natural experience of the world', quoted in Burt C. Hopkins, *The Philosophy of Husserl* (Durham, NC: Acumen 2011), p. 4

[41] Maslow's hierarchy of needs provides a useful rationale for this displacement of attention from the object itself to associations; humans concern themselves first with matters of immediate survival, then when these needs have been met they focus on social relationships and ultimately on abstract thought. A. H. Maslow, 'A Theory of Human Motivation', *Psychological Review* 50:4 (1943), 370–96

[42] M. Heidegger, *Being and Time* (1927) (Oxford: Blackwell, 1962), pp. 78–86

result of previous experiences of the world – a 'web of significance' arising from actions in the world.[43] *Dasein* is sufficiently integrated into its world as to be unable to discriminate between its own existence and that of the world around it; in Heidegger's words, it has '"fallen" into the world'.[44] So *Dasein* conceives of its environment and its own place in it in terms of significance and possibilities.[45] Its experience of the world is temporal because the engagement in the world is conducted on the basis of past experience with a view to future outcomes, and spatial because *Dasein* conducts itself in space. Actions thus flow in space through time from past knowledge to future anticipations.[46] Human (or *Dasein*'s) experience arises from being in the world, creating a web of associations or contextualisation of the world, which in turn constitute a knowledge of the world which directs responses to the world.

This immersion in the experience of being in the world, and simultaneously conceptually 'understanding' and seeking to order the world can be seen as a significant impulse in human domestication. Ian Hodder regards domestication as the manifestation of a mentality seeking to order nature, from which emerged fixed settlement and agriculture. Termed by Hodder *domus*, the house became an 'enabling, conceptual and practical mechanism for social and economic transformation', being not only the residence of a clearly defined family group but also the domain of production and a vehicle for the distribution of resources.[47] The individual house also became, in association with others, a social aggregate, literally the building block of a larger society. Hodder's choice of the term *domus* deliberately evokes linguistically the Indo-European stem *dom* and its association not only with nurturing and care but also with taming and domination, linking the appearance of the house with hierarchical social structures.[48]

The potential for human benefit from the environment – indeed, the release in a Maslovian sense from the necessity of survival in order to develop social and conceptual aspirations – has been linked by James Gibson to a perception or *affordance* of the properties of that environment.[49] This may

[43] *Ibid.*, pp. 120–1; C. Gosden, *Social Being and Time* (Oxford: Blackwell, 1994), p. 11
[44] Heidegger, *Being and Time*, pp. 219–24
[45] *Ibid.*, p. 184
[46] *Ibid.*, pp. 418–21; Gosden, *Social Being and Time*, pp. 13, 17, 34
[47] Hodder, *The Domestication of Europe*, pp. 33, 37–9, 53. Ian Hodder sees domestication as a physical and conceptual distancing from nature, and even argues that the fixed dwellings of the late Pleistocene and early Holocene periods acted as a stimulus for, rather than being consequent on, the development of agriculture and sedentism, demonstrating a shift of collective mentality towards the deferment and sharing of benefits from cultivation and animal husbandry, and societal-wide control of behaviour and durable social relations under a trusted authority. The archaeological record also shows the emergence of domestic artefacts displaying cultural signification at this time, suggesting that the house became the focus of cultural activity reinforcing shared social values
[48] E. Benveniste, *Indo-European Language and Society* (London: Faber, 1973), pp. 249–51
[49] J. J. Gibson 'The Theory of Affordances', *Perceiving, Acting and Knowing*, ed. R. Shaw

consist of the natural elements such as terrain, water, other animals and foodstuffs, or human manufacture such as shelter, fire, tools and human displays. There is a reflexive quality to affordance, which is specifically and frequently variable according to the characteristics and requirements of the affordee. Humankind is intimately involved in the nature of the affordances of the environment, having changed the environment in order to alter its affordances for its own benefit, in terms of sustenance, shelter and security, and converting earth's substances into artificial materials and distinct objects. Forms of affordance may also operate between human beings, from the beneficial to the injurious. The natural or artificial affordance of the environment is therefore a determining factor in the nature of human engagement with that environment, and the concept of affordance provides a means of embracing both the physical and psychical potential of the environment.[50]

Human existence consisting of being in and responding to the world, the domestic unit can be seen as a manifestation of a human desire to manage both nature and the social (subsistent and reproductive) group. The 'home' is both a physical and social context, and a frame of mind. The complex and interrelated components of domesticity have been elegantly theorised in Pierre Bourdieu's theory of practice.[51] In his structuralist analysis of the society of the Kabyle of North Africa, Bourdieu observed that the arrangement of the furnishings in the domestic interior clearly articulated the conceptualisation of social relationships. He therefore concluded that it was in repeated actions around objects in the home that members were inculcated with its values, a process Bourdieu calls *habitus*.[52] The individual generally acts in accordance with learnt norms, only occasionally choosing to act of their own volition. Social relationships and cultural values are thereby inextricably linked to human actions, or *practice*, in the material world.[53] Habitual actions underpin both physical and social existence, and the concepts which link these states. Knowledge is also spatial, gained by the movement around the environment of daily life.[54] In the words of Gosden: 'It is the mass of habitual actions and the referential structure they form which carries the main burden of our lives, giving them shape and direction.'[55] Bourdieu's interpretive framework is broadly applied in this study to the early modern household, observing the way in which habitual actions around objects articulate relationships and values.

---

and J. Bransford (New York: Erlbaum, 1977); J. J. Gibson, *The Ecological Approach to Visual Perception* (New York: Psychology Press, 1986)

[50] *Ibid.*, pp.127–30

[51] P. Bourdieu, *Outline of a Theory of Practice*, trans. R. Nice (Cambridge: Cambridge University Press, 1977); P. Bourdieu, *The Logic of Practice* (Cambridge: Polity Press, 1990)

[52] *Ibid.*, pp. 52–5

[53] *Ibid.*, p. 54; Gosden, *Social Being and Time*, pp. 11, 17

[54] T. Ingold, *Being Alive* (London and New York: Routledge, 2011), p. 160

[55] Gosden, *Social Being and Time*, p. 16

Within domestic 'practice' the individual then is subjected to their environment, and to the values and actions of the group, within which in turn they act. If there is a reflexive relationship between the affordance of the environment and the requirements of the affordee, it follows that in some way each acts on the other. The concept of 'agency' recognises that people and objects act on their environment; they are 'agents', defined as 'one who or that acts'.[56] Thus agency is intimately linked with the habitual actions which constitute 'practice'. Human agents act as individuals but always in the context of the social group to which they belong, and since elements of influence and control exist within the group, that agency normally takes the form of expressions and experiences of power, directed and negotiated through domestic practice. The concept of 'the self' and its boundaries vis-à-vis the group fluctuates culturally and historically. Agency is practised in the context of culture which prescribes norms of behaviour, both enabling and constraining: orthodox practices through which actions become intelligible.[57]

These norms of behaviour and the values which underpin them are communicated through actions, but also through spaces and objects within and around which actions occur, and the form and decoration with which that environment is differentiated. As human relationships are enacted, so objects engaged acquire conceptual significance. In this manner objects can be said to have identities and lives and to 'act' by inducing responses, thus possessing agency.[58] According to post-structuralists Foucault and Derrida, 'discourse' in the form of language and symbols precedes the agent and produces the conditions for agency.[59] Agency is judged by the agent and by the recipients, the *meaning* of the action conditioned by context and frequently of greater significance than the action itself. The cues of agency are often material; the setting and objects involved, and objects giving expression

---

[56] *Oxford English Dictionary (OED)*
[57] M. Dobres and J. E. Robb, eds, *Agency in Archaeology* (London: Routledge, 2000), p. 8
[58] A. Appadurai, 'Introduction: Commodities and the Politics of Value', *The Social Life of Things: Commodities in Cultural Perspective*, ed. A. Appadurai (Cambridge: Cambridge University Press, 1986); I. Kopytoff, 'The Cultural Biography of Things: Commoditisation as Process', *The Social Life of Things*, ed. Appadurai; C. Knappett, and L. Malafouris, eds, *Material Agency: Towards a Non-Anthropocentric Approach* (New York and London: Springer, 2008)
[59] J. Butler, *Bodies that Matter* (New York, London: Routledge, 1993), p. 15. In challenging structuralist assertions of the primary role of social structures in ordering human experience, French post-structuralists Michel Foucault and Jacques Derrida both made considerable use of the work of Ferdinand de Saussure (1857–1913). The Swiss linguist, considered the father of semiotics (or study of signs), analysed the symbolism invested in words and signs. Saussure argued that no word is inherently meaningful. Rather, a word is only a 'signifier', i.e., the representation of something, and it must be combined in the mind with the 'signified', or the thing itself, in order to form a meaning-imbued 'sign'. Objects and their form and decoration can be viewed as form of signification, as communication, and interpreted as such. Roy Harris, *Reading Saussure: A Critical Commentary on the Cours de Linguistique Générale* (London: Duckworth, 1987), pp. 58, 219–20

to social relationships.[60] But some writers have further ascribed agency to objects themselves.[61] Marx's concept of fetishism embraces the power invested in objects; 'the definite social relation between men themselves ... assumes here ... the fantastic form of a relation between things'; 'There the products of the human brain appear as autonomous figures endowed with a life of their own, which enter into relations both with each other and with the human race.'[62] Gell, Latour and Knappett and Malafouris all emphasise the power of objects, sometimes elevated to person status, and Kopytoff refers to the biography of objects with their own life spans and histories.[63] Anthropologists have long seen the exchange and consumption of objects as potent with agency, articulating social relationships and cultural values, not simply as passive items but like persons having distinct lives, endowed with significance and acting on the social fabric.[64] In this sense, the objects listed in the Thame probate inventories can be seen as agents, in bequest, exchange or action impacting on the social dynamic.

The question, however, arises: if domestic behaviour is governed by prescriptive norms – the *habitus* – how can these norms have originated and how can they alter? Two possible modes of innovation are offered; Derrida's notion of 'iteration' allows that each action is only an imperfect citation of the norm and the discrepancy between practice and the norm, and the passage of time gives rise to the generation of new meanings.[65] Thus, norms are necessary to mobilise action, but in their iteration lies the possibility of variance.[66] Bourdieu also allows for a degree of intentional variation (or intentionality) in the re-enactment of *habitus*.[67] By consciously varying *habitus* an agent can decide to challenge and negotiate the distribution of control and influence. According to Rapoport, just as architecture

---

[60] J. Thomas, *Time, Culture and Identity: An Interpretive Archaeology* (London: Routledge, 1996), pp. 80, 153

[61] Arguably a functional object is somewhat distinct from a word in terms of signification, having phenomenological associations relating to actions and practice.

[62] K. Marx, *Capital: A Critique of Political Economy*, trans. B. Fowkes (Harmondsworth: Penguin Books, 1976), p. 165

[63] A. Gell, *Art and Agency* (Oxford: Clarendon Press, 1998); B. Latour, *Reassembling the Social*; Knappett, and Malafouris, *Material Agency*; Kopytoff, 'The Cultural Biography of Things'

[64] M. Mauss, *The Gift: Forms and Functions of Exchange in Archaic Societies* (1925), trans. I. Cunnison (London: Routledge and Kegan Paul, 1969); M. Douglas and B. Isherwood, *The World of Goods: Towards an Anthropology of Consumption* (London: Allen Lane, 1979); Appadurai, *The Social Life of Things*, p. 5

[65] J. Derrida, *Of Grammatology*, trans. Gayatri Spivak (Baltimore and London: Johns Hopkins University Press, 1977), pp. 157–8

[66] Butler, *Bodies that Matter*, p. 15

[67] Bourdieu, *Outline of a Theory of Practice*, p. 55; Giddens also asserts the conscious rather than the conditioned engagement with *habitus*, in contrast to Talcott Parsons, *Social Systems and the Evolution of Action Theory* (New York: Free Press; London: Collier Macmillan, 1977), determinist position. A. Giddens, *The Constitution of Society* (Cambridge: Polity, 1984), pp. 63–74

encloses behaviour, so activities – and the objects around which they are centred – shape architecture.[68] In Rapoport's analysis the domestic domain comprises fixed features (buildings), semi-fixed features (furnishings) and latent features (people and meanings). Domestic activities range from the instrumental and manifest to the latent and conceptual, with increasing cultural specificity. For example, cooking is a universal manifest activity, but the social contexts of food consumption and the symbolism of food preparation and consumption are conceptual, varying widely between and within cultures.[69] The latent qualities or meanings of activities are often hard to deduce in the past, and the semi-fixed features of buildings – or furnishings – may provide more indications of activities than the fixed structures of the buildings themselves.[70] Objects become the visible part of concepts and a form of social memory, holding ideas for people who use them, and providing clues as to actions and meanings, their significance provided by the contexts and associations in which they are employed.[71]

Social theorists have debated the relative influence of structures on social relationships, or conversely of relationships of the structures that they inhabit. For structuralists, the physical and ideological frameworks of domestic life largely determine the social relationships and activities within. Rapoport describes interconnected domestic spaces as 'systems of settings', milieux which define 'a set of appropriate actions' by transmitting cues or mnemonics, physical and cognitive, to participants.[72] Within a cohesive group, cultural conventions become incorporated into segments of the built environment, which, in turn, will cue later judgements and expectations.[73] So, to employ Rapoport's terminology, *activity systems* complement and occur in *systems of settings*. In addition, there is the temporal dimension, where actions are sequenced through time. The temporal ordering of tasks is not always evident from material record but is a part of the ordering of domestic life and of the significance of actions and engagements.[74] Countering a determinist perspective of social relationships,[75] the structuralist theorist Giddens suggests that human beings have the capacity of knowledgeable interaction with the world that they inhabit.[76] The social structure

[68] A. Rapoport, 'Systems of Activities and Systems of Settings', *Domestic Architecture and the Use of Space*, ed. S. Kent (Cambridge: Cambridge University Press, 1990)

[69] *Ibid.*, p. 11

[70] *Ibid.*, p. 13

[71] Douglas and Isherwood, *The World of Goods*, p. 59

[72] Rapoport, 'Systems of Activities and Systems of Settings', p. 12

[73] D. Canter, *The Psychology of Place* (New York: St David's Press, 1977), pp. 105–60; D. Sanders, 'Behavioural Conventions and Archaeology: Methods for the Analysis of Ancient Architecture', *Domestic Architecture and the Use of Space*, ed. Kent, p. 45

[74] Rapoport, 'Systems of Activities and Systems of Settings', p. 14

[75] Parsons, *Social Systems and the Evolution of Action Theory*, p. 163

[76] A. Giddens, *Central Problems in Social Theory: Action, Structure and Contradiction in Social Analysis* (Basingstoke: Macmillan, 1979); Giddens, *The Constitution of Society*

is an expression of repeated actions, directed and constrained, it is true, by allocative (circumstantial) and authoritative (institutional) resources, but nevertheless essentially a mode of individual expression. In this process humans act both with 'practical' unconsciousness, and 'discursive' consciousness. Social engagement is driven by a desire for self-expression and power, relational and limited by available resources, and subject to dialectical tendencies and shifting over time. Giddens distinguishes between 'social *production*' – the social life produced as people engage in social practices which are the substance of their lives – and 'social *reproduction*' – the way in which social life becomes patterned and routinised. Routines, and the daily face-to-face encounters which they involve, provide individuals with a sense of ontological security. Importantly, in terms of domestic life, Giddens sees this day-to-day interaction with its spatial and temporal considerations (albeit without specific reference to the role of materiality apart from inclusion in 'allocative' resources) as central to the human experience of life and the formation of social structures.[77] An even greater emphasis is placed on the social element in the structuring and experience of life by actor-network theory (ANT), which, in the words of Latour, one of its principal authors, asserts that the search for firm social structures is futile, social identity residing in multiple relationships which leave discernible traces of networks as they are acted out. Latour adopts a phenomenological perspective claiming that human experience is formed through association with the world. Social 'order' is discerned when actions have been played out, revealing traces. Networks are observed only intermittently; sometimes visible, often invisible. Groups' identities are defined by continual action, often articulated around objects which themselves have agency, providing durable networks for relationships.[78] Ingold moves beyond the concept of ANT to assert that human beings should not be viewed as discrete entities in a network of relationships, but as an entanglement of relationships both within and outside the physical body, a meshwork which transcends the supposed boundaries of the self in a state of continual 'becoming'.[79]

Such metaphysical considerations, whilst valid, do not necessarily enable us effectively to analyse and comprehend life in the past through the available evidence. Human life, it is true, consists of a myriad of simultaneous interactions with the physical and social environment, engendering an evolving personal and collective conceptual domain. But this complexity can only be assessed and described by a sequence of inquiries identifying its

[77] *Ibid.*, pp. 5–6, and 'Acting units ... are always involved in cultural systems, which express, symbolize, order, and control human orientations through patterned meaning systems', *ibid.*, pp. 34–7; D. Layder, *Understanding Social Theory* (Thousand Oaks, CA: Sage, 1994), pp. 125–41

[78] Latour, *Reassembling the Social*, pp. 23–43, 63–74; J. Law, *Organizing Modernity* (Oxford: Blackwell, 1994)

[79] Ingold, *Being Alive*, pp. 64, 84–5

separate strands, which are then woven into a more complex description. In addition, humans also attempt to simplify this complexity through the artifice of categorisation, which acquires its own cultural validity. By identifying observable structures and the less visible relationships which underpin them, both structuration and ANT provide useful perspectives of the ordering of material and social life, and therefore of the domestic domain. Whilst structuration proposes that it is through the knowing action of agents that discernible structures or systems are articulated and reinforced, ANT asserts rather that definitive structures are elusive, and that the focus should be on the relationships that connect the various elements of life, in particular those enacted in the material environment. Although it is the enactment of relationships between people, between objects and between people and objects that undoubtedly articulate domestic life, nevertheless there exists in the household an institution which has existence beyond those actions, as concept in the form of expectations and legislation, and materialised in dwellings and their contents. What is proposed in this study, then, is a domestic culture conceived as a structured and structuring network of relationships in variably differentiated spatial settings, of shorter or longer duration and mutable through time, and as an interpretive framework identifying the relationships in order to trace networks, and the manner in which they both articulate pre-existing structures in space and through time. As a concept, 'domestic culture' owes much to Bourdieu's practice and *habitus*; however, assumptions made about the reproduction of culture in a pre-industrial society may not automatically apply in an early modern context.

A phenomenon as complex as domesticity demands a sophisticated and nuanced mode of interpretation. Not only must diverse strands of evidence be combined, but the relationship between them, and between the parts and the whole, must be comprehended. An effective approach is the employment of the hermeneutic circle – the analogy of the comprehension of the word through its context in text – which constantly refers the individual element of evidence to its context, testing its interpretation in the light of all the evidence, creating 'a dialectical movement back and forth between the parts and the totality'.[80] In the case of inventories the manner of the compilation of the document does place objects within a context, in association with other objects and in place, and in time. Thus, a hermeneutic reading of the objects listed in probate inventories will attempt not only to ascertain their ontological properties, but to grasp the contemporary epistemological conceptualisation inherent in the text, and to enrich that understanding with an appreciation of the web of associations in which that object lies. And, as Dilthey observed, the greatest comprehension of

---

[80] M. Shanks and C. Y. Tilley, *Re-Constructing Archaeology: Theory and Practice* (Cambridge: Cambridge University Press, 1987), pp. 104–5

that context and its associations will be based in an approach to the circumstances and mentalities of the time.[81]

Figure 0.1a attempts to illustrate the operation of 'domestic culture'. In the left-hand panel are the elements of which domestic culture exists: materiality in the form of the dwelling and objects, people within the dwelling and the concepts which are associated with the interaction between materiality and people. The right-hand panel states the existence of domestic culture in the dimensions of space and time. The central panel demonstrates the relationships which link these elements, through the affordance of objects, actions and the agency of people and objects, articulating social relationships, and both generated by and generating concepts which are reintegrated into objects and actions. This study will follow such a sequence: identifying the relationships between objects and actions, determining the agency of objects and people and the social relationships expressed through actions, and the attendant conceptual values in turn reinvested in objects and actions. Figure 0.1b illustrates this process in the case of commensality. Objects such as chairs and stools provide seating with different ergonomic and status affordances, possibly with the added comfort of cushions, and are placed in association with a table, with eating and drinking vessels. Candlesticks provide lighting. This assemblage is engaged in a defined space within the dwelling, giving rise to concepts of status, conviviality and comfort, which are in turn invested in the objects employed.

The Characteristics of Probate Inventories

The evidence of the past may take many forms: oral tradition, documents, biological traces and human artefacts. What do probate inventories represent, how can they be interrogated and what might they reveal of the world in which they were created? Probate inventories were legal and economic documents compiled as part of the administration of estates at the time of death, containing information on the identity of the decedent and his or her place of residence and frequently their occupation. They were designed to facilitate the smooth transition of the estate of the deceased by summarising his or her moveable assets and their value (Figure 0.2). They thus represent a record of the material culture of the household of the deceased, often listed in distinct rooms within the dwelling, indicating where such objects might be kept and employed, the way a house was furnished and the manner in which the internal space was differentiated. In relating people, occupations and status to their domestic material belongings, they might be

---

[81] Anthony Savile, 'Historicity and the Hermeneutic Circle', *New Literary History* 10:1 (Literary Hermeneutics) (Autumn 1978), 49–70, 49–50; Wilhelm Dilthey, *Hermeneutics and the Study of History*, ed. Rudolf A. Makkreel and Rodi Frithjof (Princeton and Chichester: Princeton University Press, 1996), pp. 136–7.

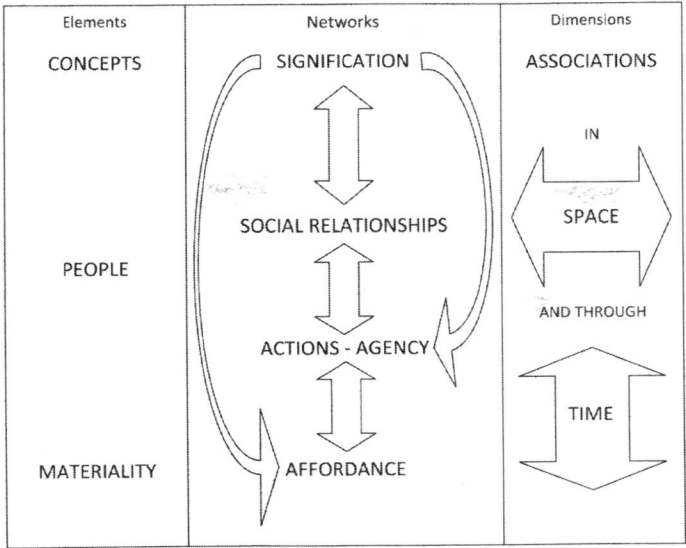

Figures 0.1a (top) and 0.1b (bottom) Schematic diagrams of the relationships between elements in 'domestic culture'

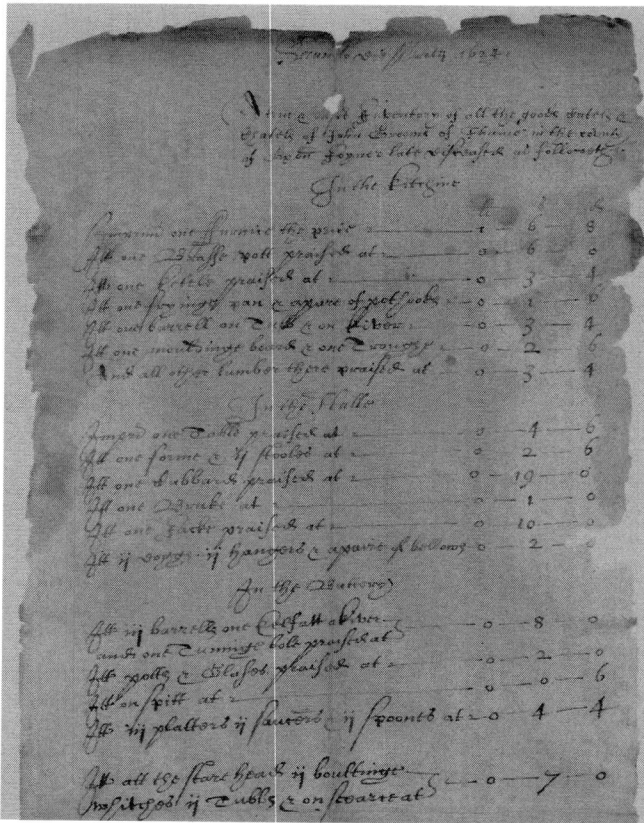

Figure 0.2
Portion of the inventory of John Groome, joiner of Thame, dated 2 March 1624 (Full transcription given in online Appendix 3)

deemed one of the most valuable sources of information on the domestic life of the early modern period, especially as they also embrace the lives of the middling ranks of society, often excluded from elite histories. Like much historical evidence they are, however, problematic, providing a wealth of data but raising considerations of reliability and of interpretation. Many of these problems arise from the documents' contemporary purpose and manner of compilation.

The process of probate – that is, the proving of the will and the granting of administration of the estates of the deceased – had come during the Middle Ages to be administered largely by ecclesiastical courts. However, only the deceased person's personal estates, consisting of moveable goods, credits and leaseholds, came under the jurisdiction of the ecclesiastical courts; their real estate, consisting of the freehold and copyhold land and property, was initially under the jurisdiction of manorial courts and later remained, in the case of disputes, under that of the civil courts. The structure of church courts was largely unaltered by the Reformation. At the lowest level was the archdeaconry court, with the diocesan consistory courts granting probate for estates with assets in more than one archdeaconry, and ultimately the prerogative courts of the archdioceses of Canterbury and York were used frequently for appeals as the senior ecclesiastical court in the land, and for the probate of estates with assets in more than one diocese. In addition to this structure there were peculiar courts outside jurisdiction of local archdeaconry. The probate inventories employed in this study come from one such peculiar archdeaconry, Thame, remaining part of the diocese of Lincoln on the creation of the diocese of Oxford in 1541.[82] Under the Tudor monarchs the church courts were employed to maintain the direction of religious reforms, but in the early seventeenth century the courts became more controversial, simultaneously weakened by the attacks by dissidents and employed to enforce Laudian doctrine. Abolished temporarily at the time of the Commonwealth and Protectorate, they were re-established on the restoration of the monarchy, but by this time more receptive to the principles of common law. Although technically not abolished until the mid-nineteenth century, they entered an irremediable decline on the granting of toleration to dissenters in 1689. The hierarchy of courts means that the wills and inventories pertaining to a particular locality can be dispersed in the archives of various courts, and the survival of documents varies widely between courts.[83] It is possibly because of the non-peripatetic nature of the Thame peculiar court that the records remained relatively intact.

As a general rule the church courts only concerned themselves with personal estates valued at over £5.[84] A large portion of those whose assets fell below this level were therefore excluded from the probate process. Estimates for the representation of the population of adult males and widows by probate inventories vary nationally between 10 and 60%, averaging 20

---

[82] Other wills and probate inventories, 101 in number, relating to parishioners of Thame between 1598 and 1698 were also lodged with the prerogative court of Canterbury, generally for decedents of the greatest wealth in the community: gentlemen, wealthy yeomen, widows and tradesmen. Their inclusion with the aggregated data of this study would have had the effect of further weighting the interpretation towards the wealthiest section of Thame society. In order to maintain, as far as is possible, a non-elite focus in this study, it was decided to exclude these inventories and employ only those brought before the archdeaconry court.

[83] T. Arkell, 'The Probate Process', *When Death Do Us Part*, ed. Arkell, Evans and Goose, pp. 3–13

[84] An Act of 1529 in Henry VIII's Reformation Parliament laid down fees payable to the church courts for the administration of estates; those valued at less than £5 were charged only a fee of 6d for registration, a 3s fee was payable for those valued from £5 to £40, 5s for those valued over £40. Church courts therefore encouraged the drawing up of probate inventories for estates worth over £5, although according to the relevant law (21 Hen. VIII, c.5) it was intended that all estates be inventoried, but for those worth less than £5 the fee be waived. Arkell, Evans and Goose, *When Death Do Us Part*, Appendix 2, p. 346; Jeff and Nancy Cox, 'Probate 1500–1800: A System in Transition', *When Death Do Us Part*, ed. Arkell, Evans and Goose, p. 26, note 65

to 30%. [85] Levels of representation can sometimes be ascertained by checking the data against relevant hearth tax or parish records. In addition, the presumption that the assets of a married woman belonged to her husband means that this category is not effectively represented in probate inventories. Thus, from the point of view of historical research, inventories provide a very partial picture of the population as a whole.

The data contained within the inventory varies in reliability and detail due to the manner in which the inventory was compiled. Under requirements laid down in Henry VIII's Reformation Parliament, the executors of the estate were required to find four honest men to 'make a trewe and perfyte Inventory of all the goodes catells wares merchaundyses as well moveable as not moveable ... and shall cause the same to be Indented'. [86] The quality of the composition was therefore dependent on the competence of those who undertook the task. Although a certain degree of custom appears to have asserted itself over the manner in which inventories were compiled by different appraisers in one region, there can be great differences in the manner and detail with which they were compiled in different areas of the country. For example, inventories in Oxfordshire normally detail items in different rooms of the house, some with individual values, whilst those of Breconshire generally provide only the barest outline of goods, with aggregated values. As inventories were principally economic instruments, descriptions of the qualities of objects were generally limited to those that would affect value: material composition, construction and occasionally decoration. As a general rule greater descriptive detail and room locations were given in wealthier households, possibly in order to differentiate between numbers of similar items. On the other hand, items of low monetary value, but not necessarily of no interest to the historian, were often brought together anonymously under such terms as 'lumber'. It also cannot be assumed that all items of the personal estate of the deceased were listed. Reasons for omission might be that household items had been bequeathed in the will and already removed by the legatee, were part of the married portion of the widow and therefore regarded as her property, were regarded as heirlooms, or had been sold prior to the compilation of the inventory to pay for the maintenance of orphans in their minority. [87] There is also no guarantee that the location in which objects were listed was their usual place of use. The omission of objects cannot thus necessarily be taken as proof of their absence, nor can the rooms listed be presumed to be the totality of those within the dwelling, especially in conditions of multiple occupancy found in urban dwellings. Meaningful comparisons between individual inventories, or between those from different parts of

---

[85] T. Arkell, 'Interpreting Probate Inventories', p. 73
[86] 21 Hen. VIII, c.5. Quoted in Barley, *The English Farmhouse and Cottage*, p. 39
[87] Overton, Whittle, Dean and Hann, *Production and Consumption*, pp. 14–18

the country, are therefore problematic by reason of variable standards of compilation and possible omissions.

In addition, the valuations placed on household goods, livestock, crops and the assets of trade, whilst useful data for the economic historian, cannot be regarded as an indicator of total wealth. Generally the inventory lists only the moveable goods of the deceased, and therefore does not include the fixed assets, such as land and leases, nor the debts of the deceased, a point illustrated by Spufford in her analysis of the frequent discrepancy between the apparent inventory 'gross' wealth and the actual 'net' wealth of decedents when debts were taken in to account.[88] As employed by Spufford, other sources such as accompanying wills and probate accounts can usefully complement inventories to establish a fuller picture of the real wealth of the deceased. Assessment of the values given to household furnishings and agricultural and trade assets in inventories do, however, provide useful data on household economics and trends in consumption and production, and the values given do show a degree of consistency with market prices.[89] Such values as are given in the inventory are frequently not for individual items but for groups of goods, either within a room, or in a category such as linen, or crops, making comparison of specific commodities difficult. The attribution of monetary value, therefore, which was the primary purpose of the inventory, is neither a comprehensive indication of the total wealth of the deceased, nor unambiguously identified with individual commodities.

The fact that inventories were compiled as a result of death also poses its own limitations. Analysis based on inventories is concerned with the activities of the living, but mortality occurs at variable points in the life cycle, and the stage reached by the deceased affects the nature of the assets that he or she has amassed, and the size and activities of the household. Such variations will inevitably have a significant impact on the conclusions drawn from the data. Indeed, unless the inventory is accompanied by a comprehensive will, or unless parish registers exist of baptisms, marriages and burials with which to establish the age, marital status and dependants of the deceased, it is difficult to know exactly the life stage at which mortality occurred. It might be assumed that the majority of deaths of householders would occur in older age, but a limited study of those leaving inventories in the village of Milton in Kent showed a strong correlation between the age of decedents and the age profile of the population as a whole.[90]

There are thus many problems for the historian employing probate inventories as the basis of research. They remain a rich and widely used

---

[88] M. Spufford, 'The Limitations of the Probate Inventory', *English Rural Society 1500–1800, Essays in Honour of Joan Thirsk*, ed. J. Chartres and D. Hey (Cambridge : Cambridge University Press, 1990), pp. 139–74

[89] M. Overton, 'Prices from Probate Inventories', *When Death Do Us Part*, ed. Arkell, Evans and Goose, pp. 132–41

[90] Overton, Whittle, Dean and Hann, *Production and Consumption*, p. 27

source, but must be used with caution. As a piece of historical evidence they are open to interpretation on a number of levels, and from a number of perspectives. The inventory can be transcribed and tabulated in such a way that the data within is allowed to speak for itself in a purely anecdotal or descriptive fashion, or the inventory or group of inventories may be trawled to answer specific inquiries. Inventories may be allowed to stand in isolation or they may be used as part of a comparative study, effectively often distinguishing the qualitative from the quantitative analysis. Following from what has been said of the variable qualities of compilation, the manner in which inventories are selected has significant implications for the direction of the inquiry and the methodology applied. It is instructive to examine studies using inventories as their principal source to see how effectively they have been employed and how valid the conclusions.

Interpretive Approaches to Probate Inventories

Solitary inventories have been employed by a number of writers, often in relation to the incidence of particular artefacts or products, in fields as diverse as furniture and cooking implements simply to illustrate the manner in which objects were present in individual households, giving a biographical association to the object.[91] Such use, characterised as 'incidence/counter-incidence', may serve a purpose in terms of illustration and evidence of the earliest known presence of such objects, but does little to indicate whether such evidence is representative, and makes little reference to the association of objects.[92]

Many studies revolving round one locality, such as that of Steer analysing inventories from the parish of Writtle in Essex from 1635 to 1749 has sought to publish every aspect of the information available in the inventories, from house layout and furnishings, to village industries and crop and stock densities.[93] Such studies might be said to follow the principles of 'total' history, yielding a comprehensive survey of the one locality, but one more descriptive than analytical. One of Steer's clearly stated motives is to explore the lives of lower social ranks to be found in underutilised inventories. Havinden also, in his county-wide survey of Oxfordshire from 1550 to 1590, emphasises the importance of inventories in exposing the life of 'ordinary people'. He analyses furnishings, wealth (in terms of furnishing value) and house size in relation to occupations and status. The time span from which the inventories are drawn provides an opportunity for analysis

---

[91] V. Chinnery, *Oak Furniture: The British Tradition* (Woodbridge: Antique Collectors Club, 1979)

[92] M. Overton, 'Computer Analysis of an Inconsistent Data Source: The Case of Probate Inventories', *Journal of Historical Geography* 3 (1997), 317–26, 318

[93] Steer, *Farm and Cottage Inventories of Mid-Essex 1635–1749*

of changing standards of living. The study also emphasises the importance of inventories in understanding the use of space in houses deduced from furnishings.[94] A more integrated descriptive approach combines the evidence of probate inventories with material evidence of extant archaeological or artefactual remains. Alcock benefits from the almost unique survival of both buildings (albeit sometimes altered), deeds, wills and inventories from Stoneleigh and Ashow in Warwickshire to construct a picture of the changing structure of the houses, and from the inventory evidence deduces the manner in which the dwelling evolved towards greater specialisation in use of space in an increased number of rooms. This enables him to draw limited conclusions about the nature of changing use of space; for example, the development in the later seventeenth century of the parlour as a place of household comfort and sociability.[95]

Thus inventories have provided through the listing of furnishings in rooms, opportunities for the study of the dynamics of space within the household, subject to the caveats given above with regards to reliability. Just as Alcock utilises inventories to construct a picture of the changing use of space in Warwickshire households, so also Havinden relates the function of dining furniture to the differentiation of space, and Earle uses inventories to describe the use of space in London houses.[96] Similarly the paper by Priestly, Corfield and Sutermeister examining the use of space in Norwich households in the early modern period, drawn from data contained in over 1,400 inventories, seeks to illustrate the conditions of urban housing, and to suggest a developing specialisation in room use.[97] A parallel approach was taken by the author, employing the properties and associations of furniture viewed as ethnographic objects, to read the social use of space in Thame households in the early seventeenth century – a catalyst for the present study.[98]

A group of studies in recent years has made considerable use of inventories to explore the themes of consumption and production: those of Weatherill, Shammas and Overton, Whittle, Dean and Hann.[99] Such an approach only functions when a number of inventories are employed for comparison. The selection of data groups requires awareness by the historians of the questions which they seek to answer, the degree of representation and, in the case of comparative studies, the comparability of data sets. Despite the

---

[94] Havinden, *Household and Farm Inventories in Oxfordshire 1550–90*
[95] Alcock, *People at Home*, pp. 202–5
[96] Earle, *The Making of the English Middle Class*
[97] Priestly, Corfield and Sutermeister, 'Rooms and Room Use in Norwich Housing, 1580–1730', pp. 93–123
[98] A. Buxton, 'Domestic Culture in Early Seventeenth-Century Thame', *Oxoniensia* 67 (2002), 76–115
[99] Weatherill, *Consumer Behaviour and Material Culture in Britain 1660–1760*; Shammas, *The Industrial Pre-Consumer in England and America*; Overton, Whittle, Dean and Hann, *Production and Consumption in English Households, 1600–1750*

estimated one million inventories archived in the United Kingdom, both their quality and their survival are uneven; those of Devon and Essex, for example, were substantially destroyed in the Second World War, and those for most London parishes are sparse and unevenly distributed.[100] Sampling is a necessary technique employed to achieve representative statistical data sets from large numbers of inventories, but given their inconsistency and uneven and partial survival, as Overton remarks, it is not possible to claim a representative sample from surviving inventories, but it is possible to create a statistical population in a selected sample.[101]

Weatherill's study draws on a sample of nearly 3,000 inventories dating from 1660 to 1760 from London and widely dispersed regions of England and Scotland. The purpose of the study is not only to examine changing patterns of consumption in diverse localities but also to explore the motivation for economic actions within the household. Items of furnishing are selected for their significance in terms of socialising (table ware), wealth (looking glasses and clocks), education (pictures) or cultural taste (books) and related to occupations, in order to establish the social basis of consumption during this period. Whilst the data does indicate the spread of 'consumer luxuries' outwards from London, Weatherill's analysis questions the assumption that the stimulation of consumption occurred through a process of emulation of metropolitan taste, concluding rather that the evidence suggests an important conduit role played by provincial towns. In addition to the statistical analysis of inventories, Weatherill places considerable stress on a parallel examination of contemporary written and pictorial sources in order to establish as far as possible the cultural basis for domestic behaviour and choices, but the household is still seen primarily as an economic entity, and the items selected to signify changes in consumption are largely viewed in isolation. Indeed, the size of the statistical sample once again removes the study from any sense of the intimate complexity of people and objects in the household.[102] Earle also employs a combination of other contemporary evidence with inventories in his study of the emergence of the middle class in London.[103] Shammas similarly seeks to identify patterns of domestic consumption in pre-industrial England and America in relation to status and wealth. Selecting categories of objects which indicate wealth, comfort and prestige and employing regression analysis (the effect of variables, such as wealth or size of house, on a given constant, such as ownership of consumer durables), she examines not only the evidence of consumption but also the likely impact of variables on consumption decisions, such as the purchase of a mirror, or the adoption of feather beds. With an emphasis

[100] Arkell, 'Interpreting Probate Inventories', pp. 72–4; Overton, Whittle, Dean and Hann, *Production and Consumption in English Households, 1600–1750*, p. 11
[101] *Ibid.*, p. 29
[102] Weatherill, *Consumer Behaviour and Material Culture in Britain 1660–1760*
[103] Earle, *The Making of the English Middle Class*, pp. 207–10

on the role of the supply side of economic life, she also utilises inventories of shopkeepers to ascertain how retailing facilitated consumption.[104] Both Weatherill and Shammas effectively use the evidence of probate inventories to demonstrate major shifts in consumption in the late seventeenth and early eighteenth centuries.

Overton et al. use a large body of probate inventories from Kent and Cornwall to test theoretical models of household production and consumption in the early modern English household. Categories of objects are used as indicators of economic production and consumption, and regression analysis is again used to determine the changing frequency of these indicators, and thus possibly the circumstances which lead to those changes. Few complementary sources are drawn upon for this study, the significance of indicative artefacts seeming to be taken as self-evident, and, notably for a study centred on the household, there is little attention to aspects of domestic life beyond the economic. This study is an example of highly competent quantitative analysis of probate inventories, and yet by its own account results in conclusions which are somewhat unrepresentative and ambiguous, not least because of the nature of the data source, neither Kent nor Cornwall (by Overton's admission) representing an economic profile characteristic of most English counties of the time.[105] So, no matter how competent the data handling and statistical analysis, an enquiry may well be circumscribed at the outset by the particular characteristics of the primary source.

Inventories have thus been employed for localised, regional and national studies, within descriptive and comparative frameworks and employing both qualitative and quantitative approaches to examine economic and social conditions and developments. The non-localised studies referred to above focus primarily on specific aspects of domestic life, especially production and consumption, whilst making reference to the influence of social relationships and the material environment of the household. The consideration of these major themes – or 'questions that count' – is perfectly valid in itself, but may encourage the researcher to impose a logic on the evidence which obscures other more sensitive interpretations. Nor do sophisticated computer programming and quantitative techniques necessarily guarantee valid outcomes, if they ask the wrong questions. Whilst, in the words of Margaret Spufford, inventories need to be approached with 'whole salt-cellars of disbelief',[106] they still form one of the most useful and versatile sources of information on the economic and social life, and thus the domestic culture, of the household in the early modern period.

---

[104] Shammas, *The Industrial Pre-Consumer in England and America*
[105] Overton, Whittle, Dean and Hann, *Production and Consumption in English Households, 1600–1750*, pp. 170–1
[106] Spufford, 'The Limitations of the Probate Inventory', p. 174

The Scale of this Study

It has been argued that human existence can be read on a number of levels, from the personal to the embracing meta-structure. Some of the historical studies examined above focussed on the larger narrative of economic and cultural activity. But much of human existence is played on a small stage, so an understanding of life can also be found in the detailed examination of the particular. One of the most significant contributions of anthropology to 'new history' was the appreciation of the way in which small groups signify, and some of the most attractive studies are those which focus on the strategies of ordinary people.[107] This does not mean that we need not guard against the counter-tendency to view the local community as self-contained nor against falling into the trap of seeing the smaller community as a microcosm of the larger.[108] It can be argued that the meta-narrative by its very scale obscures the very activities, minute and mundane, on which it is ultimately based. For Braudel, political events were no more than the foam on the waves of the sea of history, and it is in the quotidian where human life was really experienced.[109] How can we best analyse a domain of such diffuse, complex, multifaceted and non-sequential relationships?

The model selected for this study is the microhistory, limited to the domestic life in Thame in the seventeenth century. But this is a study *in* a locality, not necessarily *of* a locality.[110] Rather than restricting the scope of the study, the microhistory enables the exploration of the intimate matrix of relationships which govern human life and which must, of necessity, be excluded from a study on a larger scale. The microhistory celebrates and records the complexity of life, rather than tending to ignore it. As a result of the scale, sensitivity to the 'voice' of the evidence can be adopted; the historian becomes an ethnologist rather than inquisitor. Geertz's conception of comprehensive data as 'thick description' should focus a study on the totality of circumscribed evidence, thus reducing the temptation of initiating an inquiry with selective, large-scale interpretations. The 'thinning' of a rich body of data to extract dominant themes denies the complexity that lies within its density and ambiguity;

> To set forth symmetrical crystals of significance, petrified of the material complexity in which they were located, and then attribute their existence to autonogenous principles of order, universal properties of the human mind,

---

[107] P. Burke, 'Overture: The New History: Its Past and its Future', *New Perspectives on Historical Writing*, ed. P. Burke (Cambridge: Polity, 2001), p. 15
[108] F. Barth, 'Towards Greater Naturalism in Conceptualizing Societies', *Conceptualizing Society*, ed. A. Kuper (London: Routledge, 1992), p. 29
[109] Burke, 'Overture', p. 4
[110] C. Geertz, *The Interpretation of Cultures* (New York: Basic Books, 1973), p. 22

or vast a priori *weltanschauungen*, is to pretend a science that does not exist and imagine a reality that cannot be found.[111]

The microstudy does not seek, then, to provide neat answers to the nature of society, but celebrates the *heteroglossia* of varied and opposing voices within the complexity of social organisation – not seeking to find one 'true' perspective, but to embrace the honest divergence of views.[112] On the other hand, as Geertz also stresses, to approach an inquiry open minded does not mean intellectually empty handed; theoretical ideas should be allowed to grow on the evidence if valid, or wither if erroneous.[113] As in any social science, the extent to which we can penetrate other worlds, separated by time or cultural space, can be legitimately debated. But, by enabling a dense body of data to articulate human actions and values, we stand a chance of coming closer to the totality of that other experience.

Scale is an important factor not only of the breadth of data used in the study, but also of data itself. This study effectively employs a sequence of interpretive levels which are related to physical scale: diminishing from the wider environmental context to the household, then to the object and ascending again to the association of objects within the household. However, physical scale is not the only relationship at play. There is also the potentiating relationship between the object (and groups of objects) and people: 'the action-possibilities of objects that only make sense in relation to an agent'.[114] There is also the dynamic of different levels of social grouping, from the individual to the domestic group and beyond to the community, and the way in which those relationships both influence and are influenced by the interaction between humans and their physical environment, and the continuous relationship between the material context and time.[115] As noted above, humans operate through time; actions are undertaken with the benefit of past experience and in the anticipation of future outcomes.[116] Time can be measured as the short 'nested durations' of tasks, the frequency of habitual actions or the longer context of change.[117] An awareness of the relationship between different levels of physical scale, association and time is essential to an understanding of the complex matrix of objects and human actions, relations and values in the domestic domain.

---

[111] *Ibid.*, p. 20
[112] Burke, 'Overture', pp. 5–6
[113] Geertz, *The Interpretation of Cultures*, p. 27
[114] G. Lock and B. L. Molyneaux, 'Introduction: Confronting Scale', *Confronting Scale in Archaeology: Issues and Theory of Practice*, ed. G. Lock and B. L. Molyneaux (New York: Springer Press, 2006), p. 1
[115] *Ibid.*, p.4
[116] Gosden, *Social Being and Time*, p. 15
[117] Lock and Molyneaux 'Introduction: Confronting Scale', p. 2

Constructing and Interrogating a Relational Database

Historical inquiry may start from a theoretical point suggested by a broader narrative or from a body of potential evidence but is circumscribed by the nature of the evidence. The effective interpretation of probate inventories involves relatively complex forms of analysis, recording the information in such a manner that it is open to a broad spectrum of queries.[118] Probate inventories list a range of data: date, identity, status, spatial distinctions, individual and assemblages of objects and their collective values. As previously described, they have been used for incidental and descriptive purposes, but a superficial approach is unlikely to reveal the complex dynamic of domestic life. In order to achieve this end, we need to uncover the frequency and contexts of objects and relationships in place and in time.

As already noted, individual or small numbers of inventories impart an impression of domestic material culture, but they may be idiosyncratic and give little reliable indication of trends. Meaningful inquiry requires a body of data which can be viewed as representative for a chosen set of spatial, social and temporal parameters, according to the scale of the inquiry. Data can then be aggregated and analysed to reveal the frequency, associations and context of objects against selected variables, such as status, date or size of dwelling. The computer is a powerful tool, acting as both data storage and interrogating device, for the rapid extraction of information, conducting statistical calculations and presenting results in a variety of formats, numerical and histographic. It potentially enables the inquirer to conduct a wide range of queries of the data to reveal significant frequency and trends which can then be investigated in greater detail; for example, in the case of inventories the frequency of objects, and therefore activities in particular spaces.[119] The process of inquiry is therefore ongoing and evolving, and it is important that the database be constructed so that the widest possible range of subsequent queries is possible.

The Access software programme provides a versatile and powerful analytical tool for the recording and interrogation of both numerical and textual data, and so it is ideally suited to the analysis of probate inventories.

---

[118] Weatherill, *Consumer Behaviour and Material Culture in Britain 1660–1760*; Shammas, *The Industrial Pre-Consumer in England and America*; Buxton, ' Domestic Culture in Early Seventeenth-Century Thame'; Overton, Whittle, Dean and Hann, *Production and Consumption in English Households, 1600–1750*

[119] For the development of computing in inventory analysis, see Overton, 'Computer Analysis of an Inconsistent Data Source'; M. Overton, 'Computer Analysis of Probate Inventories: From Portable Micro to Mainframe' and L. Weatherill, 'Using "Dataretrieve" to Analyse Data from a Sample of Probate Inventories', *History and Computing*, ed. D. Hopkins and P. Denley (Manchester: Manchester University Press, 1987); M. Overton, 'A Computer Management System for Probate Inventories', *History and Computing* 7:3 (1995), 135–42 and Overton, Whittle, Dean and Hann *Production and Consumption*, pp. 19–21

The database must be as comprehensive as possible, accommodating all required data in a logical and non-repetitive manner. The data is entered into a number of tables, and the interrelation of the tables means that one element of data need only be entered once in the database to be available for any inquiry. The selection of these tables and fields is therefore critical and involves a significant element of categorisation, differentiating the data with a view to efficient recording and future inquiry.[120] In the case of the probate inventories a rationale and a form of categorisation already exists in the documents themselves. The information which appraisers were required to record – the moveable assets of the household and their value – was compiled in a manner suggested by its presentation, association and distribution. A range of information was given: date, decedent identity, occupation, spatial distinctions and groupings and valuations of individual objects. The data therefore already predisposes the design of the relational database by ordering the information in a certain manner, progressing from the common denominator of personal identity through spatial differentiation and groupings of objects to the individual objects and their qualities. To utilise this format both aids data entry and also helps to yield the contemporary meaning; for example, by employing the textual grouping of objects to reveal how they might have been associated physically in space and conceptually in the contemporary mind. The data contained in the probate inventories is therefore grouped into tables as shown in Figure 0.3, as follows:

Personal identity, location and date
Spatial distinctions within the dwelling
Textually grouped artefacts and their monetary values
Individual domestic furnishing objects
Grouped economically productive commodities and their values
Individual economically productive commodities
Monetary credits and debts
Narrative details – elements of textual description

An important additional element in the construction of the database is the inclusion of interpretive fields to facilitate inquiry. For example, grouped and individual artefacts are categorised, where it is clearly justifiable, by associated activity. Chairs, stools and benches are all categorised as 'seating furniture' in order that rapid and broad-ranging inquiries can later be made of activities without the need to specify each object. Similarly, where 'tubs' are clearly listed in association with brewing utensils they will be classified as belonging to that activity. Such categorisation is potentially

---

[120] C. Harvey and J. Press, *Databases in Historical Research* (Basingstoke: Macmillan, 1996), pp. 119–37

```
A true Inventory of all such goodes as p[er]tained to John Stone of
Morton in the p[ar]ish of Thame in the Count[y] of Oxon  Yeoman
deceased taken the 17ᵗʰ of August 1618


Imprimis in ye hall
          a table & frame  8 ioyned stooles  2 Chaires
          a Cubbord & 8 Cushions & 2 Yron doggs                    xLˢ


Item      in the p[ar]lor
          a ioyned bed  a featherbed & furniture           iijᴸⁱ
          Item   a Chest  a square Table  3 Boxes  & a forme
          xˢ
Item      in the Chamber over the p[ar]lor
          a ioyned bed  a featherbed & furniture
          2 flockbeds & bedsteds with the furniture       iiijᴸⁱ
Item      2 Chests                                                 vˢ
Item      xj paires of sheetes  3 Table clothes
          18 napkins  6 pillowbeares & one Towell          iijᴸⁱ
Item      3  dozen of pewter Great [and] small
          6 Candlesticks  one bason  5 saltcellers          xLˢ
Item      2 brasse potts  4 kettles  2 pans
          & 4 postnets  2 skimmers                            Lˢ
Item      the yron worke                                     xxˢ

Item      his apparell                                     vjᴸⁱ

Item      in Tubbes  Timber Lumber & Wood                 vijᴸⁱ
Item      plow & plowgh geares  cart & cart geares          vᴸⁱ
Item      a Malt mill                                            xˢ
Item      six kine & 2 bullocks                            xijᴸⁱ
Item      50 sheepe                                           jᴸⁱ
Item      six horses & Colts                             xviijᴸⁱ
Item      4 hoggs & piggs                                  iiijᴸⁱ
Item      powltry                                              xvˢ
Item      in corne in Wheat & Rye                           xLᴸⁱ
Item      in Barly                                          iijᴸⁱ
Item      in Beanes  fetches                                xxᴸⁱ
Item      in Hay & Lease of Land                           vjᴸⁱ


                                  Suma    Cxviijᴸⁱ  xˢ
```

The relational database

Figure 0.3a Example of transcript of probate inventory

subjective and requires a degree of familiarity with the material culture of the period and interpretive integrity. In Figure 0.3b those fields underlined are the relational component of the database, linking different tables. Those in normal font are the factual data imported from the inventories; for example, names, dates of probate, occupations, quantities, names and values of objects. Those in italics are interpretive fields as discussed above, such as occupational status categories and object activity groups. All the objects listed in the probate inventories employed in this study, grouped

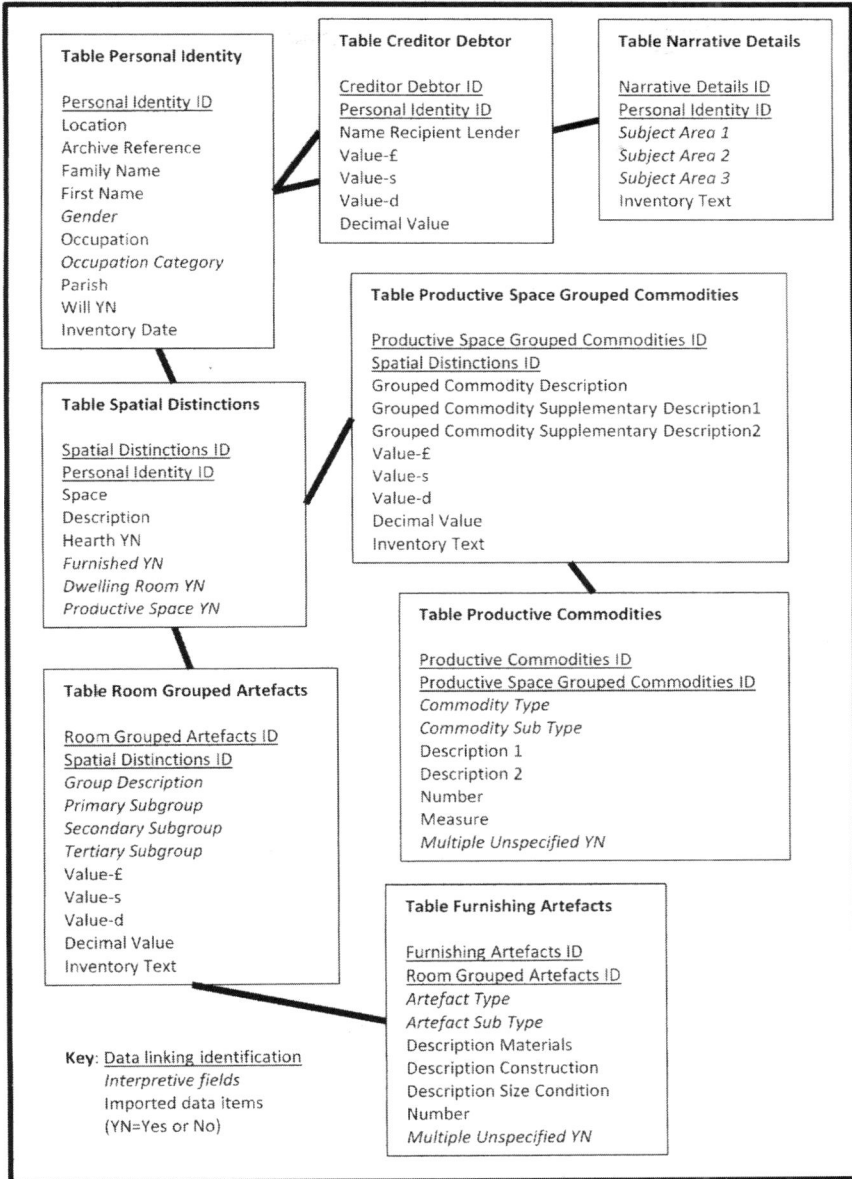

Table Personal Identity

Personal Identity ID
Location
Archive Reference
Family Name
First Name
Gender
Occupation
Occupation Category
Parish
Will YN
Inventory Date

Table Creditor Debtor

Creditor Debtor ID
Personal Identity ID
Name Recipient Lender
Value-£
Value-s
Value-d
Decimal Value

Table Narrative Details

Narrative Details ID
Personal Identity ID
Subject Area 1
Subject Area 2
Subject Area 3
Inventory Text

Table Productive Space Grouped Commodities

Productive Space Grouped Commodities ID
Spatial Distinctions ID
Grouped Commodity Description
Grouped Commodity Supplementary Description1
Grouped Commodity Supplementary Description2
Value-£
Value-s
Value-d
Decimal Value
Inventory Text

Table Spatial Distinctions

Spatial Distinctions ID
Personal Identity ID
Space
Description
Hearth YN
Furnished YN
Dwelling Room YN
Productive Space YN

Table Productive Commodities

Productive Commodities ID
Productive Space Grouped Commodities ID
Commodity Type
Commodity Sub Type
Description 1
Description 2
Number
Measure
Multiple Unspecified YN

Table Room Grouped Artefacts

Room Grouped Artefacts ID
Spatial Distinctions ID
Group Description
Primary Subgroup
Secondary Subgroup
Tertiary Subgroup
Value-£
Value-s
Value-d
Decimal Value
Inventory Text

Table Furnishing Artefacts

Furnishing Artefacts ID
Room Grouped Artefacts ID
Artefact Type
Artefact Sub Type
Description Materials
Description Construction
Description Size Condition
Number
Multiple Unspecified YN

Key: Data linking identification
Interpretive fields
Imported data items
(YN=Yes or No)

Figure 0.3b Linked relational database tables

in interpretive object-action fields, are laid out with frequencies in online Appendix 2.[121]

The Presentation of the Data

The relational database thus enables the inventory data to be interrogated to establish frequency of objects and object groups in relation to the size and occupational status of households, in place and through time. The purpose of this study is build a picture of domestic life in Thame in the seventeenth century through the evidence of the material culture, utilising the *relationships* which existed between objects and object groups to understand the habitual actions which revolved around the objects, and the consequent *structured networks* of social relationships and conceptual values, in turn invested in the objects and actions. This, then, is not a detailed statistical study, for although some 27,000 objects were listed in the Thame inventories, the households number only 188 over a period of approximately a hundred years.[122] In addition, as already noted, probate inventories cannot ever be said to be a truly representative source, being records of only a small portion of the population at best and subject to vagaries of survival and idiosyncratic composition. The purpose is to capture frequencies and trends, and although some of the data is presented in numerical frequency tables, much is presented in bar and scatter chart and histographic form, which make trends more visible whilst making fewer claims to statistical significance.[123] The process of inquiry involves the identification of variations in the frequency and association of objects to reveal not only their use, but also the important contextual associations which that use generated, and therefore the social relationships and concepts which emerge out of habitual action. The principal variables employed here are types of object, associations of objects both within a differentiated space and in the different parts of a dwelling, households of different occupational status and size, and finally associations through time. The inquiry should be seen as an evolving interrogation of the actions and meanings behind the objects listed in the inventories, a dialogue between researcher and data with the tables as a form of notes of that inquiry. The quantitative elements in the text are presented numerically in order to facilitate comparison, but occa-

---

[121] See online Appendix 2, at http://boybrew.co/9781783270415

[122] As previously noted, the database does not include a number of additional elite wills and inventories for the parish of Thame granted by the prerogative court of Canterbury

[123] For the efficacy of various types of data chart refer to M. Fletcher and G. R. Lock, *Digging Numbers: Elementary Statistics for Archaeologists* (Oxford: Oxford University Committee for Archaeology, Oxbow Books, 1991), pp. 13–30; D. I. Greenstein, *A Historian's Guide to Computing* (Oxford: Oxford University Press, 1994), pp. 128–9; P. Hudson, *History by Numbers: An Introduction to Quantitative Approaches* (London: Arnold, 2000), pp. 53–84

sionally a single entity is represented by the indefinite article in place of a '1' in order to aid the flow of the text.

The Structure of this Study

It has been argued in this introduction that the historical quotidian is a significant area of inquiry which has proved a rich vein of evidence for studies in economic history, but that the early modern home in its totality and complexity has been largely neglected as the focus of studies. An ethnographic approach recognises, after Heidegger, that human life is founded in a materiality conditioned by context and association, and after Bourdieu that values are unthinkingly embedded by the activities that surround objects in the home. The balancing of ontological with epistemological interpretation of objects is addressed by a contextual or hermeneutic reading. Probate inventories provide rich if problematic evidence of the domestic material culture of the early modern period, culled by historians for evidence of economic and social trends. However, it is the integrated approach of historical archaeology which provides a better understanding of the complexity of the intermingled material, social and conceptual dimensions of domestic life. This study takes the form of a microstudy to enable the density of the material evidence to speak through a wide-ranging interrogation of a computerised relational database, revealing the multiple associations of objects, people and conceptual values in space and time.

Chapters 1 and 2 are devoted to the context in which the domestic material evidence is set. The first chapter explores the environmental, economic, social, legal and moral culture of the community of Thame in early modern England. The Thame household was set in an agricultural and urban context which had an impact on the composition and ordering of the household. The landscape itself presented possibilities and limitations to the Thame inhabitants, depending on individual circumstance, and the community was also part of a wider economic and political culture. But context consists of not only the immediate physical environment and its economic implications but also the social structures and cultural values which enfolded the household. Ideologies were expressed by contemporary authors on the subject of good behaviour and right conduct between the ranks and sexes, but the evidence suggests that opinions were frequently challenged. The second chapter examines the household as an institution and its formation in the early modern period. On the assertion that the household forms a key component of human societies, some of the elements of the domestic life which lie at its base and justification are identified – as a mechanism for biological, social and cultural reproduction, as a focus of subsistence and productive activity, and a group sharing a dwelling space. Such factors have implications for the way in which the household was formed, developed and organised, and for its internal dynamics, including the ideology and practice of relationships between household members of different gender, age and status. The chapter then proceeds to examine the extent that the seventeenth-century English household corresponded to such archetypes. The conduct literature of the period asserted the primacy of patriarchy, and whilst such seems to have been the widely held ideology, marriage formation and relationship between husband and wife appear to have been based more on consent than coercion. Besides those of husband and wife, the early modern household comprised relationships, subject to idealisation and negotiation, between parents and children and also with servants. Finally the chapter turns to evidence for the physical structure of the domestic dwelling itself in Thame. Whilst few, if any, of the Thame inventories are related directly to identifiable dwellings, extant buildings of the period in the town can greatly enhance the understanding of the built domestic context.

Chapters 3, 4 and 5 examine the affordance and agency of household objects. A wide range of artefacts were listed in the Thame inventories relating to diverse domestic activities, responding to household needs, sourced locally or at a distance and employing diverse technologies. Although the objects listed in probate inventories are not extant, it is possible to deduce their construction and functions. Artefacts of the period, such as furniture, pottery, fabrics and ironware, whilst not directly related to those listed in the inventories, can yield highly relevant information on the materials and processes involved in their creation, and thus the culture of their use. The third chapter is concerned with the provision and processing of foodstuffs, a significant activity of early modern households, especially in an agricultural producing and trading community. The fourth chapter examines the preparation of food and drink, its consumption and the culture of conviviality. The fifth chapter is concerned with the provision of furnishings for rest, and for the ordering and storage of household goods.

Chapter 6 examines the association of objects and actions in place and through time; in effect the 'practice' of the Thame household. The Thame inventories provide evidence of the location of objects and groups of objects or assemblages in distinct parts of the dwelling. Areas were differentiated by their activities, and this indicates the wider ordering of the household in terms of habitual actions, social relationships and conceptual values. Although fixed in the individual inventory, from household to household through variations in status and time, object associations appear, change in composition and disperse. Viewed over time and in place, assemblages and activities in the household provide a picture of the domestic culture and its development.

Chapter 7 is designed to add a personal element to a study which has deliberately largely employed aggregated data of material culture (in order to establish household norms and trends), examining the spatial and material composition of a number of individual households representing the range of occupations and status in Thame in the seventeenth century, and by combining inventories and wills providing a profile of the physical and social composition of the household, and the householder's social ties, affections and anxieties.

The conclusion summarises the study's response to the principal research aims laid out at the very start of the study: to gain an insight into the experience of daily life in the early modern period, and an understanding of the operation of domestic life. The conclusion assesses the success of the study in conveying the experience of domestic life as a validation of the theoretical premise, the extent to which material culture is a factor in and able to yield evidence of the experience of daily life. It also assesses the picture painted of domestic life both in its daily operation and alterations through the seventeenth century, in the context of wider historical narratives. Finally, it addresses the effectiveness of the concept of a domestic culture as an interpretive framework, assisting an understanding of the multifaceted and complex operation of the domestic domain, one of the chief arenas of human experience.

1

The Thame Household in Context

What is meant by context? All inquiry is by its nature defined by an area of focus which does not exist in isolation but is conditional on other elements. In textual analysis it is the narrative in which the passage under consideration is embedded, but in other areas of inquiry it should include any factor which impacts on the matter under primary consideration. This study focusses on households in Thame, but they existed not in isolation but in contact with a wider world in which each household was embedded and which affected its material condition, its social structures and its values. In this chapter, then, we consider a wide range of factors which provided opportunities and constraints to Thame households: environmental conditions, economic activities, social structures and cultural ideologies. In attempting to evaluate such factors we are confronted by the distance of time which has obscured much of past *lived* experience, and by the problem of fully comprehending the *significance* of such factors for the various households in the study. Not only is much of what was known and experienced by a resident of Thame – man, woman and child – in the seventeenth century at best indistinctly and uncertainly perceived from the present, but also, paradoxically, the process of historical research and inquiry may well focus on aspects of the past which were unknown or imperfectly comprehended by those 'living the past'. For example, present understanding of Thame may be enhanced by knowledge of early settlement on the site, which would be obscured and seem largely irrelevant to the seventeenth-century inhabitant. Again, historical research may reveal processes of demographic shift or meteorological conditions in the seventeenth century which placed pressure on resources and helped to reconfigure social structures, but which the individuals living through those processes may well have experienced only as aberrations to assumed norms, as anxiety or optimism rather than tending to permanent change in their world. Contextual factors for this study are most significant in the way in which they affected the actions and mentalities of the past, not as abstracted historical facts and processes. As Muir writes, 'the sense of place is a subjective phenomenon ... the exclusion of emotion from intellect and symbol from reason in western science does not equip us to recognize and relate to sense of place factors which may have motivated our distant forebears'.[1] This chapter therefore will attempt to view the varied elements of context through the impact that they made on the lives and mentalities of the households of Thame.

The Natural Environment and its Exploitation

If the Thame householder stepped beyond their domestic threshold, they would find themselves in the urban environment of Thame, the few streets, the adjoining households with their inhabitants. Beyond, they would perceive a landscape in which the town was situated (Figure 1.1). This is not the place for a lengthy discussion of landscape interpretation, but the debate on the subject marks a shift from a purely empirical to an interpretive approach. Johnson notes the way in which a purely factual description of the elements of the landscape have given way to an appreciation of the manner in which the economic reconfiguration of the landscape can be interlinked with new ways of conceiving human relations.[2] The natural environment became, with the advent of agriculture, a domain of social relationships and concepts.[3] In an archaeological perspective, space was conceived as 'socially constructed and constitutive of social relationships' rather than 'a passive backdrop for actions'.[4] Ingold terms the landscape a 'taskscape', to indicate the impact of human involvement in its configuration, one which at any given time comprises the inheritance of the past and is simultaneously evolving under natural and human processes: 'It enfolds the lives and times of predecessors who, over the generations, have moved around in it and played their part in its formation.'[5] The landscape therefore becomes, especially in a population wedded primarily to agricultural production, a part of the biography of the individuals and groups that inhabit it: the canvas for their 'engagements, attachments and entanglements'.[6]

---

[1] Richard Muir, *The New Reading the Landscape: Fieldwork in Landscape History* (Exeter: University of Exeter Press, 2000), p. 147

[2] Matthew Johnson, *Ideas of Landscape* (Oxford: Blackwell, 2006), pp. 1–6

[3] See Ian Hodder, *The Domestication of Europe* (Oxford: Blackwell, 1990), pp. 33–9

[4] C. Robin and N. A. Rothschild, 'Archaeological Ethnographies: Social Dynamics of Outdoor Space', *Journal of Social Archaeology* 2:2 (2002), 159–72, 161; a 'post-processual' perspective.

[5] Tim Ingold, 'The Temporality of Landscape', *World Archaeology* 25:2 (October 1993) 152–74, 152; Dan Hicks, Laura MacAtackeny and Graham J. Fairclough, eds, *Envisioning Landscape: Situations and Standpoints in Archaeology and Heritage* (Walnut Creek: Left Coast Press, 2007), p. 14

[6] A. Salmond, 'Theoretical Landscapes: On a Cross-Cultural Conception of Knowledge', *Semantic Anthropology*, ed. D. Parkin (London: Academic Press, 1982), p. 66; Hicks, MacAtackeny and Fairclough, *Envisioning Landscape*, pp. 13–29

Figure 1.1 A view of Thame from the north, 1724

The visual perspective for the inhabitant of Thame would extend to the horizon, to the extremities of the shallow river valley in which the town is situated (Figure 1.1). The valley of the river Thame, a tributary joining the river Thames at Dorchester-on-Thames, runs from north-east to south-west, with the escarpment of the Chiltern Hills some three miles to the south, and one mile to the north the spurs of higher ground on which the neighbouring settlements of Long Crendon and Haddenham are situated, between which exit northern tributaries of the river Thame. The broad vale, undulating with the low Lobbersdown, Barley, Christmas and Hossenden hills around the town, gently descends from Aylesbury in the east towards Wheatley in the west. The valley floor consists of clay and the hills to the south of chalk, those to the north predominantly of (Portland) limestone.[7] The geology of the district has implications for the formation of the river valley and, with the prevailing climate, the suitability for certain forms of agriculture. In addition it provided construction materials: stone for the better local buildings predominantly from the limestone quarries of Wheatley and, from the fourteenth-century, Headington to the west. Local calcareous clays were suitable for marl and the formation of building and boundary walls known locally as *witchett*, and the lower and upper Oxford clays were suitable for brick and tile manufacture. Building sand and gravel were also available in the river terraces.[8]

To east and west, then, Thame inhabitants would have viewed an undulating valley landscape of open fields and meadows employed for a range

---

[7] British Geological Survey, *Geology of the Country around Thame* (London: HMSO, 1995), pp. 1–2

[8] *Ibid.*, pp. 122–4

of agriculture. Describing 'The rich and goodly Vale of Alsbury, / That stood So much upon her Tame', the contemporary poet Michael Drayton celebrated the agricultural fecundity of the vale in his epic description of the nation, *Poly-olbion*, in 1622:

For, Alsbury's a Vale that walloweth in her wealth,
And (by her wholesome air continually in health)
Is lusty, frim, and fat, and holds her youthful strength
Beside her fruitful earth, her mighty breadth and length,
Doth Chiltern fitly match ...
... her soil throughout so sure,
For goodness of her glebe, and for her pasture pure,
That as her grain and grass, so she her sheep doth breed,
For burthen and for bone all other that exceed.[9]

As in much of England at that time, agricultural production balanced cereal cultivation with animal husbandry.[10] The production of corn and cattle, with a significant element of dairying, was practised in the vale. Beef cattle were raised for consumption, and sheep for mutton as well as for wool. The downwash of alkaline salts from the limestone hills ameliorated the clays of the valley, providing rich loams suitable for crop production without heavy manuring.[11] Wheat and barley were grown, much of it for export down the river Thames in barges to London.[12]

In Thame, as in much of west Oxfordshire in the seventeenth century, most production was still on the township's open fields, an area totalling over 5,000 acres.[13] The term 'field system' describes a process whereby the inhabitants of a town subdivided and tilled their arable, meadow and pasture land (Figure 1.2). One of the most compelling reasons for so doing had been the pooling of resources; medieval ploughing teams required, with the technology of the time, as many as eight beasts to draw the plough. Even in the early modern period four oxen or horses would have been needed to draw the improved ploughs, a number beyond all but the most prosperous farmers. The shared investment in draught beasts, therefore, as well as tradition, may have discouraged the enclosure

[9] Michael Drayton, *The Complete Works of Michael Drayton*, introduction and notes by R. Hooper (London, 1876), pp. 182–3

[10] H. L. Gray, *English Field Systems* (London: Merlin Press, 1969), p. 7

[11] J. R. Wordie, 'The South: Oxfordshire, Buckinghamshire, Berkshire, Wiltshire, and Hampshire', *The Agrarian History of England and Wales, Volume 5(i): 1640–1750*, ed. Joan Thirsk (Cambridge: Cambridge University Press, 1984), pp. 318–24

[12] M. A. Havinden, 'Agricultural Progress in Open-Field Oxfordshire', *Agricultural History Review* 9:2 (1961), 73–83, 73

[13] J. Garlick, 'Farming Activities at Thame and Woodstock in the Early Seventeenth Century: The Evidence of Probate Inventories', *Oxfordshire Local History* 3,:7 (Autumn 1991), 291–317, 293

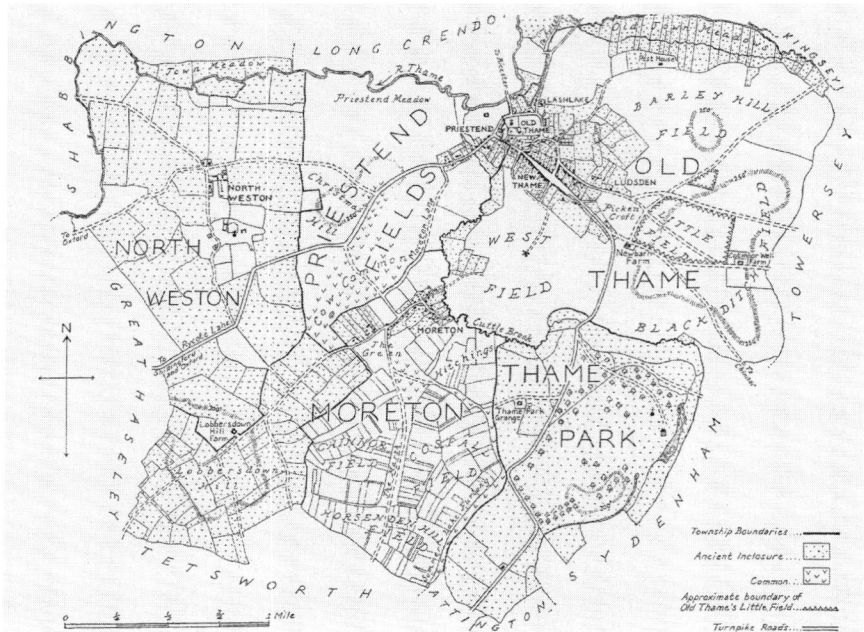

Figure 1.2 Map illustrating early enclosure and open fields in Thame and its hamlets before general enclosure, based on Richard Davis's map, 1797

of land. Part of the land would have been tilled for crop production, and sheep and cattle grazed on the arable waste and the portion of the land lying fallow.[14] The township of Thame maintained a three-field system, until enclosure by Act of Parliament in 1826, on the Old and New Thame, Priestend and Moreton fields.[15] Describing the husbandry of the clay lands on Oxfordshire, the contemporary Robert Plot wrote in 1677 'at most places where their land is cast into three Fields, it lies fallow in course every third year, and sown but two; the first with wheat, if the Land be good, but if mean with Miscelan [maslin], and the other with Barly and Pulse promiscuously'.[16]

The impression we gain of the primary agricultural activity of this community, then, is in large part a collaborative enterprise moderated by the status of the various participants, dependent on the size of holding and

---

[14] Gray, *English Field Systems*, pp. 1, 8–9

[15] Inclosure by award on 19 May 1826, Act 4 Geo. IV c. 8 (1823) Priv. K, in *A Handlist of Inclosure Acts and Awards Relating to the County of Oxford*, Oxfordshire County Council Record Publication 2, 2nd edn (Oxford, c. 1975)

[16] Robert Plot, *The Natural History of Oxfordshire* (Oxford, 1677), 2nd edn (Oxford, 1705), p. 244

manner of tenancy: freehold, a long-term copyhold, or a tenancy at will with the threat of immediate termination and right only to the crops in the ground. The open field system was under continuing threat, however, from the interests of private landowners. The inhabitants of Thame would have been conscious of the threat of enclosure, partly through instances in the locality, and partly through a prevailing culture of commoners' distrust of the landowners. As early as the mid-fifteenth century the Cistercian monks of Thame Abbey had enclosed part of their estates at Attington, and the Wenman family which acquired their lands in the mid-sixteenth century at the time of the dissolution of the monasteries continued the process. The disappearance of hamlets around Thame in the Middle Ages is thought to be primarily due to enclosure, rather than the decimation of the population through the Black Death. Attington Manor was known as 'Attington pasture' due to the preponderance of grazing land over arable, and in 1538 Sir John Clerke obtained a pardon for 'ruins, decays and voluntary devastations' as a result of land enclosure.[17]

Although Thame largely retained its open field system, there was a history of discontent at enclosure in the region. In the rebellions of 1548–49, which were largely formed around resentment at enclosure and fear of loss of common rights, the local seat of Lord Norris, Rycote House, had been sacked, and it was one of the servants of the same house who initiated and led the ineffectual Enslow Hill rebellion of 1596, prompted by the failure of Lord Norris, the lord lieutenant of Oxfordshire, to respond to grievances over malnutrition amongst the poor and failure to act against illegal enclosures. In 1607 revolt over enclosure had also broken out in the nearby county of Northampton, amongst others in the Midlands.[18] However, enclosure could occur with broad consent. The scheme to enclose Thame's Lubbersdown Field, promoted by the lord of manor Edward Wray and supported by tenants, was granted at the courts of chancery on 3 July 1651.[19] Reasons given were the distance of two miles of the field from the town requiring long haulage for manuring, and the shortage of ready timber which could be planted in new hedgerows.[20]

Making comparison with the greater incidence of enclosure in another county, Herefordshire, Gray attributes the persistence of the field system in Oxfordshire in part to the configuration of settlements.[21] In Herefordshire parishes tended to consist of a number of scattered hamlets, each with

---

[17] G. Clarke, *The Book of Thame* (Buckingham: Barracuda Books, 1978), pp. 20, 55

[18] R. B. Manning, *Village Revolts: Social Protest and Popular Disturbances in England, 1509–1640* (Oxford: Clarendon Press, 1988), pp. 53, 220–52

[19] Oxfordshire History Centre Archives (OHCA): Thame I/v/2

[20] Mary Lobel, ed., *A History of the County of Oxford, Volume 7: Dorchester and Thame Hundreds*, Victoria County History (London: Institute for Historical Research, 1962) (hereafter VCH), p. 190

[21] Gray, *English Field Systems*, p. 153

seldom more than ten tenants apiece, whilst in Oxfordshire townships consisted of as many as thirty tenants. Gaining consent to enclosure from the large number of tenants was achieved only with difficulty. Another reason for the persistence of the field system in Oxfordshire may well have been its relative success. According to Havinden, this region in the seventeenth century should not be seen as an agricultural backwater.[22] As mentioned previously, it was benefitting from the growth of the London metropolis as a market. Significant changes were made to open field cultivation with a shift from predominantly arable to animal husbandry, responding to the increased demand for meat, tallow and wool. Fodder crops were substituted for fallow, and the greater number of livestock helped to manure the land, resulting in higher crop yields. This 'convertible' husbandry introduced in the latter part of the seventeenth century – sowing fodder crops of improved ryegrass, clover, lucerne and sainfoin in 'leys' in the open fields, a process known as 'hitching' – required the consent of all parties. Legumes rested the ground without exhausting it, and wheat, beans and peas were increasingly substituted for barley, oats and rye.[23] Whilst the Thames valley was not as favourable for sheep as the neighbouring uplands, inventory analysis shows that flocks increased significantly in size in the latter part of the seventeenth century, with more modest increases in the size of cattle herds, averaging around five beasts at the start of the century.[24] The probate inventories of Thame reflect this balance of cultivation. The inventory of Edmund Tomlinson, a yeoman whose inventory was taken in 1607, shows he was cultivating 20 acres of wheat, 20 of barley, 4 of beans, 1 of maslin (a mixture of crops, usually rye with wheat, or grain with pulses) and 1 acre of peas and vetches. He also owned 5 milk cows, and 8 sows and 8 weaners. William Graunt, a yeoman whose inventory dates from 1643 had 9½ acres of wheat and 18 acres of beans and barley in the Priestend Field. Artisans and tradesmen also engaged in agriculture; John Groome, a joiner, whose inventory dates from 1624 was cultivating 5½ acres of winter corn when he died with 6½ acres waiting to be sown with barley or peas, and Joan Spindler, a widow, left 5 cattle and 2 two sheep in 1612.[25]

Across the valley bottom would also have been stands of timber such as the well-wooded Thame Park, isolated trees and significant woodland on the flanks of the Chilterns to the south. Timber was a vital commodity for a variety of purposes: for heating and cooking, for economic production, and for construction purposes in houses, for furniture and for household and agricultural implements. A number of trees with different economic signifi-

---

[22] Havinden, 'Agricultural Progress in Open-Field Oxfordshire', p. 73
[23] Ibid., pp. 74, 78
[24] Ibid., p. 80; Garlick, 'Farming Activities at Thame and Woodstock in the Early Seventeenth Century', p. 296
[25] OHCA: MS. Wills Pec. 52/3/15; MS. Wills Pec. 39/4/31; MS. Wills Pec. 39/3/35; MS. Wills Pec. 51/1/4

cance grow in the Chilterns adjacent to Thame, most abundantly beech, but also oak, and ash used in coppicing, the process of harvesting the young tree limbs close to the ground every seven years. Diverse timbers have differing uses; durable oak was widely employed for building structures and for furniture, and ash in smaller dimensions for purposes such as wattle laths and hurdles. There is evidence that beech was also extensively coppiced from the sixteenth century onwards. In the Chilterns underwood was coppiced at eight or nine years' growth – tall wood or coppices 'of which they make tall Shids, Billet etc' at no certain time.[26] One of the chief uses for the timber was fuel, shipped as far as London. The common woodlands, which were open in character, provided timber, pannage and herbage[27] for villagers in the hills and the neighbouring vale.[28] Not only were the woodlands encroached by clearance by commoners, they were also subject to extensive exploitation as the demands on their resources increased. Drayton in his *Poly-olbion* depicts the Chilterns in comparison to the vale as 'wise Chiltern',

... the world who long had try'd
And now at last had laid all garish pomp aside:
Whose hoar and chalky head descry'd him to be old,
His beechen woods bereft that kept him from the cold.[29]

In the neighbouring royal forest of Wychwood in west Oxfordshire tracts were leased out for coppicing, for the production of firewood, charcoal, laths and hurdles. Lessees cut the underwood one year and fenced the tract in with hurdles to protect new growth from deer and commoners' animals for seven years. However, a survey of 1617 found that the coppices had 'bene formerlie much abused and neglected' and 'muche spoyled by browsing'.[30] The shortage of ready timber was one of the reasons why tenants agreed to the enclosure of Lubberdown Field at Thame; enclosure provided standard trees in hedgerows which would be available to the community at a future date.[31]

The impression we gain of the landscape surrounding Thame in the seventeenth century is therefore of one which was favourable to the growth of cereal crops, fodder and pasture for livestock. Cultivation was carried

---

[26] Plot, *The Natural History of Oxfordshire*, p. 267
[27] Pannage was the foraging of pigs in woodland for food; the action of pasturing pigs in this way (*OED*). Herbage was the right to graze cattle in in woodland: '*Droict d'herbage*, herbage; or the libertie some haue to graze their cattell in other men's woods', Randle Cotgrave, *A Dictionarie of the French and English Tongues* (1611) (Menston: Scholar Press, 1968)
[28] D. Roden, 'Woodland and its Management in the Medieval Chilterns', *Forestry* 41:1 (1968) 59–71, 59
[29] Drayton, *The Complete Works of Michael Drayton*, p. 183
[30] B. Schumer, *Wychwood: The Evolution of a Wooded Landscape* (Charlbury: Wychwood Press, 1999), p. 77
[31] VCH, p. 190

out predominantly on the communal open fields, despite the presence of enclosed land which was under private ownership and the partial enclosure by consent of a limited amount of communal land for pasturage. The area was also potentially well suited to the growth of timber. However, this was not a static landscape. Pressures on resources led to the over- exploitation of the neighbouring woodlands, and similar pressure of population and economic forces beyond the region were threatening traditional methods of land ownership, management and cultivation. In west Oxfordshire the open field system persisted, but to the north considerable social tensions surrounded the development of enclosure. Nor were the inhabitants apparently averse to innovation in their agriculture, introducing new methods of cultivation and crops, and changing the balance between crop production and animal husbandry. This, therefore, was a landscape of tradition in land ownership and production, subject to forced and voluntary innovation.

Just as agriculture permeated life in Thame, so the agricultural year imposed its discipline on life in the town. Robert Plot gives an indication of the way in which agricultural activities imposed a seasonal rhythm. The first tillage for wheat, called the 'fallow', occurred about the beginning of May, or as soon as the winter barley season was over. Before the second tilth, called the 'stirring', around the end of June or the beginning of July, 'they give the land its Manure which if Horse-dung or Sheep-dung, or any from the Home-stall, or from the Mixen in the Field, is brought and spread on the land just before this second ploughing'. If the manure was from the sheep fold, 'an excellent Manure for this land', it was spread either in winter before the fallow, or in summer after its fallowing. Wheat and barley required three ploughings, other grains seldom more than one. The land was sown with wheat, 'which is its proper Grain'. The following year – 'it being accounted advantageous in all tillage to change the grain' – beans were cultivated, ploughing in bean brush at All Saints' Day. Barley and winter wheat were cultivated in following years, as well as allowing the land to lie fallow, or 'hitched' with fodder crops, grazed by the livestock.[32] The dominant rhythm of life was therefore very much that of the seasons and consequent agricultural activity.

Despite the best endeavours of cultivators, they were always at the mercy of weather. Climatic variations were reflected in harvests, sometimes beneficially, often negatively. Wet summers generally resulted in poor harvests, leading to food shortages. There is no evidence of compensatory benefits for other forms of agriculture, as for example wet summers benefitting grazing. On the contrary, wet conditions often seemed to lead to widespread diseases amongst farm animals and a consequent scarcity of dairy produce. The failure in the supply of one commodity also placed pressure on others.[33] Over the whole of the seventeenth century approximately 25% of harvests

[32] Plot, *The Natural History of Oxfordshire*, p. 244–5
[33] W. G. Hoskins, 'Harvest Fluctuations and English Economic History, 1480–1619', *Agricultural History Review* 12:1 (1964), 28–46, 42

have been classified as deficient, 35% as average, and only 40% as good.[34] To quote Hoskins:

> The yield of the harvest was the most fundamental fact of economic life in England as in all other countries. When we look at ... the fluctuations in the average price of wheat from year to year we are looking at the electro-cardiogram of a living organism. These are the heart-beats of the whole economy of England through ... generations. The health and well-being of the entire country depended upon the quality of this heart-beat more than upon any other organ and activity.[35]

In the first years of the seventeenth century there would have been clear memories of dearth. In the 1590s four good harvests, which induced the government to repeal the Anti-enclosure Act of 1563, were followed by four terrible years. In 1594 incessant rains fell, and by 1596 grain prices had almost doubled, with the Great Famine prevailing over much of Europe. There were food riots in many counties, the most serious being in Oxfordshire, in particular the Enslow Hill rebellion already mentioned.[36] Legislation in 1597 and 1598 experimented in the relief of poverty and the maintenance of husbandry and tillage.[37] In the early years of the following century the bad harvest of 1608 was also followed by the plague year of 1609, frequently a disease accompanying poverty and malnutrition.[38] Apart from those years, the first two decades of seventeenth century enjoyed average to good harvests.[39] The early 1620s were wet, leading to a disastrous harvest in 1622 and famine in 1623. The later 1620s were good, but the 1630s generally poor, resulting in inflated food prices. As a consequence, the 1640s opened with widespread agrarian disorders, but despite the disruption of the Civil War there were generally good harvests until the middle of the decade. Poor harvests in the second half of 1640s led once again to rising food prices, by nearly 50% in five years. These short-term fluctuations in the cost of living were critical to the vast majority of the population. Cromwell's years of rule during the 1650s were generally plentiful, and food prices stabilised. Harvests were poor at start of the 1660s, followed by good years later in the decade, and mixed harvests in the 1670s. A generally good sequence in the 1680s was once again followed by poor crops at the end of the century with sharp rises in food prices.[40] A critical

---

[34] W. G. Hoskins, 'Harvest Fluctuations and English Economic History, 1620–1759', *Agricultural History Review* 16 (1968), 15–31, 15
[35] Hoskins, 'Harvest Fluctuations and English Economic History, 1480–1619', 40
[36] *Ibid.*, 38
[37] *Ibid.*, 37–8
[38] Hoskins, 'Harvest Fluctuations and English Economic History, 1620–1759', 18
[39] Hoskins, 'Harvest Fluctuations and English Economic History, 1480–1619', 39
[40] Hoskins, 'Harvest Fluctuations and English Economic History, 1620–1759', 18–22

factor in the availability of foodstuffs from crops was the balance between bread corn and seed corn. A sequence of bad harvests would have a cumulative effect as the supply of seed corn was depleted. As Hoskins observes: 'The English economy in the sixteenth and seventeenth centuries was an agrarian economy that worked on a very fine margin between sufficiency and shortage.'[41] Thus, although the area surrounding Thame was in average years favourable to agriculture, the harvest was always susceptible to poor weather conditions, leading to a constant uncertainty and for the poorer members of the community the real prospect of insecurity and hunger, even if, from the latter part of the sixteenth century, the development of an integrated grain market meant that it was a fear of want rather than actual starvation.[42] In a primarily agricultural community, therefore, climatic conditions would have had a considerable impact on living conditions and, even amongst the more prosperous members of the community, the sense of well-being from year to year.

The Settlement of Thame and its Market Economy

The landscape surrounding Thame was thus a physical domain essential to the sustenance and economic viability of the community, one invested with possibilities, conflicts and uncertainties. The settlement of Thame itself, with its satellite hamlets of Attingham, North Weston and Moreton, represented a world within this world, of streets, of houses, of communal buildings and spaces, and of social dynamics, imbued with significance for the inhabitants of the town – a map of shifting and evolving opportunities and constraints. This was the world most contingent on the individual household, providing the context for its economic and social existence. Approximately three-quarters of the English population was living off agriculture during the early modern period, according to the late seventeenth-century statistician, Gregory King, and perhaps a fifth were living in the small market towns which serviced this economy.[43] According to Clark and Slack: 'Towns were the essential cogs in the machinery of rural society, providing organization, articulation and diversity.'[44] Towns such as Thame had an intimate relationship with their rural hinterland, the countryside penetrating up to the boundaries of the small urban settlement; not only was the economy of the town based on the agricultural production of the

---

[41] *Ibid.*, 17

[42] P. Glennie and I. Whyte, 'Towns in an Agrarian Economy 1540–1700', *The Cambridge Urban History of Britain*, ed. D. M. Palliser, P. Clark and M. J. Daunton (Cambridge: Cambridge University Press, 2000), pp. 179–80

[43] *Ibid.*, p. 169; P. Clark and P. Slack, *English Towns in Transition 1550–1700* (Oxford: Oxford University Press, 1976), p. 11

[44] *Ibid.*, p. 1

region, and most inhabitants, even those in trades, had some direct involvement in cultivation, but the town market also provided the outlet for the produce of the hinterland.[45]

As the term 'market town' implies, a principal distinguishing feature of Thame was its large market space, especially noted for the sale of cattle. It is known that a settlement existed here in Anglo-Saxon times on a favourable site where a sandstone spit rises above the surrounding clay, defended on two sides by water, clustered around the parish church. The original landowners, the bishops of Dorchester, transferred the manor to the see of Lincoln around 1078. Although the earliest record of a Tuesday market dates from the late twelfth century, it was in 1215 that the Bishop of Lincoln was granted permission to establish fairs and markets in his manorial possessions. Consequently, in 1221 New Thame (as opposed to Old Thame, the original settlement around the parish church) was laid out around the extensive market space, on which regular markets were established in 1227 and through which the main road from Oxford to Aylesbury was diverted (Figure 1.3). A survey of the bishop's estates at this time records sixty-three burgesses; burgage plots of some 700 feet in length existed to the south of the High Street, of lesser length to the north. By the fifteenth century the town extended as far as Friday (present-day North) Street, and by 1700 as far as the White Hound Pond.[46] The market traded a wide range of the local agricultural produce. The confirmatory grant obtained by Lord Norris in 1603 refers to it as a 'wool market', but in a Civil War raid in 1643 Royalist forces from Oxford commandeered all the fat cattle bought by London butchers, and by 1673 it was noted as being 'well frequented by grasiers and butchers from London and other parts, for the buying of cattle, for which it is eminent'.[47] The prestige of the market was embodied in the market hall, the sixteenth-century timber-framed structure with open space below for shops, rebuilt after its collapse in 1679 at the expense of the Norris family (Figure 1.4).[48] The market had thus reflected the shift towards specialist production for the growing metropolitan market. Sections of the market and remaining street names give an indication of the goods sold: Cock Row, The Drapery, Sheep Row, Butter Market, Cornmarket and Hog Fair were all recorded at various times in the seventeenth century.

A market town such as Thame did not simply act as an entrepot for local produce but performed a wide range of complementary services.[49]

---

[45] Ibid., p. 18

[46] Clarke, The Book of Thame, p. 14; VCH, pp. 162–5

[47] Richard Blome, Britannia: or, A Geographical Description of the Kingdoms of England, Scotland, and Ireland, with the Isles and Territories Thereto Belonging (London, 1677), p. 189

[48] VCH, pp. 161, 166

[49] A. Dyer, 'Small Market Towns 1540–1700', The Cambridge Urban History of Britain, Volume 2: 1540–1840, ed. P. Clark (Cambridge: Cambridge University Press, 2000), pp. 440–1

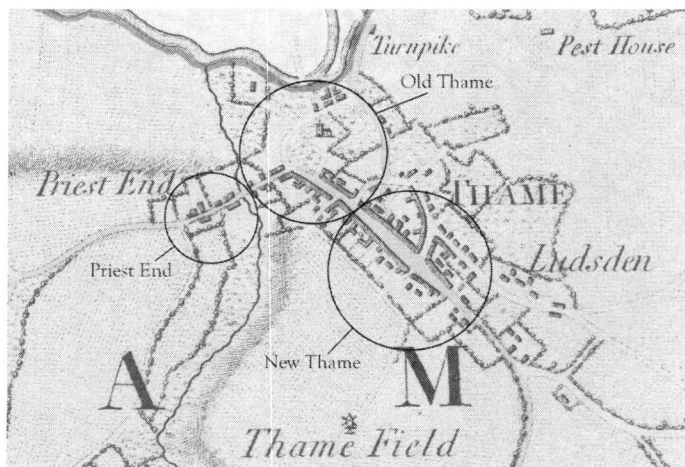

Figure 1.3 Detail from map of Oxfordshire by R. Davis, 1797

Figure 1.4 Thame sixteenth-century market hall

Amongst the decedents of the probate inventories were primary processors of local agricultural produce: butchers, curriers and cordwainers processing the livestock for meat and leather, millers grinding corn, hemp dressers processing flax and maltsters barley for brewing. Eight butchers are listed, and amongst the assets of Richard Striblehill, whose inventory was made in 1607, were a bullock, a lamb, a calf and 2 sheep in the slaughter house and 9 pigs and 2 other beasts in the stable.[50] Weavers and dyers were making and processing textiles, collarmakers and a plough-wright providing implements for farmers. The many visitors to the market were catered for by victuallers and innkeepers, trading within the comfort of inns complementing market transactions later in the century. Bakers and brewers catered for other sustenance in the town. Artisan-traders, the tailor, shoemaker

[50] OHCA: MS. Wills Pec. 50/5/36

and glover, helped to clothe the populace, the brazier provided cooking pots and the cooper barrels for a wide range of applications, including beer and the salting of food. Distributive tradesmen, such as the mercer, draper and milliner, provided a wide range of goods from outside the locality for farmers and their wives on the market or in shops. Professional services were provided by the clerks, scrivener and surveyor, personal grooming or rudimentary surgery by the barber, and spiritual care by the vicar. And the construction needs of the locality were catered for by a wide range of artisans: the mason, carpenter, joiner, locksmith and glazier. Table 1.1 shows the frequency of different occupations gathered into occupational status categories. In terms of named occupational status, it will be noted that whilst those of gentlemen, widows and agricultural producers – yeomen, husbandmen and labourers – are described collectively, the urban traders and producers make up a great diversity of occupations, even in a small community like Thame. In terms of occupational status categories that of gentlemen is self-explanatory. Clerics were those of professional status. Yeomen were those who generally owned land, and husbandmen were copyholders of land, whilst agricultural labourers were waged. Traders were those who from the inventory evidence were simply selling goods, artisans simply making, whilst artisan-traders appear to have been both making and selling. (Within individual shops there would also have been a distinction in productive labour between the master and his or her 'servants'). It should also be noted that the premises of eight innkeepers, an important market town occupation, were also inventoried. They do not form part of this study as an inn is not strictly a domicile and their inclusion would distort the evidence of purely domestic furnishings. For the same reason the significant association of shops and workshops to dwellings is referred to later in relation to its impact on domestic life, but the conduct of trade and craft is not examined in depth. Table 1.2a shows the relationship of the value of domestic furnishings to occupational status, gentlemen and clerics being the most affluent, and husbandmen, agricultural labourers and artisans least so. In Table 2.2b a point of interest is the relatively larger size of the dwellings (in terms of rooms) of urban traders and artisan-traders in comparison with those of yeomen and husbandmen.[51]

The market town, such as Thame, therefore provided an outlet for goods from its hinterland and services in return – an economic unit with spatial and relational dimensions for those engaged in its operations. A 'sense of place' in such a world was founded on the immediate locality, with its daily routines and intimate relationships revolving around a limited domain. For many this was the quotidian sphere; the household, the working world and

---

[51] Online Appendix 1, Table 1.3, 'Occupational status: distribution by date and by furnishing value', at http://boybrew.co/9781783270415 reveals (apart from gentry and clerical households) a relatively close correspondence of occupational status to varying bands of furnishing wealth relatively unchanged through the study period.

Table 1.1 Occupational status categories with mean household furnishing values and frequency of occupations of inventoried decedents

Occupational status category	Total in category	Mean value of furnishings	Named occupations	Frequency
gentlemen	5	£88.23	gentlemen	5
clerics	6	£62.46	clerk	2
			scrivener	1
			surveyor	1
			vicar	2
yeomen	41	£35.57	yeoman	41
husbandmen	12	£11.13	husbandman	11
			gardener	1
agricultural labourers	5	£5.34	labourer	2
			shepherd	3
traders	17	£30.80	butcher	6
			draper	1
			mercer	1
			merchant	1
			milliner	1
			shopkeeper	2
			victualler	5
artisan-traders	31	£30.29	baker	3
			blacksmith	4
			brasier	1
			brewer	1
			chandler	2
			collermaker	1
			cooper	1
			cordwainer	3
			currier	2
			glazier	1
			glover	2
			gunsmith	1
			locksmith	1
			malster	1
			miller	1
			plowright	1
			salter	1
			shoemaker	2
			weaver	1
			not specified	1

Occupational status category	Total in category	Mean value of furnishings	Named occupations	Frequency
artisans	23	£18.29	barber/surgeon	2
			bricklayer	1
			carpenter	3
			cordwainer	3
			dyer	1
			glazier	1
			hempdresser	1
			joiner	1
			mason	1
			miller	3
			shoemaker	1
			tailor	3
			weaver	2
widows-spinsters	37	£22.46	widow	35
			spinster	2
not specified	11	£11.28	not specified	11
Total	188			188

N.B. some occupations – for example 'miller' – are found in both artisan-trader and artisan categories, on the basis of inventory evidence suggesting whether trading was occurring in addition to artisan work.

Table 1.2a Mean value of furnishings by occupational status category

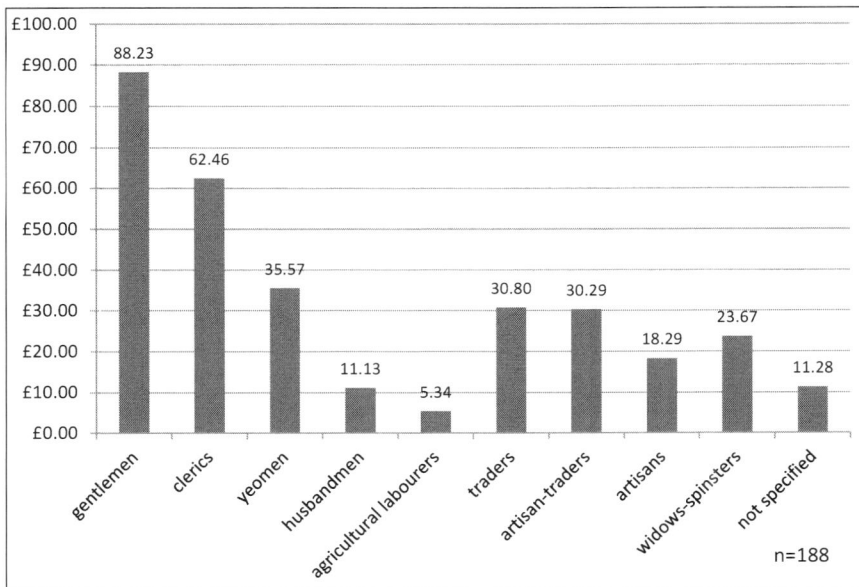

Table 1.2b Mean frequency of dwelling rooms by occupational status category

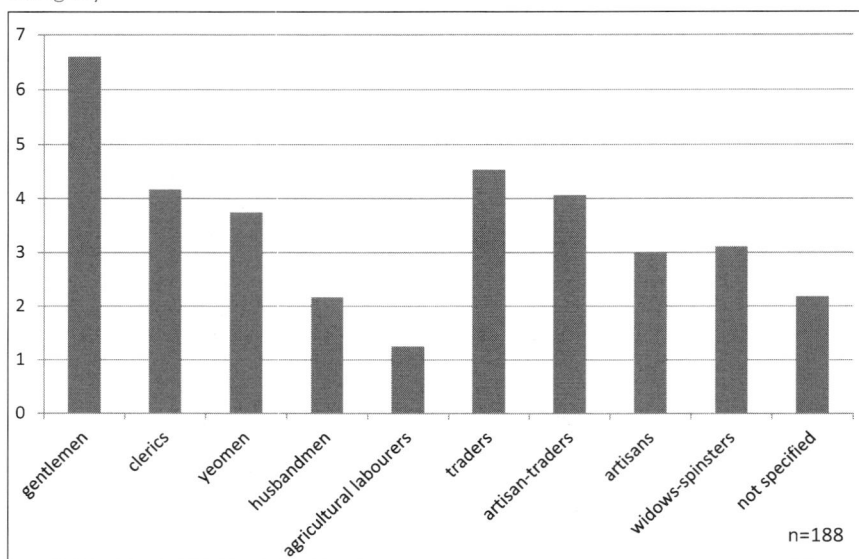

its social relationships. For most not only their occupation but also their degree of mobility would place limitations to their horizons. The distribution of the medieval market was based on the principle that a peasant would spend two-thirds of a day walking to and from market, and one-third engaged in his or her business. A pertinent indication of the implications of distance and mobility is provided by the fact that market towns tended to have a larger hinterland in areas of animal husbandry than in arable regions; getting mobile livestock to market simply involved less effort than conveying harvested crops.[52] The town of Thame was also the largest settlement in its neighbourhood, with a population in 1600 of around 800, rising by the end of the seventeenth century to approximately 1,500, compared with a village of generally fewer than 200 inhabitants.[53] But whilst this was a focussed world, it was not self-contained. As Laslett and Wrightson point out, the localism of the agrarian pre-industrial age was giving way, primarily through demographic pressures, to a growing awareness of the wider world.[54] The network of roads (Figure 1.5) that brought local villagers into the town for

[52] Dyer, 'Small Market Towns 1540–1700', p. 429

[53] P. Motla, 'The Occupational Structure of Thame c.1600–1700', *Oxfordshire Local History*, 4:2 (1993), 62; Clark and Slack, *English Towns in Transition 1550–1700*, p. 19

[54] Peter Laslett, *The World we Have Lost: Further Explored*, 3rd edn (Abingdon: Routledge, 1983), p. 76; Keith Wrightson, *English Society 1580–1680* (Abingdon: Routledge, 2003), pp. 48–52

Figure 1.5
Detail from
'A New Map
of Twenty
Miles around
Oxford'
attributed
to Benjamin
Cole, 1706

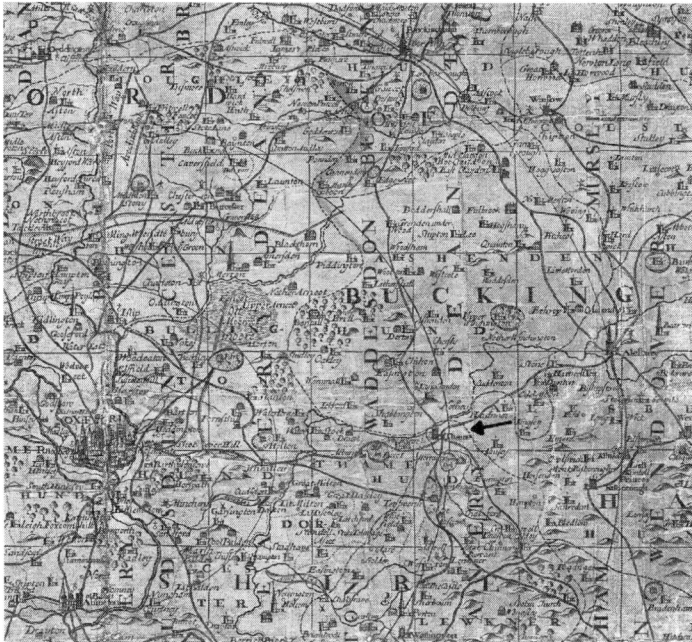

their trading also led beyond to a wider world, to the regional centres of Oxford and Aylesbury, and further still to London. The most important local communication since earliest times was the road from Aylesbury to Wallingford, with the road used by travellers from Oxford to London running three miles to the south of Thame, and the Icknield Way four and a half miles to the south-east. To the north ran the road to Long Crendon and the Buckinghamshire villages. Down these roads came the chapmen with their wares and accounts of a larger world, the manufactured goods sold by the mercer and the draper, and the London dealers in search of livestock to drive back to the great metropolis, out of sight but exerting its influence throughout the south-east, changing cultivation and developing commerce. And the population itself was far from self-contained. Service and apprenticeship led to migration out of and into the town, and marriage was frequently outside the community. Researching marriage patterns in Tudor and Stuart Shrivenham in Berkshire, Dils and Schwartz found that only 29% of the women born in the village who survived to maturity were married in the village.[55]

So, Thame need not be considered a rural backwater. It had one of the principal markets in the region, set in a fertile vale. The market was success-

[55] J. Dils and D. Schwartz, *Tudor and Stuart Shrivenham* (Reading: The Authors, 2004), pp. 107-8

fully defended against a potential market grant to Aylesbury in 1657 and the setting-up of a rival horse fair in Oxford in 1683.[56] Hints of a significant past may have lingered in the substantial parish church, the partially ruined abbey and the old prebendal chapel and hall. And, whilst not self-governing and subjected to manorial authority, a sense of reflected status may have emanated from the local landed gentry who flourished on the national stage. The most notable local figure was John Williams, the younger son of a Berkshire landowner born around 1500. Prominent in Wolsey's administration and holding positions at court, he was appointed Visitor for the Monasteries in 1539, and benefitted substantially from surrendered monastic lands, including Thame Abbey. Created Lord Williams by Queen Mary, he was for a time the lenient custodian of Princess Elizabeth, who later favoured his house of Rycote with several visits during her reign. A legacy in his will of 1559 established both almshouses and the grammar school, a valuable asset to a market town which the antiquarian William Camden described in 1610 as 'a very faire schole'.[57] Amongst the prominent students were Lord Chief Justice Sir John Holt (1642–1710), John Fell (1625–86) the dean of Christchurch and Bishop of Oxford, and the parliamentarian John Hampden (c.1595–1643).[58]

Nor could Thame isolate itself from national events when the Civil War erupted in 1642, situated as it was on the road between the Royalist forces in Oxford and those of Parliament in Aylesbury, both with an interest in accessing provisions from the market and town. A graphic account is given by Anthony Woods, then a pupil at the grammar school, of the pursuit of Royalist cavalry through the town by Parliamentarians.[59] Early in 1643 attempts were made by Parliamentary forces to achieve a permanent footing in the town. In June of that year Essex made his headquarters there, but retired to Aylesbury in July after harrying by Royalist forces under Prince Rupert, including the action on Chalgrove Field which led to the death of the wounded John Hampden six days after the engagement, on 24 June in a Thame inn. As well as the inevitable depletion of resources in the neighbourhood, as a consequence of the passage of the Parliamentary army the town suffered an outbreak of disease which led to a surge in mortality.[60] As mentioned earlier, in August 1643 Royalists commandeered all fat cattle bought by London butchers at Thame market, and in January 1644 Prince Rupert made Thame his base for an attack on Aylesbury, and Royalist forces appear to have remained in Thame until the spring of 1645. After

---

[56] VCH, p. 182
[57] Clarke, *The Book of Thame*, pp. 35–44
[58] VCH, pp. 160–5
[59] Clarke, *The Book of Thame*, p. 50; N. K. Kiessling, ed. *The Life of Anthony Wood in his own Words* (Oxford: Bodleian Library, 2009), pp. 15–16
[60] See J. Bell, 'The Mortality Crisis in Thame and East Oxfordshire 1643', *Oxfordshire Local History* 3:4 (1990), 137–52

the Royalist defeat at the battle of Naseby, Parliamentary forces again reoc-
cupied Thame in preparation for an attack on Oxford, before the Royalist
garrison there surrendered in June 1646.[61]

The Social and Moral Culture

Thus far we have looked at the way in which the environment and its
economic exploitation might have affected the Thame household. But
the physical environment was not the only context; the household also
existed in a web of social relationships. This was evidently an inequitable
society in terms of material wealth; it was also unequal in terms of social
status. A gulf of standing and opportunity separated the most privileged in
the parish of Thame from the most disadvantaged. Local landowners, of
whom the Thame householder would have been well aware both in terms
of presence and economic, political and social influence, represented the
higher echelons of English society. The township, both Old and New
Thame, originally passed to Lord Williams in 1550 after its sale by the
Bishop of Lincoln to the Protector Somerset. By the seventeenth century it
was in the possession of the Norris family, from 1682 made Earls of Abingdon, descendants through a daughter of Lord Williams, and inheritors of
Rycote House in the neighbouring parish of Great Haseley. The other elite
house in the neighbourhood, Thame Park (originally the Cistercian abbey
acquired by Lord Williams) was the seat of the Wenman family, initially
wool merchants from the Witney region and lords of Moreton manor,
descended from Richard Wenman, who had married Lord Williams' second surviving daughter.[62] It was no accident that the nobility and gentry
lived nearby amongst the rural community as elite status was very much
defined by the owning of land. The town made at least nominal deference
to their social masters, making a payment of twenty shillings from parish
funds 'for wyne for my lord of Thame for suche pleasing as he dyd to the
p[ar]yshe'. At the other end of the social scale were the indigent poor, such
as 'an Irishman, his Wife & three small children' given a shilling from
the same source.[63] Ranged in between were the prosperous yeomen and
merchant traders, husbandmen and artisans, common labourers and the
poor of the parish.

Late sixteenth- and early seventeenth-century accounts of the social order
tend to suggest a well-ordered hierarchy with clearly defined ranks, from the
titled nobility, knights, esquires and gentlemen, to the professions, citizens

[61] VCH, p. 161
[62] *Ibid.*, pp. 170–7
[63] H. Lupton, *Extracts from the Accounts of the Proctors and Stewards of the Prebendal Church of
the Blessed Virgin in Thame, Commencing in the year 1529 and Ending in the Year 1641, and of the
Churchwardens of Thame Beginning in the Year 1542* (Thame: Henry Bradford, 1852), pp. 4, 32

and burgesses, yeomen, husbandmen, artisans, labourers and servants.[64] Emanating as these accounts do from writers at the upper end of the social scale, great attention is placed on the grading of noble and gentry status; indeed, one of the main impressions gained is of the great divide which was considered to exist between genteel and non-genteel rank. However, where the two collided, the accounts show some confusion and differing interpretations of gentry status. One possible explanation is the desire for recognisable status in a world of increasing social mobility. As well by inheritance, William Harrison, writing in 1587, ascribed genteel rank to those who had studied the law, or attended university, or held rank in the armed forces. But most significantly, gentry status seems to have been equated with presentation based on wealth: any man who 'can live without manual labour, and thereto is able and will bear the port, charge and countenance … [will be] … reputed for a gentleman ever after'.[65] Wealthy merchants were placed below gentlemen, but here Harrison recognised the reality that changing economic fortunes could alter social status: 'our merchants … often change estate with gentlemen, as gentlemen do with them, by a mutual conversion of the one into the other'.[66] Yeomen were described as men of 'a certain pre-eminence and more estimation than labourers and the common sort of artificers', who 'commonly live wealthily [and] keep good houses'. Their enterprise, especially at a time of rising commodity prices when Harrison wrote, could generate

> great wealth, insomuch that many of them are able and do buy the lands of unthrifty gentlemen, and often setting their sons to the schools, to the universities, and to the Inns of the Court, or, otherwise leaving them sufficient lands whereupon they may live without labour, do make them by those means to become gentlemen.[67]

The mass of the population was condensed into 'the fourth and last sort of people in England': 'day-labourers, poor husbandmen, and some retailers (which have no free land), copyholders, and all artificers, as tailors, shoemakers, carpenters, brickmakers, masons, etc [who] have neither voice nor authority in the commonwealth, but are to be ruled and not to rule other'. Harrison does, however, acknowledge that whilst such as these have no recognisable status in a national context, they may do so at a local level; 'in villages they are commonly made churchwardens, sidesmen, alecon-

---

[64] Keith Wrightson, 'The Social Order of Early Modern England', *The World We Have Gained: Histories of Population and Social Structure*, ed. L. Bonfield, R. Smith and K. Wrightson (Oxford: Blackwell, 1986), p. 179

[65] William Harrison, *The Description of England* (1587), ed. G. Washington Edelen (New York: Folger Shakespeare Library, Dover Books 1994), pp. 113–14

[66] *Ibid.*, p. 114

[67] *Ibid.*, pp. 117–18

ners, now and then constables'.[68] Some hundred years later in 1688 the statistician Gregory King made a similar survey of the composition of the population, but now with a more overtly economic estimation of status; those who were, in his words, increasing and decreasing the wealth of the kingdom, understood not only as wealth creation but as control of wealth-producing assets. King, like Harrison, listed in detail the distinct ranks of the nobility, followed by gentlemen, office-holders and – significantly for the changing origins of wealth – greater and lesser merchants 'by sea'. Lawyers and clergy were now succeeded not by yeomen by name, but by freeholders of the 'better' and 'lesser' sort, and by farmers, reflecting the commercialisation of agriculture. Again, changes in trading were reflected by the identification of shopkeepers as a category, with tradesmen followed by artisans and makers of handicraft. Those in the armed forces were followed by labourers and servants, cottagers and paupers, with 'vagrants, as gipsies, thieves, beggars etc' firmly located at the lowest level of the table. By an estimation of numbers in each category, King reckoned that half of the population, labourers, servants, cottagers and paupers, insecure in employment and land tenure, were effectively a deficit to the wealth of the kingdom. His table thus has elements of a table of precedence, with the distinction of 'ranks, degrees, titles and qualifications', but this is far more a table of occupation, as though King was paying deference to old concepts of status whilst estimating the new.[69]

Given that Harrison and King showed little concern with the finer gradations of social status at the lower levels of society, what kind of social dynamic operated within a community like Thame? In the rural community and small town the most elevated social position after the local gentry was that of yeoman, defined as someone who could lay freehold claim to what had been in early Tudor times land worth forty shillings per annum in revenue. The term came in time to represent any person of substance, generally a freeholder of land. Wealthy tradesmen also laid claim to the title. It was therefore a reflection of substance in the community, but also guarded as a mark of respect. William Snow of Thame, who died in 1621, described himself as a yeoman in his will, but was recorded, doubtless more accurately and reflecting his fallen condition, as labourer in the inventory of his modest two-roomed dwelling.[70] As Harrison noted, there were also local positions of authority available to the inhabitants of towns and villages. If Thame had been an incorporated borough the townsmen could have achieved pre-eminence in their community as aldermen, often as part of a powerful self-perpetuating oligarchy, but even within a seigneurial possession positions existed which brought local prestige, as constable, ale-conner

[68] *Ibid.*, p. 118
[69] G. M. Trevelyan, *English Social History* (1944) (London: Longman, 1978), pp. 240–3
[70] OHCA: MS. Wills Pec. 51/1/35

or summoned on to the jury of the leet court.[71] High local status could be enjoyed by being appointed a trustee to town charitable institutions, such as the almshouses re-endowed in Lord Williams' will or the grammar school named in his memory. But the body which most represented public prestige was the vestry of the parish church, administering the most important building in the town, charitable collections and adopting the important role of poor relief.

One place where the social dynamics of the community would have been experienced weekly was in the seating arrangements in the parish church. In the words of Susan Amussen, 'The placement of people in the church was the visible representation of the local hierarchy.'[72] In theory a clear order existed with gentry at the head, followed by yeomen, husbandmen and finally labourers. But changed local fortunes could create presumptions of changed status, even involving the church seating of servants, which on occasions became the subject of legal dispute. In addition, in the latter part of the seventeenth century precedence became increasingly embodied in enclosed pews reserved for one family or household, such as the leading Stribblehill family in Thame. But this tension should not necessarily be viewed as the result of a rigid social order but perhaps the reverse; Amussen suggests that church seating became so critical because the social order was being challenged outside the church.[73] Attendance at church was an opportunity to attempt to restate through seating the ideal social hierarchy. But not all parishioners attended church on Sunday, as they were theoretically obliged to do. There are many accounts of clerical alarm at poor attendance, and whilst Archbishop Grindal's injunctions in 1571 emphasised the desirability of householders' attendance, servants and the poor were considered beyond recall. Reasons for non-attendance included ignorance, indifference and scepticism.[74] Attempts to remedy the situation included Sabbatarian legislation in 1625 making games and sports on Sundays punishable with fines or spending three hours in the stocks. By an Act of 1593 recusants had to register with the parish constable, and the parish constable had to make annual presentments to justices for those who failed to attend church once a month by an Act of 1606.[75] In 1670 ninety Thame parishioners were accused of non-attendance and subsequent non-payment of fines to the vicar.[76]

---

[71] Clark and Slack, *English Towns in Transition 1550–1700*, p. 128
[72] S. D. Amussen, *An Ordered Society: Gender and Class in Early Modern England* (Oxford: Blackwell, 1993), p. 138
[73] *Ibid.*, pp. 138–44
[74] K. Thomas, *Religion and the Decline of Magic* (London: Weidenfeld and Nicolson, 1971), pp. 159–73
[75] Joan R. Kent, *The English Village Constable 1580–1642* (Oxford: Clarendon Press, 1986), pp. 33, 34
[76] Clarke, *The Book of Thame*, pp. 109–10

Another aspect of church seating was the increasing segregation of men and women during the seventeenth century, and maidens from married women. Women's condition in theory varied according to marital status.[77] Until marriage the woman should be under the authority of her father or male relative, and during marriage under the authority of her husband. The evidence suggests that marital relations varied widely; wives in the working households of Thame would have exercised considerable authority in the conduct of the house and work. However, in the public domain the woman was supposed to act in a subservient manner to her husband.[78] Only widows enjoyed a considerable degree of personal status in the community, due to their independence and accumulated financial assets. With marriage lasting on average some twenty years, and widowhood some ten years, widows represent around 19% of the decedents in Thame. In her study of the economic status of widows in Thame and Woodstock in the seventeenth century, Mary Hodges identified them as major sources of finance for family and neighbours.[79] In the working environment of a small market town many relationships would have revolved around reciprocal need. Vertical ties of patronage and clientage in the traditional hierarchy appear to have been complemented by strong horizontal bonds of day-to-day contact and shared interests.[80] Nevertheless, Wrightson emphasises 'the pervasive influence of relative social position on the life experiences and opportunities of individuals'.[81]

What then of the values that were supposed to inform social relationships? One might imagine that the established church, charged as it was with the conduct of the rites of baptism, marriage and burial, would be the fount of moral conduct. The very title of the Book of Common Prayer, first published in 1549 and republished in 1559, was designed to emphasise the unity of the congregation and its shared beliefs. Sermons provided an opportunity for the priest to convey moral instruction to their flock. Not all parish priests were licensed to preach, and books of homilies were intended to provide moral instruction. Bishop Jewel's *Second Book of Homilies* contained exhortations towards greater religious observance – 'Of the place and time of Prayer' and 'Of Repentance and true Reconciliation unto God', for example – and also instructions on the conduct of a godly life – 'Against gluttony and drunkenness', 'Against excess of apparel', and 'Of the state of Matrimony'.[82] Religious instruction was also part of the culture of Lord

---

[77] Thomas, *Religion and the Decline of Magic*, p. 152
[78] Wrightson, *English Society 1580–1680*, pp. 98–101
[79] M. Hodges, 'Widows of the Middling Sort and their Assets in Two Seventeenth-Century Towns', *When Death Do Us Part: Understanding and Interpreting the Probate Inventory Records of Early Modern England*, ed. T. Arkell, N.Evans and N. Goose (Oxford: Leopard's Head Press, 2000), p. 308
[80] Keith Wrightson and D. Levine, *Poverty and Piety in an English Village: Terling 1525–1700* (New York: Academic Press, 1979), p. 192
[81] Wrightson, 'The Social Order of Early Modern England', pp. 186–7
[82] John Jewel, *The Second Tome Book of Homilies* (London, 1571)

Williams Grammar School: daily prayers were held 'for inculcating piety or for checking the frivolity of the young'. The pupils attended church each Sunday and were given a test on the sermon on their return.[83] But there are indications that such instruction appealed only to the educated elite. Writing in *The Christian Divine* in 1631, Edmund Reeve noted that 'there are extant in English sundry books very profitable, which few of the common people do make use of, for that their style and words for the most or a great part are for scholars only'.[84] There were also those who chose to make their own compact with God. Thame had a tradition of nonconformity; some of the upper members of Thame society had Puritan leanings, including the Petty family (who were related to the Cromwells), the Hampdens, Ingoldsbys and Wallers, and the church incumbent, Thomas Hennant was Puritan in sympathy in early Stuart times. From the mid-seventeenth century a strong strand of nonconformity existed. The Compton Census of 1676 recorded that there were 100 'utter' dissenters, including Quakers, Presbyterians and Anabaptists.[85] If Durkheim is correct, and it is by religious ritual that society affirms its collective unity, then the divergence of religious opinion and practice reflected an increasingly fragmented community.[86]

More informally the parish priest sought to act as the guide and mentor to his congregation. He would usually try to adjudicate in disputes, having consulted with members of the congregation; 'whenever any controversie is brought to him', wrote George Herbert, 'he never decides it alone, but sends three or four of the ablest of the Parish to hear cause with him'.[87] Secular literature also provided some guidance for everyday conduct. Gervase Markham's *A Way to Get Wealth by Approved Rules of Practice in Good Husbandry and Huswiferie* suggested that:

> our English Hus-wife must bee of chast thought, stout courage, patient, untyred, watchful, diligent, witty, pleasant, constant in friendship, full of good neighbourhood, wise in discourse, but not frequent therein, sharpe and quicke of speech, but not bitter or talkative, secret in her affaires, comfortable in her counsels, and generally skilfull in the worthy knowledge which do belong to her vocation.[88]

Significantly, the author does not offer any advice on desirable qualities in the man. Another more accessible source of guidance to conduct was

---

[83] Clarke, *The Book of Thame*, p. 44
[84] Thomas, *Religion and the Decline of Magic*, p. 163
[85] VCH, pp. 211–12
[86] Thomas, *Religion and the Decline of Magic*, p. 172
[87] George Herbert, *A Priest to the Temple* (1652), ed. H. C. Beeching (Oxford: Blackwell, 1908), p. 89
[88] Gervase Markham, *The English Housewife* (1615), ed. M. R. Best (Kingston and Montreal, McGill-Queen's University Press, 1986), p. 6

the broadside ballad sheet. Some, with titles such as *A Prospective Glass for Christians to Behold the Reigning Sins of the Age: or, The Complaint of Truth and Conscience Against Pride, Envy, Hatred and Malice; which is too Much Practis'd in this Present Age* (Figure 1.6) were straightforward exhortations to a godly life. Others presented a fable to be sung to a popular tune for entertainment, but conveying nevertheless instruction in right conduct and describing the consequence of failure to conform to prescribed roles. In *The Carefull Wife's Good Counsel: or, The Husband's Firm Resolution to Reform his Life, and to Lay up Something Against a Rainy Day* (Figure 1.7) the wife counsels her husband against the passing attractions of ale-wives and 'jovial boon companions' who will desert him once he has 'wast his youthfull strength', each verse ending with reminder of 'the rainy day' to come. There was thus a spectrum of counsel in personal conduct from the pulpit to fables of common sense. However, all conduct literature must be considered as a possible indication of anxiety surrounding challenges to established authority and the inscribed modes of conduct. And the exclusion of large sections of the population from the educated discourse does not necessarily imply a lack of moral awareness, but the growth and message of the dissenting community indicates that, in their opinion at least, moral instruction was to be found outside the established church and exercised in everyday conduct.

Right conduct was not simply a matter of personal behaviour, but also of the law. The Thame householder had concerns for harmonious relationships with his or her neighbours and the security of his household and property. Civil matters were dealt with by the successors to the medieval manorial courts, held at regular intervals. Records exist for courts baron

Figure 1.6
Broadside ballad
engraving 1683–96

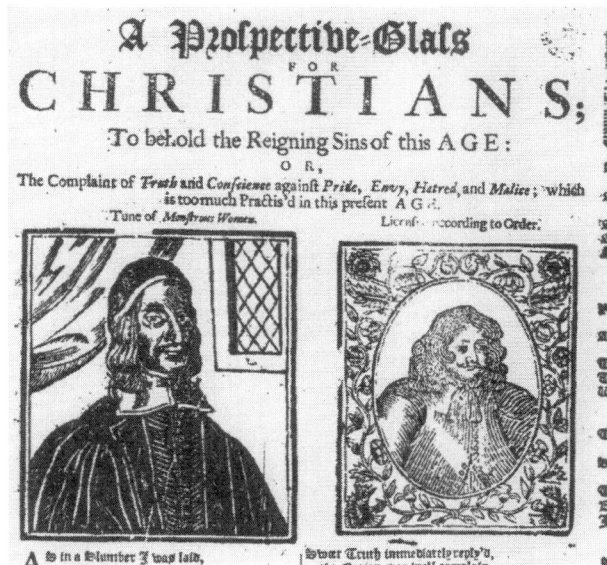

THE CAREFULL

Wife's Good Counsel :

OR, THE

Husband's firm Resolution to Reform his Life,' and to lay up something a-
gainst a Rainy Day.

To the Tune of The Spinning-Wheel.   Licensed according to Order.

Figure 1.7
Broadside ballad
engraving 1683–96

for Old Thame, Priestend, North Weston and Moreton. During the seventeenth century the vestry grew in importance as an administrative body, but
frankpledge – the binding together of a tithing or small unit of households
to be held responsible for each other's good conduct – and manorial courts
continued to be held by the bishop's successors to the lordship. Their main
business was the admission of tenants, the regulation of the open field system and the appointment of the offices of fieldsmen, hogsherds, haywards
and mole-catchers. Courts were also vested with the upkeep of the roads
and the enforcement of sanitary rules about the streets and market place.
At Old Thame court in 1608 2 scourers of watercourses, 2 meat-tasters and
4 tithingmen were elected. At the October court for 1649 nineteen jurors
dealt with presentments which included killing bulls unbaited (mostly by
men from neighbouring villages), bloodshed, killing sheep and calves and
emptying paunches in the shambles, contrary to the regulations. Town
officers were also elected at the October courts, in 1676 including 2 sealers
of leather, 2 constables, 2 ale-tasters, 2 fleshtasters, 2scavengers and 4 tithingmen.[89] The tithing system placed an emphasis on the role of neighbours
in the maintenance of harmonious civic relations. As part of a culture of
mutual benefit, neighbours were a central element in social relationships
and support, providing – in the words of Wrightson – 'mutual recognition of reciprocal obligations' and assurance of 'proper behaviour between
neighbours', although when relationships turned to the bad, neighbours

---

[89] VCH, p. 195

could and did resort to acrimonious and frequently long and expensive actions in the courts of law.[90]

More forcible daily reminders of the law and its sanctions, the gallows, the whipping post and stocks, were visible to the inhabitants of Thame. It is also possible that the Birdcage Inn had been used as a prison in the sixteenth century.[91] The apparatus of punishment was the responsibility of the town constable, the figure invested with the prestige of the law and the local representation of authority. He it was who was responsible for the maintenance of law and order in the township and the enforcing of government statutes.[92] Although the constables appear to represent a clear legal process for misdemeanours, in practice much misconduct was dealt with by conciliation. At a time when the theft of goods valued at a shilling was punishable with hanging, price inflation had made a man's life cheap. Justices were often berating constables for their inefficiencies but there is evidence to suggest that they not infrequently chose to substitute reprimand for the harsh penalties of the law. The constable was himself a member of his community, and he had to live with the social consequences of his actions, including accusations of malicious intent. For the same reasons in a small community there was often unwillingness to report neighbours' misdemeanours; rather, remedy was sought by informal means.[93] The operation of justice was therefore often mediated in favour of good community relations.

In an increasingly commercial culture in the seventeenth century there was another aspect to neighbourly relationships which will be discussed at greater length in the context of domestic hospitality. In his seminal work on the operation of credit in this period, Muldrew identifies the convergence of financial viability and trust: 'a strong notion of reciprocity in exchanges and communal bonds of neighbourliness coexisted with free movement of prices'.[94] Sociability was a form of currency, in commensal entertainment and the formation of social bonds thorough patronage and marriage. 'Trust had to be generated, communicated and negotiated by each household involved in the market', and the operation of the Thame household in the seventeenth century arguably adapted to meet this demand.[95]

For one group of people there was little sympathy, however: the indigent poor. Demographic changes were principally responsible for the growth in the late sixteenth century of a large body of 'the poor' perpetually living on the verge of chronic poverty, and the anxiety of civil disorder that

[90] Wrightson, *English Society 1580–1680*, p. 59
[91] Clarke, *The Book of Thame*, p. 19
[92] Kent, *The English Village Constable 1580–1642*, pp. 24–33
[93] Wrightson, *English Society 1580–1680*, p. 165–6
[94] Craig Muldrew, *The Economy of Obligation : The Culture of Credit and Social Relations in Early Modern England* (Basingstoke: Macmillan, 1998), p. 124
[95] *Ibid.*, p. 151

accompanied it amongst the more prosperous. In some English villages as much as a third of the population was considered to belong to this category and in need of relief, especially in a bad year.[96] Distinction was made between the deserving and undeserving poor, the 'rogues and vagabonds' who were a common enough sight on the roads. A statute of 1601 sought 'to prevent misdemeanours in lewd and idel people' such as 'unlawfull cuttynge or taking awaye of corne and grayne growynge, robbynge of orchards or gardens, dygginge upp or taking awaye fruite trees, breakynge of hedges, poles or other fences, cuttynge or spoiling of woodes and underwoodes', punishable by whipping, and another statute of 1604 called on all persons to assist in the apprehension of rogues, and convey them to the nearest constable or tithingman. In what was probably a vain attempt to reduce the poor's movement around the country, justices were supposed to issue authority for the poor to travel, and the constable to convey the diseased poor to the next parish.[97] For the deserving poor there was provision of parish relief, administered by the constable and vestry, as much precautionary as charitable. The world outside the household was therefore one which presented considerable insecurity to the householder, only partially addressed by local and national legal remedies, and the impression gained is one of security founded largely on individual and community resources.

In conclusion, the context of the Thame household was complex and multifaceted. The landscape and settlement set the physical parameters of life outside the dwelling, intimately linked to its existence through the affordance of livelihoods, subject to the vagaries of nature and the economic and political influences of the wider world. The social environment also structured social engagement without, and the expectations of relationships and conduct within the dwelling. And this was not a static cultural environment, but one which was undergoing significant change, presenting both challenges and opportunities. The household was thus not distinct from, but interdependent with and considered a key component of the early modern world. When Gregory King sought to survey the population of England in 1688 he did so by estimating the number of households, and the orderly household was in many ways taken as the archetype for the well-ordered society. It is to the household itself and its formation that we now turn.

---

[96] Wrightson, *English Society 1580–1680*, p. 157
[97] Kent, *The English Village Constable 1580–1642*, p. 31–2

2

The Early Modern Household in Context

Having examined the broader physical, economic, social and cultural context of Thame, we turn now to the household itself. On the assertion that the household is a key component of human societies, this section aims to identify the essential functions which determine domestic life: as a mechanism for biological and cultural reproduction, as a focus of subsistence and productive activity and as a social group sharing a dwelling space. Such characteristics have implications for the way in which the group is formed, is organised and develops, and for its internal dynamics, including the ideology and practice of relationships between members of different gender, age and economic status. This chapter will also examine the extent to which the formation, composition and social dynamic of the seventeenth-century English household corresponded to such archetypes. Finally it turns to the nature of the dwelling itself, based on the archaeological evidence of extant seventeenth-century buildings in Thame.

As argued in the introduction to this study, human life largely consists of experience of the intimate material and social environment, and therefore the domestic arena in which much of life is experienced should logically form a significant area of study. The domestic sphere is one which forms an important source for historical research and is regarded as a fundamental component in early modern society, and yet not infrequently it is taken simply as a given part of that wider world, its internal dynamics unexplored, its characteristics restricted to a brief description and definitions privileging certain aspects, as a residential group, as a dwelling space or as an economic unit.[1] It may be that it is the commonplace nature of the household that

---

[1] For example Peter Laslett, 'Introduction: The History of the Family', *Household and Family in Past Time*, ed. P. Laslett and R. Wall (Cambridge: Cambridge University Press, 1972); J. Boulton, *Neighbourhood and Society: A London Suburb in the Seventeenth Century* (Cambridge and New York: Cambridge University Press, 1987); P. Earle, *The Making of the English Middle Class: Business, Society and Family Life in London, 1660–1730* (London: Methuen, 1989); L. Weatherill, *Consumer Behaviour and Material Culture in Britain 1660–1760* (London: Routledge, 1988); M. Overton, J. Whittle, D. Dean and A. Hann, *Production and Consumption in English Households, 1600–1750* (London: Routledge, 2004)

leads to this oversight, or that the very complexity of the household and the diversity of activities which take place within it contribute to the fragmented nature of inquiry.[2] There are authors who have attempted to address this complexity, generally from the anthropological and archaeological perspective rather than the historical.[3] It may thus be profitable, whilst recognising the variation in its form and operation through time and place, to attempt to discern *core* characteristics in order to determine its *modus operandi* and to understand the role that the domestic group plays in human life. To avoid ambiguity, in the ensuing discussion the term 'family' will refer specifically to the conjugal pair and their offspring, and 'domestic group' to the frequently more extensive body residing together for the purposes not only of procreation but also of subsistence.

The Domestic Group as Reproductive and Social Unit

This study is based primarily on documentary evidence of material culture and asserts its centrality in developing an insight into the domestic culture of the period. Nevertheless, the household also comprises social elements and it is important to understand the role that they played in domestic life and in the formation and culture of the early modern household, as a significant part of the context for actions in the material world. With the focus on kinship, anthropologists have traditionally tended to see the domestic unit as a reproductive mechanism to manage the replenishment of the biological stock of the social group and through the acculturation of succeeding generations to inculcate behavioural norms and values. The formation of the domestic group is determined by the reproductive biology of the human species; the birth of vulnerable offspring initially needing intensive care and protection by the mother, followed by a prolonged period of physical and cultural maturation. The matricentral cell, the mother and her child, itself requires protective support, generally from the biological father. In return, in most societies the male is given rights over the fertility of his wife, over her assets and labour, and over his offspring and their

---

[2] J. Carsten and S. Hugh-Jones, 'Introduction', *About the House: Levi-Strauss and Beyond*, ed. J. Carsten and S. Hugh-Jones (Cambridge: Cambridge University Press, 1995), pp. 3–4
[3] J. Goody, 'The Evolution of the Family', *Household and Family in Past Time*, ed. P. Laslett and R. Wall (Cambridge: Cambridge University Press, 1972); P. J. Wilson, *The Domestication of the Human Species* (New Haven and New York: Yale University Press, 1988); I. Hodder, *The Domestication of Europe* (Oxford: Blackwell, 1990); M. Johnson, *Housing Culture: Traditional Architecture in an English Landscape* (London: UCL Press, 1993); M. P. Pearson, and C. Richards, 'Ordering the World: Perceptions of Architecture, Space and Time', *Architecture and Order: Approaches to Social Space*, ed. M. P. Pearson, and C. Richards (London and New York: Routledge, 1994); J. Deetz and P. S. Deetz, *The Times of their Lives* (New York: Freeman, 2000); V. Buchli, 'Architecture and the Domestic Sphere', *The Material Culture Reader*, ed. V. Buchli (Oxford: Berg, 2002)

labour. This distinction in roles leads to the division of labour between the man and woman, and their offspring, establishing itself in an ideology of correct modes of behaviour according to gender and age, and giving rise to internal hierarchies and discourses of power within the family and domestic group.[4] Since the support given to the mother and child is material as well as affective, the family group becomes a centre of subsistence, and the status and gendered division of labour is also frequently expressed in economic activity. There is therefore in the pre-industrial household a conjunction of biological and economic functions with role-based hierarchies and ideologies.

The domestic group generally exists within a larger social group for protection and for mutually beneficial cooperation, providing a cultural consensus on social organisation and modes of behaviour. For Fortes the domestic group is primarily a mechanism of *social* reproduction. 'In all human societies the workshop, so to speak, of social reproduction, is the domestic group', a means whereby the group replaces its membership and transmits its values to its new members.[5] It may also be the institution that provides the individual with emotional support and a sense of identity.[6] Society thus replenishes itself by providing a robust structure for the physical and cultural maturation of the next generation – the reproductive pair plus their offspring.[7] Human mortality and the lifespan of the individual determine that the family is perpetually changing its personnel and composition. Fortes proposes a paradigm of three principal phases to its development. The family is initiated by the establishment of the reproductive pair on a recognised basis or marriage, leading to the production of offspring. This reproductive phase is limited by the term of fertility of the pair, principally that of the woman, and during this phase the offspring are economically, jurally and affectively dependent on their parents. Following this first phase of establishment and enlargement, the second phase, which may well overlap the first, is one of dispersal or fission of offspring at maturity. The third phase is one of closure, the dismantling of the reproductive pair with the death of one or both members, and the replacement of this group with others. (This study is particularly focussed on this third phase of closure as the process of probate marks the legal termination of one form of the domestic group). The cyclical nature of the family means that each generation claims in succession rights over productive and reproductive resources. It follows that at each stage of its existence the composition

---

[4] M. Douglas, *Man in Society: Patterns of Human Organisation* (London: Macdonald & Co., 1964), p. 85

[5] M. Fortes, 'Introduction', *The Developmental Cycle in Domestic Groups*, ed. J. Goody (Cambridge: Cambridge University Press, 1958), p. 2

[6] Douglas, *Man in Society*, p. 82

[7] Fortes 'Introduction', p. 8

of the group will be different, not only in terms of personnel but also the relationship between the parties.[8]

Reproduction is thus usually the significant factor in the initial formation of domestic groups. However, as the composition of the domestic group shifts through time it frequently assimilates members beyond the nuclear family: past-reproductive or non-reproductive members who do not fit into the paradigm of the nuclear family. And, as already stated, the domestic group also frequently acts as the primary source of subsistence for the individual members of a society, and as such is the focus of productive activity involving members beyond the kinship group. The nature of the relations will thus vary within the group, from direct bonds of marriage, filiation and siblingship to less direct kinship, jural, affectional and economic bonds.[9] And these bonds may well shift and overlap, where, for example, a dependent child matures to become economically productive, where an ageing widowed parent becomes dependent on the domestic group of an adult offspring, or where a subservient male economic member of the group marries a widow, thereby shifting to a dominant position within the group.

As already observed, the reproductive family is enmeshed in the wider society, receiving validation and support in return for providing members of that society. The individual therefore is simultaneously a member both of the domestic group and of a wider society.[10] The relative strength of these relationships varies according to the status of the member of the domestic group – the head of the household generally being more significantly linked to external structures than, for example, his spouse or offspring – and the balance varying from society to society, and changing through time, the relative strength of social and domestic relationships being seen as an indication of the complexity of a society. It is argued that in the simpler society the domestic group plays a more significant part in the life of the individual than the wider social group, whilst in the more complex society that polarity tends to be reversed.[11] It is part of the purpose of this study to see whether the evidence of the domestic culture in early modern Thame provides any evidence of such a shift.

The Household as a Residential and Productive Unit

In most human societies the domestic group ideally occupies a distinct space, and the residential configuration provides a physical indication of the relationship between the social and domestic group, including economic and affective ties. The nature of dwelling also often reflects the

---

[8] *Ibid.*, pp. 2–10
[9] *Ibid.*, pp. 8–9
[10] *Ibid.*, p. 2
[11] *Ibid.*, pp. 3, 8

status of any domestic group and the stage in its developmental cycle. It was the limitations of viewing the domestic group solely through the perspective of kinship in certain societies that prompted Levi-Strauss to examine the role of the dwelling or house within the social structure. In his view, greater emphasis is placed on economic and political considerations in the formation of a household in societies in transition from one governed predominantly by kinship, based on prescriptive rules pre-determining choice of marriage partners, to complex class-based societies where the choice of marriage partner is only governed by proscriptive rules, excluding certain categories of marriage partner.[12] According to Levi-Strauss, the 'sociétés à maison' of the aristocratic houses of Medieval Europe evolved a mode of social organisation which fused social identity and continuity with the fabric of the house. The dwelling became the domain within which social and material circumstances and the conflicting loyalties to the wider social group, the household and the individual could be regulated. Much more than dwelling space, the structure of the house became an indication of the social standing of its inhabitants, the expression of the *identity* of members of the group.[13] Levi-Strauss therefore placed an emphasis on long-term historical analysis of the domestic unit with a view to identifying mechanisms for and processes of establishment, consolidation and dissolution of households – in so doing neglecting short-term ethnographic observation of the quotidian activities on which these processes are based.[14] But for Carsten and Hugh-Jones, social and material existence are intimately interwoven in the domestic domain: 'If the language of the house is *about* kinship, it is no less *about* economy, and just as much about joint subsistence production and consumption as it is about property'. Shared activity, with its attendant roles and hierarchies, is as much a part of identity of the domestic group as shared residence.[15] And those activities are centred on the objects which furnish the dwelling, themselves invested with the affective significance of social relationships that those activities articulate: 'the person–object relationships that emerge from the various uses by actors of tangible (and also intangible) phenomena'.[16] To fully understand how the domestic domain operates, it is therefore essential to investigate the physical house and its material contents in parallel with the social 'house', 'examining the processes, which may be both cyclical and incremental, by which relationships

---

[12] Carsten and Hugh-Jones, *About the House*, p. 1

[13] *Ibid.*, pp. 11–12; C. Lévi-Strauss, *Anthropology and Myth: Lectures, 1951–1982*, trans. R. Willis (Oxford: Basil Blackwell, 1987)

[14] *Ibid.*, pp. 158, 193–4; Susan D. Gillespie, 'Beyond Kinship: An Introduction', *Beyond Kinship: Social and Material Reproduction in House Societies*, ed. R. A. Joyce and S. D. Gillespie (Philadelphia: University of Philadelphia Press 2000), p. 11; Susan. D. Gillespie, 'Levi-Strauss: *Maison* and *Societé á Maisons*', *Beyond Kinship*, ed. Joyce, and Gillespie, p. 32

[15] Carsten and Hugh-Jones, *About the House*, p. 18

[16] Gillespie, 'Beyond Kinship', pp. 2–3

between people, and between people and their houses, are enacted and transformed over the lifetime and beyond of a living individual'.[17]

For other writers the house assumes yet greater importance as the seat of a culture which defined and continues to define human society. Hodder sees domestication as a physical and conceptual distancing from nature, and even argues that the fixed dwellings of the late Pleistocene and early Holocene periods acted as a stimulus for, rather than being consequent on, the development of agriculture and sedentism, demonstrating a shift of collective mentality towards the deferment and sharing of benefits from cultivation and animal husbandry, and societal-wide control of behaviour and durable social relations under a trusted authority.[18] As discussed in the Introduction, Hodder interprets early domestication as an attempt to impose order on the natural and social worlds, both physically and conceptually.[19] The archaeological record also shows the emergence of domestic artefacts displaying cultural signification at this time, suggesting that the house became the focus of cultural activity reinforcing shared social values.[20] This archaeological perspective on the role of the house in acculturation corresponds with Bourdieu's observation of *practice* amongst the Kabyle; in the words of Carsten and Hugh-Jones, 'through habit and inhabiting each person builds up a practical mastery of the fundamental schemes of their culture'.[21] There is no Cartesian distinction between thought and sensation, only an environment of overlapping significance and experience; 'House, body and mind are in continuous interaction, the physical structure, furnishing, social conventions and mental images of the house at once enabling, moulding, informing and constraining the ideas and activities which unfold within its bounds'.[22] It is this interaction between the material and the social environment, and their conceptual associations, which makes for the complexity of domestic culture.

We have, then, in the domestic group and its residence a number of inter-linked and shifting relationships. Its primary purpose is as a mechanism for the control and distribution of resources, reproductive and subsistence, within a larger society. Set in the context of human mortality, the domestic group guarantees the physical reproduction of the group and its cultural values, generally based around the elementary family of mating pair and offspring, involving division of labour, status and rights, and the emergence of the fixed dwelling in association with the development of agriculture and sedentism. The house itself becomes a highly significant component

[17] Gillespie, 'Levi-Strauss: *Maison* and *Societé á Maisons*', p. 46; Carsten and Hugh-Jones, *About the House*, p. 19

[18] Hodder, *The Domestication of Europe*, pp. 31, 37–8, 53

[19] E. Benveniste, *Indo-European Language and Society* (London: Faber, 1973), pp. 249–51

[20] Hodder, *The Domestication of Europe*, p. 34

[21] Carsten and Hugh-Jones, *About the House*, p. 2

[22] *Ibid.*, p. 2

of human experience, underlying new mentalities and leading to the creation of complex social structures enmeshed in a built environment and engendering cultural dichotomies between the world within the house and without, between culture and nature and between social cohesion and differentiation.[23] With its attendant activities, the dwelling structure becomes a significant and transmissible component in the composition and culture of the domestic group, a seat of social values, leading to the notion that individuals, their actions and their attitudes, are unwittingly forged in a fusion of the environment and practices of the house and its occupants. The household does not generally leap into the world newly formed, but, as is suggested by the cyclical development of its domestic group, emerges from and cements pre-existing social and physical structures and is in turn replaced by others. The mechanism of transition varies from culture to culture depending on environmental and cultural factors. The manner in which material assets are redistributed between generations in life and at time of death also constitutes an important element in the formation of the new domestic group. Douglas argues that in the shift to more complex societies the significance of kinship links diminishes as that of the wider social group and material assets increases.[24] For the individual, life in a sedentary domestic group will therefore consist of a combination of experiences, of relationships with kin and associated members of the social group mediated through hierarchies of status and culturally prescribed modes of engagement, of quotidian existence dependent on material circumstances and shared production and consumption of the household, and of the physical environment of the dwelling and its functionally and culturally determined differentiation of space. These overlapping experiences will take place in the context of cultural assumptions of behaviour and attitudes which are articulated as much in actions as in dialogue and symbol.

The Early Modern Household

It is relevant here to explore the extent to which the English seventeenth-century household corresponded to an archetypal domestic group. In general terms it could be described as a 'house' society; a discrete social unit, within a distinct dwelling, centred on the elementary family and often augmented with non-kin members associated through household activities, exercising a degree of social and economic autonomy under the jurisdiction of the head of the household. As well as acting as a hub for the distribution of resources and consumption, the early modern household was frequently

---

[23] *Ibid.*, p. 5
[24] Douglas, *Man in Society*, pp. 100, 102. This observation is particularly pertinent in relation to the study of household material culture.

a centre of economic production.[25] Following the demographic work of Laslett and Wall it has become well established that the early modern household predominantly consisted of a nuclear family of modest size, the mean household size from the late sixteenth to the early eighteenth century in a sample of parishes being some 4.75 persons.[26] Approximately one-tenth of households had resident extended kin, and one-third of households had servants, who made up one-quarter of the population.[27] This evidence contradicts previous assumptions that the English early modern domestic group was in a state of evolution from an earlier extended family, supported by collective land ownership by a kin group.[28] It is important to identify this flawed analysis as it has a tendency to promote *a priori* assumptions of the extended nature of the pre-industrial as opposed to the post- industrial household. It now seems clear that the early modern household was relatively small in size and focussed on the nuclear family consisting of one conjugal link.[29]

Murdock argues that such small domestic units are found in societies which practise bilinear descent.[30] In theory the lack of strong external affiliation, not tied specifically to patrilineal or matrilineal kinship and residence, fosters greater autonomy in succeeding generations and independent residence. Early modern England accords with this model despite the preferential distribution of assets through the eldest male heir due to the practice of patrimony. A culture developed of autonomous households with relatively weak links to other kin households, especially at lower social status. The practice of patrimony underpinned the superior jural status of the man within the household. The predominant practice of primogeniture materially favoured the household of the elder male heir, although it is evident from wills that considerable efforts were made by parents to ensure the prospects of younger siblings through the bequest of subsidiary properties and financial assets.

An examination of the formation of the early modern household may assist in an understanding of its operation and values. The ideology of marriage and household formation was expressed by a number of contemporary

---

[25] Laslett, 'Introduction: The History of the Family', *Household and Family in Past Time*, ed. Laslett and Wall, pp. 1, 25-6; Keith Wrightson, *English Society 1580–1680* (Abingdon: Routledge, 2003), p. 74

[26] The study by the Cambridge Group for the History of Population and Social Structure employed the demographic profile of 100 communities in pre-industrial England

[27] Laslett, 'Introduction: The History of the Family', pp. 76, 81–2

[28] Burges and Locke identified three chief historical stages in the evolution of the family: the large patriarchal family, the small patriarchal family and the modern domestic family, E. W. Burges, and H. J. Locke, *The Family, from Institution to Companionship* (New York: American Book Company, 1945), pp. 18–21

[29] Laslett, 'Introduction: The History of the Family', pp. 8–9, 28; Wrightson, *English Society 1580–1680*, p. 52

[30] G. P. Murdock, *Social Structure* (New York: Macmillan, 1949), p. 2

authors.[31] Wrightson's review of the advice from conduct books concludes that parity of age, status, wealth, reputation and religion were considered to make the best conjugal match, but that weight might be given to any of these qualities.[32] Significantly for the social dynamic of the early modern household, the woman was seen as being in some respects the equal of the man, although with a different and primarily supportive role, a view generally sanctioned by religion. It is unlikely that the ideology expressed in conduct books always corresponded to actual family formation and life.[33] The very presence of such advisory texts might indicate a lack of culturally embedded norms of marriage and household formation, or an anxiety that the ideal was not always followed.

To what extent was marriage the result of social prescription or of free choice, with implications for the relationship between the conjugal couple? In his controversial analysis of marriage formation in the early modern period, Stone identified a shift from a culture of prescribed choice influenced by the extended kin group, implying a low level of personal affection between partners, to one of individual choice and greater affection.[34] But, as Ingram points out, Stone based his analysis largely on a change of courtship culture amongst the aristocracy during this period and extended it by implication to lower social ranks.[35] It is more fruitful to see any change in courtship culture as part of a dialogue between official and popular culture. The internal hierarchy of the household was viewed as analogous to that of the state, and Tudor and early Stuart ideologies sought to encourage due obedience to authority within the household, as within the state. The importance of domestic piety was also emphasised by the church. But in popular culture a presumption was emerging towards more 'compassionate and caring relationships'. The evidence of diaries, letters and wills indicates that in the middle ranks there was a considerable degree of conjugal affection and cooperation.[36]

In reality there was a significant variation in the courtship culture and attitude towards household formation according to social rank.[37] The parental sanction of unions was generally greater where there were economic

[31] K. Davies, 'Continuity and Change in Literary Advice on Marriage', *Marriage and Society*, ed. R. B. Outhwaite (London: Europa Press, 1981), pp. 58–80; Sir Robert Filmer, *Patriarcha and Other Works of Sir Robert Filmer* (London, 1680)

[32] Wrightson, *English Society 1580–1680*, pp. 80, 83

[33] Laslett, 'Introduction: The History of the Family', p. 63

[34] L. Stone, *Family, Sex and Marriage in England 1500–1800* (London: Weidenfeld and Nicolson, 1977)

[35] According to Ingram, Stone was influenced by Robert Muchembled's *Culture Populaire et Culture des Elites*, itself influenced by the writings of Jean Delumeau and Michel Foucault. M. Ingram, 'The Reform of Popular Culture? Sex and Marriage in Early Modern England', *Popular Culture in Seventeenth Century England*, ed. B. Reay (London: Croom Helm, 1985), pp. 129–30

[36] *Ibid.*, pp. 132–34

[37] Wrightson, *English Society 1580–1680*, p. 80

assets at stake. Even here, however, allowance was generally made for personal preference but with the proviso of parental consent.[38] Foreign visitors were surprised by the degree of freedom given to English women; their status appears not to have been subordinate to male authority to the extent indicated in patriarchal ideology.[39] Women were often accorded a degree of financial independence, with parental assistance, varying according to rank, status and wealth.[40] Lower in the social scale there is little indication of direct parental involvement in matchmaking, men taking the initiative in their choice of partner whilst women consulted to a greater degree with their parents. This was in part a consequence of the operation of inheritance by primogeniture, forcing younger offspring to seek employment in service or apprenticeship at a distance from the natal home, and thus enabling them to form relationships with the opposite sex without parental involvement. In addition, the culture of the autonomous household meant that there was considerable pressure for prospective marital partners to establish their own economic viability before setting up a home. As a result, marriage age was relatively late in the lower social ranks, often in the mid-twenties at the conclusion of apprenticeship, curtailing the period of conjugal fertility and number of offspring and thus the size of the family.[41] Women also could bring a significant economic contribution to the marriage through their portion in goods or money, either granted in the lifetime of the parent or provided for in their will. With early mortality parents might even be dead before their offspring entered into marriage. Personal economic considerations were complemented by public pressure to inhibit the creation of households dependent on parish support through profligate marriages, demonstrated by contemporary concerns over pre-marital sexual activity and informal betrothals (often linked) and discouraged by the institution of banns and marriage licences.[42] A socially sanctioned marriage and an economically viable household indicated a well-ordered society, whilst impulsive union endangered social fabric and the well-regulated redistribution of resources.[43]

From an anthropological perspective the emergence of a new generation to social maturity can involve tension between generations; the redistribution of authority and resources must be carefully channelled to avoid conflict.[44] There is copious evidence from wills and contemporary

---

[38] Ingram, 'The Reform of Popular Culture?', p. 135
[39] Ibid., pp. 133, 135
[40] Wrightson, English Society 1580–1680, p. 81
[41] This dynamic also raises the possibility that wives had experienced a degree of autonomy prior to marriage and might see themselves more as partners than as subordinates in the marriage
[42] Ibid., pp. 55–7, 81–2; Ingram, 'The Reform of Popular Culture?', pp. 135, 145–6; R. Houlbrooke, Church Courts and the People during the English Reformation, 1520–1570 (Oxford: Oxford University Press, 1979), pp. 56–7
[43] Ingram, 'The Reform of Popular Culture?', pp. 137–44
[44] Fortes, 'Introduction', p. 5

correspondence of the readiness of early modern parents to assist their offspring in the establishment of their own households.[45] The Thame wills consisted largely of mechanisms to ensure, as far as assets allowed, the viability of offspring's households, sometimes expressed in the bequest of household items. A pattern of matchmaking frequently predicated on economic considerations thus had significance for the operation of the domestic group in terms of attitudes and behaviour. It would be wrong, however, to suppose that marriage was always the result of cool calculation. The evidence indicates a mixture of viability, affection and consent to varying degrees, usually according to the financial stakes involved.

Social Relationships within the Household

Turning to the relationship between the man and woman in the home, the evidence suggests the assertion of the principle of patriarchy, in ideology, law and practice, moderated by individual circumstance and character. Religious teaching and nature conspired to convince women, in the words of ideologues, that their subordinate role in life was pre-ordained. The biblical account of Eve's creation from the rib of Adam and her role in their fall from grace suggested her weaker moral character. Her natural childbearing physiology and the subsequent need for male protection and support also indicated her primary role in life. Men were divinely endowed to be morally, physically and intellectually stronger and a woman's moral fallibility could corrupt man's higher nature. The proper place of women was in the home, raising children and managing the household, whilst men's role was 'abroad'.[46] According to Sir Thomas Smith in *The Common-wealth of England*, the man and woman together were the fundamental component of society, each with clearly defined roles:

> the husband and ... the wife ... each having care of the family, the man to get, to travail abroad, to defend; the wife to save that which is gotten, to tarry at home, to distribute that which commeth of the husband's labour, for the nurtiure of their children and family of them both and to keep all at home neate and cleane.[47]

The ballad *The Woman to the Plough and the Man to the Hen-Roost: or, A Fine Way to Cure a Cot-Quean* (Figure 2.1) tells of the dire consequences of

[45] Wrightson, *English Society 1580–1680*, p. 83
[46] B. S. Capp, *When Gossips Meet: Women, Family and Neighbourhood in Early Modern England* (Oxford: Oxford University Press, 2003), pp. 4, 8, 15
[47] Sir Thomas Smith, *The Common-wealth of England and the Maner of Gouernement Thereof* (London, 1609)

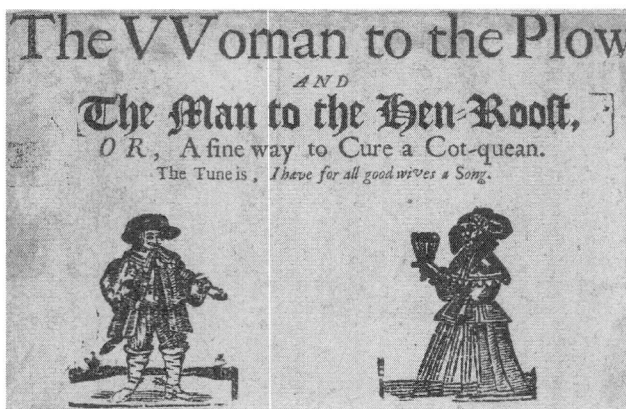

Figure 2.1
Broadside ballad
illustration
1678–80

an inversion of roles in the household, again an indication of the ambiguity and anxiety surrounding gender relationships.[48]

The subordinate status of women was enshrined in law, and on marriage the legal responsibility and property of the wife passed to the husband. If husband and wife jointly committed a crime she was considered not legally responsible for dutifully following his instructions, and he was able to dispose of her property without her consent or even her knowledge. A widow was entitled to one-third of her deceased husband's estate (half if there was no issue from the union) but this was frequently forfeit if she remarried, whilst a widower was entitled to the whole of his wife's property. Consequently, concerned fathers devised trusts to protect a daughter's economic independence, especially from spendthrift husbands, and in some marriages husbands would consent to the wife retaining control of the economic assets she brought into or earned within the marriage.[49] Outside London, single women – apart from widows – were excluded from the most profitable trades, and any earnings that the wife made within the marriage were expected to be under the control of her husband. However, since wives were expected to manage the household and were an integral part of the economic productivity of those of middling and lower rank, they frequent had control of budgets and, as expressed in the ballad *The Carefull Wife's Good Counsel*, were not infrequently compelled to safeguard the household finances from the husband's improvidence.[50] Conduct literature, however, written by and aimed at the literate elite and middling household, repeatedly warned of the consequences of female emancipation, especially in light of the opinion that, compared to the rest of Europe English women already

[48] Bodleian Libraries, University of Oxford (Bod.), accession number: MS Douce Ballads: 2(247b)
[49] Capp, *When Gossips Meet*, p. 6
[50] *Ibid.*, p. 10; Bod., accession number: MS Douce Ballads: Don.b.13(8)

enjoyed unparalleled liberties.[51] In *The English Housewife*, published in 1615, having first enjoined the housewife to be 'a godly, constant and religious woman, learning from the worthy preacher and her husband', Gervase Markham further advised,

> it is meete that our English Hous-wife be a woman of great modesty and temperance ... as in her behaviour and carriage towards her husband, wherein she shall shunne all violence of rage, passion and humour, coveting lesse to direct then to be directed, appearing ever unto him pleasant, amiable and delightful.[52]

The husband's role was to show love, care and forbearance. As the divine Thomas Gataker opined: 'Love goeth downward; duty cometh upward'.[53] Marital violence towards women, which undoubtedly frequently occurred, especially in lower-status households by the evidence of court depositions, was regarded by the authors of conduct literature as shameful; however, it was regarded as a lesser evil to the social inversion of husband beating, which could result in the shamed couple being forced to leave the neighbourhood.[54] Ballad sheets echo these themes; 'Hold your Hands, Honest Men' to be sung to the tune of 'Keep a Good Tongue in your Head'; the rhyme to the latter continuing 'Here's a good woman in every respect, / But only her tongue breeds all the defect.'[55] The householder was considered to be in effect the lord of his domain, and correct conduct and loyalties within the household were considered analogous to order in the wider society and state.[56]

What strategies could women adopt to assert themselves against the dominance of men? Scott suggests that in situations of ideological dominance ways will be found by the subordinate to challenge and circumvent authority without directly confronting its principles, by creating physical, social and cultural spaces beyond its control.[57] Women did enjoy a certain degree of autonomy in the running of the household and in those of lower status undertook economic activities abroad; they could seek the moral

---

[51] Capp, *When Gossips Meet*, p. 7

[52] Gervase Markham, *The English Housewife* (1615), ed. M. R. Best (Kingston and Montreal, McGill-Queen's University Press, 1986), p. 7

[53] Thomas Gataker, 'Marriage Duties Briefly Couched Together', *Certaine Sermons* (London, 1637), p. 195

[54] Capp, *When Gossips Meet*, p. 10; D. Underdown, 'The Taming of the Scold: The Enforcement of Patriarchal Authority in Early Modern England', *Order and Disorder in Early Modern England*, ed. A. Fletcher and J. Stevenson (Cambridge: Cambridge University Press, 1985), p. 131

[55] British Library, Roxburghe 1.514–15, 1.512–13

[56] Capp, *When Gossips Meet*, p. 4

[57] J. C. Scott, *Domination and the Arts of Resistance: Hidden Transcripts* (New Haven: Yale University Press, 1990), pp. 108–24 passim

support of servants who were also of subject status, and alliance with kin and neighbours beyond the household. Evidence exists of many situations of marital discord, showing that women could and did exercise opinions and actions contrary to the wishes of their husbands.[58] Recognising the ability of women to challenge their spouses vigorously and verbally, Markham advised that the housewife,

> though occasions, mishaps, or the misgouvernement of his will may induce her to conatrarie thoughts, yet virtuously to supresse them, and with mild sufferance rather to call him home from his error ... calling in her minde that evil and uncommly language is deformed though uttered even to servants, but most monstrous and ugly when it appears before the presence of her husband.[59]

Women were often afforded more respect in Puritan households, where they were frequently recognised as moral guides, and they held influential positions in nonconformist congregations. By the late seventeenth century there were a few female authors who were prepared to challenge in print the patriarchal order, and even the institution of marriage.[60] In conclusion, we can see the sway held by the prevailing patriarchy underpinned by ideology, law, history and custom. But against this ideology gender relationships were played out in households according to the values, status, circumstance and character of the individuals involved. And contemporaries held that it was within the household that patriarchy was most effectively challenged by women. In the words of Capp, 'we should think of gender relations in early modern England in terms of uneasy equilibrium rather than stasis'.[61]

Not all households were, however, headed by men. Widows formed a substantial section (19%) of the inventoried Thame decedents, from some of the poorest to the moderately wealthy.[62] As Mary Hodges points out in her study based on Thame and Woodstock in the seventeenth century, widows played a significant role in town life, both socially and economically. With wives tending to survive their husbands, and with the majority of men bequeathing the bulk of their estates to their wives, widows had a significant role as a source for finance for family and neighbours, as is evidenced by credits mentioned in inventories. A few widows appeared to carry on their husband's businesses after their demise.[63] Wealthy young

[58] Capp, *When Gossips Meet*, pp. 88–9, 125
[59] Markham, *The English Housewife*, p. 7
[60] Capp, *When Gossips Meet*, p. 18
[61] *Ibid.*, p. 25
[62] For the purpose of the data analysis in this study two spinsters listed as the decedents in probate inventories have been amalgamated with the thirty-five widows, in a category entitled 'widow-spinsters'
[63] M. Hodges, 'Widows of the Middling Sort and their Assets in Two Seventeenth-Century Towns', *When Death Do Us Part: Understanding and Interpreting the Probate Inventory Records of*

widows were considered to be socially disruptive and were often the butt of malicious gossip. The inventory and other evidence indicate also that widows maintained themselves by small-scale husbandry and sale of food-stuffs. Other widows were too poor to support themselves and formed a significant proportion of those receiving parish relief.[64] To a certain extent the widow within her household occupied the same position as a male head, but on remarriage ceded authority, in theory at least, to her spouse. A household headed by a widow was one of those factors that helped to undermine continually the patriarchal ideal.

The evidence suggesting the status of children and the relationship between parents and offspring in the early modern household is opaque. Probate inventories provide limited clues; apart from a few mentions of small versions of adult furniture there seems to have been little specific provision for their needs. Studies relying primarily on literary sources have resulted in diverse opinions. The work of Linda Pollock based on diaries of the period has revealed an anxiety on the part of parents for the formation of the moral character of their offspring, matched with pride and affec-tion, and a relative absence of physical correction.[65] The diarists display an awareness of the developing abilities of their children, who were, at least in elite households, not expected to have adult capabilities. Children were commonly referred to as 'comforts', unsurprisingly in a world where they were regarded as an insurance against the insecurity of older age.[66] Their physical and moral dispositions were also a source of anxiety; Henry Newcome (1627–95) was concerned that 'my children be kept in health, or from sad and grievous distempers' and that they 'be not a cross and exercise to us, by rebellious untowardliness'.[67] As Pollock points out, the modelling of the moral character of the child, especially in Puritan households, was not so much adult repression as part of a general concern with the virtue of the whole household.[68] This is of relevance to this study in light of the fact that Thame had a distinctly Puritan culture in the mid-seventeenth century. Perhaps not surprisingly in view of their opinion that a child was the outcome of original sin, whose character therefore had to be forcibly remodelled, Puritan parents tended to be stricter and more ready to penalise their children's misdemeanours, either with moral censure or with physical

Early Modern England, ed. T. Arkell, N. Evans and N. Goose (Oxford: Leopard's Head Press, 2000)

[64] Capp, *When Gossips Meet*, p. 38

[65] L. Pollock, *Forgotten Children: Parent–Child Relations from 1500 to 1900* (Cambridge: Cam-bridge University Press, 1983)

[66] The word 'comfort' was employed up to the eighteenth century primarily in an affective, medicinal and nutritional sense, rather than applying to personal amenity. See J. E. Crow-ley, *The Invention of Comfort: Sensibilities and Design in Early Modern Britain and Early America* (Baltimore and London: Johns Hopkins University Press, 2001), pp. 3–4

[67] Quoted in Pollock, *Forgotten Children*, pp. 100–1

[68] *Ibid.*, p. 102

punishment. In the case of Thomas Ellwood it was his adolescent tendency towards Quakerism that brought a violent response from his father; during the day Thomas sat in the kitchen of the farmhouse at Crowell (close to Thame under the Chilterns) to avoid his father, who, seeing him there with his hat on, 'first violently snatched off my hat, and threw it away; then giving me some buffets on my head, he said "Sirrah, get you up to your chamber". I forthwith went; he following ... and now and then giving me a whirret on the ear'.[69] Fathers are recorded as the main administrators of physical punishments, sometimes against the remonstrations of their wives. Mothers, however, could be strict judges of moral character, and frequently the absence of parental affection appears to have been the most effective punishment, suggesting a normal state of affection of parents towards their offspring.[70] The evidence from literate households thus suggests that serious attention was given to raising children, with a concern for the child's social, and – especially in Puritan households – moral character. At a lower social level children's activities would be more closely integrated into the life of the adult household, taking their part in the productive activities of the house.

The early modern household was not simply a nuclear or elementary family unit, despite the fact that that function generally lay at its heart and gave it justification. It could also in a limited number of instances comprise extended kin, recorded in Laslett and Wall's sample in an average of some 10% of all households between the late sixteenth and early eighteenth centuries.[71] It also frequently comprised 'inmates' or members associated for economic reasons; Laslett and Wall calculate that 28% of households in this period included servants, and Kussmaul also calculates that two-thirds of the population aged fifteen to twenty-four were servants.[72] The term 'servant' must not be understood in its nineteenth-century connotations of domestic service; in 1587 Harrison referred to yeomen having servants to get 'both their own and part of their master's living', as opposed to 'idle servants as the gentlemen do'.[73] In the early modern period the term tended to apply to all those who provided labour for a certain period, generally of more than a year, whilst labourers were those hired by the day or week.[74] The most significant servants in the culture of the household were those accommodated within the dwelling, either trade apprentices or servants

[69] Quoted in M. W. Barley, *The English Farmhouse and Cottage* (London: Routledge & Kegan Paul, 1961), p. 147
[70] Pollock, *Forgotten Children*, pp. 100–1, 149–56
[71] Laslett and Wall, *Household and Family in Past Time*, p. 81
[72] Laslett, 'Introduction: The History of the Family', p. 56; Laslett and Wall, *Household and Family in Past Time*, p. 83; A. Kussmaul, *Servants in Husbandry in Early Modern England* (Cambridge: Cambridge University Press, 1981), p. 3
[73] William Harrison, *The Description of England* (1587), ed. G. Edelen (Washington and New York: Folger Shakespeare Library, Dover Books, 1994), p. 117–18
[74] Kussmaul, *Servants in Husbandry in Early Modern England*, p. 6

in husbandry. The terms and conditions of these two categories varied significantly. Whilst apprentices were taken by the master, who undertook to lodge, board, clothe and teach the apprentice the trade for a set number of years on receipt of a premium from parent or guardian, the servant in husbandry was generally taken by the master with a verbal or tacit agreement for a period of a year, in return for a wage, board and lodging. In both cases the servant lived in the household of the master and was subject to his authority. Service generally occupied the period of adolescence, a prelude to adulthood, serving an economic and demographic function. By drawing in servants, households were not dependent on the number and abilities of offspring for labour, and equally children surplus to the productive requirements of their natal household could find employment elsewhere.

The institution of service meant that the culture of the household was as much economic as affective.[75] However, although it is now recognised that husbandry service was the experience of the majority of male youth, the transitional nature of the arrangement means that servants rarely figure in documentary records. Contemporaries regarded them as being absorbed into the households to which they belonged; in his economic survey of 1688 Gregory King subsumed servants under heads of households. The tasks of servants in husbandry, and their reward, varied according to age, gender and the size of the establishment. Men traditionally worked with draught animals, ploughing and harrowing, and cared for cattle and sheep. Women ran the dairy, milked the cows, cared for small animals, including poultry, and performed household tasks ancillary to agriculture, cooking and brewing. The youngest servants simply performed a range of minor tasks in return for board and lodging.[76] Although living under the roof of the master the relationship seems to have been potentially charged with resentment on both sides. Timothy Nourse wrote of the need of farmers for their servants, 'the Hands by which the Good Husbandman does subsist and live', but also complained that 'There is not a more insolent and proud, a more untractable, perfidious and a more churlish sort of people breathing, than the generality of our servants'.[77] And George Herbert wrote of the country parson, 'To his Children he shewes more love than terrour, to his servants more terror than love'.[78] But the long-term older servant, unmarried or widowed, enjoyed a different status, according to Herbert, to be treated more like a child. Perhaps it is indicative that servants tended to be valued more for their character than for their labour; to Herbert it was 'Truth, and Diligence, and Neatnesse, or Cleanlinesse' which made

---

[75] Ibid., p. 3
[76] Ibid., pp. 34–5
[77] Timothy Nourse, *Campania Foelix: or, A Discourse of the Benefits and Improvements of Husbandry* (London, 1700), pp. 204–5
[78] George Herbert, *A Priest to the Temple* (1652), ed. H. C. Beeching (Oxford: Blackwell, 1908), p. 41

the complete servant.[79] Service also provided an opportunity for acquaintance between the sexes without the constraints or censure of their parents, which alarmed moralists. In the words of Richard Mayo, 'How often has Opportunity and Privacy exposed Men and Maids that live together to the Devil's Temptations.'[80] Despite these tensions, all members of the household, kin and servants, were commonly referred to as 'family'.[81] This not only indicates a different terminology, but also reflects the patriarchal nature of the early modern household, both kin and servants under the authority of a male head, and a personal identity based primarily on the household, its shared residence and activities. A distinction was drawn earlier in this chapter between the biological and social reproductive functions of the domestic unit, and its productive role. In the domestic service of the early modern period, with the placement of adolescents in other than their natal households, of economic service to the householder but simultaneously acquiring knowledge the culture of that household, we have both productive and social reproductive functions combined. The early modern domestic unit was thus a complex institution comprising reproductive, subsistence and productive activities, normally based on and drawing its social justification from the elementary family unit but in many cases having a more complex social composition owing to economic considerations and wider kin obligations.

The Early Modern Household in the Community: Proximity and Interdependence

The household rarely exists in isolation, neither physically, socially nor economically, and as noted above can be viewed as the fundamental component in the creation of larger communities. In early modern England the relative weakness of kinship ties seems to have been reflected in a greater dependence on neighbours. Analysis of parish registers of the period indicate no resident clusters of kin in English parishes, rather the opposite.[82] Recognised and strong kinship links were generally limited and few, especially amongst lower social ranks where the support of close neighbours was of greater significance. The system of tithing referred to in the last chapter represented the operation of neighbourly interdependence for mutual security. Since

---

[79] Ibid.; Kussmaul, *Servants in Husbandry in Early Modern England*, p. 45

[80] Richard Mayo, *A Present for Servants, from their Ministers, Masters, or Other Friends* (London, 1693), p. 40

[81] N. Tadmoor, 'The Concept of Household-Family in Eighteenth Century England', *Past and Present* 151 (May 1996), 111–40, 111–12

[82] K. Wrightson and D. Levine, *Poverty and Piety in an English Village: Terling 1525–1700* (New York: Academic Press, 1979), pp. 84–7; A. Macfarlane, *The Origins of English Individualism* (Oxford: Blackwell, 1978), pp. 197–8

women were responsible for much of the interaction of the household with the outside world at the domestic level, good neighbourliness was a desirable virtue; as Markham advises, 'our English hus-wife must be ... full of good neighbourhood'.[83] Significantly, the Tudor Poor Laws assumed the obligation of kin support to exist only between parents and children, and grandparents and grandchildren respectively.[84] The household was also considered a key element in civic administration, and the position of householder also bestowed a position and potential influence in the community. The strength of neighbourhood links and the enmeshing of individual households in the structures of political, social and economic urban life are illustrated in the study by Boulton of early modern Southwark, Muldrew's analysis of the significance of social relationships in the establishment of trust as a basis for financial credit, and the day-to-day interaction of neighbours revealed by court depositions as revealed by Orlin.[85] Membership of the household and of the neighbourhood therefore superseded that of extended kinship groups, and we can see the early modern household as a partially discrete but funda-mental component of the wider community.

The household was thus not an autonomous body. In this chapter we have seen that its existence was justified and maintained by social tradition and legal norms. In succeeding chapters we will see how the environment provided for the subsistence of its members, the dwelling frequently provid-ing the setting for the processing of natural materials not only for internal consumption but for sale back into the immediate and more extended economic community. In addition, the household was drawing on the external world for products which it was unable, or, with greater specialisa-tion, unwilling to produce internally. Social engagement for members of households therefore was both economic and affective, balanced between external and internal requirements. Through the seventeenth century in Thame the evidence suggests that the partial economic and social autonomy of the household was being challenged, and its relationship to the wider world and community appears to have been significantly altered.

Households exist in physical as well as social proximity. Although of later date, the map in Figure 2.2 still usefully illustrates the early modern layout of dwellings and plots around the market place in New Thame. The devel-opment of the settlement, particularly around the market place with thin elongated burgage plots, created extended proximity, dictating the associa-tion of households and people. Dwellings lay side by side along streets, but to the front lay the shared street or market space, routes of passage and

---

[83] Capp, *When Gossips Meet*, p. 29; Markham , *The English Housewife*, p. 6

[84] Wrightson, *English Society 1580–1680*, p. 55

[85] Boulton, *Neighbourhood and Society*; Craig Muldrew, *The Economy of Obligation: The Cul-ture of Credit and Social Relations in Early Modern England* (Basingstoke: Macmillan, 1998); L. C. Orlin, 'Boundary Disputes in Early Modern London', *Material London, ca. 1600*, ed. L. C. Orlin (Philadelphia: University of Pennsylvania Press, 2000)

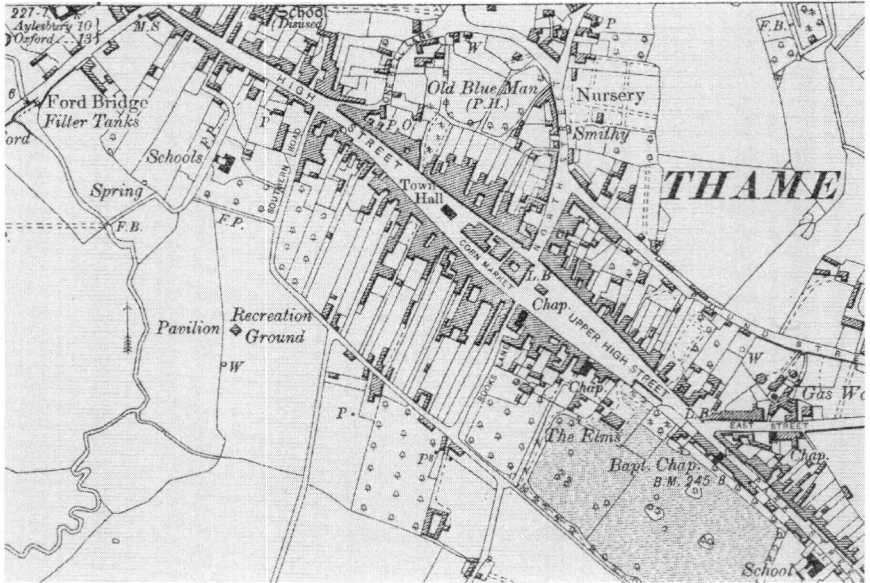

Figure 2.2 Map of Thame, 1897–99

potential places of encounter, whilst to the rear of most properties lay the fields representing the world of subsistence and work. To the front of the dwellings lay the urban, to the rear the agricultural world. Social engagement was therefore physically organised along axes which also served as focal points and lines of communication.

The Thame Dwelling House

Households therefore were units existing in close physical and social proximity to other households. But what can we deduce of their physical entity? A dwelling is a structure devised to accommodate and to shelter, and to facilitate the daily activities of the domestic group. It may also spatially define the territorial domain of the group, and the exercise of its internal hierarchies and relationships. (Although these relationships, such as that of parent and child, extend into the outside world, their dynamic may be subtly altered in different contexts.) As already noted in the Introduction the form of the dwelling therefore is an expression of the domestic group and its dynamics, and also acts as a physical constraint on its activities; in the words of Lawrence, 'the morphology of a vernacular building is inseparable from its social meaning and its use'.[86] The basic structure of

---

[86] R. J. Lawrence, 'Interpretation of Vernacular Architecture', *Vernacular Architecture* 14

most early rural dwellings, up to the late Middle Ages, was a simple timber-framed structure of rectangular form infilled with wattle-and-daub panels, with a thatched roof. The evidence suggests that these were predominantly divided into a more public area, or hall, for eating, cooking and entertaining guests, and more private space for sleeping and storing goods. The basic rectangular form was extended both outwards and upwards to create more accommodation, especially for service and private use. The relationship between significant elements of the dwelling – the location of the entrance, the access between spaces and the source of heat – dictated how it related to the outside world and operated internally. The entrance was commonly located either in the end wall, or at the corner or centre of a side wall, in the latter case frequently entering a screened cross-passage dividing the hall from the service area. Heat was initially provided by an open paved hearth venting smoke through the open roof. Due to the relative lack of space in the small dwelling the hearth migrated to the end wall, where the smoke was either vented through one bay, the smoke bay, of the roof or, persisting in poor houses into the eighteenth century, a smoke hood, which in effect created an inglenook around the fire. The staircase, where employed, was located either beside the fire place or within the living space. Urban plots were frequently constrained by the limited space and by the requirements of trade. The form of burgage plots meant that the building, unlike many rural dwellings, could be only one room wide and had to expand both down the elongated plot, the different rooms connected by a passage, and upwards. The space in the house dedicated to trade – the shop or workshop – was usually located at the street front of the dwelling, with living accommodation in the form of a parlour behind the shop, or in an upper chamber.[87] Other dwellings within Thame sat on larger plots, with a hall set along the street and service wing at right-angles to the street. In the later part of the sixteenth century a shift in the internal organisation of dwelling space can be observed, with greater functional specialisation and subdivision, and provision of greater privacy for the household.[88] This process was termed by Hoskins the 'Great Rebuilding', based on his observation of the significant number of improved houses dated between 1570 and 1640 in the Midlands and south of England.[89] Other authors have argued that the evidential base used by Hoskins was too incidental and unrepresentative in view of the attrition of older houses,[90] and that in any case the rebuilding extended for

(1983), 19-28, 25-6
[87] R. W. Brunskill, *Houses and Cottages of Britain: Origins and Development of Traditional Domestic Design* (London: Victor Gollancz, 1997), pp. 50-1, 108-10
[88] *Ibid.*, p.50
[89] W. G. Hoskins, 'The Rebuilding of Rural England, 1570-1640', *Past and Present* 4 (1953), 44-59
[90] C. R. J. Currie, 'Time and Chance: Modelling the Attrition of Old Houses', *Vernacular Architecture* 19 (1988), 1-9

a longer period, peaking at the end of the seventeenth century.[91] Hoskins did, however, note a significant shift in the quality of accommodation and furnishings in the period, particularly in middling-ranking houses. He identifies the introduction of chimney flues within the house, releasing space in the upper region of the hall for chambers accessed by new staircases, the availability of glass and the creation of distinct social and economic areas (service rooms, replacing outbuildings) of the dwelling as particularly important developments. The motivation, according to Hoskins, was a desire to emulate the comfort and privacy already enjoyed in the houses of the gentry, made possible by demographic, economic and social change. He suggests that it was the early sixteenth-century rise in population combined with the low cost of long-term tenancy agreements that both forced food commodity process upwards at the end of the century and gave rural yeomen and husbandmen the opportunity to invest, firstly in an enlargement of their landholdings, and subsequently in improved dwellings and furnishings. Machin indeed found from the evidence of north Oxfordshire that there was a correlation between varying agricultural commodity prices and building improvements.[92] Both Machin and Alcock noted that settlements with free copyhold or even tenancy without security – conditions obtaining in Thame – could offer the same advantages.[93] The contemporary commentator William Harrison, rector of Radwinter in Essex, noted in 1587 that 'within their sound remembrance' old men in his parish had noted 'the multitude of chimneys lately erected ... [and] the great (although not general) amendment of lodging'.[94]

In his survey of the Great Rebuilding debate, Johnson credits the attempt to identify and understand a marked development in vernacular domestic building, but criticises Hoskins, Machin and Currie for placing too much focus on economic factors relating to the physical structure of the buildings themselves, and neglecting, or seeing as relatively inconsequential, the life lived within.[95] Both built and documentary evidence *does* suggest that economic circumstances in some parts of early modern society provided the financial means to alter and improve dwellings, the primary evidence of which is provided by extant rural dwellings. These changes afforded additional and differentiated internal space and comfort. In attributing these changes to a desire for privacy and to the emulation of elite custom,

---

[91] R. Machin, 'The Great Rebuilding: A Reassessment', *Past and Present* 77 (November 1977), 33–56

[92] *Ibid.*, 48

[93] *Ibid.*, 52–3; N. Alcock, 'The Great Rebuilding and its Later Stages', *Vernacular Architecture*, 14:1 (1983), 45–8, 45

[94] Harrison, *The Description of England*, pp. 200–2

[95] M. Johnson, 'Rethinking the Great Rebuilding', *Oxford Journal of Archaeology* 12:1 (1993), 117–25; Hoskins, 'The Rebuilding of Rural England, 1570–1640'; Machin, 'The Great Rebuilding'; Currie, 'Time and Chance'

Hoskins leaves the possible motivation largely unexplained.[96] Indeed, Johnson identifies in the practice of vernacular architectural history (at the time that he was writing) a bias towards the physical characteristics of buildings, whereas he argues that the physical environment was the setting for a complex set of relationships embracing economic, social and cultural life which should be subjected to theoretical appraisal.[97] He identifies within the early modern dwelling a 'closure' of space, creating greater internal segregation and a corresponding diminution of social inclusiveness. The built evidence suggests that this process was not simply an emulation of elite houses but was promoted by the lesser gentry and 'middling sort'.[98] The alterations in the arrangement of domestic space, of the ground plan and internal circulation, were stimulated by changing social and cultural identities, affording greater spatial (and therefore social) distance, segregation and polarity within the dwelling, and what Johnson describes as potentially changed 'constructions of gender' between master, mistress and servants.[99] These changes were ultimately linked to an ethos generated by the rise of commerce and individualism, underpinned by religious ideology.[100] King identifies this as the process whereby the 'middling sort' sought to separate themselves as a distinct class;[101] to quote Tönnies, a shift from *Gemeinschaft* (community) to *Gesellschaft* (society),[102] according to this narrative, resulting in a greater emphasis on the personal environment, on personal possessions and the physical well-being that they provided. King critiques Johnson for a 'totalizing presentation', describing broad social and cultural shifts without sufficient recognition of variations between regions and communities.[103] Certainly, some features of the Great Rebuilding were already found in medieval urban dwellings: multistoried construction, internal chimney stacks, habitable attic spaces and modified halls, and where the evidence still exists urban dwellings show a continuing gradual adaptation and development through the early modern period. However, Johnson does acknowledge that different localities responded in varying ways to larger economic and cultural impulses.[104] In his analysis of the Great Rebuilding

---

[96] Hoskins, 'The Rebuilding of Rural England, 1570–1640', 122

[97] Johnson, 'Rethinking the Great Rebuilding', 120–2

[98] C. King, '"Closure" and the Urban Great Rebuilding in Early Modern Norwich', *Post-Medieval Archaeology* 44:1 (2010), 54–80, 56

[99] Johnson, 'Rethinking the Great Rebuilding', 122–4; King, '"Closure" and the Urban Great Rebuilding in Early Modern Norwich', 56, 58

[100] Johnson, 'Rethinking the Great Rebuilding', 124

[101] King, '"Closure" and the Urban Great Rebuilding in Early Modern Norwich', 56–7

[102] Concepts evolved by Ferdinand Tönnies in *Gemeinschaft und Gesellschaft*, first published in 1887 in Leipzig, theorising the values underpinning social relationships in pre-modern and capitalist society. In the former, *Gemeinschaft* describes the desire of the individual, directed by ideology, to serve the social group; in the latter *Gesellschaft* the reorientation of social relationships towards self-interest, now regulated by the instruments of law

[103] King, '"Closure" and the Urban Great Rebuilding in Early Modern Norwich', 57

[104] *Ibid.*, 57–8; Johnson, 'Rethinking the Great Rebuilding', 122

debate and his identification of profound economic, social and ideological changes in the early modern period, Johnson nevertheless provides a useful analytical perspective, against which in this study the evidence of the changing nature of domestic culture in seventeenth-century Thame will be assessed. He argues the necessity of rethinking relationships between archaeology and history, and with Alcock emphasises the value of examining buildings in conjunction with documentary evidence which can help to illuminate the values of the household.[105] To quote Johnson, 'in order to make the houses speak we have to think more carefully ... about what actually goes on in building and living in a house, about the relationship between housing and social, economic and cultural change'.[106]

Although there is no specific relationship between the Thame wills and probate inventories and any extant dwellings, a number of houses still exist in the parish originating from the early modern period which give an indication of methods of construction and the form of dwellings. Thame urban housing appears to have conformed to the typology suggested by Pantin of hall alignment both parallel and, on burgage plots at right-angles to the street.[107] Approximately thirty extant buildings of the period listed by the Department of the Environment are broadly consistent in construction and form, the majority timber-framed structures originally infilled with wattle-and-daub panels, on an uncoursed rubble plinth. The majority of the roofs were originally thatched, and brick ridge stacks are found predominantly to the centre of the dwellings. Size varies from one to seven bays, the majority falling between two and four bays and two-storeyed, or of single storey with attic, and a significant number have a single-storey extension (see Figure 2.8).[108]

A house in Thame High Street dating from the second quarter of the sixteenth century, with seventeenth-century alterations, has been well documented by Malcolm Airs and John Rhodes.[109] The earliest structure was a timber-framed house, originally with wattle-and-daub infilling, of four bays parallel to the street with a two-bayed cross-wing (Figure 2.3). It was of two storeys throughout and the absence of smoke blackening to the roof trusses indicates that the large axial chimney stack serving both floors was part of the construction from the outset, although the quality of the carpentry in the upper chamber indicates that it was also originally open to the roof. A spacious staircase was incorporated into the same bay as the chimney stack.

---

[105] Ibid., 117; Alcock, 'The Great Rebuilding and its Later Stages'

[106] Johnson, 'Rethinking the Great Rebuilding', 122–3

[107] W. A. Pantin, 'The Development of Domestic Architecture in Oxford', Antiquaries Journal 27 (1947), 120–50

[108] Department of the Environment, List of Buildings of Special Architectural or Historical Interest; District of South Oxfordshire; Town of Thame (London: Department of the Environment, 1988)

[109] M. Airs and J. Rhodes, 'Wall-Paintings from a House in Upper High Street, Thame, Oxoniensia 45 (1980), 235–59

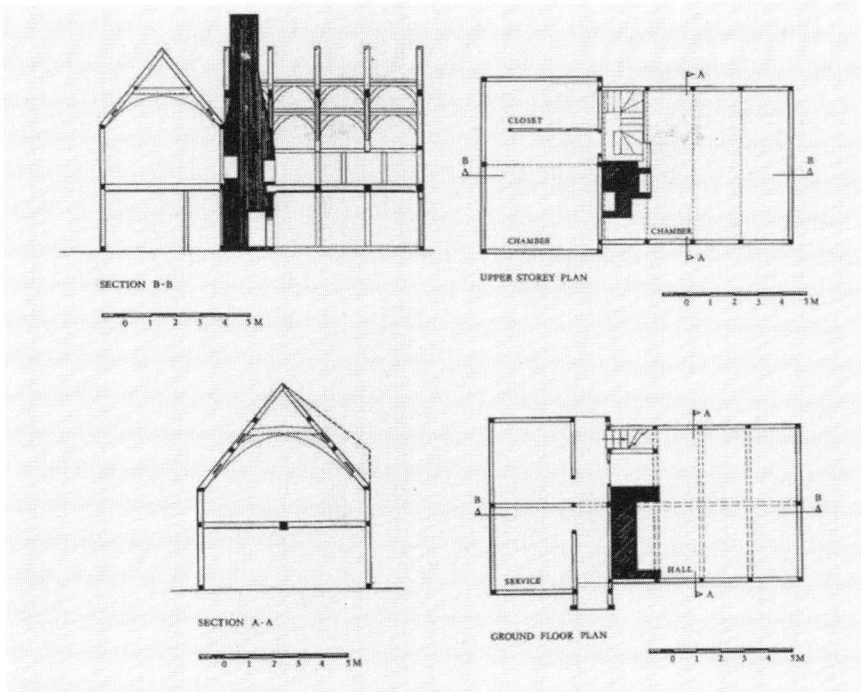

Figure 2.3 The original configuration of the house in Upper High Street, Thame

The house was accessed by an original porch into a service passage, with the large ground floor hall to the right (indicating a reluctance to break with medieval patterns) and two service rooms to the left. The staircase leads to the two chambers on the upper storey; that to the right over the hall was probably the principal chamber to judge by its size and the quality of its carpentry, and to the left a smaller chamber subdivided to create a closet.

In the seventeenth century a wing was added either to create a greater division of space or to create a separate dwelling (Figure 2.4). This is a timber-framed structure of two bays, at right-angles to the street, of two storeys with an attic, both floors heated by a chimney stack set outside the side wall. The building was further extended with a wing at the service end in the later seventeenth century, and the whole building rendered to disguise the by-then old-fashioned timber framing. The tall wagon entrance in the new section to the left of the original structure of the house is an indication of continuing involvement in agriculture.[110]

---

[110] *Ibid.*, passim

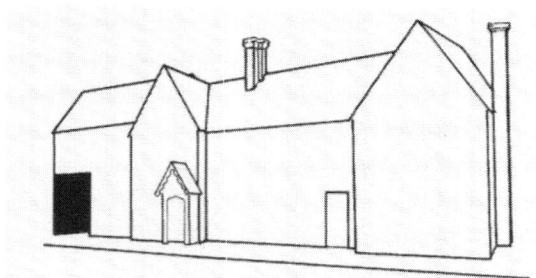

Figure 2.4 Seventeenth century extensions to the right of the house in Upper High Street, Thame

The home of the seventeenth-century diarist Thomas Ellwood still exists in the adjacent village of Crowell as an example of a substantial rural dwelling: a timber-framed structure consisting of a hall, parlour and service wing accessed by a cross-passage, with lateral chimney stacks to the hall and kitchen. The upper-storey rooms correspond to those on the ground floor, reached by a staircase in the passage. According to the contemporary diaries, the family eat in the parlour, the servants in the kitchen.[111] The modifications to the roof made to the house in the High Street (Figure 2.5) are a good indication of seventeenth-century improvements, providing greater accommodation on the second storey; the end wall shows a possible ridge line which has been extended upwards. The actual process of improvement is well described in the household accounts from 1618 of Robert Loder of Harwell in north Berkshire, not far from Thame: 'Money layd out about my Chimney ... [and] making my staires, my window & selling [ceiling] and plastering'.[112] The will of the Thame widow Margaret Greene in 1638 indicates that dwelling improvements were not yet considered permanent: 'And further my will is yt ye bords in ye floor in ye lower chamber should not be remooved but remaine to my son John if it may please god he survive me'.[113] The relative novelty of window glass is evidenced by its listing in eleven households between 1603 and 1645 belonging to six artisan-traders and three widows, the last being for that of a yeoman.

The listing of rooms in the Thame probate inventories also illustrates the process of subdivision of the internal space of the dwelling, with indications of the creation of upper-storey chambers with the nomenclature of 'chambers over' various ground-floor rooms – the hall, parlour and kitchen

[111] Barley, *The English Farmhouse and Cottage*, pp. 147–8
[112] G. E. Fussell, 'Robert Loder's Farm Accounts, 1610–20', *Camden Society* Third Series, 53 (1936), 157–8
[113] OHCA: MS. Wills Pec. 39/4/26

Figure 2.5 Timber-framed house in Thame High Street, showing original roof line on end wall

– and the social differentiation of space expressed in such terms as 'high', 'great' and 'privy' chamber.[114] The complex nature of structural alterations to domestic dwellings over time is exemplified by analysis carried out on an extant dwelling house in Priestend in Thame (Figure 2.6). The evidence suggests a medieval hall-house on the site to which was added in the late sixteenth century a chamber and parlour range with a 'service house' to the rear, the medieval building itself being replaced in the late seventeenth century, and in turn 'improved' in the eighteenth century.[115]

As discussed in the Introduction, the spatial ordering of the dwelling played a significant role in the structuring of habitual actions and social relationships; the differentiated use of internal space will be examined

[114] A. Buxton, 'Domestic Culture in Early Seventeenth-Century Thame', *Oxoniensia* 67 (2002), 76–115, 82–4
[115] D. R. Clark, *Oxfordshire Buildings Record Report No. 90* (Oxford: Oxfordshire Buildings Record, 2010)

Figure 2.6 No. 54 High Street, Thame, consisting of the seventeenth-century block to the right, the sixteenth-century range centre and service house to the left. St Mary's church is left background

in detail in Chapter 6. In the last two chapters we have established the physical, economic, social and cultural context of the seventeenth-century Thame household. In the next three chapters the scale of the study focusses on the objects listed in the inventories in detail to establish the domestic practice that they represent.

3

Foodstuff Provisioning, Processing and Cooking

The following chapters, 3, 4 and 5, turn to an examination of the objects listed in the Thame inventories. We examine their properties and the extent to which production technologies were simple or complex, local or distanced, and assess through contextualisation and reference to other contemporary sources their role in the life of the household.

The Provisioning of the Household

This section commences with those objects and actions pertaining to the important aspects of provisioning the household with foodstuffs, their processing and cooking. In terms of material culture, food can very much be seen as the 'stuff' of life. Food and drink are some of the principal forms of affordance for the household, using the local environment or obtaining by trade and exchange the raw ingredients, processing and preserving them, and transforming them through cooking into palatable nutrition to sustain the members of the household and to enhance its standing through hospitality. Foodstuffs therefore mark the very fundamental interdependence of the Thame household with its immediate environment. As already mentioned in relation to archetypal domestic life, the manner of the preparation and consumption of food is inextricably entwined with the social structure and expression of the collective values of the household. Foodstuff and its management also have an impact on the configuration of the dwelling through the existence and location of food processing and storage, the hearth and cooking and commensality. Unsurprisingly, food occupies a significant place in sociological and anthropological literature, seen as a method of control and an expression of power.[1] Functionalist approaches place an emphasis on the relationship of foodstuffs to social relationships

---

[1] P. Kropotkin, *The Conquest of Bread* (1892) (London: Allen Lane, 1972); H. Spencer, *The Principles of Sociology*, 3rd edn (London: Williams and Norgate, 1898–1900); T. Veblen, *The Theory of the Leisure Class* (1899) (New York: New American Library, 1953)

and the structure of groups; food is vital not only for survival but for the
construction of culture,[2] with 'foodways' symbolising social relationships,
part of 'pattern-making rules' encoding social events, and maintaining
social relations both within and beyond the household.[3] Seeing all tasks
as culturally controlled and shaped, structuralist analysis focusses on the
conceptual associations of food, as text in the social dialogue, and as part
of the structure of human thought. Particular emphasis is placed on the
changing states of food through its acquisition, processing and consumption, and food also occupies an important place in Bourdieu's concept
of *habitus*.[4] From a developmental perspective the availability of food, its
nature and consumption are also subject to ecological and cultural conditions, including prevailing physical and social circumstances discussed here
in Chapter 1.[5] In the wider sphere, social, political and economic changes
embracing the process of emulation can also influence the choice of diet.[6]
The acquisition of food, its processing and consumption constitute not
only significant activities of the household, but also its social, cultural and
spatial structuring.

As noted in Chapter 1, Thame lies in a rich agricultural area, and
the inventories provide evidence of the agricultural production of the
householders producing a mixture of crops and livestock in the seventeenth century (Figures 3.1 and 3.2). Although there are indications in
the early eighteenth century that a significant proportion of the livestock
production was destined for London meat markets,[7] it might justifiably
be assumed that a fair portion of the local agricultural production still
found its way to the local population. For example, the mixed agricultural
assets of John Parkin,[8] a yeoman who died in 1635, included of livestock
4 beasts and a bullock, 13 sheep and 7 lambs, 2 hogs and poultry, and
of crops acreage of wheat, maslin, barley, beans and oats. It was not only
primary agriculturalists – yeomen, husbandmen and agricultural labourers – who had agricultural assets, however. Table 3.1 shows agricultural
assets distributed through all the occupational categories. Although gentry were disproportionately wealthier in terms of agricultural assets (some
four times those of yeomen), all other occupational status categories had

[2] C. Gosden, 'Introduction', *The Prehistory of Food: Appetites for Change*, ed. C. Gosden and
J. Hather (London: Routledge, 1999), p. 1
[3] S.Mennell, A. Murcott and A. H. van Otterloo, *The Sociology of Food: Eating, Diet and Culture*,
(London: Sage, 1992), p. 9; C. Counihan and P. Van Esterick, 'Introduction' *Food and Culture:
A Reader*, ed. C. Counihan and P. Van Esterick (London: Routledge, 1997), pp. 2–3
[4] C. Lévi-Strauss, *The Raw and the Cooked* (London: Jonathan Cape, 1969); P. Bourdieu,
Distinction: A Social Critique of the Judgment of Taste, trans. R. Nice (London: Routledge, 1984)
[5] Mennell, Murcott and van Otterloo, *The Sociology of Food*, pp. 14–15
[6] *Ibid.*, p. 17
[7] Henri Misson, M. *Misson's Memoirs and Observations in his Travels over England* (London,
1719), pp. 145–7, 313–14
[8] OHCA: MS. Wills Pec. 48/2/32

Figure 3.1
'Husbandry'

Figure 3.2 'Grazing'

roughly comparable assets, with traders, including butchers, actually holding more than husbandmen. Given the retention of the open field system,
land was not yet largely restricted to primary agriculturalists, but still
available to traders and artisans. Gentry and yeomen, unsurprisingly, had
the greatest assets in terms of livestock and crops, but traders and artisan-
traders appear to have held assets on a par with those of husbandmen, and
widows were also significantly involved, especially in animal husbandry.
For example, Joan Spindler,[9] a widow who died in 1612, possessed 4 hogs,
5 beasts (cattle) and 2 sheep, and John Groome,[10] a joiner in 1624, winter
corn, barley and peas. Involvement in agricultural production and the
holding of agricultural assets therefore seems to have permeated every

[9] OHCA: MS. Wills Pec. 51/1/4
[10] OHCA: MS. Wills Pec. 39/3/35

Table 3.1 Agricultural assets: mean value by occupational status category

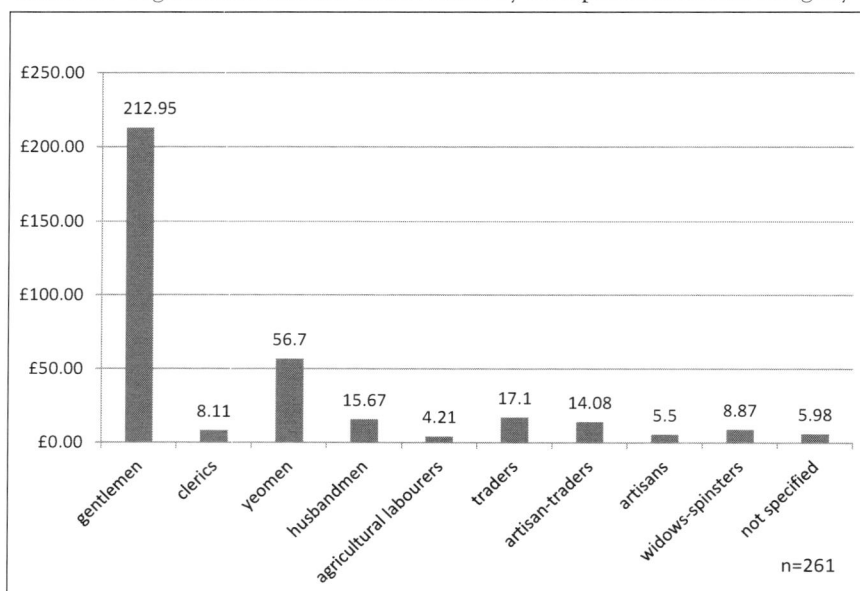

occupational category amongst inventoried decedents to varying degrees. The provision of one other element was of vital importance to the sustenance of the household and the execution of many household tasks: water. There is scant evidence of this from the inventories, apart from reference to the 'Pumpe & Troffe' in the backside of Peter Willmot[11] in 1626, and the 'Well bucket & chayne' of Edmund Maund[12] in 1661, both yeomen. We might deduce, then, that water might have been generally drawn from subterranean sources close to the habitation, in part avoiding the health risks in ground water polluted by craft processes and sanitary habits.

Foodstuff Processing

Having established the local availability of agricultural foodstuffs, we turn to the processing of such commodities. Agricultural output represented in large part the wealth of the town and individual households, but it was seasonally harvested and also frequently perishable. In addition, apart from a few commodities such as fruit, it was harvested in a form

---

[11] OHCA: MS. Wills Pec. 54/2/36
[12] OHCA: MS. Wills Pec. 46/2/24

that required further processing for human consumption. There were, therefore, a number of reasons for processing agricultural foodstuffs: preservation and reconstitution for human consumption, continued supply of food during the winter and spring months, and also for sale. Processing of specific foodstuffs was manifested not only by specific locations in which dairying, baking and brewing were the most frequent[13] – the spatial implications of which will be examined in greater detail in Chapter 6 – but also by implements specifically involved in various processes. The processes which were indicated by locations and utensils were salting (preservation of meat), dairying, boulting (sifting of milled grain) and baking, malting and brewing. Cooking of food, also a foodstuff processing activity, which the evidence suggests was common to all households, will be examined later in this chapter. As opposed to cooking, the processing of specific ingredients was found only in certain households. In all households brewing was the most prevalent processing activity (found in 49% of all households), with salting (26%), malting (24%), and dairying (21%) and baking (21%) less so, but still present in a considerable number of households.[14] Foodstuff processing was found on average in approximately a quarter of all households but differentially according to the occupational status. Salting utensils were found in some 60% of gentry households, 35% of husbandmen and artisan-trader households, and in the region of 20 to 25% of other households. However, there was a complete absence of salting utensils in the households of agricultural labourers, despite evidence of their ownership of small quantities of livestock. Dairying implements were found in approximately 40% of gentry and yeoman households, with a much lower incidence, approximately 20%, in the households of husbandmen, agricultural labourers and widows. Traders, artisan-traders and artisans show a less than 10% incidence of dairying implements, possibly indicating that the commitment required in dairying did not fit easily with the principal activities of these trade households. Baking utensils (Figure 3.3c) were less common, found in a third of husbandmen's and a quarter of traders' households, with boulting and baking utensils found in approximately 20% of gentry, yeoman, artisan-trader, artisan and widow dwellings. Turning to malting, this process was found in approximately 25% of all households, with the highest average frequency of approximately 40% of gentry and yeoman households, 30% amongst artisan-traders and 23% of both traders' and widows' households. Husbandman and artisan households showed an average incidence of only 17% and 13% respectively. Brewing was the most common form of foodstuff processing. All inventoried gentry house-

---

[13] See online Appendix 1, Table 3.3, 'Service houses: frequency', at http://boybrew.co/9781783270415
[14] See online Appendix 1, Table 3.4, 'Domestic foodstuff processing: mean percentage occurrence by occupational status category'

holds had evidence of brewing, as did 76% of traders and over 60% of the households of clerics, yeomen and artisan-traders. Artisans, husbandmen and widows all had a 29 to 35% frequency of brewing activities. Only agricultural labourers showed no evidence of this activity.

The incidence of food processing, then, appears to have been more a factor of household status than of occupations specifically linked to agriculture. Although gentry, yeomen and husbandmen were well represented, so were traders, artisans and widows. The evidence suggests a close correspondence of frequency of processing utensils to house size.[15] Most marked is the evidence of greater brewing activity in larger households. The data appears to suggest that food processing was linked to the internal requirements of the household (apart possibly from the malting activity of widows which, based on other contemporary evidence, may indicate the provision of beer for sale) and to the ability of the household to afford the equipment and dedicated space for processing. The distribution of the various foodstuff processing varied according to dwelling size, with dairying found in dwellings of all sizes, salting and baking in most bar the smallest, but brewing increasing quite possibly in line with the size of the human household. The implications of distribution of foodstuff processing through place and time will be discussed in Chapter 6.

We turn now to the nature of the artefacts employed in the processing of various foodstuffs. The knowledge of actions which flowed from historical objects is not always open to us, even when confronted by the object itself.[16] In the case of this study we have only the text to serve as evidence, and frequently, as technologies and practices change, knowledge of actions which centred on certain objects ceases to be current. As previously discussed, the process of naming involves the connection of perceived properties shared by objects to a word. The deduction of properties from a textual source requires cautious interpretation. The use of certain terminology may still be current. We may believe that we understand the properties of an object called a 'table' as being largely identical in the seventeenth century and the present: a horizontal surface and its support used for a variety of purposes. But such apparent familiarity can be misleading. For example, the word 'table' in the seventeenth century could refer only to the top board of such a piece of furniture, or to a picture or a games board. Affordances of objects can change and can also become obsolete. Sometimes an indication of the affordance attached to an obscure term may be revealed by contextual proximity to another of term of known quantity, such as a 'copper' (vessel) to 'brewing vessels' or 'brew-house'.[17] It may also be possible to examine an extant example of the object in order to determine its physical properties,

---

[15] See online Appendix 1, Table 3.5, 'Domestic foodstuff processing distribution: mean percentage occurrence in households by dwelling size'
[16] T. Insoll, *Archaeology, the Conceptual Challenge* (London: Duckworth, 2007), pp. 16–18
[17] OHCA: MS. Wills Pec. 48/3/7

but we will still be little nearer to appreciating its contemporary meaning, since we do not approach the objects ourselves immersed in seventeenth-century 'practice'.

It may, however, also be possible to employ contemporary written and pictorial sources to illuminate an historical object and attendant actions. In the case of the processing and preparation of food there are books of household management from the later sixteenth and seventeenth centuries outlining not only recipes but also household tasks. But all contemporary written and pictorial evidence must be employed with caution, as representing the perspectives of a single contemporary commentator, in a particular social and cultural context, and often with a subjective agenda. It may be a moralising or prescriptive work, expressing the author's prejudices rather than an objective account of contemporary practices. In addition, such supplementary contemporary evidence should be used only to illuminate the primary inventory evidence, not to inflate it. Of the considerable number of contemporary cookery books, use is made here of Gervase Markham's *The English Housewife*, published in 1615.[18] Household instruction books, being literary sources for the literate, tended to focus on elite households, and Markham did indicate that he had drawn on other elite sources on the subject of herbal physic and wines.[19] However, although of genteel (but relatively impecunious) origins, Markham and his wife did engage in husbandry as a living for a number of years: 'Now for myself, although a piece of my life was scholar, a piece soldier, and all horseman; yet did I for nine years apply myself to the plough, followed it with earnestness.'[20] His work differs in two respects from others: it praises simple country fare, giving recipes for what he calls the 'ordinary' housewife – 'forasmuch as our housewife is intended to be general, one that can as well feed the poor as the rich'[21] – and it assumes that the housewife will herself be engaged in the daily chores that he describes.[22] Pictorial evidence of domestic processes is also provided by *Orbis Pictus Sensualium* by Johann Amos Comenius, originally a Latin-German grammar published in Nuremberg in 1658, and subsequently in English, including the third London edition of 1672 employed here.[23] This study also uses both images and descriptions of objects in Randle Holme's *The Academy of Armory*, published in 1688.[24]

---

[18] Gervase Markham, *The English Housewife* (1615), ed. M. R. Best (Kingston and Montreal, McGill-Queen's University Press, 1986)
[19] M.R. Best, 'Introduction' in Markham, *The English Housewife*, pp. xvii–xxii
[20] Markham, *The English Housewife*, p. 3
[21] *Ibid.*, p. 74
[22] Best, 'Introduction', pp. xxxvii–xxxviii
[23] Johann Amos Comenius, *Orbis Sensualium Pictus* (London, 1672)
[24] Randle Holmes, *The Academy of Armory; or, A Storehouse of Armory and Blazon* (1688), ed. I. H. Jeayes (London: Roxburghe Club, 1905)

Figure 3.3 'Butchery'

Salting

Salting was an important method for the preservation of seasonally slaughtered livestock. Figure 3.3 shows on the left the scalding of a swine carcass and on the right the stunning of a beast prior to slaughter with the knife. On the wall behind are various joints of meat. The most frequent salting utensils listed[25] were troughs and tubs for the application of salt to the carcass, and barrels for the storage of the salted meat. It is possible that the sacks mentioned were for the salt, although strangely, given the prevalence of the process of salting, there is no incidence of salt per se in the probate inventories. Salt was obviously an important commodity in domestic life, preserving foodstuffs and making food more palatable. In the early modern period salt was derived from coastal pans in France and the south of England. In addition, a finer grade was obtained from salt springs in Cheshire, supplying the inland north and west. However, salt evaporation was hindered, as in other industries, by the lack of timber for charcoal, and salt producers were forced to adopt the use of coal which, however, was too hot for the traditional lead evaporation pans. By the sixteenth century an industry had emerged in Scotland using iron pans, and Elizabeth I granted a patent to salt makers in

---

[25] See online Appendix 1, Table 3.6, 'Salting utensils: frequency'

Tyneside in order to attempt to imitate their success.[26] Given the high cost of inland transport, it is probable that the salt used in Thame would have come from coastal sources by river, and may have been distributed by travelling chapmen. The salting process required a tub or trough which was large enough to contain an entire side or flitch of bacon. Grooves were run into the bottom of the vessels for brine to drain away, and salt was rubbed into the flesh over several weeks, with curing sometimes completed by hanging the meat in the chimney over the wood fire.[27] Meat was likely to be very salt, especially in winter months. Markham recommended, 'you shall take the whitest and youngest bacon; and cutting away the sward, cut the collops into thin slices; lay them in a dish, and put hot water unto them, and so let them stand an hour or two, for that will take away the extreme saltness'.[28]

Dairying

Markham dealt at length with the process of dairying in the household, with instructions on 'the ordering and government of dairies', 'the cattle ... the hours of milking, and the ordering of the milk, and the profits arising from the same'.[29] He recommended 'kine of the best choice and breed ... deep in milk, gentle, and kindly' and hours of milking, in the spring and summer between five and six in the morning, and between six and seven in the evening.[30] He stressed the importance of the good ordering of the dairyhouse:

> Touching the well ordering of milk after it is come home to the dairy, the main point belonging there unto is the housewife's cleanliness in the sweet and neat keeping of the dairy house; where not the least mote of any filth may by any means appear, but all things either to the eye or nose so void of sourness of sluttishness, that a prince's bed chamber must not exceed it'.[31]

To this must be added 'the sweet and delicate keeping of her milk vessels' and the materials of which they may be made,

> whether ... of wood, earth or lead, the best of which is yet disputable with the best housewives; only this opinion is generally received, that the wooden vessel which is round and shallow is best in cold vaults, the earthen vessels principal for long keeping, and the leaden vessels for yielding much cream.

---

[26] www.saltsense.co.uk/salt-history (accessed 4 July 2015)
[27] D. Everleigh, *Brass and Brassware* (Princes Risborough: Shire, 1995), pp. 3–5
[28] Markham, *The English Housewife*, p. 67
[29] *Ibid.*, pp. 166, 169
[30] *Ibid.*, p. 169
[31] *Ibid.*, pp. 169–70

Figure 3.4 Milk pail

However 'any and all these must be carefully scalded once a day, and set in the open air to sweeten, lest, getting any taint of sourness into them, they corrupt the milk that shall be put therein'.[32] Dairying utensils listed in the probate inventories can be grouped according to the processes of transporting and cleaning the milk, making butter and cheese.[33] Of buckets were 12 listed, 43 milk bowls (or bowls), 12 milk pan (or pans) and 19 kivers, shallow containers. There were 36 churns, 31 cheese vats (or vats), 14 cheese tubs (or tubs), 19 cheese presses, 15 cheese boards (or boards) and 33 cheese shelves (or shelves).

In the following account of the various dairying processes we can note (my italics) some of these implements which are listed in the inventories. The first dairying process was the straining or siling: 'after your milk is come home, you shall as it were strain it from all unclean things through a neat and sweet kept *siledish*, the form whereof every housewife knows', 'the broader it is and the shallower the better it is, and yieldeth ever the most cream, and keepeth the milk longest from souring', filtered with 'a very clean washed fine linen cloth, such as one as will not suffer the least mote or hair to go through it'.[34] From the filtered milk could be processed the 'profits' arising from dairying: butter, cheese and milk. In the production of 'fleeting cream' 'the milk which you did milk in the morning you shall with a fine thin shallow dish made for the purpose take off the cream about five in the evening' or evening milk at five o'clock the next morning, and

---

[32] *Ibid.*, p. 170
[33] See online Appendix 1, Table 3.7, 'Dairy utensils: frequency'
[34] Markham, *The English Housewife*, p. 170

Figure 3.5 Woman at churn with dog

'the cream so taken off you shall put into a clean sweet and well leaded earthen pot close covered, and set in a cool place'.[35] In the churning of butter (figure 3.5) the importance of cleanliness was stressed again; 'For your butter which only proceedeth from the cream, which is the very heart and strength of the milk, it must be gathered very carefully, diligently and painfully.'[36] The organisation of the external mercantile world dictated some of the regulation of household dairying processes: 'Your cream being neatly and sweetly kept, you shall ... *churn* it on those usual days which are fittest either for your use in the house, or the markets adjoining near unto you, according to the purpose for which you keep your dairy.'[37] It was recommended that churning should be done the day before market, on a Monday in the case of the Thame Tuesday market. Correct temperature was important in the churning process, carried out for this reason early in the morning or late in the evening in the summer, and in the warmest place in the dairy in the winter. If churned too hot the resultant butter would be crumbly and bitter. The nature of the strokes of the churn was also important – slow in hot and rapid in cold weather. Butter could be kept fresh or salted. Fresh butter was hand-washed to remove the buttermilk: 'After your butter is ... gathered well together in your *churn*, you shall then open your *churn*, and with both your hands gather it well together, and take it from the buttermilk, and put it into a very clean *bowl* of wood, or pancheon of

---

[35] *Ibid.*, pp. 170–1
[36] *Ibid.*
[37] *Ibid.*, p. 171

Figure 3.6 Cheese tub

earth.'[38] Or the butter could be salted and potted unwashed into 'clean earthen pots, exceedingly well leaded' laid on and covered with a layer of salt, 'then closing up your pot let it stand where it may be cold and safe'. It was recommended that a lump of May butter should be set aside as a medicinal salve.[39] The buttermilk could be charitably bestowed on poor neighbours, or used to make buttermilk curds – buttermilk heated in a large 'earthen dish' with new milk, let stand and separated from the whey, eaten with cream, ale, wine or beer. The whey could be kept to make curds or used to feed swine, given to poor neighbours, or stored in a stone vessel and drunk cold, when it was called 'whig' and recommended as a summer drink for labourers.[40]

The manufacture of cheese converted milk into a more enduring consumable product. Markham noted the existence of various forms of cheese: new milk or morrow cheese, nettle cheese, flotten milk cheese and eddish or aftermath cheese. To make cheese, rennet had to be obtained from the 'cheeselip bag', the stomach bag of a young suckling calf. 'Of these bags you shall at the beginning of the year provide yourself a good store', the curd washed and cleaned, salted and returned to the bag, which was to be potted and matured a year before use.[41] New milk cheese, 'the best cheese made ordinarily in our kingdom', was made from milk 'early in the morning as it comes from the cow', sieved or siled 'into a clean *tub*' (Figure 3.6) and

[38] *Ibid.*, p. 172
[39] *Ibid.*, pp. 173–4
[40] *Ibid.*, pp. 174–5, 178–9
[41] *Ibid.*, pp. 175–6

added to cream from the previous night's milking scalded with water, with the rennet added, left to stand for half an hour. The cheese curd was then to be pressed in the cheese vat under a cheese board to remove the remainder of the whey, then placed in a large cheese cloth and pressed in the cheese press. In new dry cloths it was to be turned five or six times in the first day, and after two days in the press placed in a kimnel (kiver) and rubbed with salt, lain on a shelf or table to dry, for two or three days more, wiping off the brine. Nettle cheese, 'the finest summer cheese which can be eaten', was laid on a bed of fresh nettles. Flotten milk cheese, 'which is the coarsest of all cheeses', was made from sour milk. Eddish or winter cheese was similar to new milk cheese but because of the season of the year remained soft.[42]

Boulting and Baking

Markham wrote that 'our English housewife ... must not then by any means be ignorant in the provision of bread and drink',[43] and the two processes, baking and brewing, central to the sustenance of the household, were linked through the vital ingredient of yeast. After milling and prior to baking, the ground meal had to be sifted from the bran, or boulted. This was sufficiently dusty, and dangerous by reason of fire, to merit a separate boulting house, of which eight were listed in the inventories. The boulting process may have been combined with that of baking. Markham recommended,

> in your bake-house you shall have a fair bolting house with large pipes to bolt meal in, fair troughs to lay leaven in, and sweet safes to receive your bran: you shall have bolters, searces, ranges, and meal sieves of all sorts both fine and coarse; you shall have fair tables to mould on, large ovens to bake in'.[44]

The aggregated inventory evidence[45] lists firstly 2 millstones for grinding the grain along with various containers, 2 bushels and 9 tubs, and the 6 meal troughs (or troughs). Boulting is indicated by vessels, possibly of different capacities: 12 boulting wyches, a form of shallow dish presumably used for the sifting process, 3 boulting vats (or vats) and 3 boulting hutches (or hutches, a form of chest). The baking process is indicated by the listing of 21 dough or kneading kivers and 5 moulding boards, the term given to the forming of the dough. The 1 searce was a form of sieve and the 1 peel was a flat wooden shovel used for inserting the loaves into the oven, and there is finally one mention of a bread bin.

[42] *Ibid.*, pp. 177–8
[43] *Ibid.*, p. 204
[44] *Ibid.*, p. 211
[45] See online Appendix 1, Table 3.8, 'Boulting and baking utensils: frequency'

Figure 3.7 Dough brake, kneading trough and bread basket

With a number of cereal grains available, the quality and status of bread was determined by the nature of the flour: 'is meet that you cleanse your meal well from the bran, and then keep it in sweet vessels'.[46] A number of breads were described by Markham: simple wheat or rye bread, or compound meal of rye and wheat mixed together, or rye, wheat and barley. Markham recommended that the oldest meal was best, sweet and untainted. 'Manchet', a white bread, was considered best. Meal was ground 'on black stones if it be possible, which makes the whitest flour', boulted 'through the finest bolting cloth' and put into a clean kimnel (kiver). 'Opening the flour hollow in the midst, put into it the best ale barm [yeast] the quantity of three pints to a bushel of meal, with some salt to season it with ... and knead it very well together with both your hands' (Figure 3.7). Markham also recommended folding the dough in a cloth and working it with the feet.[47] 'Cheat' bread was made with coarser meal boulted through coarser cloth, using sour leaven from a previous batch of leaven, well salted and left to sour overnight: 'thus ... you may bake any bread leavened or unleavened whatsoever, whether it be simple corn, as wheat or rye of itself, or compound grain as wheat and rye, or wheat, rye, and barley, or rye and barley, or any other mixed white corn'.[48] Brown bread, 'bread for your hind servants, which is the coarsest bread for man's use', was of a different quality, made of grain and pulses; 'you shall take of barley two bushels, of pease two pecks, of wheat or rye a peck, a peck of malt'.[49] This was passed through a meal sieve, put into a 'sour trough' and hot liquid worked in with a 'mash-rudder', left to stand until the following day and 'then mould it and bake it into great loaves with a very strong heat' (Figure 3.8), with the recom-

[46] Markham, *The English Housewife*, p. 209
[47] *Ibid.*, pp. 209–10
[48] *Ibid.*, p. 210
[49] *Ibid.*

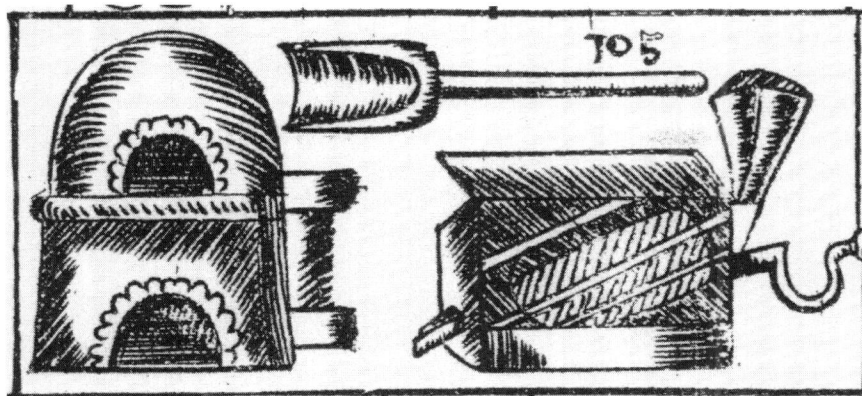

Figure 3.8 Oven and meal shovel

mendation that the sourer the leaven 'the less will the smell or rankness of the pease be received'.[50] There was thus a clear status distinction within the household, even in a staple such as bread.

Malting

As already mentioned, baking and brewing were closely associated with the malting process. Markham noted that 'It is most requisite and fit that our housewife be experienced and well practiced in the well making of malt, both for the necessary and continual use thereof, as also for the general profit which accrueth and ariseth to the husband, housewife, and the whole family.'[51]

> This office or place of knowledge belongeth particularly to the housewife ... for it is housework, and done altogether within doors, where generally lieth her charge ... for the art of making the malt ... even from the vat to the kiln, it is only the work of the housewife and the maids-servants to her appertaining.[52]

Only two malt houses, those of Edward Kent, yeoman 1658, and Robert Alnett, carpenter 1626, were listed in the Thame inventories,[53] against fourteen brew houses, whilst ten inventories listed malt, suggesting that that it might have been bought from local suppliers. Markham indicated

[50] *Ibid.*, p. 211
[51] *Ibid.*, p. 180
[52] *Ibid.*
[53] OHCA: MS. Wills Pec. 44/4/9; MS. Wills Pec. 32/1/28

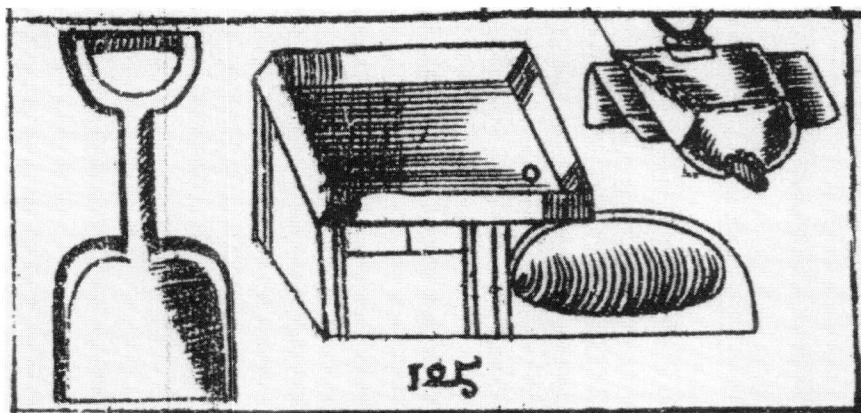

Figure 3.9 Malt shovel and cooler

that the building and equipping of a malt house, situated for good ventila-tion with drying floor, kilns and cisterns, was a considerable investment.[54] Edward Kent possessed both a malt house and a larger quantity of malt, 960 gallons, than other households. It is interesting to note that evidence of malt occurs only in the first half of century, but brew houses appear throughout the century. Materials listed for malting[55] include 33 bushels of barley and a small quantity, 2 bushels, of wheat, and various implements for handling and sorting the fermenting grain, 2 malt kivers, 1 malt screen and 1 malt shovel. The 40 malt mills – the most numerous evidence for the malting process – would have been used for grinding up the roasted grain, in association with the listed 59 bushels of finished malt. Progressing to the brewing process, there were 50 generic listings of 'brewing vessels', utensils which may have been similar to the 50 mash vats or mash tubs (or tubs) used to hold the 'mash' after it had been watered with the liquor from the copper (2) or kettle (2) over the furnace (9), and then let into the 8 cool-ers (Figure 3.9) or cool tubs. The strained liquor was fermented in the 25 brewing vats or ale vats (or vats) before storage in vessels of various sizes, the most common of which were the 99 barrels (or drink barrels), 7 firkins, 34 kilderkins, 12 runlets and 44 hogsheads (containing over 50 gallons) stored in the 60 stands of various descriptions.[56]

In the malting process grain was soaked and warmed to allow germina-tion, releasing natural sugars. The malt was heated and dried in a kiln, a process which affected the colour and flavour of the resultant beer, and when dry milled into a powder. The milled powder was mixed with hot

[54] Markham, *The English Housewife*, pp. 180–9
[55] See online Appendix 1, Table 3.9, 'Brewing utensils and materials: frequency'
[56] See online Appendix 4 for relative volume measures

water and left in the 'tun' whilst the sugars in the malt dissolved. This 'wort' was boiled with hops in the copper, cooled and run into fermentation tanks where yeast was added. Markham indicated the correct time taken in the making of malt: 'from first steeping to the time of drying' as a fortnight to three weeks. Any temptation to shorten the process should be resisted, for 'in less than three weeks a man cannot make perfect malt'. Stopping the germination process too early meant 'you shall have half malt and half barley, and that is good for nothing but hens' and hogs' trough'. Markham cautioned against too much liquid to speed the germination process 'because it hath so much moist substance as doth make it both apt to corrupt and breed worms in most great substance'. The malt was normally turned with a shovel for convenience, but 'there are others (and they are for the most part women maltsters) which turn all with the hand, and that is the best, safest and most certain way'.[57] Problems arose from 'mixed grain' of old and new barley, and Markham's advice highlights the potential problems of sourcing foodstuffs from the market place:

> But if it so fall out that you buy your barley, and happen to light on mixed grain, some being old corn, some new corn, some the heart of the stack, and some of the staddle, which is an ordinary deceit with husbandmen in the market, then you may be well assured that this grain can never come or sprout equally together.[58]

In cold weather Markham recommended the covering of the malt heap or couch with 'some thick woolen cloths, as coarse coverlids, or such like stuff, the warmth whereof will make it come presently'. Grain, barley (of which the best grew on clay soils) and wheat, was most commonly malted, and also peas. Malting was an activity which both provided the staple drink of the household but also gave the potential for profit – from the production of malt 'is made the drink, by which the household is nourished and sustained, so to the fruitful husbandman (who is the master of rich ground, and much tillage) it is an excellent merchandise'.[59] Malt production was thus the preserve of wealthier households, and its acquisition placed other households into dependency on outside supply.

Brewing

The most commonly brewed drinks were beer and ale, and perry and cider were also produced. Various tastes and strengths of beer existed, according to the proportions of malt and hops and the ageing of the

[57] Markham, *The English Housewife*, pp. 195–6
[58] *Ibid.*
[59] *Ibid.*, p. 180

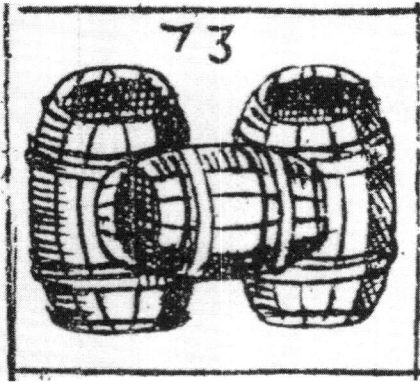

Figure 3.10 Tuns

beverage. 'Ordinary' beer was 'that wherewith either nobleman, gentle-men, yeomen, or husbandman shall maintain his family the whole year'. The traditional strength, according to Markham, was one quarter of malt producing three hogsheads of beer, 1 hogshead equalling 54 gallons.[60] In the brewing of ordinary beer ground malt was put into the 'mash vat' with water or 'liquor' in the 'lead' ready to heat. Boiling liquor was added little by little 'with scoops or pails' to the malt, let stand for an hour or so and then well stirred or 'mashed'. The first liquor was replaced into the emptied lead and boiled for an hour with added hops. This 'wort' was then sieved into a cooling vessel, and run into a dish containing the yeast, or 'barm'. The scum or 'mother' on the barm was removed and the beer 'tunned' up in cleaned hogsheads, bunged up after the beer had 'purged' or cleared for a day or two (Figure 3.10). Weaker 'small beer' could be made by adding a second liquor to the wort and hops. The best March beer was brewed with peas, wheat and oats mixed with the malt, produc-ing a strong ale with fewer hops.[61] According to Robert Plot, the local water was not best suited to brewing: 'But at Thame, where there never is a well in the whole Town whose water will ... brew' 'why then Beer will stink within fourteen Days wherever they attempt to brew with this water'.[62] This deficiency did not seem to inhibit the numerous drinking establishments catering for the town and its market trade.

In conclusion, foodstuff processing was essential to the subsistence of the Thame household, involving considerable economic investment in imple-ments and in space. The processes involved recquired knowledge and discourse of best practice and were exercised through habitual actions and

[60] *Ibid.*, pp. 204–5
[61] *Ibid.*, pp. 206–8
[62] Robert Plot, *The Natural History of Oxfordshire* (Oxford, 1677), 2nd edn (London, 1705), p. 37

considerable physical effort on a daily basis – for example, turning malt by hand or working dough with the feet. There is a clear presumption, constantly restated by Markham, that these, apart from salting, were the tasks of the women of the household: 'it is only the work of the housewife and the maids-servants to her appertaining'.[63] They therefore indicate the way in which labour and knowledge were apportioned, and how roles were presumed to be divided along gender lines, thus structuring social relationships within the household. Foodstuff processing also linked the household to its immediate environment, responding to the rhythms of agriculture, drawing in and processing materials for internal consumption, or sending them out again for economic benefit. The slaughter of livestock before the winter and the act of butchery marked the transition from a symbiotic relationship between farmer and beast to that of consumer and consumable, and dairying the close alignment to the hourly requirements of the dairy herd, also responding to the economic rhythms of the market place. The perishability of foodstuffs exerted a discipline of regularity, when milk would spoil within hours. Markham even equated the correct ordering of the dairy and its very necessary cleanliness to social status, the disordered housewife falling into the moral opprobrium of a slattern or slut. The tasks of dairying, malting and brewing required extensive acquired knowledge of, and expertise in, the ordering of tasks; of correct temperatures or degrees of humidity, and of the time to allow for processes. Foodstuff processing can thus be seen as an example of 'practice', knowledge transmitted through the habitual actions supporting life, certainly open to discourse, but also defining identity and articulating relationships and values.

Foodstuffs Listed in Households

In addition to evidence of foodstuff processing, some foodstuffs were also listed in the inventories. Foodstuffs, as other more durable objects, were commodities sourced from natural materials and 'manufactured' for exchange and for consumption. The relative lack of evidence of such commodities which must have been commonplace in households indicates that there were small quantities and may reflect perishability and relatively low monetary values. As with agricultural assets, the presence of foodstuffs would to a certain extent depend on the season in which the inventory was compiled; for example, salt fish was associated with Lent, although the '2 coople of ling & 2 cople of Colefishe' in the servants' chamber of the cordwainer Vincent Hester[64] were recorded in November 1605. Nevertheless,

---

[63] Markham, *The English Housewife*, p. 180
[64] OHCA: MS. Wills Pec. 41/1/38

the listing of foodstuffs does provide a partial picture of diet in the household, the most frequent items being bacon, cheese, various grains and fruit – all forms of agricultural produce which could be preserved, and stored for home consumption or for the market.

The twenty-two incidences (in some 12% of inventories) of bacon in dwellings ranged from one piece in the household of William Evans, a yeoman in 1694, to twelve flitches in that of Philip Burton the elder, a mason in 1662 – an average in the region of 3.25 flitches per listing.[65] Of this number, 11 were yeomen, 2 husbandmen and 3 widows. The frequency of cheeses (twenty-one in number, again some 12% of households) ranged from 3 in the inventory of Humphrey Gibbins, a yeoman in 1637, to 130 cheeses in that of Edward Kent, another yeoman in 1658.[66] The average quantity was in the region of 25 cheeses, 12 listed in the households of yeomen, and 3 in those of widows. Unsurprisingly perhaps, bacon and cheese were thus listed predominantly in the dwellings of agriculturalists. The cereals listed were barley, corn, wheat and non-specific meal. Barley was widely used for brewing, and associated with brewing utensils in six of the ninety-three households where this activity occurred. Quantities ranged from one bushel in the inventory of Frances Griffin in 1631, whose status was not given but likely to have been a widow, to twenty bushels in that of Edward Kent, a yeoman, in 1658.[67] Barley was listed in the inventories of 2 yeomen, 2 widows, 1 carpenter and 1 cordwainer, indicating the cross-occupational status nature of brewing. Corn was listed in two inventories in unspecified amounts, and wheat in six inventories, ranging from one bushel in that of John Corner, a yeoman in 1619, to six bushels in those of John Burton the senior, a baker, and John Louch, a victualler, both taken in 1643.[68] Listing of maslin (five instances) ranged from one bushel in the inventory of Anthony Nore, a yeoman in 1627 to one quarter in that of Nicholas Powell, a butcher in 1627.[69] Meal, ground cereal, was only listed in three inventories, ranging in quantity from two bushels in that of Reynold Graunt, a yeoman in 1618, to one quarter in that of Richard Striblehill, a butcher in 1607.[70] Unspecified bakery was listed in the inventory of John Carter, a yeoman in 1643.[71] Pulses in the form of beans were listed in five inventories, ranging in quantity from one bushel in that of William Tipping, a shoemaker in 1640, to ten bushels in that of Reynold Graunt, a yeoman in 1618.[72] The six shillings' worth of

[65] OHCA: MS. Wills Pec.33/2/28; MS. Wills Pec. 38/1/11
[66] OHCA: MS. Wills Pec.39/4/23; MS. Wills Pec. 44/4/9
[67] OHCA: MS. Wills Pec. 39/4/14; MS. Wills Pec. 44/4/9
[68] OHCA: MS. Wills Pec. 34/4/32; MS. Wills Pec. 33/2/18; MS. Wills Pec. 45/2/15
[69] OHCA: MS. Wills Pec. 47/1/77; MS. Wills Pec. 48/2/18
[70] OHCA: MS. Wills Pec. 39/3/26; MS. Wills Pec. 50/5/36
[71] OHCA: MS. Wills Pec. 35/1/19
[72] OHCA: MS. Wills Pec. 52/3/12; MS. Wills Pec. 39/3/26

beans listed in the household effects of Thomas Francklin,[73] a labourer in 1611, gives a rare indication of part of the diet of a poorer member of the community. The quantities given of cereals were therefore variable, but rarely less than one bushel, a storage quantity.

Fruit was found in the inventories in the form of apples, generally in unspecified quantities apart from the three quarters (twenty-four gallons) listed in the effects of Reynold Graunt,[74] the yeoman in 1618, although there are indications of the consumption of fruit at table in the form of fruit dishes, listed in twenty-five inventories, through the whole century from 1598 to 1693, in quantities varying from just one to twenty-four in a household, with an even spread in terms of occupational status and dwelling size. Apples (generally crab) could also be crushed for the production of verjuice, which was used in the cooking process. One verjuice press was mentioned, in the household of John Vickers, a husbandman in 1643, and two listings of verjuice barrels, quite possibly the same ones, belonging to William Tipping and his widow Anne in 1604 and 1605.[75] Markham instructed that :

> To make verjuice, you shall gather your crabs as soon as the kernels turn black, and, having laid them a while in a heap to sweat together, take them and pick them from stalks, blacks, and rottenness: then in long troughs with beetles for the purpose, crush and break them all to mash: then make a bag of coarse haircloth as square as the press, and fill it with crushed crabs; then put it into the press, and press it while any moisture will drop forth, having a clean vessel underneath to receive the liquor: this done, tun it up into sweet hogsheads ... and then bung it up, and spend it as you shall have occasion.[76]

Given the indication of widespread brewing activity in a large number of households it is perhaps surprising to find only five listings of beer in household effects, amongst which were two victuallers, for whom the beer could constitute a trade asset. The quantity was generally unspecified but James Cowden, a barber, possessed three barrels of beer at the time of his death in 1691 and William Apowell, a victualler, two hogsheads in 1658.[77] It is of course possible that beer in the household would have been consumed as part of the customary drinking at the deceased's dwelling before the 'forth-coming' of the corpse to the burial service and interment. Indeed, contemporary sources indicate that the wake was one of the significant community events, drawing together family and neighbours.[78]

[73] OHCA: MS. Wills Pec. 38/3/16
[74] OHCA: MS. Wills Pec. 39/3/26
[75] OHCA: MS. Wills Pec. 52/3/12; MS. Wills Pec. 52/3/13
[76] Markham, *The English Housewife*, p. 134
[77] OHCA: MS. Wills Pec. 35/3/35; MS. Wills Pec. 32/1/43
[78] F. Heal, *Hospitality in Early Modern England* (Oxford: Clarendon Press, 1990), p. 373

Besides listings of actual foodstuffs, there are also indications of consumables from objects directly connected with certain commodities. The inventory evidence reveals a limited presence of oatmeal, mustard, pepper and spices, and their storage prior to culinary use. Contemporary recipes suggest that oatmeal was commonly used to thicken stews and broths: 'If you will make Pottage of the best and daintiest kind, you shall take Mutton, Veale or Kidde ... you shall put in a good handful or two of small Oatmeal.'[79] On this very limited sample neither the mustard nor the spice mill appear to have been restricted to higher-status households. The six listings of mustard mills were in dwellings ranging from two to eight rooms belonging to a gentleman, two yeomen and tradesmen. The ten spice mortars were found in dwellings ranging from one to five rooms belonging to a gentleman, yeomen, widows, a husbandman and a cordwainer. The pepperbox appropriately belonged to the merchant Zachariah Hames in 1686.[80]

Two further strands of evidence exist which suggest elements of the diet: salad and fruit dishes. Salad dishes were found in only five inventories, all of relatively lower status, in households of four dwelling rooms[81] or fewer belonging to 1 yeoman, 2 artisan-traders, 1 widow and 1 shepherd. They also occurred only in the first two decades of the century, suggesting an object or a terminology falling out of use. However, Markham emphasised the importance of a knowledge of the garden for the housewife, and herbs and vegetables occurred frequently in recipes: 'To proceed then to this knowledge of cookery, you shall understand that the first step thereunto is to have knowledge of all sorts of herbs that belong to the kitchen, whether they be for the pot, for sallats, for sauces, for servings.'[82]

No herbs or vegetables were listed in the probate inventories, presumably being perishable and of low monetary value. We must turn again to the contemporary recipe to gain some indication of those that might have been employed in the Thame household. Markham advises,

> First then to speak of sallats, there be some simple, and some compounded
> ...your simple sallats are chibols [onions] peeled, washed clean, and half of
> the green tops cut clean away, so served on a fruit dish; or chives, scallions,
> radish roots, boiled carrots, skirrets [water parsnips], and turnips, with such
> like served up simply; also, all young lettuce, cabbage lettuce, purslane [the
> herb Portalaca oleracea], and divers other herbs which may be served up
> simply without anything but a little vinegar, sallat oil, and sugar.[83]

---

[79] Robert Morris, *The Book of Pottage and Broth 1580–1660* (Bristol: Stuart Press, 2006), p. 4
[80] OHCA: MS. Wills Prob. 4 15794
[81] In the inventory analysis of domestic space the 'dwelling room' – employed primarily for residence and sociability – was differentiated from 'productive space' with practical and economic potential
[82] Markham, *The English Housewife*, p. 60
[83] *Ibid.*, p. 64

We therefore have an indication of the components of the Thame diet in the seventeenth century, based on locally sourced and processed foodstuffs: meat, dairy produce, cereals and pulses, complemented by fruit and possibly also 'salad' in the form of vegetables and herbs, and beer to drink. Pennell's research into the consumption of food in early modern England also established the generally abundant supply of food staples in Oxfordshire.[84] We will now look at the evidence, in the form of cooking utensils, of the way in which these ingredients were prepared for consumption, and possible variation in diet according to occupational household status.

Cooking – from Ingredients to Consumable Food

The cooking process is evidenced in the inventories by objects for preparing food for cooking, and for placing in or on whilst cooking. The cooking process involved the exposure of ingredients to heat, generally in the form of a household hearth. The ability of humans to combust material in order to provide heat, security and a means of making a wider range of foodstuffs more digestible was fundamental to the process of domestication, and the fire occupied a central functional and conceptual place in the household. The hearth was thus a pivotal place in the spatial and diurnal organisation of the household, and in the identity of the home. This study has made the not infallible assumption that hearths were indicated in the Thame inventories by the listing of fire and cooking irons and other hearth tools in a particular location, cooking irons being those specifically dedicated to the cooking process, such as pothooks and spits, as opposed to fire irons such as fire dogs which simply facilitated the combustion process. This is likely to have yielded an underestimate due to the absence of irons from some hearths at the time of appraisal; a comparison with Thame hearth tax records show that the nine inventoried households also listed in the 1662 hearth tax had on average 1.8 more hearths per household than object evidence suggests, and the seventeen inventoried households in the 1665 tax records 1.5 more hearths on average. Of 211 hearths thus indicated in the inventories, 149 (71%) had cooking irons and 45 (21%) only fire irons, the remaining percentage (8%) being indicated by other hearth tools such as fire shovels and bellows alone. It is also possible that fire and cooking irons were displaced prior to appraisal; however, the inventories show no irons in improbable locations such as cocklofts. Where *cooking* irons are indicated, 102 hearths (68%) were in halls, 36 (24%) in kitchens and 5 (3%) in chambers. The location of the cooking process is highly significant in terms of the physical and social organisation of the household, but this aspect will

[84] S. Pennell, 'The Material Culture of Food in Early Modern England, circa 1650–1750', D.Phil. thesis (University of Oxford, 1997), p. 181

be examined in detail in Chapter 6. In Thame in the seventeenth century it appears that wood was the normal fuel on the household hearth. Within the 89 listings of fuel, 50 referred to 'wood', 28 to 'firewood' and 9 to 'billets' – 'a thick piece of wood cut to a suitable length for fuel'[85] – in quantities, where specified, ranging between nine and a half loads – equivalent to a wagonload of wood – and a 'small parcel'. The sole mention of 'one quarter of coales' was in the possession of a blacksmith, Leonard Yates,[86] in 1606, probably charcoal in the terminology and technological context of the time, rather than coal as now understood, which in the seventeenth century was commonly referred to as 'seacoal'. Within the the 89 listings of wood fuel 16 were in service houses (8 in a specific woodhouse), 27 in the backside, barn and stable, 'without doors' or yard, 3 in the kitchen, 2 in the cellar, 4 in chambers or the 'house' and 37 where the location was not specified.

The cooking process is indicated by the utensils for the preparation of ingredients, boiling, frying, roasting, grilling or toasting and baking.[87] Firstly there were fire irons in cooking hearths which served to aid the process of combustion – 173 listings of andirons (Figure 3.11) and 120 of fire dogs. The development of the side hearth on a wall employing a chimney stack (Figure 3.12) instead of the central down hearth in the middle of the room made it feasible to hang cooking vessels over the fire. Chimney stacks were an innovation of the later sixteenth century, part of Hoskins' Great Rebuilding and incorporated into buildings in Thame from the late sixteenth century, referred to at the end of the previous chapter.[88] William Harrison wrote in 1587 of 'the multitude of chimneys lately erected'.[89] Side hearths could accommodate, and are indicated in inventories by, mechanical aids: hooks and hangers for pots and cobirons for spits. They were thus a technological advance, refining the hearth into an effective and versatile cooking zone frequently incorporating an oven which had previously been a separate structure. Other portable forms of heating which appeared in the inventories were thirty-six chafing dishes and twenty-three furnaces. The chafing dish was small receptacle for hot coals (usually charcoal) or other fuel (Figure 3.13). In *The Compleat Angler* Izaak Walton wrote,'Let ... [a Chub] then be boiled gently over a Chafing-dish with wood coles'.[90] A furnace was a combustion device frequently associated with a cauldron or boiler.

---

[85] *OED*
[86] OHCA: MS. Wills Pec. 56/4/2. In addition there was one instance of 'log' and one of 'stackwood'
[87] See online Appendix1 , Table 3.10 a), 'Cooking utensils' and 3.10 b) 'Cooking irons'
[88] W. G. Hoskins, 'The Rebuilding of Rural England, 1570-1640', *Past and Present* 4 (1953), 44–59; M. Airs and J. Rhodes, 'Wall-Paintings from a House in Upper High Street, Thame', *Oxoniensia* 45 (1980), 235–59
[89] William Harrison, *The Description of England* (1587), ed. G. Edelen (Washington and New York: Folger Shakespeare Library, Dover Books1994), p. 201
[90] Izaak Walton, *The Compleat Angler* (London, 1653), p. 58

Figure 3.11 Andirons

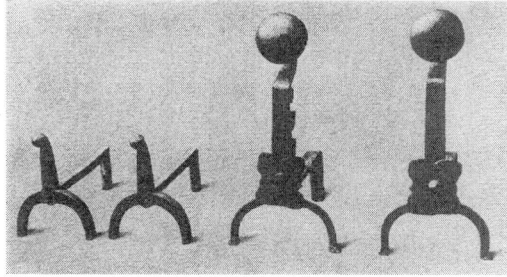

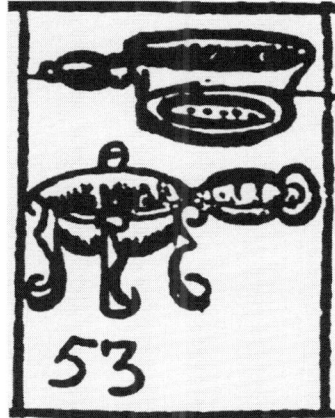

Figure 3.12 Reconstructed seventeenth-century fireplace at the Weald and Downland Museum. Note the pothanger centre right and oven door on the left

Figure 3.13 Chafing dish on stand

In order to cook foodstuffs, the ingredients needed to be held in proximity to a source of heat. The materials therefore had to be durable, heat- and liquid-resistant, and preferably non-toxic. Some pottery utensils could be placed close to the heat but were not very robust. Two metals were predominantly used for cooking utensils and vessels – iron and brass. In the Thame inventories, of the approximately 20% of cooking vessels where the material is specified, 403 were of brass as against 35 of iron. Of a total of 1,422 cooking irons, the material was specified as iron in 75 cases, but it must be assumed that the remainder of these objects would have been, as the name suggests, of iron. So iron was predominantly used in fire and cooking irons, in small cooking vessels and frying pans. Larger cooking vessels (Figure 3.14) were made of brass.[91] Of the two materials iron, at

[91] N. Cox, '"A Flesh Pott, or a Brasse Pott or a Pott to Boile in": Changes in Metal and Fuel Technology in the Early Modern Period and the Implications for Cooking', *Gender and Material Culture in Historical Perspective*, ed. M. Donald, and L. Hurcombe, Studies in Gender and Material Culture 3 (London: Macmillan, 2000), p. 152

Figure 3.14 Pot or cauldron in pot metal

approximately one and a half pence, was considerably cheaper than brass at four and a half to six pence per pound[92] and the technology of iron production was well established in this country. There were two forms of iron, cast and wrought. Wrought iron was fibrous in structure and could be reworked when heated, whilst cast iron, containing more carbon, was more crystalline in structure and thus harder. The late fifteenth-century development of the charcoal-fired blast furnace in the Weald, with the use of water-powered bellows, facilitated the reduction of the carbon content in order to produce wrought iron. The early Tudors supported the development of a domestic cast iron industry especially for the manufacture of cannons, and cast iron found a domestic market in the supply of fire backs and fire irons in the late sixteenth century and a limited production of smaller cooking vessels such as mortars, skillets and posnets. But through the sixteenth and seventeenth centuries no more than 5% of iron output was used for cast work.[93] The relatively high melting point of iron made it unsuited to the casting of larger objects and it was not until the early years of the eighteenth century when Abraham Darby developed the use of coke in the blast furnace, combined with reusable sand moulds in place of the traditional loam moulds, that larger iron cooking pots became widely available. Prior to those developments there is evidence of charcoal-smelted iron pots, in the 1690s using local ores at Leighton in Shropshire and on the river Wye at Redbrook. Frying pans, however, were made using 'battery' – water-powered hammers – on wrought iron. The Hallen family was making frying pans by battery in Staffordshire in the seventeenth century.[94]

As a result of these limitations of casting iron in the seventeenth century, larger cooking vessels, pots and kettles, were made of brass, which has a lower melting point and so flows more easily into the mould. But brass is also toxic, causing anaemia, a fact that was recognised with the

---

[92] *Ibid.*, p. 150
[93] J. Fearn, *Cast Iron* (Princes Risborough: Shire, 1990), pp. 3–5
[94] Cox, 'A Flesh Pott, or a Brasse Pott or a Pott to Boile in', pp. 149–52

tinning of the inside of the vessel.[95] Brass is an alloy of copper and zinc, although Everleigh suggests that the term 'brass' referred to any alloy of copper until the eighteenth century, when it came to represent this specific combination.[96] By the fourteenth century Austria, Germany, France and the Low Countries all had flourishing brass industries, where reserves of copper ore and calamine (zinc ore) were found in association with water power for the battery or beating of the metal; the scale of the enterprise required capital investment and specialist skills. No brass was produced in England until the sixteenth century, and up to the end of that century much brass was imported from the Low Countries. Copper alloy goods were produced in England by craftsmen using imported raw brass, called latten, but most brassware was still shipped from the Low Countries until the early eighteenth century.[97] In order to foster a domestic industry, the Company of Mines Royal and the Mineral and Battery Works, royal monopolies, were formed in 1568, the charter of the latter granting it the sole right to manufacture and produce brass ingot, sheet and finished battery goods. Up to the Civil War in the seventeenth century English copper mining and brass production was largely financed by foreign money and employed foreign workers. Early mining for copper ore was in Cumbria, and zinc ore was discovered in the Mendip Hills. Latten was produced at Tintern on the river Wye for making folded wares and containers, but the brass was not malleable enough to be worked by battery and the works were abandoned.[98] Nationally the enterprise was thus not a success, domestic manufacturers being forced to accept raw brass from monopoly holders of a quality inferior to that of imported brass.[99] However, in 1582 a new brass manufacturing enterprise was established at Isleworth in Middlesex, spawning a local industry making brass products,[100] amongst them the first domestic production from native brass of kettles and pans.[101] Records show that in 1601 the Merchant Adventurers were still importing considerable quantities of copper, latten and brassware – pans and kettles – and a 1635 parliamentary petition complained at the significant quantities of such manufactured goods being exported to this country by Dutch and German merchants.[102] In widespread violation of the Mineral and Battery Works monopoly, 'brass works' were established across the country using imported

---

[95] Ibid., pp. 149–50

[96] Everleigh, *Brass and Brassware*, p. 3

[97] R. Gentle and R. Feild, *Domestic Metalwork 1640–1820* (1975), rev. and enlarged B. Gentle (Woodbridge: Antique Collectors Club, 1994), pp. 15–16; Everleigh, *Brass and Brassware*, p. 4

[98] Gentle and Feild, *Domestic Metalwork*, p. 34; Everleigh, *Brass and Brassware*. p. 5

[99] Gentle and Feild, *Domestic Metalwork*, pp. 22, 34, 19

[100] Ibid., pp. 34, 43

[101] Everleigh, *Brass and Brassware*, p. 5

[102] H. Hamilton, *The English Brass and Copper Industries to 1800* (London: Cass and Co., 1967), pp. 57–8

raw materials, and by the outbreak of the Civil War brass smelting and manufacture was established at a number of sites nationally, making use of coal resources and transport by water.[103] However, again in the 1660s, latten and brass works in Nottingham had fallen into decay due to Swedish competition.[104] The Mines Royal Act of 1689 abolished the royal monopoly over mining, and copper mining, smelting and brass making began to be organised by private enterprise.[105] By 1694 copper ore from Cornwall was being smelted at Conham near Bristol on the river Avon, and around 1702 Abraham Darby started brass production at Baptist Mills on the river Frome in Bristol.[106]

Brassware was thus both cast in moulds from molten copper and fashioned by braziers by hand from cold sheet material. Thomas Burges[107] was recorded as a brazier in New Thame in 1664. Both trades were widely distributed through Britain, utilising sheet or ingot brass or wire. Founders specialised in the production of round-bottomed pots, and braziers in straight-walled and flat-bottomed pans and kettles, the latter for suspension over the domestic hearth from a loop and used mainly for heating water. Founders and braziers were regarded as separate trades but in practice worked in close cooperation, braziers being responsible for the finishing and assembly of cast brassware. Domestic utensils were cast from a copper alloy of lead with only a small tin content called 'bell metal', also known as 'crock metal' or 'pot metal' (Figure 3.14). There were similarities in bell and pot casting techniques, both using moulds made of clay mixed with dung, and both trades frequently combined; those who restricted their production to pots were called 'potters'. Other utensils which were produced from metal by casting from the mid-sixteenth century were brass spoons and candlesticks.[108]

In metallic cooking irons and vessels we see the provision of distanced materials and sophisticated technologies in Thame household activities. Throughout the period cooking vessels represented a significant household investment, ranging from approximately 8% to 24% of the value of all domestic furnishings. However, metallic cooking vessels were durable and repairable and therefore would have been frequently inherited, or brought to a household as part of a bride's portion on marriage. Pennell also identifies a market in used cooking and eating and drinking vessels, the exchange of 'new for old' and their perpetuation through repair.[109] When William

[103] Gentle and Feild, *Domestic Metalwork*, pp. 34, 42–3
[104] Hamilton, *The English Brass and Copper Industries to 1800*, pp. 61–2
[105] Gentle and Feild, *Domestic Metalwork*, p. 50
[106] Everleigh, *Brass and Brassware*, p. 5
[107] OHCA: MS. Wills Pec. 33/2/32
[108] Everleigh, *Brass and Brassware*, pp. 9–11
[109] Pennell, *The Material Culture of Food in Early Modern England, circa 1650–1750*, pp. 135–41

Figure 3.15 Chopping knives

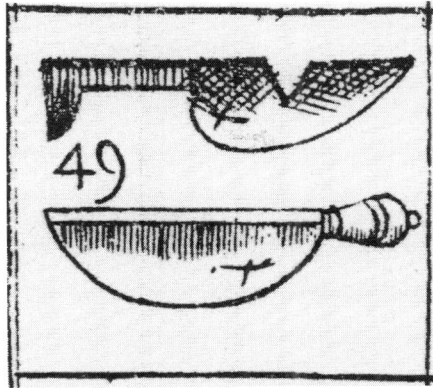

Tipping[110] made his will on 11 June 1604 he bequeathed a number of goods to two daughters of his friend Stephen Smyth, items of furniture, bedding and cooking wares which appear to have constituted the basic requirements of household life, included amongst which were for Grace 'my best brasse pot ... my best kettle' and 'my best frying panne', and similarly for Mary 'my seconde brasse potte and a brasse panne ... one kettle' and 'the lesser fryinge pane'.

Preparation Implements

Implements listed in the inventories indicate the techniques involved in the preparation of foodstuffs for cooking.[111] We see here the interface of objects and ingredients and the resultant transformation: cutting through by chopping, slicing and shredding, or reducing and modifying by grinding, grating and sieving. There is also indication of the surfaces required to work against and on: chopping, shredding and dresser boards. Cleavers were employed in the chopping of meat, and the heavy chopping knife (Figure 3.15) could have been used with the chopping board. Ingredients including meat could also have been minced or shredded with the mincing and shredding knife, on the shredding board. Other dry ingredients could have been ground fine using the mortar and pestle (left foreground in Figure 3.16). Wet ingredients might be drained in the colander or forced through the sieve. In Robert Morris' recipe for 'a pottage without sight of herbs' the cook was instructed to 'take your herbs and oat-meal, and after it is chopt put it into a stone-morter, or bowle, and with a wooden pestel beat it exceedingly, then with some warm liquor in the pot, strain it as hard as may be, and so

---

[110] OHCA: MS. Wills Pec. 52/3/12
[111] See online Appendix 1, Table 3.10, 'Cooking utensils and irons: frequency, a) Cooking utensils: vessels'

Figure 3.16 'Cookery'. The cook is shown 'scumming' a pot, whilst a kettle hangs over the fire. In front of the fire is a gridiron (18). A pestle and mortar sit under the hearth (13, 14). On the table (which could serve the same purpose as a dresser board) are a shredding knife (27), a frying pan on a trivet, or brand-iron (19, 20) and a chopping board. Hanging on the wall above the table are a grater (15) and a colander (28). The illustration is taken from the 1658 Nuremberg Latin-German edition of Joannes Amos Comenius, *Orbis Sensualium Pictus* and depicts a hearth substantially different from an English domestic version of the period.

put it in and boyle it'.[112] Contemporary recipes also indicate that grated bread, employing the bread grater, was used to thicken pottages and sauces. Finally, when the meal was cooked, the dresser board would have been used to 'dress' food preparatory to serving, as indicated by a contemporary use of the word:

> ... at their savoury dinner set
> Of herbs, and other country messes,
> Which the neat-handed Phillis *dresses*'[113]

[112] Morris, *The Book of Pottage and Broth 1580–1660*, p 3
[113] John Milton, 'L'Allegro' (1631), in John Milton, *The Poetical Works of John Milton*, ed. H. C. Beeching (Oxford: Clarendon Press, 1900)

There is evidence to suggest that the dresser board may have been free standing, incorporating shelves and enclosed storage space, although this may apply only to pieces of that name in elite households.[114] The dresser board should not be confused with the eighteenth-century dresser, a cupboard and shelves which existed for display and storage.

Cooking Processes

Cooking vessels and irons indicate the process of placing foodstuffs in a container to undergo transformation through heat. The most frequent were those for boiling (pots and kettles, skillets and posnets, pothangers and hooks), for roasting (spits and jacks, dripping pans and basting ladles), for frying (frying pans) and grilling (gridirons).[115]

Boiling

The largest number of utensils related to the boiling of ingredients, principally for pottages and broths – pots, kettles, skillets, posnets and skimmers. The pot was a rounded cast vessel, usually of brass and often fitted with loop handle for hanging over the fire (Figure 3.17). The kettle was also made of brass, but brazed from sheet material to create a flat-walled and flat-bottomed vessel, again with a loop handle for hanging over the fire, and frequently used for boiling water. Pothangers and pothooks were wrought-iron devices built into the hearth, often in pairs, for the suspension of cooking vessels over the heat. Note in Figure 3.18 the manner in which the hanger permitted the pot to be raised or lowered relative to the heat of the fire. The skillet (Figure 3.19) was a deep pan, usually of cast iron, and fitted with three feet and a long handle for insertion into the fire. The posnet was a smaller version of the skillet. Pans also appear to have been used for boiling: 53 pans are listed, in addition to 1 stew pan and 1 pudding pan. The skimmer was a long-handled flat disc used to skim the top off the broth. The inventories listed 122 unspecified multiples of 'brass': 292 pots and 387 kettles, and 300 pothangers and 158 pothooks. In addition there were 81 posnets and 134 skillets, 62 skimmers and 24 ladles. In Figure 3.16, the cook is 'scumming' a pot of broth.

Contemporary recipes provide a picture of the interplay of foodstuffs, the hearth, cooking vessels and bodily actions, part of the 'practice' of the household. Markham's *The Country Housewife* gave a recipe for 'boiled meats ordinary' using pots:

[114] J. Gloag, *A Short Dictionary of Furniture* (London: George Allen and Unwin, 1977), p. 299
[115] See online Appendix 1, Table 3.10, 'Cooking utensils and irons: frequency, a) Cooking utensils, and b) Cooking irons'

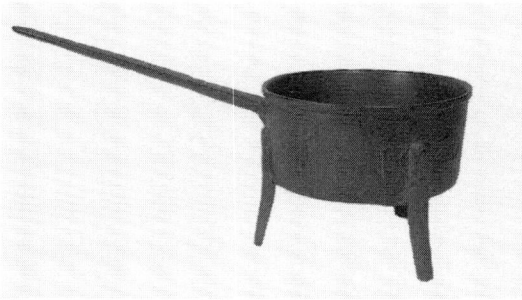

Figure 3.17 (*Top, left*) Cast-iron cooking pot with wrought-iron handle c. 1620–50
Figure 3.18 (*Right*) Pot on pothanger
Figure 3.19 (*Bottom, left*) Copper alloy skillet made by Thomas Sturton II of South Petherton Somerset, cast with initials of owner and date of 1670. The original legs have been replaced with iron

It resteth now that we speak of boiled meats and broths ... we will begin first with those ordinary wholesome boiled meats, which are in use in every goodman's house; therefore to make the best pottage, you shall take a rack of mutton cut into pieces, or a leg of mutton cut into pieces; for this meat and these joints are the best, although any other joint, or any fresh beef will likewise make good pottage; and, having washed your meat well, put it into a clean pot with fair water, and set it upon the fire; then take violet leaves, endive, succory, strawberry leaves, spinach, langdebeef [the herb Picris echoiides, 'oxtongue' or 'bugloss'], marigold flowers, scallions, and a little parsley, and chop them very small together; then take half so much oatmeal well beaten as there is herbs, and mix it with the herbs, and chop all very well together: then when the pot is ready to boil, scum it very well, and then put in your herbs, and so let it boil with a quick fire, stirring the meat oft in the pot, till the meat be boiled enough, and that the herbs and water are mixed together without any separation, which will be after the consumption of more than a third part: then season them with salt, and serve them up with the meat either with sippets or without.[116]

Another form of boiled foods was the pudding, consisting of various ingredients inserted into an animal stomach. Markham gives a recipe for calf's mugget (or entrails) pudding:

Take a calf's mugget, clean and sweet dressed, and boil it well; then shred it as small as is possible, then take of strawberry leaves, of endive, spinach, succor, and sorrel, of each a pretty quantity, and chop them as small as is possible, and then mix them with the mugget; then take the yokes of half a dozen eggs, and three whites, and beat them into it also; and if you find it is too stiff, then make it thinner with a little cream warmed on the fire; then put in a little pepper, cloves, mace, cinnamon, ginger, sugar, currants, dates, and salt, and work all together, with casting in little pieces of sweet butter one after another, till it have received good store of butter, then put it up in the calf's bag, sheep's bag, or hog's bag, and then boil it well, and so serve it up.[117]

For smaller puddings the ingredients were inserted into 'farmes' or cleaned intestines:

fill it up in the farmes, according to the order of good housewifery, and then boil them on a soft and gentle fire, and as they swell, prick them with a great pin, or small awl, to keep them that they burst not: and when you serve them at the table (which must be not until they are a day old) first boil them a little, then take them out and toast them brown before the fire, and so serve them.[118]

The recipe for blood pudding provides a picture of the actions and implements involved in the preparation of the ingredients and cooking of a dish, from the slaughtering of the beast, the gathering and chopping of herbs, filling the intestines and the interaction with the hearth.

Take the blood of a hog whilst it is warm, and steep it in a quart, or more of oatmeal grits, and at the end of three days with your hands take the grits out of the blood, and drain them clean; then put to those grits more than a quart of the best cream warmed on the fire; then take mother of thyme, parsley, spinach, succor, endive, sorrel, and strawberry leaves, of each a few chopped exceeding small, and mix them with the grits, and also a little fennel seed finely beaten; then add a little pepper, cloves and mace, salt, and a great store

[116] Markham, *The English Housewife*, p. 74
[117] *Ibid.*, p. 73
[118] *Ibid.*, pp. 71–2

of suet finely shred, and well beaten; then therewith fill your farmes, and boil them, as hath before been described.[119]

Roasting

The process of boiling could involve a wide range of ingredients; roasting was a cooking process for meats of various kinds and its prominence indicates the important place of meat in the diet. The inventorieslisted 286 spits, 29 cobirons used for holding the spits in front of the fire and 40 racks possibly for holding spits when not in use; however, the incidence of 1 'coldrack' might indicate that the 'rack' could also be used to hold spits whilst roasting meat.[120] Contemporaries suggested varying definitions: Minsheu offered 'A racke is properly that which is of yron which hath a long ranke of barres in it, and a Cobborne or Coleburne [cobiron] are the little ones of wood',[121] whilst Phillips' *New World of Words* described a rack as 'a Wooden Frame ... to lay Spits on in a Kitchin'.[122] It is, of course, always possible that the words were used interchangeably; Randle Cotgrave gave the definition for 'Rotissoir' as 'a Cobiron, or little Racke' – an example of the potential unreliability of words as ontological evidence.[123] Whatever the overlap in terminology, the principle of roasting was the placing of meat on spits before the fire, positioned on a cobiron or rack. The process could be mechanised by the application of a jack, sometimes weight driven. The inventories listed 30 jacks, 3 jacks and chains and 8 jack weights, in households of every occupational status apart from those of husbandmen and agricultural labourers, between 1607 and 1694. The description of it as a device 'to turne spitt' in the inventory of Richard Somers[124] in 1665 suggests that some explanation was still necessary at that date. These were relatively simple mechanical devices and yet marked a significant step towards the lessening of manual labour in the cooking process. Finally, there were dripping pans to catch the fat falling from the meat on the spit of which eighty-nine were listed; where materials are given, 12 are of iron, 11 of tin, 2 of brass and 1 each of lateen and plate.

Markham stressed the importance of the cleanliness of the roasting implements and the meat: 'First, the cleanly keeping and scouring of the spits and cob-irons; next, the neat picking and washing of meat before it

[119] *Ibid.*, p. 73
[120] See online Appendix 1, Table 3.10, 'Cooking utensils and irons: frequency, b) Cooking irons'
[121] John Minsheu, *The Guide into Tongues etc.* (London, 1617 and 1627)
[122] Edward Philips, *The New World of English Words; or, A General Dictionary* (1658), ed. J. Kersey (Menston: Scholar Press, 1969)
[123] Randle Cotgrave, *A Dictionarie of the French and English Tongues* (1611) (Menston: Scholar Press, 1968)
[124] OHCA: MS. Wills Pec. 51/3/18

Figure 3.20 Dressed pig

is spitted'.[125] A knowledge of the nature of the fire was also important: 'The roasting of meats differeth nothing but in the fires', with a necessity 'to know the temperatures of fires for every meat, and which must have a slow fire, yet a good one, taking leisure in roasting...and which would lie long at the fire and soak well in roasting'.[126] The meat to be roasted had first to be properly butchered: 'for the ordering, preparing, and trussing your meats for the spit or table, in that there is much difference', including which meats required the bones to be crushed when roasting, which parts of the body should be detached or retained.[127] The meat was then to be placed properly on the spit (Figure 3.20): 'then the spitting and broaching of meat, which must be done so strongly and firmly that the meat may by no means either shrink from the spit, or else turn about the spit; and yet ever to observe that the spit do not go through any principal part of the meat, but such as is of least account and estimation',[128] with the grease running off into the dripping pan. This may be the grease that found its way into the grease bag in the inventories.[129] The meat had to be basted during the roasting process, using the basting ladle. 'Then to know the best bastings for meat, which is sweet butter, sweet oil, barreled butter, or fine rendered up seam [clarified animal fat] ... There be some that will baste only with water, and salt, and nothing else.'[130]

Meats could be eaten with sauces, for which Markham provided recipes. 'The sauce for chickens is divers, according to men's tastes: for some will have only butter, verjuice, and a little parsley rolled in their bellies mixed

---

[125] Markham, *The English Housewife*, p. 83
[126] *Ibid.*, pp. 83, 88
[127] *Ibid.*, p. 88
[128] *Ibid.* p. 83
[129] OHCA: MS. Wills Pec. 38/1/7
[130] Markham, *The English Housewife*, p. 84

together: others will have butter, verjuice, and sugar boiled together with toasts of bread'.[131]

Sauces had appeared in elite English cookery books from the sixteenth century, and the appearance of the saucepan in the household effects of the middling ranks is taken as an indication of the downward spread of elite culinary habits.[132] But only two households featured saucepans in Thame, both more affluent households at the very end of the seventeenth century: a copper saucepan belonging to John Striblehill, a gentleman, in 1692, and three saucepans of Thomas Middleton, a comfortably housed clerk in 1694,[133] possibly indicating the persistence in most households of the side hearth, as saucepans were better suited to the innovation of a cooking range.[134]

Frying and Grilling

Frying, heating ingredients over the fire in the medium of butter, fat or grease, was evidenced in the inventories by the presence of sixty-two frying pans, and was one of the principal cooking processes identified by Markham: 'Now to proceed to your fricasses ... which are dishes of many compositions and ingredients, as flesh, fish, eggs, herbs, and many other things, all being prepared and made ready in a frying pan'.[135] Frying pans were shallow flat-bottomed vessels, generally of beaten iron, with a long handle for placing in the fire, possibly on one of the twenty-two trivets, cast- or wrought-iron tripod supports (Figure 3.16). Grilling is indicated by the seventy gridirons and by two toasting irons: 'Then take a manchet and cut it into toasts, and toast them well before the fire.'[136]

Baking

The side hearth could incorporate an oven used for baking items other than bread. Markham recommended that 'our English housewife must be skilful in pastry, and know how and in what manner to bake all sorts of meat, and what paste is fit for every meat [and] which would be in the finest, shortest and thinnest crust,' with recipes for meat pies, spinach and apple tarts .[137] However, the inventories listed only two objects specific to

[131] Ibid., p. 90
[132] L. Weatherill, Consumer Behaviour and Material Culture in Britain 1660–1760 (London: Routledge, 1988)
[133] OHCA: MS. Wills Prob. 4 11085; MS. Wills Pec. 46/3/18
[134] Weatherill, Consumer Behaviour and Material Culture in Britain 1660–1760, p. 205
[135] Markham, The English Housewife, p. 67
[136] Ibid., p. 69
[137] Ibid., p. 96

baking: a peel or flat wooden oven shovel for placing loaves in the oven in the inventory of William Eeles, a glazier, in 1683 and two pasty pans belonging to John Striblehill, gentleman, in 1692.[138] This could indicate a relative absence of baked items in Thame diet in the seventeenth century. Or it is possible that, since there is evidence of boulting and the production of dough, baking was done in public ovens such as those of the three bakers showing in the inventory record in 1637, 1643 and 1698.[139]

Evidence for the Nature of the Diet

It might be expected that the nature of people's diet, then, both in quality and variety, would differ according to social status. We have already seen, for example, that foodstuff processing was more frequent in larger households. Given the infrequent listings of foodstuffs it is not possible to establish the relationship of particular ingredients in the diet to social status. However, it may be possible to draw some dietary evidence from cooking irons and vessels on the basis that they indicate the preparation and consumption of different types of food. Spits represent the cooking of meats only, whereas pots were used for dishes which, from contemporary evidence, may have incorporated meat but generally in combination with pulses and vegetables. In Table 3.2 we see that there is a varying frequency per household of spits and pothooks and pothangers according to status. Pots or mixed diet predominates in number over spits, or pure meat diet, in every category. However, the greatest congruence of the two forms of cooking appears in the households of clerics and yeomen, and the greatest differentiation in favour of the pot, or mixed diet, in those of artisans. The households of agricultural labourers did not possess a single spit. If it is anticipated that a diet rich in meat was associated with higher social status then it is surprising that gentry households had no greater differentiation in favour of meat than those of artisan-traders or widows and spinsters. The tentative conclusions to be drawn are that, on the evidence of these two categories of cooking irons, the dietary habits of Thame were, at least in these higher social echelons, remarkably consistent across varying social and occupational status. There may have been a slight increase in meat consumption in the households of yeomen, where the nature of the livelihood would have made that ingredient more easily available. And for agricultural labourers, even those possessing livestock, roasting whole meat was not customary, even if it was consumed as part of pottage, possibly reflecting the diet and culinary habits of those still lower in the social scale.

[138] OHCA: MS. Wills Pec. 38/1/7; MS. Wills Prob. 4 11085
[139] OHCA: MS. Wills Pec.48/3/7; MS. Wills Pec. 33/2/18; MS. Wills Pec. 52/1/11

Table 3.2 Spits, pothooks and pothangers: mean frequencies per household by occupational status category

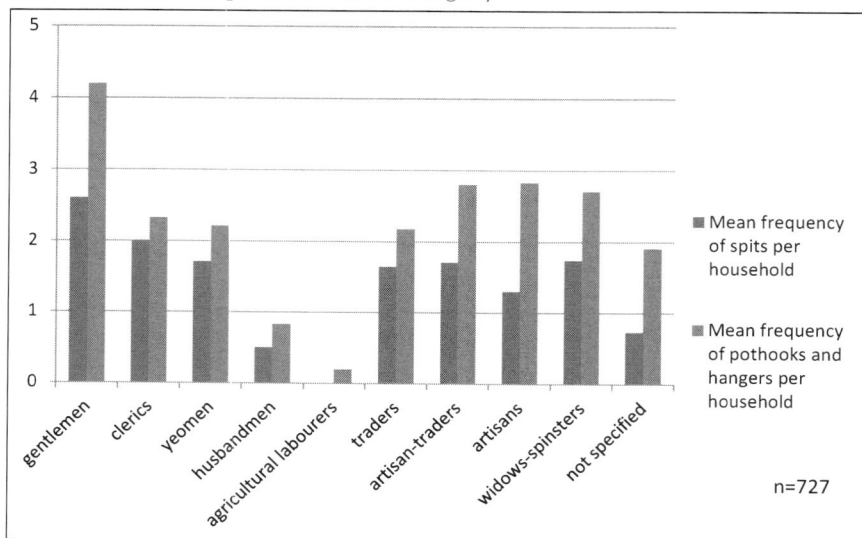

Cooking in the Domestic Culture

What can we deduce of the habitual actions of cooking from the evidence of the inventories and complementary information from contemporary sources, principally Markham's *The English Housewife*? The cooking process first involved the marshalling of resources, large-scale and occasional investment in the hearth, the cooking vessels and irons, inherited, sourced locally and at a distance, and small-scale and frequent acquisitions of food and fuel, transactions which regularly traversed the threshold of the dwelling. Cooking required a culture of regularity and organisation, with a high degree of knowledge, of implements and actions, acquired and also amenable to discourse, and subject to continual fluctuations in the availability of foodstuffs according to season or opportunity, and the varying requirements of food for simple sustenance, or for conviviality, which will be examined in the next chapter. And there was a clear presumption in the contemporary (male) author that this was, at least in the ordinary household, solely women's work. It was not only part of her skill and knowledge, of the gendered division of labour within the household, but also a statement of her moral character and virtue. 'To speak then of the outward and active knowledges which belong to our English housewife, I hold the first and most principal to be a perfect skill and knowledge of cookery, with all the secrets belonging

132

to the same, because it is a duty really belonging to a woman.'[140] It was also, like foodstuff processing, physical work and a sensory experience: lighting and tending the fire, lifting and scouring heavy metal vessels, exposure to warmth in winter and heat in summer, stirring pots or turning spits, the senses of taste and smell, and the social engagement of the shared tasks and the taking of the prepared food to the table. As cooking equipment became more specialised and spatially defined with the appearance of the side hearth and its accessories, we are possibly seeing a shift of cooking from a central place in the household to a physical, social and conceptual marginalisation, along with a greater domestic role differentiation according to gender. Cox makes the observation that the male technologies of iron and brass production both refined the cooking process but also potentially marginalised women.[141] However, Pennell cautions against a simple interpretation which characterises changes in the technology and location of food preparation as a diminution of women's power and influence. Cooking and housewifery manuals, admittedly focussed on a literate minority, assumed specialisation and social and moral power (sometimes epitomised by religious texts cast into the metalware) through competent management of the domestic domain. Such expertise, in Pennell's view, rendered women far from passive in the early modern household.[142] But this debate is perhaps to predict later developments; with cooking still frequently carried out on the hall hearth at the centre of the Thame household, custom would appear at least in part to have resisted change. The spatial and temporal significance of the processing and preparation of food within the household will be considered in Chapter 6. The purpose of obtaining and preparing foodstuffs was to sustain the household. We turn now to the objects which evidence their consumption.

---

[140] Markham, *The English Housewife*, p. 61
[141] Cox, 'A Flesh Pott, or a Brasse Pott or a Pott to Boile in', pp. 143, 148
[142] Pennell, *The Material Culture of Food in Early Modern England, circa 1650–1750*, pp. 203, 217, 240–42, 283–4

4

Commensality and Conviviality

The Furniture of Commensality

The provisioning of the household, the processing and the cooking of foodstuffs were the initial phases in the sustenance of the household. The ultimate purpose was often consumption, although in many households some foodstuffs were processed for economic benefit. We might feel justified in making the assumption that food and drink were consumed in a manner historically established, of the household group seated around a table. Engravings of the period (Figure 4.1) do show such scenes, providing one strong strand of evidence. However, since this study is based primarily on the inventory evidence, this assumption should be tested against the listed furnishings. Seating and tables of various types were well represented; in addition, cupboards, used for the storage and display of drinking vessels might also be taken as valuable indicators. The association of these three elements of furnishing in a household space might then be seen as a fair indication of commensality. It should be noted that in the compilation of the probate inventories these three furnishing elements were frequently listed and valued as a group, suggesting not only physical association in place but also conceptually in the minds of the appraisers. The great majority of tables were listed with seating of some sort; those that were not were frequently in service areas such as the kitchen and buttery, or in chambers.[1] Similarly a very high percentage (89%) of all seating was found in the same space as table furniture, and 54% when cupboards were also present. It could be argued that the simple listing of seating and tables in a particular space does not necessitate their use together; seating could be used independently of tables in the same room, and a table could be one used either in conjunction with seating or not. In addition, seating and tables together could be used for purposes other than the consumption of food and drink, although in the domestic setting this does seem from pictorial evidence

---

[1] See online Appendix 1, Table 4.3, 'Seating, table and cupboard furniture: percentage associations', at http://boybrew.co/9781783270415

Figure 4.1 Dining scene

to be the probable reason for a household group to be seated around a table. Only cupboards served a fairly unambiguous purpose – for the display and storage of drinking vessels – although again the assumption that consumption was occurring where they were located is open to question. (The interpretation of the function of objects is always liable to an element of doubt, and deductions of use are based on the balance of probability.) In order to determine more exactly those types of furniture which might fairly be assumed to have been brought into association for consumption and conviviality, and the nature of that engagement, we will now therefore explore the different types of seating, table and cupboard furniture listed in the Thame inventories.

Furniture Materials and Construction

The term 'furniture' in the seventeenth century was closely linked with the concept of furnishing, or equipping, and thus applied to a wide range of household goods. Furniture is understood here in the present sense as the larger objects, sometimes attached to the dwelling structure but generally free standing, which furnish human habitats for the purpose of facilitating bodily actions and the conduct of domestic life. The affordance and agency of the furniture listed in the inventories depended on materials, construction, variations of types and context. Objects were conceived in order to perform a function, which was not only ergonomic but also cultural. Different and evolving ways existed to make things, with materials more or less difficult to work, locally available or accessed from a distance and demanding differing skills and use of tools. Construction implies affordance: the suitability to perform a task, durability, adaptability and status. The furniture listed in the inventories is now accessible only as a record rather than as physical objects, so our understanding of its physical properties is bound to be speculative. However, by referring to illustrations of the period, especially those found on broadside ballad sheets which, according to the subject of the ballad, might be assumed to illustrate less elite domestic scenes, and to extant pieces of the period, it is possible to construct a general picture of the likely characteristics of the pieces listed in the inventories. Historically, furniture has predominantly been constructed of wood, with additional metal components. It is probable that most furniture, apart from that in elite houses, would have been constructed if not within Thame itself, at least within the locality of materials sourced nearby. The Thame inventories generally listed the furniture object only and are economical with descriptive detail, including the nature of the timber employed. The most prized furniture timber of the period was oak, being hard-wearing and impervious to the depredations of wood worm, and there are a small number of chests and bedsteads which are listed as being of that wood. The only other mention of furniture timber is found in two chests of cypress wood (valued for the fact that its resinous odour kept fabric-destroying insects at bay) in the chambers of Thomas Striblehill, a butcher in 1598, and of Thomas Hennant, the vicar deceased in 1664, the elm chest in the chamber over the shop of Katherine Benson, a widow in 1616, and 'two plancks of Ashe' listed amongst the assets of John Groome, a joiner in 1624.[2] The indigenous timbers (excluding the cypress) may well have been sourced from local woodland or hedgerow standards.

The simplest form of furniture construction was termed 'boarded', being the nailing of slabs of wood or boards together. This technique could be used to construct simple seating such as stools and containers such as chests (Figures 4.5a and 5.16). Carpenters who made such pieces principally employed chopping and boring tools such as the 'augers' and 'hatchett' as well as a 'sawe & other Tooles' listed in the inventory of Robert Alnett,[3] a carpenter deceased in 1634. Figure 4.2 shows seventeenth-century carpenters at work. This was also generally the method of construction employed for the internal wooden fitting of dwellings such as doors and shelves, and for a wide range of domestic articles such as troughs, bins, boxes and stands. In addition to Robert Alnett, two other carpenters were listed in the

[2] OHCA: MS. Wills Pec. 50/5/20; MS. Wills Pec. 41/4/13; MS. Wills Pec. 32/4/61; MS. Wills Pec. 39/3/35
[3] OHCA: MS. Wills Pec. 35/1/1

Figure 4.2 Carpenters

Thame records; Robert Collenridge and John Greene, deceased in 1626 and 1627 respectively.[4] Joined construction, the work of the joiner, was a more complex method of building wooden objects, distinguished by the use of the mortice and tenon joint in the creation of a frame, frequently in combination with panels where it was desired to form an enclosure (Figure 4.3). This technique was employed within the house in the panelling of rooms, referred to as 'wainscot'. The joiner, employing more complex technology than the carpenter and tools such as chisels and planes (Figure 4.4, bottom), could thus create more sophisticated objects such as joined table frames, stools, chairs, benches, chests and bedsteads. In place of the nails used by carpenters the joiners' structures were secured with wooden pegs (Figure 4.3). Only one joiner appears in the Thame inventories: John Groome,[5] deceased in 1624. Turning was a method of wood conversion employing a lathe to rotate a piece of wood between fixed centres and with a chisel to reduce it into a cylindrical shape. Components could be attached to other members by insertion into drilled holes. A number of turned chairs were listed in the inventories. Turning was traditionally considered a separate trade, but John Groome possessed amongst his trade tools 'a

---

[4] OHCA: MS. Wills Pec. 32/1/28; MS. Wills Pec. 39/3/37
[5] OHCA: MS. Wills Pec. 39/3/35

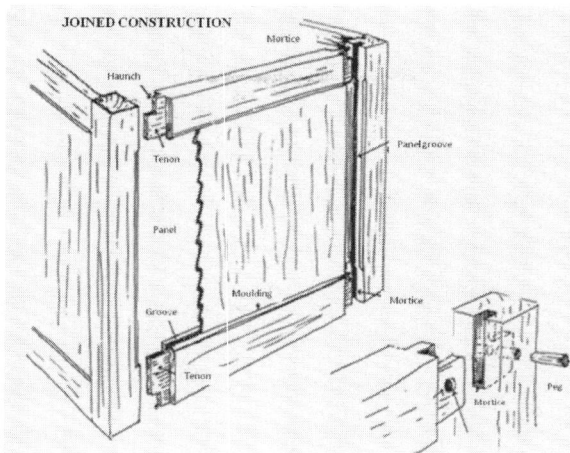

Figure 4.3 Mortice and tenon construction

Figure 4.4 Turner and joiner

lathe to turne with all', suggesting that in a small town a variety of skilled woodwork was done by the joiner.[6] The use of the simple pole lathe (Figure 4.4 top) to shape small wooden components in the woods or workshop was one which was commonplace in the nearby Chiltern beech woods into the twentieth century, and Daniel Defoe noted the prevalence of this local industry early in the eighteenth century: 'the vast quantity of beechwood

[6] *Ibid.*

which grows in the woods of Buckinghamshire more plentifully than any other part of England ... [provides] beech quarters for diverse uses, particularly chair makers and turnery wares'.[7]

Seating Furniture

The seat is an object devised to hold the human body in a semi-recumbent position. As such the use of a seat poses considerations of the posture adapted by the sitter, in activity or rest and comfort, and the attitude of the sitter vis-à-vis others in a company, standing or seated, and thus the creation of a social dynamic. Seat furniture may also incorporate materials, construction, style or decorative detail which conveys indications of status. From the inventory evidence of seating,[8] stools and chairs were by a significant margin the most numerous, together making up nearly 80% of seating, followed by a smaller proportion of forms and benches (just over 20%) and a few instances of settles, although it must be remembered that – in contrast to stools and chairs – forms, benches and settles accommodated more than one person. Using only the documentary evidence to attempt to comprehend the functional and cultural affordance of each type of furniture, we are restricted to the terminology employed, and its connotations in the minds of the appraisers. Apart from the simple name given to an object, the inventories also sometimes ascribed other qualities: material used, method of construction and size or condition. The purpose of the inventory was to indicate the value of objects, so where a description was given it may have been in order to distinguish that object from other similar objects in the same space, or to justify its valuation. Sometimes, however, it takes the form of a simple observation; for example, the chair 'by the fire side' in the hall of Phyllis Greene in 1643.[9]

The most numerous type of seating, the stool was a backless seat for one person, constructed either of nailed boards or of a seat board located on four or three riven or turned framed legs (Figures 4.5a and b). Of 861 stools in total, 478, or 55%, were listed as 'joint' or joined. No indication was given of the structure of the other stools. This may simply be an omission, or it may indicate that the remainder were of a simpler boarded construction. Joined and non-joined stools were listed together in the same space, for example in the chamber of William Apowell[10] in 1658, but 'joined' stools were also contrasted with 'low' stools, of which fifteen were listed,

[7] Daniel Defoe, *The Complete English Tradesman* (1726) (Gloucester : Alan Sutton, 1987), pp. 299–300
[8] See online Appendix 1, Table 4.3, 'Seating, table and cupboard furniture: percentage associations'
[9] OHCA: MS. Wills Pec. 39/4/30
[10] OHCA: MS. Wills Pec. 32/1/43

Figure 4.5a (*Left*) Boarded oak stool, sixteenth century
Figure 4.5b (*Right*) Joined oak stool, early seventeenth century

and twenty-six 'high' stools, possibly for the use of children. Stools were also described as 'small' (5) and 'little' (14) and as 'old' (3). Stools were found in inventories across the entire century and in households of all sizes and status (see Table 4.1a). The majority were found in halls, and to a lesser extent in chambers.

The chair was another type of single seat with a back. A certain degree of complexity existed even in the minds of contemporaries as to the exact distinctions of different types of chair. Holme opined, 'If the chaire be made all of Joyners worke, as back and seat then it is termed a Joynt chaire, or a Buffit chaire. Those which have stayes on each side are called arme chaires or chaires of ease.'[11] The chair is defined by Gloag as a seat with a back for one person with or without arms.[12] However, in the Thame inventories there is no reference to either configuration, and unless we are to assume a complete absence of chairs with arms, then in this context it seems that 'chair' was a generic term for a single seat with a back of various types, with and without arms. This interpretation is supported by the fact that the 678 chairs listed in the inventories have the greatest descriptive variety of any type of seating, some 27% linked to adjectives describing materials and construction, and fifteen different types of chair listed, in contrast to two types of stool. This may partly be explained by the fact that the chair was an

[11] Randle Holme, *The Academy of Armory; or, A Storehouse of Armory and Blazon* (1688), ed. I. H. Jeayes (London: Roxburghe Club, 1905), Book III, Chapter XIV, p. 14
[12] J. Gloag, *A Short Dictionary of Furniture* (London: George Allen and Unwin, 1977), p. 196

Table 4.1a Seating: mean frequency of single seating per household by occupational status category

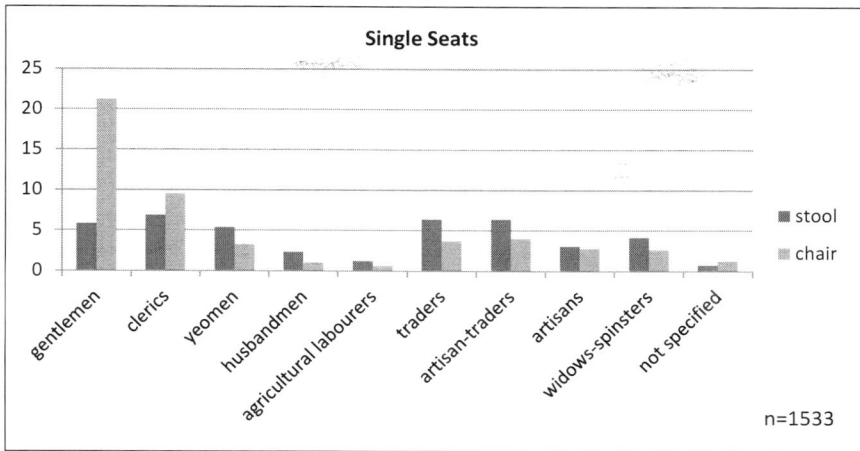

Table 4.1b Seating: mean frequency of multiple seating per household by occupational status category

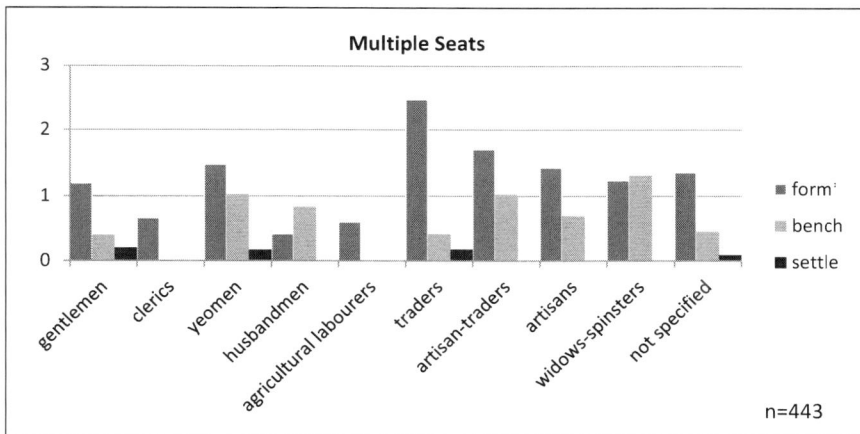

object employing a variety of materials and constructional techniques, but also more likely to be used in a variety of settings, and thus invested with diverse status and cultural significance. In contrast to the high number of stools thus described, only thirty-two (5%) chairs were listed as being of joined construction, found throughout the century in dwellings of all sizes, predominantly in halls, but also in chambers and parlours. One chair in the chamber of Anthony Nore,[13] yeoman, in 1627 was described as

[13] OHCA: MS. Wills Pec. 47/1/77

Figure 4.6 (*Left*) Joined armchair, mid-seventeenth century

Figure 4.7 (*Centre*) Boarded chair

Figure 4.8 (*Right*) Turned chair

'framed', which may also have referred to joined construction (Figure 4.6). Only two chairs were described as being of boarded construction: one seat and one chair in the hall of Peter Willmot and 'by the fire side' of Phyllis Greene, yeoman and widow, deceased in 1625 and 1643 respectively.[14] Holme describes this (Figure 4.7) as 'the old way of making the chaire ... being so weighty that it cannot be moved from place to place, but abideth in its owne station',[15] a reflection on the mobility, or otherwise, of objects. Another seventeen (3%) of the chairs were described as 'turned', found predominantly in the houses of yeomen and artisan-traders, and also those of widows, in halls and chambers. Turned chairs (Figure 4.8) occurred in the inventories from 1616 only up until 1661, which may suggest that this form of chair construction fell out of favour and use in the latter part of the century. However, later in the century, in 1693, three chairs in the hall of the widow Deborah Bigg[16] were described as 'old' and 'flaggen-bottomed', which may possibly also have referred to a turned chair seated with rushes.

Another type which was represented in a small number of seats was a woven construction, 7 'matted' of straw (1%) and 12 'wicker' of withe (2%). In the hall of the widow Elizabeth Heybourne[17] four chairs were described as 'flagen', which may have indicated a woven construction using rushes. Four chairs were also described as 'rodd' or 'rodden', which may

[14] OHCA: MS. Wills Pec. 54/2/36; MS. Wills Pec. 39/4/30
[15] Holme, *The Academy of Armory*, Book III, Chapter XIV, p. 14
[16] OHCA: MS. Wills Pec. 33/4/31
[17] OHCA: MS. Wills Pec. 42/1/34

also have referred to seats woven of withe.[18] Matted or straw chairs occurred predominantly in the hall in the dwellings of widows and artisan-traders, and Gilbert suggested that, being more comfortable and sometimes incorporating a hood, this type of chair might have been by the hearth and used by nursing mothers and the elderly,[19] and of the nineteen listed, twelve (63%) were in a space with evidence of a hearth. Holme noted that 'these chaires [are] called Twiggen chaires because they are made of Owsiers, and Withen twigs: haveing round covers over the heads of them like to a canopy ... are principally used by sick and infirm people, and such women as have bine lately brought to bed'.[20] Wicker chairs were associated with a broad range of householder occupational status, in halls, chambers and kitchens. The materials and technique used in the construction of woven chairs made them articles which potentially could have been produced locally, even within the household itself. The listing of both straw and wicker chairs ranges in date from 1636 and 1643 respectively up to 1670, again suggesting perhaps from this very limited sample that, as with the turned chair, the incidence of furnishing objects of local production and of limited durability was declining in the latter part of the seventeenth century, either through changing taste or the more distanced supply of superior commodities. As in the case of the stools, of those chairs which have no description of the materials used the presumption must be that they were made of an unspecified timber. 'Wooden' chairs were only listed in four households: those of an artisan, artisan-trader and two widows, at different times in the century.[21] There is no apparent contrast being made in any of these instances to seating in the same room of other materials, and this description perhaps should be put down to the idiosyncrasies of a few appraisers.

From the middle to the latter part of the century, between 1644 and 1690, forty-six (7%) chairs were listed with leather seats. These were found in the halls, chambers and parlours of gentry, yeomen and artisan-traders' dwellings. Twenty-one chairs in the parlour of Thomas Middleton,[22] clerk, in 1694 were described as being of Russian leather, reputedly at that time the highest quality. There is also limited evidence of fabric upholstered seating; eleven chairs had 'Turkeywork' covering: two in the parlour of Richard Somers,[23] a gentleman, in 1665 and nine in the best chamber of Thomas Baker,[24] a maltster in 1689. 'Turkeywork' was the name given to a woollen

[18] OHCA: MS. Wills Pec. 52/3/15; MS. Wills Pec. 37/4/17; MS. Wills Pec. 35/2/10
[19] C. Gilbert, *English Vernacular Furniture 1750–1900* (New Haven, London: Yale University Press, 1991), p. 148. His suggestion arose from nineteenth-century images depicting the straw chairs in such use
[20] Holme, *The Academy of Armory*, Book III, Chapter XIV, p. 14
[21] OHCA: MS. Wills Pec. 35/1/1; MS. Wills Pec. 51/4/15; MS. Wills Pec. 46/2/18; MS. Wills Pec. 52/4/14
[22] OHCA: MS. Wills Pec. 46/3/18
[23] OHCA: MS. Wills Pec. 51/3/18
[24] OHCA: MS. Wills Pec. 33/4/25

fabric employed as seat upholstery developed by English carpet weavers in the sixteenth century in imitation of the rich pile texture and patterns of Turkish carpets. At first the process consisted of hand-knotting the woollen pile, but by the seventeenth century a method of knotting the pile in the course of weaving was developed.[25] Six chairs in the hall of the blacksmith John Shreeve[26] were described as 'serge fringed' in 1682, and Thomas Stribblehill[27] possessed two embroidered stools in the chamber over his parlour in 1598. As examples of exotic and high-quality seating, two japanned chairs, employing a decorative technique in imitation of oriental lacquer, were listed in the best chamber of John Stribblehill,[28] gentrified scion of the family of butchers, and he also had sixteen cane-seated chairs in his dining room in 1692, the cane being a relatively novel import from the Far East, all almost certainly of London manufacture and representative of the elite furnishing fashions of the time. Furnishing and other household commodities were therefore increasingly sourced from specialist producers and as elements of personal 'comfort', in a Marxian sense, becoming increasingly fetishised.[29]

Forms, benches and settles were all types of multiple seating with and without backs. The opinion amongst modern furniture historians seems to be that the terms bench and form were interchangeable.[30] However, the Thame inventories suggest they were distinct to those appraisers; in the hall of John Simons[31] in 1605 were listed 'one table with the frame a bench [and] a forme'. Gloag implies that benches were wider, forms narrower and therefore possibly longer.[32] In other words, the bench was more commodious and thus possibly a higher status seat. However, where separate valuations exist for forms and benches they show no marked variation in value. Holme himself refers to an illustration (Figure 4.9) of a long multiple seat as 'a Joynt Forme, or Bench', perhaps suggesting the superior structural qualities of the bench.[33] The contemporary consensus seems to have been that the settle was a backed seat, frequently with arms.[34]

The inventories provide some indications of the construction of forms and benches. Of the 268 forms listed, sixty-two (23%) were described as

---

[25] Gloag, *A Short Dictionary of Furniture*, p. 684; R. Edwards, *The Shorter Dictionary of English Furniture* (1964) (Twickenham: Spring Books, 1987), p. 625
[26] OHCA: MS. Wills Pec. 51/4/15
[27] OHCA: MS. Wills Pec. 50/5/20
[28] OHCA: MS. Wills Prob. 4 11085
[29] K. Marx, *Capital: A Critique of Political Economy* (1867), trans. B. Fowkes (Harmondsworth: Penguin Books, New Left Review, 1976), p. 165
[30] Gloag, *A Short Dictionary of Furniture*, p. 135; Edwards, *The Shorter Dictionary of English Furniture*, p. 47
[31] OHCA: MS. Wills Pec. 50/5/30
[32] Gloag, *A Short Dictionary of Furniture*, p. 135
[33] Holme, *The Academy of Armory*, Book III, Chapter XIV, p. 15
[34] Gloag, *A Short Dictionary of Furniture*, p. 597; Edwards, *The Shorter Dictionary of English Furniture*, p. 464

Figure 4.9 Bench

Figure 4.10 Wainscot bench, oak, sixteenth century

joined. None of the 168 benches listed was described as joined, but five were described as being 'wainscot'. The term wainscot could refer to the timber used; Chinnery suggests that it could derive from the Dutch term 'waggen schot', or wagon wood, thus referring to oak.[35] However, there is some debate over the accuracy of this interpretation and it appears more likely that 'wainscot' referred here to panelled construction, employed as it was in many inventories as a term on its own describing the wall panelling. The inventory of Elizabeth Francklin[36] in 1622 listed 'the benches & backe of wainscote' in the chamber over the buttery. The use of the adjective 'wainscot' in association with these benches may therefore indicate that they had enclosed panelled bases or backs (Figure 4.10), and that the other benches and forms which were not 'joined' were of boarded construction. Benches were also described as 'little' (6), 'low' (1), 'short' (1) and 'old' (4). A terminological overlap between benches with backs and settles is indicated by the listing of two 'settle benches'.[37] We could perhaps therefore speculate that the twelve settles listed were distinguished by the presence of arms. The apparent ambiguity in the inventories in respect of the nomenclature of seating illustrates graphically the way in which typological boundaries are blurred. There are a number of spatial references for seating: benches 'about the hall',[38] 'against the wall'[39] and 'next the Buttery',[40] in association

[35] V. Chinnery, *Oak Furniture: The British Tradition* (Woodbridge: Antique Collectors Club, 1979), p. 154
[36] OHCA: MS. Wills Pec. 38/4/7
[37] OHCA: MS. Wills Pec. 45/2/15
[38] OHCA: MS. Wills Pec. 45/2/15
[39] OHCA: MS. Wills Pec. 39/4/30
[40] OHCA: MS. Wills Pec. 51/3/14

with other furniture 'at the end of the table'[41] and 'beehinde the teable'.[42] Also in association with actions and the senses, the bench 'at the fier side',[43] the chair and seat 'by the fire side'[44] and 'by ye Fyer',[45] which indicate the significance of semi-permanent positioning of furniture within the room providing cues and settings for the social dynamic in relation to all the associations invested in the hearth; warmth, sustenance and conviviality.

The variety of types of seating presented a number of options in type of construction and configuration, quality of materials, and also possibly decoration, which is not mentioned in the inventories. Members of a company could be seated in close proximity or distanced from others, on seating which was moveable or relatively immoveable and affording varying postures and degrees of comfort, or in the terminology of the time 'ease'.[46] Stools and chairs were singular seats providing distinction for the sitter, with a higher degree of comfort and status in the chair. Stools were mentioned in contemporary literature in a manner which suggested a lower status than chairs; the fool in Shakespeare's *King Lear* mocks the absent treacherous daughter Goneril in an imaginary trial: 'Cry you mercy, I took you for a joint-stool',[47] and an account of the Privy Council in the time of James I referred to younger councillors sitting 'by like children at joynt-stooles'.[48] Forms, benches and settles were collective seats with implications for physical comfort, status and social engagement. These distinctions will play an important part in the analysis of the differentiation and meaning of domestic space in Chapter 6.

Tables 4.1a and 4.1b show that different types of seating were distributed differentially according to the various occupational status of households. In single seating (Table 4.1a) we note a high representation of chairs in gentry and, to a lesser extent in clerical households in comparison to other occupational status categories, whilst stools predominated over chairs as the type of single-seating type in all other households. The elite ownership of chairs may indicate the role that chairs played in defining status: a greater degree of material wealth or innovation versus tradition in furnishing. Presumably, as a more comfortable type of seating, chairs might have been deemed more desirable, and indeed this type of seating increased in frequency through

---

[41] OHCA: MS. Wills Pec. 39/4/30
[42] OHCA: MS. Wills Pec. 51/3/14
[43] OHCA: MS. Wills Pec. 54/3/44
[44] OHCA: MS. Wills Pec. 39/4/30
[45] OHCA: MS. Wills Pec. 54/2/36
[46] The terms 'comfort' and 'ease' appear to have effectively exchanged significance between the early modern period and present day, the former previously signifying affection and the latter physical amenity. J. E. Crowley, *The Invention of Comfort: Sensibilities and Design in Early Modern Britain and Early America* (Baltimore and London: Johns Hopkins University Press, 2001), pp. 3–4, 69–70
[47] William Shakespeare, *King Lear*, Act III, Scene vi, *The Globe Illustrated Shakespeare: The Complete Works Annotated* (New York: Greenwich House, 1986)
[48] Sir Nicholas L'Estrange (1603–55), quoted in Gloag, *A Short Dictionary of Furniture*, p. 408

the century. Few stools and chairs were listed in the households of husband-men and agricultural labourers. In multiple seating (Table 4.1b) there was a numerical preponderance of forms over benches, with a few instances of settles, often associated with panelled rooms in the elite households of gentlemen, yeomen and traders. The occupational status distribution of multiple seating presents a very different profile to that of single seating, with the highest representation amongst traders and others of the urban trad-ing community, as well as yeomen, but a lower representation amongst the gentry and clerical elite. Husbandmen and agricultural labourers again had a paucity even of multiple seating. Apart from the relative abundance of single seating in higher status households, the overall impression gained is one of a combination of single and multiple types of seating within dwellings. The seating thus could provide varying options in one space for social engage-ment: singular and mobile seating with degrees of personal comfort and higher (albeit differentiated) status, and multiple seating, less mobile, socially inclusive, with less personal comfort and lower status. The range of seating types in one space could thus articulate the relative social status of members of a company. Only in gentry households, socially segregated within their own households, did a greater homogeneity of seating types within specific domestic spaces appear to exist, as the set of sixteen chairs in the dining room of John Striblehill[49] in 1692 testifies. The existence of different types of seating thus provided structure to the social dynamic of domestic life.

Cushions

Cushions supplied a degree of physical comfort for hard wooden seats. The discomfort felt from protracted periods on such a seat is indicated by Sir John Harrington's comment in the early seventeenth century that 'great plank forms ... and waynscot stooles [are] so hard that since great breeches were layd aside, men can scant endewr to sitt upon'.[50] In total 428 cush-ions were listed, and of eighty-four listings through the entire period only two were of unspecified multiples. Seven blue velvet cushions were listed with two forms in the parlour of Thomas Striblehill, a butcher, in 1598, and two gilded cushions, either of metallic thread or of gilt leather were possibly associated with two joined chairs in the chamber over the hall of Henry Page, a baker in 1637.[51] The possession of cushions related closely to status; they were found in a high proportion of gentry and clerical households, and in a fair proportion of yeomen's, traders' and artisan-traders' dwellings, but were completely absent from those of husbandmen

---

[49] OHCA: MS. Wills Prob. 4 11085
[50] Quoted in R. Fastnedge, *English Furniture Styles from 1500 to 1830* (Harmondsworth: Penguin Books, 1955), p. 31
[51] OHCA: MS. Wills Pec. 50/5/20; MS. Wills Pec. 48/3/7

and agricultural labourers. The highest mean frequency (7) was found in gentlemen's households, reflecting the high incidence of chairs, followed by clerics (3.8) and those of traders, artisan-traders, widows and yeomen (2.5 to 3.1). It does appear therefore that the possession of cushions and the number per household not only provided greater comfort, but was a mark of status. The types of seating most frequently associated with cushions are often obscured by their inclusion in a group of diverse seating furniture. However, association is occasionally indicated by equal numbers of cushions and a category of seating; for example, in the hall of John Stone, [52] a yeoman, in 1618 '8 ioyned stooles' were listed with '8 Cushions' and in the parlour of Walter Cotton, [53] also yeoman, in 1643 'fower ioynd stooles' were listed with 'fower olde Cusshens'.

Table Furniture

Tables can be viewed as elevated horizontal surfaces for various actions, of different shapes and of different materials and construction. Their size and shape affect the way in which they are used, predicating the actions of people, the use of space and the meanings invested in it. Sixteen different types of table were listed amongst the total of 551 items of table furniture in the inventories. The nomenclature indicated construction, shape and possible use. But two types predominated: 233 (42% of the total) 'tables and frames' and 228 (41%) 'tables'.[54] The generic nature of the latter term presents problems. The term 'table' was employed for the top of the table (as also was 'board' with frames or trestles in a small number of examples), but also apparently by this period for the entire item of furniture. This does not appear to be a case of the substitution of one meaning for another; both the terms 'table and frame' and 'table' were found in households from the entire spectrum of occupational status, and from the beginning to the end of the seventeenth century. These were not apparently alternative terms: eleven examples, in eight halls and three chambers between 1598 and 1670 listed both 'table and frame' and 'table' in the same space. It is true, as Chinnery points out, that 'table' could also refer to playing tables for a game or to pictures;[55] the widow Dorothy Matthews owned 'a pair of playeing tables' in her hall, in 1643.[56] But in the Thame inventories all the 'tables' were embedded in the text with items of seating furniture; for example, the widow Elizabeth Coles had in her hall 'a Table forme and

[52] OHCA: MS. Wills Pec. 51/1/23
[53] OHCA: MS. Wills Pec. 35/1/21
[54] See online Appendix 1, Table 4.3, 'Seating, table and cupboard furniture: percentage associations'
[55] Chinnery, Oak Furniture: The British Tradition, p. 280
[56] OHCA: MS. Wills Pec. 46/2/18

Figure 4.11 Table and frame, oak, mid-seventeenth century

the bench' in 1614,[57] and there appears to have been a clear association of 'tables' with seating. [58] The term 'table and frame' gives a clear indication of construction, of a top or 'table' of end-clamped boards lain on a joined supporting frame, and also usually of the rectangular shape (Figure 4.11), as is shown in contemporary illustrations (Figure 4.1). We therefore have an indication of the hierarchical social dynamic that might have existed around a table of this shape. It is possible that the term 'table and frame' was used to distinguish the joined construction of the frame from some other, simpler type of table construction, such as the trestle table (Figure 4.12) although nine tables were given this specific description in poorer agricultural and artisan households between 1603 and 1616. A comparison of the relative frequencies of 'tables and frames' and 'tables' shows that the 'table and frame' predominates in the households of traders, artisan-traders and widows-spinsters, but not in those of gentlemen, clerics, yeomen and artisans.[59] Apparently there was no status distinction between different nomenclatures, apart from the high incidence of 'tables' amongst the gentry and clerics, which may indicate that they included smaller occasional tables in more affluent households.

Other types of table occurred less frequently and differed by shape: 13 round tables (2.3% of the total number of tables), 12 square tables (2.1%)

---

[57] OHCA: MS. Wills Pec. 34/4/19
[58] Online Appendix 1, Table 4.3, 'Seating, table and cupboard furniture: percentage associations'
[59] See online Appendix 1, Table 4.4, 'Tables: mean frequency by occupational status category'

Figure 4.12 Trestle table, oak, late seventeenth century

and 5 oval tables (0.9%) were listed.[60] Both round and square tables were found through most of the century from 1613 to 1689 in households of a wide range of occupational status, from agricultural labourers to gentlemen, in halls, chambers and parlours. The size of these tables was not specified, but where used for a gathering the social dynamic would have been significantly altered by the shape. This may be of special significance in the case of the few oval tables listed, in the households of 3 gentlemen, 1 malster and 1 clerk at the end of the century, between 1688 and 1694, and located solely in parlours and a dining room. The oval table might initially appear to create a more equitable social dynamic than the hierarchy suggested by the rectangular 'table and frame'. However, it seems that this particular type, in all probability consisting of a joined frame with swing legs to support hinged side leaves (Figure 4.11), was an innovation of the second half of the century in elite circles and chosen to express equality of engagement amongst peers, when social distinctions within the household were becoming more spatially accentuated and the family commensality was frequently separated from the rest of the household.[61] All of these oval tables were associated solely with chairs with seats of leather or cane, in sizeable companies ranging from seven to twenty-one in number in the room. Oval tables and individualistic seating therefore clearly demonstrate the agency of furniture in the structuring of a changing social dynamic.

---

[60] See online Appendix 1, Table 4.5, 'Frequency of other tables'
[61] Fastnedge, *English Furniture Styles from 1500 to 1830*, pp. 55–7

Figure 4.13 Oval table, oak, 1680–1700

Another small group of tables related directly, through the descriptive terminology employed, to the serving of food and drink in a wide range of status households; 4 side tables (0.7% of all table furniture) were found in halls and a parlour in the first half of the century, 4 sideboard tables (0.7%) in parlours and a chamber, 1 dressing table (0.2%) and 9 dressers or dresser boards (1.4%) predominantly in the kitchen and hall all in the second half of the century, perhaps again indicating the growing spatial separation between cooking and commensality. These 'dressing' tables suggest the movement of cooked food from the hearth and oven to the table, its presentation and the social distinctions which indicated those who served, and those who were served. There were also small numbers of adaptable tables – six cupboard-tables (1.1%) and three chair-tables (0.5%) – possibly reflecting a more versatile use of space. They were found mainly in chambers, cupboard-tables in the first half of the century and chair-tables the latter part.

Table Cloths

Most contemporary illustrations of eating and drinking scenes feature table cloths (see Figure 4.14), suggesting that this was a significant part of the 'setting' of the table. As Crowley notes, cleanliness was taken to indicate respect, and dirt disrespect;[62] the provision of fresh linen was therefore a relatively easy way to indicate both the self-respect of the household and that

---

[62] Crowley, *The Invention of Comfort*, pp. 4–5

Figure 4.14
Dining furniture with cupboard. The women's décolleté attire does, however, suggest that this is a tavern of dubious repute, rather than a domestic setting!

due to guests. There were 491 table cloths listed in 130 Thame households (or 70% of inventoried households), without distinction of size or material. Ownership of table cloths was spread across all occupational status categories, but in particular those of yeomen, traders, artisan-traders and widows-spinsters. [63] The average mean frequency was 3.78, ranging from one to twelve per household. The top quartile which owned six or more table cloths featured yeomen, traders and widows prominently.

In conclusion, tables played an important part in the definition of space, the organisation of actions and social relationships. As one of the largest objects in a room, and semi-permanent in its location, the table could substantially define the culture of that space. The size and shape of the table determined the potential company and their social dynamic. The 'table and frame' usually took the form of a large rectangle lending itself to the articulation of the social hierarchy. Other tables came in a variety of shapes, and the round and oval would have permitted a very different and less hierarchical but more differentiated commensality.

Display-Storage Furniture: Cupboards

The meaning of the word 'cupboard' (Figure 4.14, right) was still in the seventeenth century mainly a 'board for cups'. Harrison celebrated the fact that in his time 'the inferior artificers and many farmers ... have for the most part learned also to garnish their cupbords with plate'[64] and in his *Defence of Conny Catching* Robert Greene recounted that a 'mistress ... set all her plate on the

---

[63] See online Appendix 1, Table 4.6 a–l), 'Commensality objects: mean frequency per household by occupational status category, table cloths, c) mean frequency and d) percentage occurrence per household by occupational status category'
[64] William Harrison, *The Description of England* (1587), ed. G. Edelen (Washington and New York: Folger Shakespeare Library, Dover Books, 1994), p. 200

Figure 4.15 (*Left*) Court cupboard, oak, mid-seventeenth century
Figure 4.16 (*Right*) Livery cupboard, oak, mid-seventeenth century

cubboorde for shewe'.[65] The 'court cupboard' (Figure 4.15), consisting of a series of open shelves for display, was distinguished in the Thame inventories from the simple 'cupboard', which was probably similar to the livery cupboard in Figure 5.16. Gloag is of the opinion that the cupboard was still primarily for the display of vessels in the seventeenth century but shifting towards a piece with some enclosed compartments and thus primarily for storage, whilst Chinnery suggests that by this time the term cupboard already referred to the modern understanding of a side table with compartments enclosed with doors.[66] The latter interpretation seems to be implicit in the 'table', 'press' and 'safe' cupboards listed in the Thame inventories, a press being a storage container with doors, and a safe a (generally wall hung) ventilated food storage container. The 'side', 'dresser' and 'table' cupboards suggest a role in the serving of food to the table. Numerically the simple 'cupboard' (195, 71% of the total number) predominates in the Thame inventories. There are 65 instances of court cupboards (23%), and also side (3), press (6), safe (2), hanging (1), table (1) and dresser (2) cupboards.[67]

A clue to the distinction in function and meaning between the cupboard and court cupboard may lie in their different locations. In the inventories, 64% of 'cupboards' were found in halls, 13% in parlours and 13% in chambers whilst the great majority of court cupboards (71%) were in chambers, with only 14% in halls and 12% in parlours. Both the 'court cupboard' and 'cupboard' appeared in many households in different rooms. The chamber

[65] Robert Greene, *Defence of Conny Catching* (London, 1592), Part III, p. 10
[66] Gloag, *A Short Dictionary of Furniture*, pp. 277–8; Chinnery, *Oak Furniture: The British Tradition*, p. 319
[67] See online Appendix 1, Table 4.7, 'Display storage furniture: frequency'

Table 4.2 Cupboards and court cupboards: mean frequency per household by occupational status category

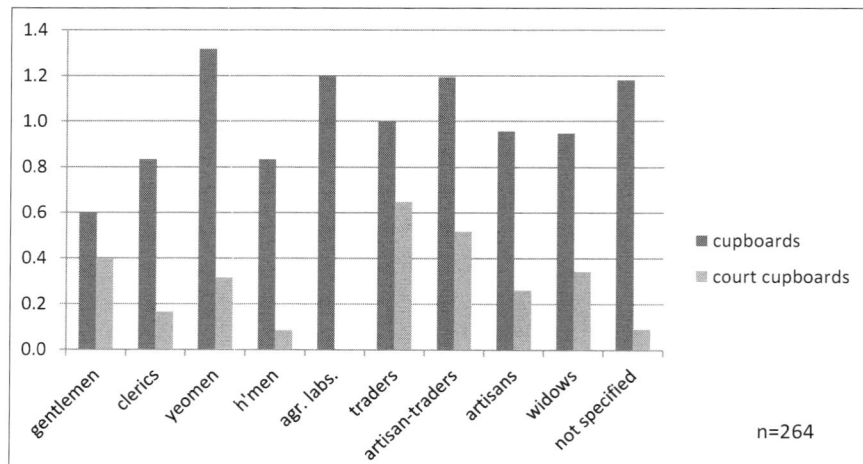

location of the court cupboard, which will be discussed further in Chapter 6, appears to have been the place of discriminating entertainment in imitation of elite households, may reflect the adoption of a culture of hospitality which the open display of vessels was designed to advertise. The significant absence of court cupboards in halls may lend credibility to Chinnery's assumption, above, that the hall cupboard was not primarily for display but, partially enclosed, for food service in the hall. The cupboard and the court cupboard also appear to have held different associations with occupational status (see Table 4.2). The cupboard was present in households across the occupational spectrum, in every household in varying frequencies between 1.3 in yeomen households and paradoxically gentry with the lowest at 0.6 per household. All other categories fell between 0.8 to 1.2 per household: artisan-traders and agricultural labourers 1.2, artisans and widows 1.0, and clerics and husbandmen 0.8 cupboards per household. The mean frequency of court cupboards was lower, possibly as it was a more prestigious item, but it appears to have been more closely related to status: traders' households with a mean frequency of 0.65, artisan-traders' 0.52, gentlemen 0.40, widows' 0.34 and yeomen 0.32. Significantly, none was listed in the dwellings of agricultural labourers. It may be a reflection of the connotations of traditional largesse conveyed by the cupboard that none was listed with the oval tables which appear to have heralded a new style of discriminating hospitality at the end of the century. Only two serving tables were listed in the parlour of Anthony Price, gent, in 1688.[68]

---

[68] OHCA: MS. Wills Pec. 49/1/23

Cupboard Cloths

A cupboard cloth can be seen in Figure 4.14. Linen may have conveyed associations of propriety, hospitality and status, as it was the furnishing item which could be presented clean for each occasion. Fifty-seven cupboard cloths were listed in thirty-four (19%) households between the years 1598 and 1665. They were predominantly found in the households of yeomen and widows, and some in those of gentlemen, clerics and husbandmen. There was virtually no representation in the households of the trading and artisan community – traders (1) and artisan-traders (1). Cupboard cloths were found in 40% of gentlemen's households, between 35% and 25% of yeomen's, clerics', widows-spinsters' and husbandmen's households, and only 6% of traders' and 3% artisan-traders' households. Their prevalence in the agricultural households and disappearance later in the century could suggest that they were a traditional but fading form of 'dressing' of commensality and conviviality, of old-fashioned hospitality in contrast to the hubristic display of plate on the court cupboard, possibly revealing the existence of two diverse cultures, amongst the more traditional agricultural occupations in contrast to that of the urban merchants and artisans. The cupboard cloth could thus perhaps be seen as an indicator of social and cultural divergence within a small community.

Commensal Washing Vessels

One small group of objects provides a reflection on the original and perhaps diminishing significance of the cupboard – the advertisement of largesse. Basins and ewers, twenty-one of which occurred in fourteen households, were traditionally employed during the meal for the host and company to wash their hands, a process in elite households attended with some ceremony. They could therefore be seen in the Thame context as indicating a desire to emulate such a culture. As dirt was taken to indicate a lack of respect, such a custom showed respect due to the occasion and its participants.[69] These items were listed not as might be expected in the gentry households, but in those of yeomen, and also equally of wealthier widows, traders and artisan-traders. However, their use, first noted here from 1598, appears to have been in decline, only found in households of yeomen after 1626, and last listed in 1658. This seems, then, to provide further evidence of a lingering but fading culture of traditional hospitality in the dwellings of yeomen.

We have then examined the frequency, the functions and meanings of the various types of the seating, table and display-storage furniture. To what

---

[69] Crowley, *The Invention of Comfort*, pp. 5–6

extent do the inventories confirm the spatial association of these types of furniture? The inventory evidence reveals that nearly 90% of all seating was found in association with tables, and around 50% in association with cupboards and with tables and cupboards combined.[70] Over 75% of tables were found in association with seating, and around 40% in association with cupboards, and seating and cupboards. Over 80% of cupboards were found in association with seating and with tables, and nearly 90% with seating and tables combined. By more specific types of furniture, there was a close association of all types of seating with tables, but especially benches (94%), stools (91%) and forms (87%), whilst chairs (82%) associated at a slightly lower level. Where cupboards were also present, stools and benches were most frequently found in association (63%), and approximately 45% of chairs and forms. 82% of *all* tables were found with seating, with 93% 'tables and frames' and 79% of 'tables' and 74% of other types of table. Of 'tables and frames' 58% were associated with seating and cupboards, but only 36% of other types of table, linking the former type of table with companies assembled for drinking as well as the consumption of food. The great majority of both cupboards and court cupboards were associated with seating and tables. We could justifiably deduce from these figures that there was a clear association between seating, table furniture and cupboards which appear to have been employed as complementary items of furnishing. We thus have, just as for the processing and cooking of foodstuffs, an assemblage of objects acting in association to enable the consumption of food and drink: tables, elevated surfaces on which the vessels of consumption could rest and around which the assembled company could sit, socially engaged, on a variety of seating providing degrees of individuation or comfort, and thus indicating status, and as a facility for the storage of vessels the cupboard standing nearby – all powerful signifiers of commensality and conviviality.

The Association of Food Preparation and Consumption

Since context is a central element of meaning and agency,[71] the proximity of one action will impact on the significance of another. The connotations of commensality, inclusive or exclusive, will have been affected by the proximity of the cooking process. Indeed, one aspect of domestic life which will be examined in Chapter 6 is the extent to which sociable consumption was segregated from the foodstuff processing activities of the household, and what such spatial segregation might indicate in terms of social hierarchies and relationships within the household. Where food consumption was in the hall it was often in close proximity to the hearth, the location of the cooking of

---

[70] See online Appendix 1, Table 4.3 'Seating, table and cupboard furniture: percentage associations'

[71] M. Heidegger, *Being and Time* (1927) (Oxford: Blackwell, 1990), pp. 418–21

the food.[72] Seating and table furniture in association were found with cooking irons in 62% of halls and in 41% of kitchens, infrequently in 5% of parlours and never in chambers. When cupboards were also present the hall was still the place where there was the greatest association, 64%, with cooking irons. In parlours there was a small association (9%) and again not at all in chambers. So it was in the hall that the furniture which represents commensality and conviviality was found most frequently side by side with the cooking of the food. The not insignificant evidence of consumption in chambers (37% of all spaces with commensal furnishings) was apparently never accompanied by cooking activity, and cooking was seldom in parlours (12%). This could represent the conscious creation of physical distance between the mundane and the social activities of the household. If this were so we might expect to see a greater distance created in higher-status households. However, there was no clear status differentiation in the proximity of food consumption to cooking. [73] The conjunction appears to have diminished in the latter part of the century, from the 1660s to 1680s as the incidence of kitchen cooking hearths increased, suggesting that the distancing of foodstuff consumption from its preparation may have been a trend, in the process moving female labour from the central position of the hall hearth to a more marginal position in the kitchen. This spatial differentiation of activities could be a consequence of, or a stimulus to, changing social relationships – spatial and social differentiation intertwined. Nevertheless, two of the latest examples of conjunction of consumption and cooking are in the households of a gentleman and a wealthy widow.[74] Where the association of seating, tables and cupboards was distanced from food preparation, it is also important to note, as above, that they may not primarily have been for food consumption but sociable drinking. Only 4% of seating was found with cupboards alone, suggesting that even if the consumption was primarily drinking, the assemblage of furniture still comprised seating with a table.

Vessels of Commensality: Eating Vessels, Cutlery and Condiments

Having established the furniture which provided for the consumption of food and drink, we turn now to the vessels from which both were consumed. Unlike furniture, eating vessels – being highly moveable objects – were not necessarily listed in the inventories where they were employed, but where they were stored ready for use. The listing and grouping of objects in the same location illustrates the manner in which most household objects were ordered, both physically and cognitively. Some of the vessels, serving dishes

---

[72] See online Appendix 1, Table 4.8, 'Spatial association of food consumption to preparation'
[73] See online Appendix 1, Table 4.9, 'Spatial association of food consumption to preparation by occupational status category and date'
[74] OHCA: MS. Wills Pec. 49/1/23; MS. Wills Pec. 42/1/34

and flagons were actually designed to transport food and drink from one location to another. Eating vessels were listed most frequently in the hall (36%), and also in the kitchen (21%), chambers (16%) and the buttery (9%). Drinking vessels were also found in halls (30%), chambers (16%), kitchens (15%) and butteries (14%), but a significant number, 19% of the total, were listed in brew houses, when drink containers are also included.[75] Eating and drinking vessels, then, were stored where they would be used, in halls, and also where comestibles were prepared and other foodstuff preparation equipment kept, in kitchens. However, a significant proportion were located and kept in chambers, reinforcing the evidence for the role of chambers in foodstuff consumption. Butteries also feature as the location of drinking vessels, possibly not only for storage but also sociable drinking. The small incidence of drinking vessels in shops and barns, working locations, might also suggest drinking in association with the world of masculine work.

We turn now to eating vessels.[76] There were sixteen distinct types of eating vessels listed, seven different generic types, and salt and mustard containers. Most eating vessels were given their actual numerical value, but the nature of the compilation of the inventories, sometimes valuing a group of items without count of their number, means that generically listed vessels or 'ware' will be underrepresented numerically. The generic 'ware' does, however, provide a good indication of the various materials from which the vessels were made: pewterware, earthenware, woodenware and white- or chinaware. Pewter and plate appear to have been interchangeable terms for metallic wares – plate originally implying vessels of precious metals but extended to all metallic eating vessels. Pewterware was listed in 88 inventories, 403 pieces counted and 64 entries of unspecified multiples (given the nominal value of 2 per entry in the frequency table), and 7 listings of plateware consisted of 13 items counted and 10 unspecified multiples. Monetary value was given to the unspecified grouped objects such as the £2 'in pewter' of William Smyth, a gunsmith, in 1644 and the £20 'in plate' of Thomas Hennant, a vicar, in 1665.[77] However, the value of metallic vessels was also often calculated by weight, such as the '102lbs of pewter' belonging to Thomas Crues, a blacksmith, in 1643 and the 'one hundred sixty nine ounces of plate at 5Li ounce' to John Striblehill, a gentleman, in 1692, both very significant quantities and values.[78]

Pewter is an alloy of tin and other metals. The finest quality consisted of 112 pounds of tin to 26 pounds of copper (effectively a 4:1 ratio), the maximum quantity that tin would assimilate, resulting in a hard resonant pewter that was easily burnished. 'Trifle' or 'common' pewter was an alloy

[75] See online Appendix 1, Table 4.10, 'Eating and drinking vessels: listed location by space and quantity'
[76] See online Appendix 1, Table 4.11, 'Eating vessels: frequency'
[77] OHCA: MS. Wills Pec. 41/4/13; MS. Wills Pec. 51/2/48
[78] OHCA: MS. Wills Pec. 35/1/22; MS. Wills Prob. 4 11085

of 83 pounds of tin to 17 pounds of antimony. Tavern ware or 'black metal' pewter was also made of an alloy of tin and lead – 112 pounds of tin to 26 pounds of lead (effectively a ratio of 4:1), but sometimes with a ratio as high as 3:2 for bowls, pots, cruets and candlesticks.[79] Pewter vessels were produced by pouring the melted alloy into metal moulds of 'bell-metal' or bronze, hammering the metal from plate form, or turning on a lathe, after which processes it was cleaned and burnished.[80] The best work came from London, where strict control of quality was exercised by the Worshipful Company of Pewterers, established by royal decree in 1348. An Act of 1503 made the marking of ware compulsory, and 'London quality' established as standard. In the early seventeenth century the power of the Worshipful Company of Pewterers declined in the face of increased competition from provincial makers, for example in Bristol.[81]

Pottery vessels are indicated by the four listings of unspecified quantities of earthenware, and one listing each of unspecified quantities of china and whiteware. All of these listings occurred in a brief period, between 1658 and 1669. In the household of Edward Kent, a yeoman, in 1658, '4 White basons & other White Earthen were' were recorded and in that of Charles Quarles, surveyor, in 1661, 'the Cheney and Whitt Ware'.[82] It is probable that much of the earthenware would have been sourced from the potteries at nearby Brill in Buckinghamshire, established in the fourteenth century and still active in the seventeenth century.[83] Using locally obtained clays, the ware is of a pale colour, close textured and generally finished with an olive-green glaze. The most common vessels produced in this period were bowls, dishes and plates; in addition there is evidence from the excavations of the kiln sites of pots, jugs (Figure 4.17), chamber pots and cups.[84] There were nine listings of earthenware between 1637 and 1670, predominantly in the households of artisan-traders and clerics, but also including a yeoman's and a shepherd's household.

Another material traditionally used for eating vessels was wood. Harrison in 1587 noted the prevalence of wooden eating vessels in the past; 'so common were all sorts of treen stuff in old time that a man should hardly find four peeces of pewter (of which one peradventure was a salt) in a good farmers house ... in my time [he have] a fair garnish of pewter on his cupboard, a silver salt, a bowl for wine (if not a whole nest) and a dozen of spoones to furnish up the sute'.[85] There were three listings of unspecified quantities

[79] H.J.L.J. Masse, *Chats on Old Pewter* (New York: Dover, 1971), pp. 51–2

[80] *Ibid.*, pp. 56–7

[81] *Ibid.*, pp.81–2

[82] OHCA: MS. Wills Pec. 44/4/9; MS. Wills Pec. 49/4/2

[83] M. Farley, 'Pottery and Pottery Kilns of the Post-Medieval Period at Brill, Buckinghamshire', *Post-Medieval Archaeology* 13 (1979), 127–52, 129

[84] *Ibid.*, 132, 137–42

[85] Harrison, *The Description of England*, pp. 201–2

Figure 4.17 Earthenware jug, Brill/Boarstall ware

of wooden ware in the households of a yeoman, a blacksmith and a widow between 1646 and 1662.[86] Trenchers and a trencher rack also featured in a number of the inventories, terms which applied traditionally to a flat circular wooden eating vessel and which Philips defined as 'a square, thin Plate of Wood, for People to cut their Meat upon'.[87] There were ninety-five pieces in seven listings (one of which was of an unspecified multiple). Despite the opinion of Harrison regarding the growing use of pewterware, wooden vessels were listed in Thame up until 1670. Nevertheless, other forms of vessel, of metal and pottery, were becoming more accessible, with implications of convenience, cleanliness (being easier to clean) and status through the acquisition of more sophisticated commodities. (It should be noted that the term trencher was also sometimes applied to similar pewter vessels.)[88] Widows, yeomen, husbandmen and artisan-traders were listed as owners of wooden vessels, but very much in the poorer section of the inventoried householders with a mean total value of household goods of only £1.97 in comparison with a mean value of all inventoried households of £28.19.

Food comes in a variety of forms, sizes, consistencies and temperatures. The various types of eating vessel presented a range of dimensions (Figure 4.18) for the collective presentation of food, personal consumption and adapted to elements of the diet by size and shape. The distinction between eating vessels was also emphasised by the manner in which the quality of pewter had been regulated according to the prescribed weight of different

[86] OHCA: MS. Wills Pec. 35/1/22; MS. Wills Pec. 37/4/16; MS. Wills Pec. 35/2/5
[87] Edward Philips, *The New World of English Words; or, A General Dictionary* (1658), ed. J. Kersey, .6th edn (Menston: Scholar Press)
[88] See online Appendix 1, Table 4.11, 'Eating vessels: frequency'

Figure 4.18
Group of pewter
vessels

vessels: chargers, platters, dishes and saucers.[89] Larger vessels such as the charger, of which three were listed – perhaps aptly in the households of two butchers, Thomas Striblehill and Richard Bennet in 1598 and 1633 respectively – were employed to convey large portions of cooked meat to the table.[90] For consumption at table, 763 platters in total were listed in 76 households (only 2 listings or 3% of which were unspecified multiples), 365 dishes in 47 households (6, or 13% unspecified multiples), 88 plates in 16 households (4, or 25% unspecified multiples), 43 basins in 27 households (1, or 4% unspecified multiple), 21 bowls in 8 households (1, or 13% unspecified multiples) and 14 generic 'vessels' in 3 households (no unspecified multiples).[91] In addition there were ninety-five trenchers already discussed as wooden vessels. Platters, dishes and plates were broad flat vessels of various sizes, whilst basins and bowls were vessels with raised sides, providing receptacles for a variety of foodstuffs, dry and wet. Pots were listed with eating vessels, but the general usage of the term seems to have implied drinking vessels (which will be discussed below) rather than eating vessels.

There were also vessels which by name indicated a specialised use related to elements of the diet. Saucers, numbering 253 in fifty-one (or 27% of)

---

[89] The weight of eating vessels – chargers, platters, dishes, saucers – was governed by ordinances laid down in of 1348: chargers 2¾ to 7lbs a piece, 13in. plus in diameter; platters 22lbs to 30lbs a dozen, 8 to13in. in diameter; dishes 10 to 18lbs a dozen; and saucers 4 to 9lbs a dozen, with a diameter down to 4in. F. R. Michaelis, *Antique Pewter of the British Isles* (London: G. Bell and Sons, 1955), pp. 14–16

[90] OHCA: MS. Wills Pec. 50/5/20; MS. Wills Pec. 33/1/24

[91] Out of a total of 188 households

households, were relatively commonplace. Spread evenly between yeomen's, husbandmen's, artisan-traders' and artisans' (but not gentlemen's) households, the medieval term was apparently no longer linked to an elite connotations of sauces, but applied simply to a smaller side dish, a case of changing custom with the retention of nomenclature but loss of original associations. Six of the listings were for a dozen saucers. The terms porringer and pottinger appear to have been interchangeable for a small circular dish with one or two side lobes (Figure 4.19), described by Holme as

> a half round vessel in the belly without a brime, some having two eares, but most onely one eare of handle or stouke as the country term is, by which it is carried from place to place; It hath its name from the bearing or holding of pottage: being very much in use for that liquor or Broth.[92]

The inventories list 202 porringers in 38 households, distributed in terms of status in a similar manner to the saucers. Four porridge dishes were noted in the household of William Fletcher,[93] a shepherd in 1670 – a small incidence but perhaps indicating that porridge existed as a meal distinct from pottage, or broth. There were also 166 fruit dishes listed in twenty-four households across a similar range of status, whether larger dishes to hold a collection of fruit on the table, or dishes for the individual diner is not clear from the inventories, but an average of nearly seven per household would suggest the latter. A small number of salad dishes, twenty-seven in five households, were listed, and 1 cheese plate, providing indications of other elements of the diet. Markham also suggests employing a fruit dish for the serving of salad.[94]

One other vessel that had a close relationship to the consumption of food was the chafing dish (Figure 3.13), described by Holme as

> a kind of round Iron, made hollow like a Bason, set on feet, either 3 or 4 with an handle to move it from place to place; its office is to hold hot coals of fire in, and to set dish-meates thereon, to keepe them warme till the tyme of serving them up to the table, or to heat a cold dish of meate, on the table.[95]

Chafing dishes,[96] of which fifty-one were listed in forty-three households across yeomen's, artisan-traders', artisans' and widows' households, give an indication of the problems of keeping food at a palatable temperature,

[92] Holme, *The Academy of Armory*, Book III, Chapter XIV, p. 5
[93] OHCA: MS. Wills Pec. 38/4/32
[94] Gervase Markham, *The English Housewife* (1615), ed. M. R. Best (Kingston and Montreal, McGill-Queen's University Press, 1986), p. 4
[95] Holme, *The Academy of Armory*, Book III, Chapter XIV, p. 11
[96] Listed both under cooking implements in online Appendix 1, Table 3.10 and eating vessels in Table 4.11

Figure 4.19 Porringer

especially where consumption was moving for reasons of convenience and prestige away from the hearth. In the majority (37) of the households where they are found they were evenly distributed between the hall and the kitchen.

Cutlery

One of the aspects of the Thame household which might strike the modern reader as anomalous is the relative paucity of cutlery compared to the number of eating vessels, an average of only 2.06 cutlery items per household in comparison with 15.45 eating vessels. Harrison noted in 1587 the probability of finding 'a dozen of spoones' in a farmer's house.[97] The only type of cutlery listed was the spoon (Figure 4.20), presumably utilised for conveying moist food to the mouth, whilst the prevalence of napkins, examined below, suggests that drier food was being consumed by hand. A knife might have been available for food consumption as a personal possession, but the only knives listed in the inventories as household goods were dedicated to the preparation of food, such as the chopping and shredding knives already described. The absence of the table fork, which was only in the latter part of the century being introduced as a part of genteel dining etiquette, would have given a very different dynamic to commensality, depending on the

---

[97] Harrison, *The Description of England*, p. 202

Figure 4.20 Pewter spoon, late seventeenth century

manners and personal hygiene of the diners. Holme described the variety of spoons as 'made plaine, but with wrought shanks, and heads with diverse devises, others have flat, or round cube heads, and many no heads at all'.[98] The inventories listed 387 spoons in forty-six households (with three unspecified multiples). Widows (3.5), yeomen (3) and traders (2.4) possessed the highest mean frequency per household.[99] Paradoxically it was the artisan-traders (0.4) who appeared to own the fewest. These figures could well be unreliable due to the possibility that spoons would have been items of very personal association which may have been bequeathed prior to death, and also as small items they might not always have been inventoried. Status could be indicated by the material of the spoon: eighty-five spoons in fifteen households were of silver, including those of six widows and five yeomen. The most prestigious items of cutlery listed in the inventories were the eighteen gilt-tipped spoons of Thomas Striblehill, butcher, in 1598.[100] A more common material was pewter; eighty-seven pewter spoons were listed in four households, including those of two widows and a yeoman.

Condiments

Salts and salt cellars also featured significantly in the inventories. Traditionally placed in the centre of the table, they could play a part in the indication of social hierarchy around the table, conveyed by the expression 'above' and 'below the salt'.[101] Seventy-nine 'salts' and eighty-four 'salt cellars' were listed in sixty-nine households across all occupational status categories, and

[98] Holme, *The Academy of Armory*, Book III, Chapter XIV, p. 6
[99] See online Appendix 1, Tables 4.6 e) and f), 'Commensality objects: mean frequency of per household by occupational status category, spoons'
[100] OHCA: MS. Wills Pec. 50/5/20
[101] I. H. Evans, ed., *Brewer's Dictionary of Phrase and Fable* (1870) (London: Cassell 1981), p. 990

Figure 4.21 Pewter salts, c. 1685

throughout the century.[102] (Paradoxically, as with spoons, there was little representation in gentry and clerical households, suggesting that they may have been listed generically with other vessels as 'pewter'). Eleven were listed as being of pewter (figure 4.21), and one of silver. One was described as 'great' and another as a 'double' salt. In the household of Thomas Strible-hill, butcher, in 1598,[103] five pewter salts were listed with a spoon. One mention of a mustard pot is found in the inventory of Zachariah Hames, a merchant, in 1686.[104] Salts, as objects, speak of the distanced acquisition of foodstuffs, of the status and largesse of the householder, of the collective and individual nature of the commensal company, acting as foci of social interaction as they were passed around the table, but also permitting seasoning of the meal according to personal taste.

Vessels of Commensality: Drinking Vessels

Drink formed a significant part of consumption in addition to, or distinct from, food. We have seen that the domestic production of ale and beer, customary daily beverages, was an important activity of many Thame households. Listed in all inventories were three generic and twenty-five separate types of drinking vessel;[105] there existed therefore a wide range of vessels for holding, serving and consuming drink. Although drinking vessels were less numerous in the inventories than eating vessels, they still formed an important part of household furnishings: eating vessels numbered in total 2,899

---

[102] See online Appendix 1, Tables 4.6 g) and h), 'Commensality objects: mean frequency of per household by occupational status category, salt cellars'
[103] OHCA: MS. Wills Pec. 50/5/20
[104] OHCA: MS. Wills Prob. 4 15794
[105] See online Appendix 1, Table 4.12, 'Drinking vessels: frequency'

in 180 households (including unspecified multiples – 105 given value of 2), whereas drinking vessels numbered 408 in 93 households (with 17 unspecified multiples). Generic wares were small in number but give an idea of the materials employed, such as pottery and pewter, discussed above in relation to eating vessels. Some of the vessels listed were dedicated to the storage of drink. Apart from the eighty-nine barrels listed in association with brewing utensils (of which 9 entries were unspecified multiples counted as 2), six drinking tuns, large storage casks, were listed in the buttery of Elizabeth Francklin, a widow deceased in 1622 and possibly engaged in the brewing and sale of ale or beer.[106] The total of 94 bottles listed might have served for storage or serving drink, as would the 54 jugs, 52 flagons and 6 flaskets. Bottles (Figure 4.22) were originally of leather, and three were listed as being of this material between 1625 and 1689.[107] Latterly they were also fashioned of metal, and a pewter bottle is listed amongst the possessions of Katherine Benson, a widow in 1616,[108] and eight of brass in two households in 1641 and 1691.[109] Flagons (Figure 4.23) were tall cylindrical serving vessels with a handle and a lid. 'Pots' appear to have served a purpose both as serving and drinking vessels, since two were differentiated as 'drinking pots', presumably as distinct from non-drinking pots. Twenty-eight were described simply as 'pots', whilst two were described as being of pewter and one of brass. Twenty-one pots in five households were described as being of 'stone'; this is possibly a description of Rhenish stoneware vessels (Figure 4.24), originally containing imported wine, and indicating the economic and cultural engagement with a wider world. These stone pots were listed predominantly in yeomen's households; for example, 'i stone pott with a silver cover' in the parlour of Reynold Graunt, a yeoman, in 1618.[110] Although these pots might have been converted to use with ale and beer, and one 'porter' (beer) pot is listed in the possession of Eleanor Crues, a widow, in 1669, one wine pot was also present amongst the belongings of Zachariah Hames, a merchant, in 1686.[111]

Pots were also categorised by their capacities – 1 gallon pot, 20 quart pots, 14 pint pots and 5 half-pint pots – indicating an ordering of volume in the culture of drinking. It would seem probable that only the pint and half-pint pots would have been used for personal drinking, which suggests that the gallon and quart pots were used for serving drink, an indication of the important part played in economic and social life by the consumption of alcohol. Two pots were described as 'band' pots, which may refer to pewter pots which were decorated with incised bands (Figure 4.25). Cups

[106] OHCA: MS. Wills Pec. 38/4/7
[107] OHCA: MS. Wills Pec. 42/1/34; MS. Wills Pec. 50/2/10; MS. Wills Pec. 46/2/9
[108] OHCA: MS. Wills Pec. 32/4/61
[109] OHCA: MS. Wills Pec. 35/3/35; MS. Wills Pec. 51/2/39
[110] OHCA: MS. Wills Pec. 39/3/26
[111] OHCA: MS. Wills Pec. 35/2/18; MS. Wills Prob. 4 15794

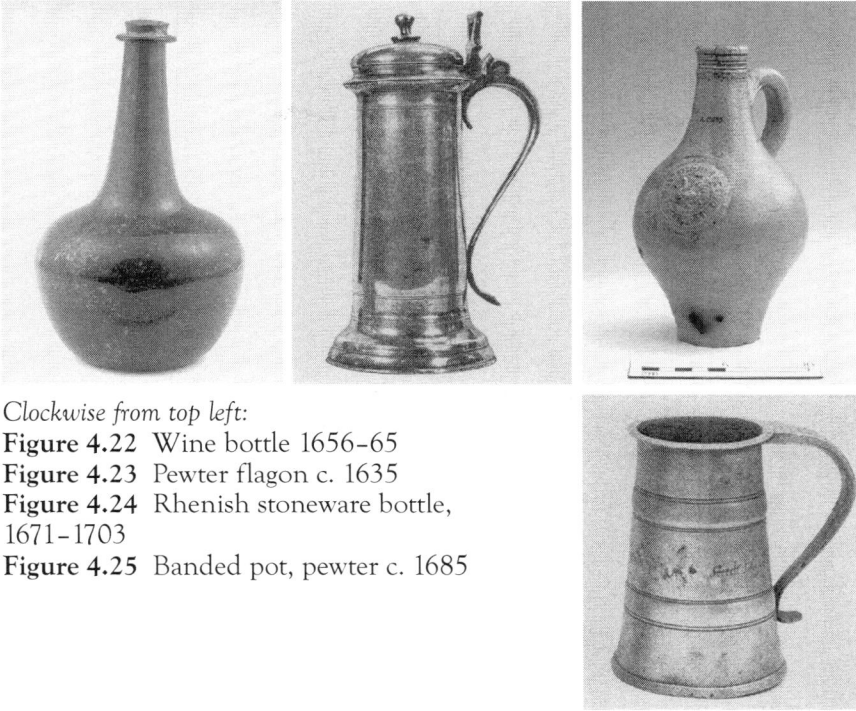

Clockwise from top left:
Figure 4.22 Wine bottle 1656–65
Figure 4.23 Pewter flagon c. 1635
Figure 4.24 Rhenish stoneware bottle, 1671–1703
Figure 4.25 Banded pot, pewter c. 1685

and tankards, however, were clearly drinking vessels. Twenty-nine cups and three 'drinking cups' were listed in nineteen households. For a number of cups the materials were specified: earthen (1), wooden (2), pewter (8) and silver (1). Cups (Figure 4.26) were bowl-shaped vessels with handles, standing on a foot. Tankards (Figure 4.27, and see also Figure 2.2) were cylindrical vessels, usually fitted with a handle and a lid, until later in the century when lidless versions appeared.[112] Of the twenty-one tankards listed in eleven households, across a range of household status occupations, 1 was listed as pewter, 2 as silver. Bowls and basins in a variety of materials were also listed amongst the drinking vessels. Harrison noted, 'a bowl for wine (if not a whole nest)'.[113] Twenty bowls were listed in eleven households, 4 of which were described as wooden, 2 of pewter and 1 of silver. The three basins listed in three households were 'earthen' or pottery (1) and pewter (1). A drinking vessel of similar shape could therefore be made of widely differing materials, with associations of status surrounding the same action. Eleven tasters, a shallow cup to taste wine, were listed in eight households, one of pewter. Other pewter drinking vessels listed were two goblets. Only

[112] Michaelis, *Antique Pewter of the British Isles*, pp. 20–1
[113] Harrison, *The Description of England*, p. 202

Figure 4.26 Pewter cup, c. 1685

Figure 4.27 Pewter tankard, c. 1670

twelve glasses were listed, although ten glass cases occurred, mostly in halls (7), also in 2 parlours and a chamber, half belonging to artisan-traders, 2 to clerics, between 1638 and 1694. There was also one instance of a glass cupboard, in the hall of Elizabeth Francklin, a widow, in 1622.[114]

In summary, although more limited in number than eating vessels, the variety of drinking vessels, from humble pottery to precious vessels for service and consumption, suggests an important part was played by the consumption of drink in early modern life, with marked status associations. There appears to have been a strong masculine bias of sociable drinking (Figure 4.16); of 101 drinking vessels of various types – cups, tankards, glasses, goblets – in fifty-seven households only six were listed in four widows' households. Notwithstanding the existence of inns in Thame, eight of which are inventoried, as we have seen, there is evidence of extensive brewing and drinking in private dwellings, and indications of dedicated drinking spaces. The inventory of Peter Willmot, a yeoman, in 1625 noted a 'drinking room next to the street'[115] and that of John Burton senior, a baker, in 1643 his 'outward drinking room'.[116] Giving some indication of the level of alcoholic drink consumption, Smyth quotes the evidence of the account books of Robert Loder, a Berkshire farmer of substance, between 1611 and 1618; the eight to eleven individuals working his 300 acres consumed between six and eight pints of ale and beer a day.[117] Ale and beer were therefore not simply safe beverages; they were also the context for social engagement, often with a strong gender bias, produced predominantly by women (see Figure 3.2) for significant consumption by men.

[114] OHCA: MS. Wills Pec. 38/4/7
[115] OHCA: MS. Wills Pec. 54/2/36
[116] OHCA: MS. Wills Pec. 33/2/18
[117] A. Smyth, 'Introduction', A *Pleasing Sinne: Drink and Conviviality in Seventeenth Century England*, ed. A. Smyth (Cambridge: Brewer Press, 2004), p. xviii

Furnishings of Commensality and Hospitality

We have looked in some detail at the wide range of objects which provided the context for the activities of eating and drinking, their affordance and the way in which their functions and variations might have acted on the people engaged with them. But consumption is an activity that can range from the solitary to the collective, with considerable social and affective implications. Indeed, one of the primary contexts in which the household expressed itself as a collective unit was in the group consumption of food and drink. To what extent is it possible to determine the scale of commensality from the frequency of objects within the household? Consumption could be restricted to the household, expressing its cohesion, or could be an act of largesse towards outsiders, intended to assert the significance of the householder and to reinforce external social networks. For this purpose we can examine[118] what might be considered indicators of the scale and manner of consumption: the number of seats, and of what nature, single or multiple, the number of eating and drinking vessels available, and on the basis that they indicate a more elevated dining etiquette, napkins and candlesticks, all in relation to the occupational status and number of dwelling rooms and therefore the presumed population of the household. To estimate the probable household population in relation to dwelling size, one- and two-roomed dwellings generally indicated a hall used for all purposes, or a hall and chamber, potentially accommodating a similar number; a six-roomed dwelling generally comprised a hall, parlour and four chambers. (See Table 6.4 for the mean distribution of rooms by dwelling size). The potential population indicated by the number of chambers in dwellings of six or more rooms could therefore be expected to be approximately four times that of the smallest.

The inventory evidence[119] shows that the number of multiple seats (forms, benches, settles) increased by a factor of approximately 4.5 from the smallest single dwelling room to largest of six or more dwelling rooms, but single seats (stools and chairs) increased by a factor of 16. The level of multiple seating thus increased by approximately the same factor, 4.5, as probable household size from the smallest to largest dwellings, in line with the internal commensality requirements of the household. However, single seating, stools and chairs – with higher status associations – multiplied by a factor of 16, implying that where this surplus existed, in larger households and those of gentlemen and clerics (Table 4.1a), they could have served for external hospitality.

Accurately assessing the mean number of eating vessels in households poses a problem as a fair percentage – for example, in 45% of gentlemen's and 50% of clerics' households (as opposed to a level amongst other

---

[118] See online Appendix 1, Table 4.13, 'Food consumption objects: frequency in relation to dwelling size'
[119] See online Appendix 1, Table 4.13, 'Food consumption objects: frequency in relation to dwelling size'

occupational status categories of 14% to 22%) – were listed as unspecified multiples, for the purpose of the study database entered with the value 2. As a result, not only will total numbers be underestimates, but there will be an inverted misrepresentation in favour of lower-status households. This might grossly underestimate the number of vessels in wealthier households, where the mean of the top quartile of households with *quantified* eating vessels is 15.72. The mean for *all* households with *quantified* eating vessels is 6.26. For the purposes of revaluing the numbers of vessels, therefore, multiplication of all unspecified multiples by 5 is taken as a reasonable readjustment, in many cases probably still an underestimate. On this basis, traders possessed the highest mean number of eating vessels (26.3), followed by artisan-traders (19.9), widows (16.7) and yeomen (16), artisans (15.5) and agricultural labourers (15.6). As discussed above, the figures for gentlemen (14.5) and clerics (15.7) may be substantial underestimates. The number of eating vessels thus increases in line with dwelling size, by a factor of 3.5 from around seven eating vessels in one-roomed dwellings to around twenty-five in a dwelling of six rooms or more.[120] This factor is in the region of the expected increase in the population by dwelling size, therefore suggesting that the food consumption was generally dedicated primarily to the occupants of the household. On the other hand, there are evidently a number of households – twenty-three with over thirty-six eating vessels – with ample provision of eating vessels for the entertainment of outsiders, including those with unspecified multiples of vessels. For example, Thomas Striblehill, a butcher (deceased in 1598), had 157 vessels, Cecilie Benson, a widow (1626), 73 vessels, and James Cowden, a barber (1691), 51 vessels.[121]

Lower mean frequencies, as well as much lower levels of unspecified multiples (0% to 17%) are manifested in the record of drinking vessels: artisan-traders (3), artisans (2.7), traders (2.2), widows (2.0). Adjusted figures for clerics show 2.3 per household, but only 0.8 for gentlemen, which appears anomalous. Amongst agriculturalists, yeomen's households had a mean of 1.8 drinking vessels, husbandmen 1.9 and agricultural labourers only 0.4. These figures tentatively suggest a stronger urban drinking culture, exemplified by the dedicated drinking spaces in Thame already noted above.

Napkins

Napkins potentially provide a better indication of the social nature of the food consumption. As already noted above in the discussion of cutlery, consumption in the absence of forks would have involved a fair amount of handling of food. As Crowley notes, dirtiness of place or person was taken

---

[120] See online Appendix 1, Table 4.13, 'Food consumption objects: frequency in relation to dwelling size'
[121] OHCA: MS. Wills Pec. 50/5/20; MS. Wills Pec. 32/5/18; MS. Wills Pec. 35/3/35

as a mark of disrespect, and therefore manners and accoutrements leading to cleanliness would have indicated respect both for the household and for the guests, raising the social tenor of the occasion.[122] Large numbers of napkins, 2,770 in 139 households, were listed in the inventories, in some households numbering many dozens; John Striblehill, gent, deceased in 1692 possessed ten dozen napkins.[123] Napkins were generally listed in dozens, or fractions of dozens, only ten out of 144 listings (or 7%) are given as unspecified multiples. High mean frequencies of napkins[124] were found in gentry (33) and clerical households (27). In the households of yeomen, traders, widows and artisan-traders the mean frequency ranged from eighteen to fifteen napkins. Napkins were found in approximately 80% of houses of the occupational status categories of gentlemen, yeomen, artisan-traders, artisans and widows-spinsters, and in 50% to 65% of the households of clerics and traders. The relationship between napkin numbers and dwelling size reveals that the larger households with six or more dwelling rooms had on average thirty-four napkins, some four times the eight napkins in the smallest dwellings, which is in line with the probable difference in household population between the largest and smallest households, suggesting that commensality may have been focussed on the household rather than entertainment of outsiders. Once again, however, this average conceals the fact that, as with John Striblehill above, there were twenty-seven households of yeomen, clerics, traders, artisan-traders and widows with more than three dozen napkins, well in excess of those simply required for the household.

Candlesticks

In the form of candlesticks (Figures 4.28 and 4.29) lighting is an indication not only of the essential provision of light after dark for productive purposes but of the possibility for extended hours of socialisation. However, the fact that candlesticks do not occur in every inventory perhaps suggests that they were objects which on occasion were omitted as individual items. Candlesticks were listed in 40% of agricultural labourers' households; 50% of artisans' and clerics', 63% of yeomen's, 67% of husbandmen's, 71% of traders', 77% of artisan-traders' and 92% of widows-spinsters' households. The highest mean frequencies per household, between 2.5 and 2.2, were found in those of artisan-traders, traders and widows. In the households of yeomen, artisans and husbandmen mean frequency ranged from 1.8 to 1.2 candlesticks. The households of agricultural labourers only averaged 0.8. The figures for the households of gentlemen and clerics appear to

---

[122] Crowley, *The Invention of Comfort*, p. 4
[123] OHCA: MS. Wills Prob. 4 11085
[124] See online Appendix 1, Table 4.6 i) 'Commensality objects: mean frequency of per household by occupational status category: napkins'

Figure 4.28 Pewter candlesticks, c. 1685

Figure 4.29 Engraving from an early seventeenth-century broadside ballad sheet

be somewhat anomalous, at mean values respectively of 1.0 and 0.8, and candlesticks were listed in only 20% of gentry households. (Where goods of higher value were proximate, it is possible that smaller items were amalgamated as 'lumber'). However, if the frequency is based on those households within which candlesticks were listed, the mean value for the smallest dwellings was 2.4 and for the largest of six or more rooms 7.3, indicating plentiful provision of light after dark. Of materials specified, pewter (in 21% of all 341 candlesticks listed) was the most frequent, followed by brass (20%), with others described as brasen (7%), wood (4%), tin (3%), lateen (2%) and wire (2%). The quality of lighting varied between dimmer smoky tallow, and brighter wax. William Tipping, a shoemaker, deceased in 1604, possessed a tallow pan and tub, and the hempdresser Thomas Fletcher in 1672 'foure dossen of Wickyearne'.[125] The only records of actual candles feature in the inventories of Vincent Hester, cordwainer, in 1605, who pos-

---

[125] OHCA: MS. Wills Pec. 52/3/12; MS. Wills Pec. 38/4/33

sessed thirteen, and Henry Cope the elder, a cordwainer who possessed twenty-four in 1659.[126]

As far as commensality and hospitality were concerned, then, the objects which might be considered as indicators – the number and type of seating, of eating and drinking vessels, of napkins and candlesticks – suggest that commensality, of food at least, in general met the requirements of the household without an evident surplus for the entertainment of guests. The consequence in terms of ambience during meals would therefore have been one of household consolidation rather than external social engagement. The household might have engaged significantly with the external world rather more in the consumption of drink. However, there were a significant minority, in the region of one-fifth of households, from the gentry, professionals and upper echelons of both the agricultural and mercantile culture, that possessed these indicators in ample quantities for hospitality. In fact, there is written contemporary evidence that suggests that home entertainment was an important part of good neighbourliness and the reinforcement of status, social relationships being enacted and enhanced in commensality, and as outlined in Chapter 1 the Thame household was indeed set in a web of significant relationships in the community.[127] Keeping house and keeping hospitality could be seen as synonymous. Harrison noted that 'the artificer and the husbandman are sufficiently liberal and very friendly at their tables'.[128] Although it was thus a process that undoubtedly enhanced the status of the male householder in the outside world, hospitality was an opportunity for both housewife and husband to combine in the welcoming of outsiders to their table. Women apparently played active roles as hostesses, and it was customarily their responsibility to ensure that the food and drink were prepared for the occasion.[129] Household hospitality was prompted by a variety of occasions: feasts in the religious year such as Christmas, and in an agricultural community harvest home and sheep shearing. Rites of passage, such as the churching of women, childbirths – at which much gossiping of the women was observed – and marriages also provided an opportunity for the household to celebrate its place in the community. Funeral wakes were generally held in local taverns, but mourners were invited to the deceased's dwelling for a drink prior to the 'forth-coming' of the corpse for burial.[130] The household's use on such occasions meant that

[126] OHCA: MS. Wills Pec. 41/1/38; MS. Wills Pec. 35/2/4

[127] F. Heal, *Hospitality in Early Modern England* (Oxford: Clarendon Press, 1990), p. 6; Craig Muldrew, *The Economy of Obligation : The Culture of Credit and Social Relations in Early Modern England* (Basingstoke: Macmillan, 1998), pp. 149–50; A. Flather, *Gender and Space in Early Modern England* (Woodbridge: Royal Historical Society, 2007), pp. 96–8

[128] Harrison, *The Description of England*, p. 131

[129] Flather, *Gender and Space in Early Modern England*, pp. 96–8

[130] Heal, *Hospitality in Early Modern England*, pp. 356–74

the commodities of foodstuffs were thereby transformed into the social and conceptual dynamic of the household.[131] In addition, informal drinking in the dwelling could be a way of cementing relationships with neighbours, or sealing a commercial deal. This was apparently popular with widows whose gender, despite their status as head of their household, hindered them from drinking in the local taverns.[132] The hospitality was lent significance by its location, and a number of differentiated spaces or rooms within a dwelling could provide more subtle social connotations. Chambers (like the hall chamber of the house studied by Airs and Rhodes)[133] and parlours with hearths and suitable furnishings were enhanced as places of retreat and hospitality.[134] The consumption of food and drink in the Thame household, it seems, ranged from a bowl of porridge to a lavish feast, from a solitary pot of ale to slake the thirst to a consolidation of the social peer group.

Cultural Diversions

Indications of the leisure activities of the inventoried households of Thame are slight, apart perhaps from the sociable drinking discussed in this chapter. Outside the house there are indications of shooting and fishing, presumably by male householders both for sport and to provide extra food for the table, in the four instances of birding guns, and four of fishing tackle, between 1637 and 1690 in the inventories of 5 yeomen, 2 gentlemen and 1 draper. Within the dwelling there were a few instances of objects which indicate the playing of games: the dice listed in the parlour of the widow Ann Flaxman in 1603, the 'tables and the tablemen belonging to them' in the hall of another widow Dorothy Mathewes, in 1643, and the shovel board table in the kitchen of William Sumner, a miller, in 1679.[135] In the 'One paire of Virginoles' in the parlour of Edward Cope, a gentleman, there is an indication of musical culture at an elite level.[136] Perhaps of more serious turn and indicating literacy were the twenty-five listings of fifty-four books, ranging between one and five in number per household, and thirteen listings of unspecified multiples of books, in a total of thirty-two households. Unspecified multiples indicating a larger number of books were found in the households of 1 gentleman, 2 clerics, 4 yeomen, 3 traders and 2 artisan-traders between 1626 and 1694. Twenty-one (or 41%) of the listed books were bibles, ranging between one

---

[131] S. Pennell, 'The Material Culture of Food in Early Modern England, circa 1650–1750', D.Phil thesis (University of Oxford, 1997), pp. 254–64
[132] Flather, *Gender and Space in Early Modern England*, p. 102
[133] M. Airs and J. Rhodes, 'Wall Paintings from a House in Upper High Street, Thame', *Oxoniensia* 45 (1980). pp. 235–59
[134] Flather, *Gender and Space in Early Modern England*, p. 98; M. Johnson, *An Archaeology of Capitalism* (Oxford: Blackwell, 1996), p. 169
[135] OHCA: MS. Wills Pec. 38/3/8; MS. Wills Pec. 46/2/18; MS. Wills Pec. 51/4/9
[136] OHCA: MS. Wills Pec. 34/4/26

and four in the households of 5 yeomen, 3 artisan-traders, 2 widows, a trader and an artisan between 1619 and 1690. Two psalters were listed in the inventories of John Calcott, a glover, in 1625 and Henry Cope the elder, a cordwainer, in 1659.[137]Although the absence of books from a household cannot automatically be assumed as a sign of illiteracy, since books were expensive items and might also have been gifted by the decedent before his or her demise, nevertheless it is interesting to note that books were only listed in 20% of inventoried households, themselves representing only the same proportion of the total population of Thame. On this evidence books were possibly therefore only found in a small proportion of all Thame households. The apparent absence of other recreational objects does indicate that life consisted primarily of work and that recreation, where taken, might have consisted mostly of conversation and sociable drinking.

Conclusions on Commensality and Conviviality

In the present age when food supplies are considered secure and consumed at several removes from the environment of their production, it requires an effort of the imagination to appreciate the importance in the early modern period of the intimate and personal engagement with the landscape from which the rural population directly obtained most of its sustenance, and the providential value placed on its abundance and on shared consumption. The provision, processing, preparation and consumption of food and drink were a fundamental part of the domestic culture of the Thame household of this period. Natural ingredients were thereby converted not only into comestible commodities but into culture, whose consumption was structured by other commodities which furnished the practice of commensality. The habitual actions of food consumption was structured by the type of furniture employed, serving a company of a certain number and composition, with degrees of inclusivity and hierarchy, in varying proximity to the preparation of the food, consumed from vessels of certain types reflecting diet, manners and status. Large numbers of objects were involved in these activities, engaged singly and in combination, with ergonomic, social and cultural implications emerging from the variations found within one type of object, asserting agency on the household in terms of cues for expected behaviour. The spatial and social context in which these objects were engaged was also critical in their function and meaning, dictating which member of the household performed a certain task, and where, implicating investment in assets and time, skills and knowledge learned and transmitted. The entire process of obtaining, preparing and consuming foodstuffs therefore constituted a central, if variable, part of the 'practice' of the Thame household.

---

[137] OHCA: MS. Wills Pec. 34/4/40; MS. Wills Pec. 35/2/4

5

Rest and Security

We come now to household objects providing rest and security. Just as the sharing of food for sustenance is an important indication of participation in a social group, so also the right to a habitual place of repose grants to the individual a sense of inclusion and security. The affordance of rest also has implication in terms of degrees of comfort, and social and affective associations. (The differentiation of space within the household for retirement, rest and sleep will be examined in detail in Chapter 6). In this chapter we will also examine the objects which facilitate another aspect of security, the ordering and storage of household and personal belongings. As with all of the domestic actions that we have examined thus far, there were a number of objects with different properties which were brought together to enable rest, and the ordering and storage of household goods, and variations within those types of objects subtly altered their agency.

Furnishings of Retirement and Rest

Sleeping Furniture

Sleeping furniture consisted of various types of bedsteads; a wooden structure supporting the items of bedding on which and under which the sleeper lay. The total sleeping furniture of various types numbers 599, a mean of approximately 3.2 per household (ranging from one to sixteen per household).[1] Here we encounter again, as with seating furniture, a considerable variety of objects which all ostensibly serve the same purpose, suggesting that variations in construction and quality address conceptual as well as functional requirements, lending these objects agency. And once again we encounter ambiguous nomenclature; the term 'bedstead' and 'bed' both occurred in relation to the furniture on which the bedding lay,

---

[1] See online Appendix 1, Table 5.8, 'Bedsteads: frequency', at http://boybrew.co/9781783270415

Figure 5.1
Joined oak
tester bedstead,
mid-seventeenth
century

although the term 'bedstead' predominated. 'Bedstead' was unambiguously applied to the wooden structure, but the term 'bed' was also used for the linen envelope, filled with feathers, flock or straw, placed over the base of the bedstead and on which the sleeper lay. Gloag notes that the term 'bedstead' meant literally in its original medieval usage 'a place for the bed', being the location of the soft bedding on which the sleeper lay, only subsequently coming to mean the structure supporting that bedding.[2] The bedstead could be a low structure for the bedding alone, or could feature a superstructure so that the sleeping area could be enclosed with curtains, and also covered with a panelled tester or roof (Figure 5.1). Chinnery asserts that the bedstead was frequently enclosed from the sixteenth century onwards.[3] In the Thame inventories the term bedstead was used both for a structure with curtains, and also extensively apparently without a curtained superstructure. Of the 381 'bedsteads', only sixty-one or 16% were clearly listed with bed hangings. The term 'bed' was employed for thirty-seven items which were clearly a framed structure from their textual association with other 'beds', feather and down filled, in the text, of which only three were clearly associated with curtains. John Stone in 1618, a yeoman, had in the chamber over his parlour 'a ioyned bed', clearly a wooden structure.[4]

[2] J. Gloag, A Short Dictionary of Furniture (London: George Allen and Unwin, 1977), p. 129
[3] V. Chinnery, Oak Furniture: The British Tradition (Woodbridge: Antique Collectors Club, 1979), pp. 385–6
[4] OHCA: MS. Wills Pec. 51/1/23

Figure 5.2 Broadside ballad illustration
Figure 5.3 Low bedstead

There therefore appears to be no clear structural distinction between 'bedstead' and 'bed' as sleeping furniture, but a clue may lie in the distribution of the listings. The term bedstead was current through the entire study period whilst 'bed' was employed from 1613 to 1649. It is possible that the displacement of the term 'bed' for the structured support for the bedding by 'bedstead' (contrary to our current usage) marks an appreciation of the relatively recent introduction of this more sophisticated arrangement, and thus the evolution towards a more sophisticated material culture.

In addition to those bedsteads which appear through association with bed hangings to have been canopied, there is also a clearer indication of this configuration through those sixteen listed as 'high' and four as 'tester', the term employed for the canopy. A canopied bedstead would consist of the horizontal base frame on which the mat and bedding was laid on a lattice of cords, with a headboard and two extended columns at the feet supporting the canopy, or 'tester' (Figure 5.1). The curtains were suspended on curtain rods or rails, listed in the inventories. Valances were pieces of cloth hung from the frame of the bed (Figure 5.2). In modern usage the term often describes the cloth which drapes the base of the bedstead concealing the void underneath; however, in the seventeenth century it seems likely that the term was applied to the decorative fabric which hung down from the canopy. Including curtained 'bedsteads' and 'beds' only, some 14% (84) of the total sleeping furniture in the Thame inventories thus consisted of curtained and canopied bedsteads. In the collective domestic culture of the seventeenth century the creation of privacy through a curtained sleeping space would have been a mark of privilege and differentiated status. Gentlemen and clerics enjoyed the highest mean frequencies, of 2.5 and 1.5 respectively, of canopied bedsteads (Table 5.1). The more affluent members of the mercantile community, traders and artisan traders, both had approximately 0.7, and yeomen, husbandmen, artisans and widows

Table 5.1 Curtained bedsteads: mean frequency per household by occupational status category

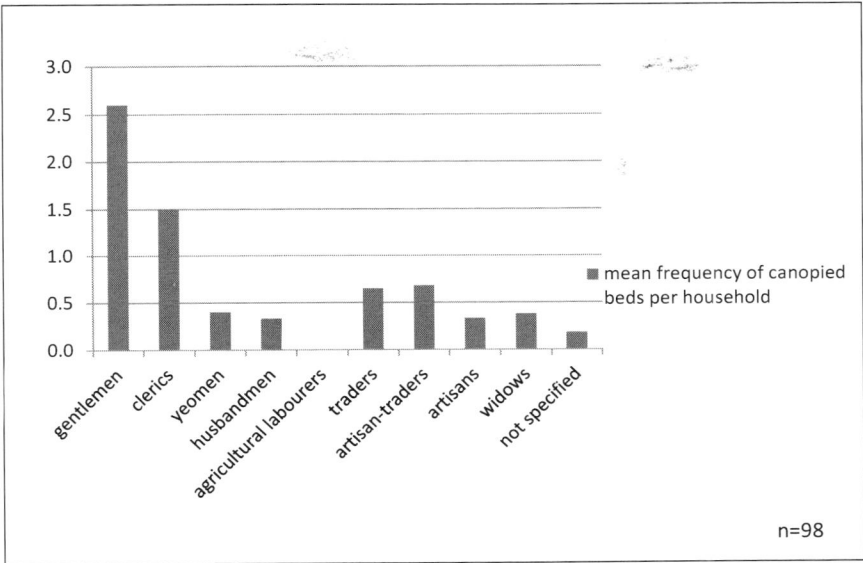

Bar chart showing mean frequency of canopied beds per household. Categories (x-axis): gentlemen, clerics, yeomen, husbandmen, agricultural labourers, traders, artisan-traders, artisans, widows, not specified. Y-axis: 0.0 to 3.0.

n=98

Table 5.2 Curtained bedsteads: chronological occurrence by occupational status category

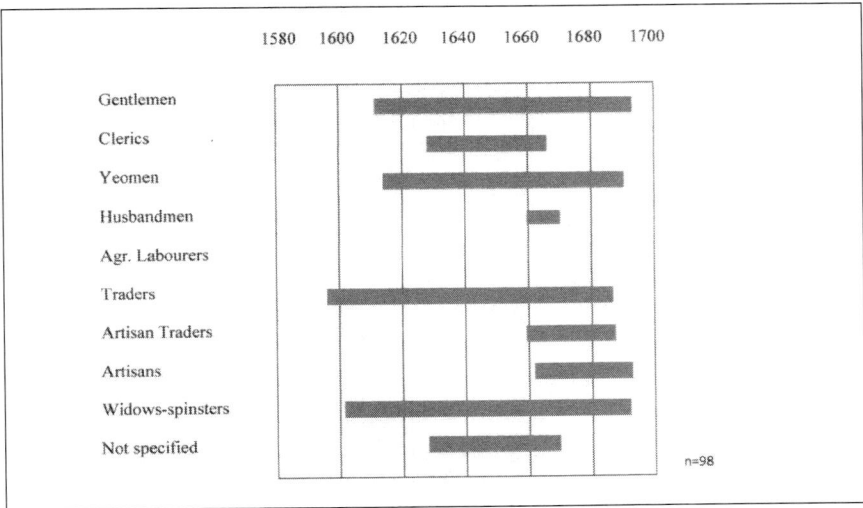

Timeline chart (1580–1700) showing occurrence by category: Gentlemen, Clerics, Yeomen, Husbandmen, Agr. Labourers, Traders, Artisan Traders, Artisans, Widows-spinsters, Not specified.

n=98

only around 0.35 mean frequencies, although in Table 5.2 we see that the ownership of canopied bedsteads percolated down the social scale as the century progressed, to husbandmen, artisan-traders and artisans. Only agricultural labourers were apparently unable to furnish their dwellings with such distinction.

The inventories also list twenty-five 'half headed bedsteads', with a lower headboard and without a canopy. The remaining 311 items (or 52%) of the sleeping furniture appear to have consisted of low bedsteads (Figure 5.3). Eight were described as being of joined construction, and one of wainscot. One 'bed' was described as boarded, or simply nailed together, and we could speculate that many of these lower bedsteads not described as joined were of this cruder form of construction. A small number of bedsteads, twenty or 5% of the total, were described as 'standing', a term which occurred in relation to a number of different types of furniture, but the significance of this is not entirely clear. The contemporary meaning, especially in relation to bedsteads, may have been a comparison with temporary and moveable furniture; in *The Merry Wives of Windsor* Sir John Falstaff had in his chamber 'his Castle, his standing bed, and truckle-bed' – the latter being moveable.[5] One standing bedstead was described as carved and One as joined. In contrast, there was one 'field bed' in the chamber over the entry of William Cozens,[6] a yeoman, in 1630, which indicates a structure which could be dismantled, providing versatile accommodation, usually in more elite households. There were further indications of the construction of bedsteads; eighty-nine, or 23% of all bedsteads were described as being of a joined construction, employing joints with a pegged mortice and tenon. Three were also described as being of 'wainscot', or panelled, which might have related both to the headboard and the canopy (Figure 5.1). Thirty-eight were described as being old, and two small, possibly a rare example of furniture to accommodate children.

A further category of sleeping furniture was the truckle, or trundle bed (Figure 5.4), of which 104 were listed, 17% of the total number of bedsteads. Gloag defines this as a low bed that could be wheeled under a bed of ordinary size (Figure 5.5), frequently used by servants, and Chinnery sees in this item of furniture the close relationship between the master and mistress and their servants.[7] It may also have served for children. Tables 5.3a and 5.3b show that the frequency of truckle beds was highest in gentlemen's, yeomen's, traders', artisan-traders' and widows' households, but that they appeared more frequently in larger dwellings presumably housing more servants. Rare indications of the presence of children in the Thame households are five listed cradles. All were in larger households

[5] William Shakespeare, *The Merry Wives of Windsor*, Act IV, Scene v, 6, *The Globe Illustrated Shakespeare: The Complete Works Annotated* (New York: Greenwich House, 1986)
[6] OHCA: MS. Wills Pec. 34/4/52
[7] Gloag, *A Short Dictionary of Furniture*, p. 680; Chinnery, *Oak Furniture*, pp. 395–6

180

Table 5.3a Bedsteads and truckle beds: mean frequency by occupational status category

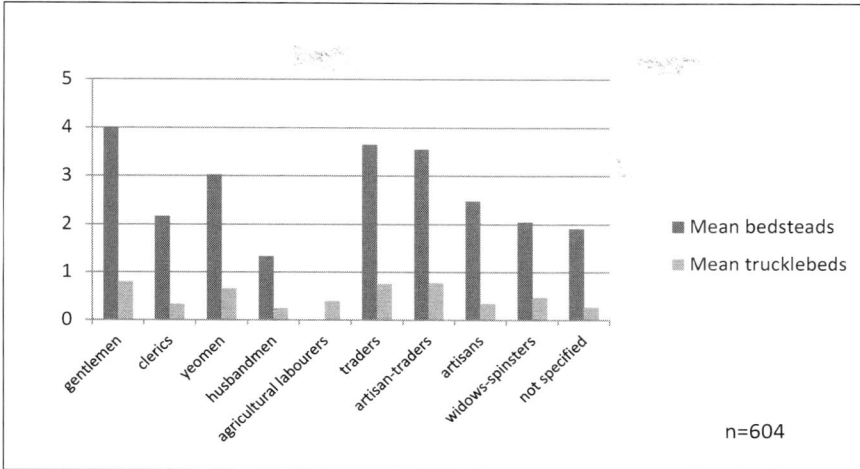

Table 5.3b Bedsteads and truckle beds: mean frequency by dwelling size.

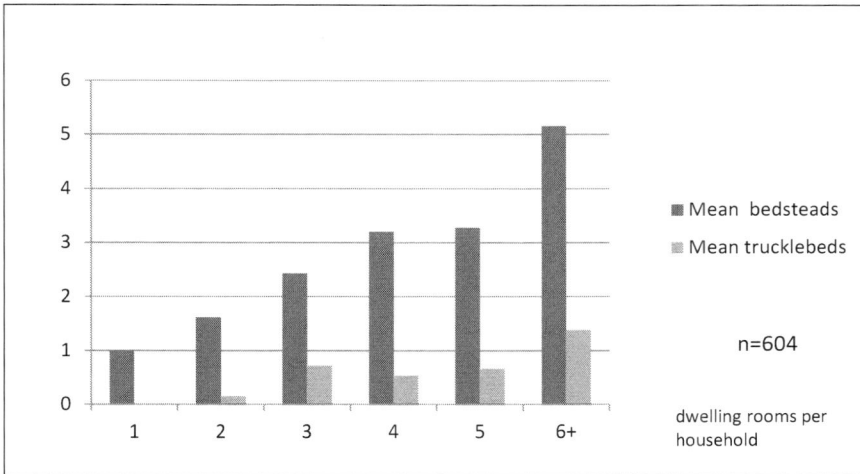

with more than three dwellings rooms and of relatively elevated social standing, the households of a gentleman, yeoman, victualler, gunsmith and carpenter, between 1626 and 1697. It is possible that the cradle would have been one item of furniture which was customarily handed down to a succeeding generation prior to the demise of the grandparent, and thus not often found amongst a decedent's personal belongings. Apparently the humblest form of sleeping furnishing was provided by a simple bed

Figure 5.4 Truckle or trundle bed, joined oak, seventeenth century

Figure 5.5 Reconstruction of a bedchamber in Bayleaf Farmhouse, Weald and Downland Museum, showing bedding and a truckle bed under the main bedstead

without a bedstead and therefore upon the floor. There was no bedstead listed in the inventory of Thomas Clerke, a shepherd deceased in 1602, but 'one flockbedd' was listed in his hall, his sole dwelling room, along with '2 Coverlids two blanketts on[e] bolster and 2 pillowes'.[8] Such simple accommodation appears also to have been the lot of the servants of Edmund Tomlinson, a yeoman, in their servants' chamber in 1607, with the inventory noting 'One old flockbed' with 'a Cov[er]lid'.[9] This may indicate the level of furnishing available to the poorer majority of Thame households which were not inventoried.

The relative status significance of sleeping furniture and furnishings is best indicated by the sums invested in them in relation to the total value of household furnishings (Table 5.4), between approximately 25% for agricultural labourers' and 40% for gentlemen's households, with yeomen and artisan traders also manifesting a high relative investment of approximately 36%. This suggests that bedsteads and bedding were an important part of the furnishing of every level of household and that the quality and comfort of sleeping furniture was significantly related to status.[10] Bedding, and the

8 OHCA: MS. Wills Pec. 34/3/24
9 OHCA: MS. Wills Pec. 52/3/15
10 As already noted, the term 'comfort' is used here in its current sense of personal physical

Table 5.4 Bedsteads and bedding: value as a percentage of total value of inventoried household goods by occupational status category

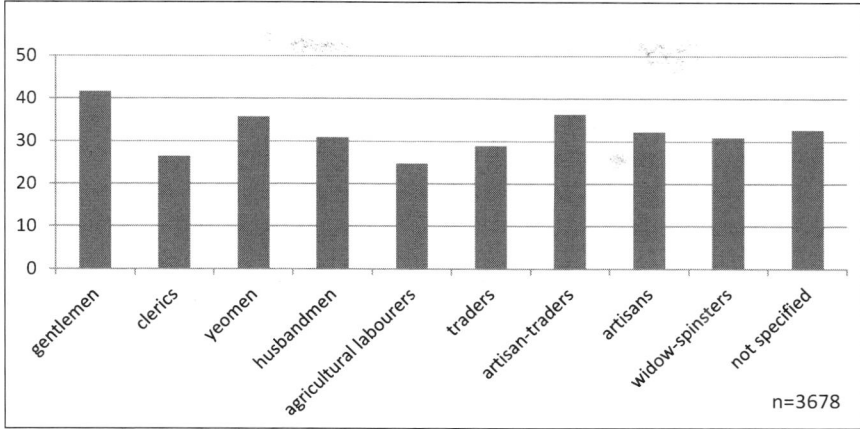

fabrics and fillings of which it was made, were the most valuable furnishings. The comparative value of the bedstead and its furnishings are difficult to determine since both were usually valued together, and similar items could vary widely in their valuation. Bedsteads valued alone ranged from eight shillings for 'one bedsted' belonging to Emanuel Slatter, a glazier, in 1664[11] to four pounds for 'one bedstede and a matte' belonging to Edward Bundocke, a tailor, in 1630,[12] whilst truckle beds were valued much lower, such as the three shillings for 'One Trundle bed' belonging to Henry Page, a baker, in 1637.[13] However, as a general rule it seems to have been the bedding and bed furnishing which substantially exceeded the value of the wooden bedstead on which they lay.

Bedding

Having examined the frequency of bedsteads, we turn now to the furnishings which lay on these structures (Figure 5.5). The inventory evidence reveals a wide range of bed furnishings, from the seventy-one listings of bedding as generic group (all unspecified multiples), through items of bedding,

---

amenity; in the early modern period a more likely term for such qualities would have been' ease'. J. E. Crowley, *The Invention of Comfort: Sensibilities and Design in Early Modern Britain and Early America* (Baltimore and London: Johns Hopkins University Press, 2001), pp. 69–70
[11] OHCA: MS. Wills Pec. 51/3/13
[12] OHCA: MS. Wills Pec. 33/1/17
[13] OHCA: MS. Wills Pec. 48/3/7

beds, pillows, bolsters and various bed coverings, to the furnishings found on the canopied bedsteads.[14] All of these objects, and the bed linen, were created from linen and wool cloth, and there is evidence of the production of textile yarn and the weaving of cloth in some of the inventoried Thame households. The yarn was derived from both plant and animal sources: from the fibrous content of the flax and hemp plant, and from the wool of sheep. To provide yarn for weaving cloth and sewing, it was necessary to spin the raw fibres together on a spindle and distaff, or on a wheel. The flax plant, *Linum usitalissimum*, yielded both the fibres and the seeds that provided linseed oil, and the hemp plant, *Cannabis sativa*, a vegetable fibre coarser than that from flax. Eleanor Pitman, a widow, possessed 'the hempe in the hemphouse' in 1623.[15] The linen yarn was derived from the fibres in the bast, the layer under the outer bark. Flax harvested when the stems were still green and the seeds unripened yielded a superior yarn but no seeds for oil. If left until the seeds ripened it yielded a greater quantity of coarser fibres. These coarser fibres produced linen described as 'harden'. Harvested flax was subjected to a process known as 'retting', whereby it was laid in bundles immersed in specially dammed rivers, ponds or pits for two or three weeks in order to break down the cellulose structure of the stems. The dressing of the flax involved the removal of the fibres from the woody core and exterior bark, 'scutching' with wooden blades to shear the fibres off the bast to which they were attached with a 'brake' (Figures 5.6 and 5.7) such as that belonging to Thomas Striblehill in 1598.[16] Peter Willmot, a yeoman, had a quantity of hemp 'stripped and unstripped' in his barn in 1626.[17] Finally the fibres were 'hackled', passed through a board set with spikes, or 'hatchel' (Figures 5.6 and 5.7) as belonged to Thomas Fletcher, a Thame hempdresser, in 1672, cleaning out the remains of the woody waste, separating and aligning the fibres prior to spinning and so leaving the 'twelve dossen of drest hemp & Flax and foure hundred of Ruse hemp & Tooe' amongst his assets.[18] Scutching, hackling and the spinning of linen yarn are shown in a contemporary illustration in Figure 5.7.

Wool yielded the yarn for the other textiles in much evidence in bedclothes. The inventories list flocks of sheep, ranging from those of prosperous yeomen such as Peter Willmot, who owned 'three scoare & Eight sheepe' in 1625, and William Baker with 'One hundred and twentye eight sheep' in 1660, to the more modest holding of 'Thirty sheep' belonging to the shepherd William Fletcher in 1670 and the 'one sheepe' of the

---

[14] See online Appendix 1, Table 5.9, 'Bedding and bed furniture: frequency'
[15] OHCA: MS. Wills Pec. 48/2/10
[16] OHCA: MS. Wills Pec. 50/5/20
[17] OHCA: MS. Wills Pec. 54/2/36
[18] OHCA: MS. Wills Pec. 38/4/33; P. Baines, *Spinning Wheels: Spinners and Spinning* (London: Batsford, 1977), pp. 15–21; H. Osborne, ed., *The Oxford Companion to the Decorative Arts* (Oxford: Oxford University Press, 1975), p. 770

Figure 5.6 Brake (*lower right*) and hatchel (*left*) for scutching and hackling flax

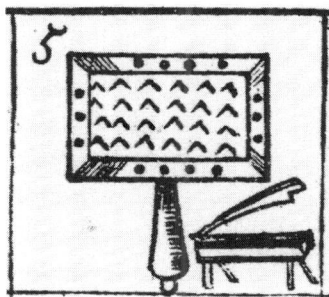

Figure 5.7 Harvested flax (*left*), hackling and scutching (*centre*) and spinning (*right*)

carpenter John Greene in 1627.[19] The flocks found on the Thame fields in all probability would have been some form of 'folding' breed: Chilterns, Oxford Heights or Old Cotswold. Owned in Thame primarily by general farmers rather than sheep masters, they were kept as much for the benefits of their urine and manure – where they were 'folded' on arable land (when the crops had been harvested) at night after the day spent on pasture – as for their meat and fleece. These sheep yielded on average around two pounds of wool of a short staple suitable for the production of woollen cloth. The nature of the textile produced therefore reflected both the environment and the wider requirements of the agriculturalist.[20]

The sheep would have been sheared by hand to release the fleece in one piece; 'three Sheepe with thene flixes' belonged to Charles Quarles, a surveyor in 1661.[21] Wool was also taken from slaughtered and dead sheep;

---

[19] OHCA: MS. Wills Pec. 54/2/36; MS. Wills Pec. 38/4/32; MS. Wills Pec. 33/2/23; MS. Wills Pec. 39/3/37

[20] E. Kerridge, 'Wool Growing and Wool Textiles in Medieval and Early Modern Times', *The Wool Textile Industry in Great Britain*, ed. J. J. Gerraint (London: Routledge and Kegan Paul 1972), pp. 19-23

[21] OHCA: MS. Wills Pec. 49/4/2

Figure 5.8 (*Left*) Wool stock card and flax comb
Figure 5.9 (*Right*) Woollen wheel

'six sheepes skines in the wooll' were listed in the inventory of John Cal-cott, a glover in 1625.[22] The wool would have been subjected to processes of sorting and cleaning: separating coarser wool from the finer, and longer from shorter fibres, scoured to remove dirt, rinsed in fresh water, wrung out and hung up to dry. The dried wool was then beaten to clear out dust and debris, a process sometimes called 'willowing'. To facilitate spinning, washed wool was oiled using a variety of fats such as sheep tallow, melted pig's fat, butter or goose grease. The wool could then be combed, remov-ing shorter and aligning longer fibres to produce worsted yarn, or roughly carded to produce the coarser warmer woollen yarn – the more likely pro-cess given the probable nature of the Thame flocks.[23] Grace Andrews, a widow deceased in 1641, had amongst her belongings a pair of wool cards (see Figure 5.8).[24]

The inventories provide evidence of these textile raw materials, flax, hemp and wool, in a number of households; hemp was listed in nine households, including those of 4 yeomen, 2 gentlemen and 2 widows between 1617 and 1645, and wool in eight households, including those of 4 yeomen, 2 widows and 1 tanner between 1604 and 1663. In only three of these households, however, were both materials found, suggesting that households tended to specialize in the production of one yarn only. There is also considerable evidence of the spinning (Figure 5.9) of yarn as a household activity; linen wheels were listed in fourteen households between 1604 and 1694, pre-dominantly in those of yeomen and widows, and woollen wheels in eleven households between 1598 and 1694 in a range of working households of artisans, artisan-traders and widows. Six households had both woollen and linen wheels. Harrison recommended that wool yarn should be spun 'upon great wool wheels, according to the order of good housewifery; the custom

[22] OHCA: MS. Wills Pec. 34/4/40
[23] Baines, *Spinning Wheels*, pp. 28–31
[24] OHCA: MS. Wills Pec. 32/1/39

whereof must be got by practice'.[25] Nineteen non-specific 'wheels' were listed in ten households between 1612 and 1669, and thirteen 'spinning wheels' in six households, those of a gentleman, scrivener, wealthy butcher, cooper, carpenter and widow between 1598 and 1663, possibly reflecting that it was a more genteel female activity in wealthier households. Some households also owned several spinning wheels, suggesting a focus on this activity to create income and that there were several women in the household both available and skilled in the work; for example the household of William Tipping, a shoemaker, possessed one woollen wheel and two linen wheels in 1604.[26] Spinning wheels, however, did not appear in the three recorded weavers' households between 1607 and 1661, suggesting that spinning was a domestic activity utilising raw materials produced by the household.[27] Also listed in the inventories are one set of winding blades, for winding the yarn, and one tod stone, a weight employed in the wool yarn trade.

Linen yarn was listed in six households – those of of 3 widows, 1 husbandman and 2 artisans between 1604 and 1663, with one mention of flax yarn. As described above, linen yarn was of different quality according to the time of harvesting. Ann Tipping, a widow, had 'xij pounds of course lynnen yarne' amongst her household effects in 1605.[28] The five listings of 'yarn' in varying quantities and in a range of occupational households between 1616 and 1669 could refer either to linen or to woollen yarn; the widow Katherine Benson possessed 'Certaine yarne spunn' in 1616,[29] but linen is suggested by the association of 'yarne and hempe' amongst the belongings of Leonard Messenger, yeoman, in 1635.[30] There is scant mention of woven cloth amongst the assets listed in the inventories but an indication of that produced may be provided by single instances of sackcloth belonging to Thomas Fletcher the hempdresser in 1672, and linen cloth, linsey woolsey and lockram to the widows Mary Wheeler and Martha Smith in 1664.[31] Linsey woolsey was a popular and hard-wearing blend of linen and woollen yarn, and lockram a finer linen suitable for sheets and personal wear. But there is no mention of looms in these households, only one in the dwelling of the weaver William Boorne in 1607 and three in the shop of the weaver Thomas Ridley in 1625, suggesting that it was these artisans (Figure 5.10) who wove the domestically produced yarn, the latter bequeathing 'to my sonne Edward Reydley my Broade Loome & all suche

[25] William Harrison, *The Description of England* (1587), ed. G. Edelen (Washington and New York: Folger Shakespeare Library, Dover Books, 1994), p. 150
[26] OHCA: MS. Wills Pec. 52/3/12
[27] OHCA: MS. Wills Pec. 32/4/30; MS. Wills Pec. 50/2/10; MS. Wills Pec. 47/2/10
[28] OHCA: MS. Wills Pec. 52/3/13
[29] OHCA: MS. Wills Pec. 32/4/61
[30] OHCA: MS. Wills Pec. 46/2/9
[31] OHCA: MS. Wills Pec. 38/4/33; MS. Wills Pec. 54/4/12; MS. Wills Pec. 51/3/14

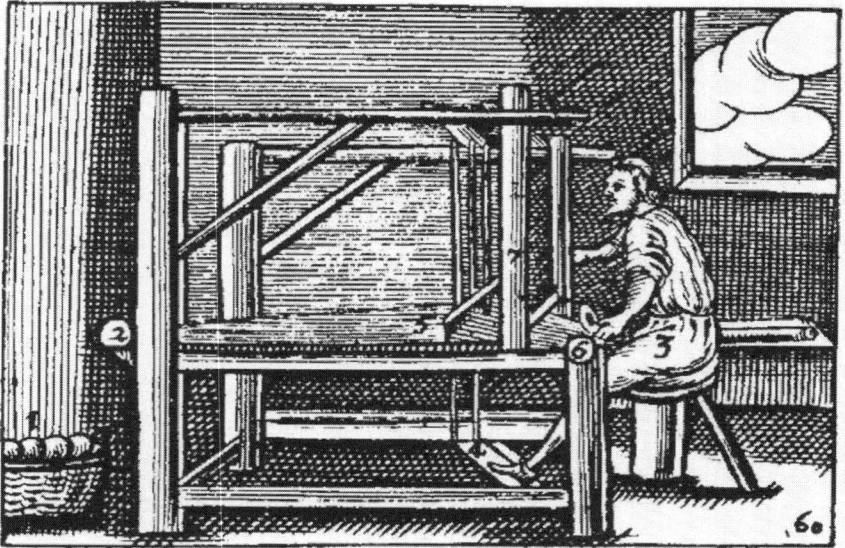

Figure 5.10 'Weaving'

tacklings as belonge to the said loome'.[32] A third weaver mentioned in the inventories is John Newberry, deceased in 1661.[33] Markham advised the housewife, 'after your yarn is wound and weighed, you shall carry it to the weavers ... knowing this, that if your weaver be honest and skilful he will make you good and perfect cloth'.[34]

Having discussed the possible local sourcing of the materials for bedding, we return to the arrangement of the bedsteads. Furnishings were placed on cords, of which twenty-four were listed, run through holes in the boards of the lower bedstead frame. Fifty-five mats and three mattresses were listed, which would have been place on top of the bedcords. On these were placed the 'beds', linen coverings with a filling of feathers, flock or straw. The majority of the 546 beds, 263 (or 48%) were feather filled; 221 (40%) with flock (including wool) and 37 (7%) with straw. A combination of bolsters and pillows supported the sleepers, customarily in a semi-recumbent position (Figure 5.11). Further evidence for this arrangement is provided by the fact that only the upper section of the bedstead headboards of the period were decorated.[35] There generally only being one bolster per bedstead we might possibly anticipate an increased number of pillows per household

[32] OHCA: MS. Wills Pec. 32/4/30; MS. Wills Pec. 50/2/10
[33] OHCA: MS. Wills Pec. 47/2/10
[34] Gervase Markham, *The English Housewife* (1615), ed. M. R. Best (Kingston and Montreal: McGill-Queen's University Press, 1986), p. 164
[35] Chinnery, *Oak Furniture*, p. 392

Figure 5.11 Broadside ballad engraving of a low or 'stump' bedstead

to reflect higher levels of comfort. Rather, the evidence indicates that the mean number of pillows per household increased in line with the expected increase in accommodation (the largest dwelling having on average four times the number of chambers of the smallest), from 1.29 to 3.85, and the proportion of pillows to bolsters actually declined in the largest dwellings, possibly a reflection of meaner sleeping provision for more servants.[36] Within the social spectrum represented by the inventories, therefore, the provision of pillows does not appear to have significantly increased in line with wealth and status.

However, both bolsters and pillows had fillings of various qualities, from down to straw, affording varying degrees of comfort. Of the 518 bolsters, 212 (or 41%) were filled with feathers, 209 (40%) with flock, 33 (6%) with straw and 6 (1%) with wool. Of the 385 pillows, 142 (37%) were filled with feathers, 18 (5%) with down, 7 (2%) with flock and 3 (1%) with wool.[37] The filling of the pillows and the resultant comfort thus appear to have clear status implications. Although the down filling, the most luxurious, accounted for only 5% of the total number of pillows, it was found significantly in the households of gentlemen and clerics, with a small incidence in those of traders, artisan-traders and widows-spinsters. Feather pillows were also well represented in the households of gentry, and of artisan-traders, with fewer instances in those of yeomen and widows. It would seem, therefore, that comfort was a desirable feature of bedding, and associated with status. The numbers of pillows listed with bedsteads could also provide an indication of the size of beds and the number of occupants: 28% of bedsteads had

[36] See online Appendix 1, Table 5.10, 'Pillows and bolsters: mean frequency by dwelling size'
[37] See online Appendix 1, Table 5.11, 'Pillow fillings: ratio to occupational status category'

single pillows, 40% had two pillows, 32% three or more. This tentatively suggests that a little over one-quarter of the bedsteads had single occupancy, and three-quarters were shared.

Bed linen constituted some of the most significant and valuable assets of the household, averaging some 25% of the total value of household goods, and found in nearly all (181) of the 188 inventoried households. Of the total 329 listings, twenty-three were recorded simply generically as 'linen' of unspecified multiples. The 2,808 sheets were generally listed as pairs, including only six listings of unspecified multiples (valued as 2). There were also 535 pillowbears, the contemporary term for pillowcases. Bed linen appears to have been closely associated with storage furniture. Of the 191 distinct spaces where bed linen was listed, in 65% or 124 instances it was associated with storage furniture; 32 with boxes, 80 with chests, 69 with coffers and 22 with trunks. The majority of bed linen, 65%, was listed in chambers, and one-third of that percentage in the principal bedchamber, reflecting its safe keeping as a valuable asset or availability for use.[38] In 16% of listings it was not specified where the linen was stored as appraisers treated this valuable part of household furnishings as a distinct commodity; otherwise small percentages in the region of 10% were found in halls, parlours and lofts.

The quality of the sheets and pillowbears was defined by the nature of the linen, made from yarn of different qualities, as described above, flax being superior in quality and comfort to hemp, and the quality of the latter being determined by the time of harvest, later in the season coarser and described as 'harden'. The majority of the listings of bed linen[39] did not distinguish the nature of the yarn, but those that did identified the yarn as hemp or hempen, and we might therefore reasonably infer that the rest were of flax. Of the total of 2,808 sheets 192 were described as hemp or hempen in fourteen households across range of occupational status households, but predominantly those of widows. Sixty-nine sheets and pillowbears described as 'coarse' or 'harden' were distributed between eleven households, those of traders, artisan-traders, widows, an artisan and yeoman between 1598 and 1683. Edward Kent, the yeoman, possessed ten harden sheets and pillowbears, presumably for his men servants, in 1658.[40] Of superior quality was the flaxen linen described as 'holland', named after the source of superior flaxen cloth, and sixty-four sheets and pillowbears were so described (or in one instance as 'hallen') in thirteen households between 1603 and 1694, in the households of yeomen, traders, artisan-traders and widows. Perhaps the finest linen in the inventories were the

[38] See online Appendix 1, Table 5.12, 'Bed linen storage: location'
[39] See online Appendix 1, Table 5.13, 'Sheets and pillowbears: description of material qualities'
[40] OHCA: MS. Wills Pec. 44/4/9

two lace pillowbears belonging to Eleanor Crues, a widow, in 1669.[41] The listings for linen in the household of Thomas Striblehill, a butcher, in 1598 give a good indication of the different qualities and values of bed linen which could be found in one household, appropriate for the different ranks of the household, from master to servants: 'viij pare of flaxane shetes were valued at £3 4s, 'viij pare of hempen shetes' at £2 and 'v pare of Course shete for labourers beds' at 12s 6d. The value per sheet therefore was 4s for the flaxen, 2s 6d for the hempen sheet and 1s 3d for the coarse hempen sheet, the master's linen having approximately three times the value of that of his labourers. We might reasonably expect the quantity of bed linen to have reflected the size of the dwelling and thus the population of the household, but how was it related to occupational status?[42] The mean frequency of sheets per household for all occupational status categories fell between approximately eighteen for yeomen and thirteen for clerics, with eight for husbandmen and five for agricultural labourers. For pillowbears the same pattern applied; all categories fell between a mean frequency of five in the households of gentlemen and two in those of clerics, apart from those of 0.5 for husbandmen and a negligible 0.2 for agricultural labourers. This would seem to indicate that in the inventoried households, all at the upper end of the spectrum of material status in seventeenth-century Thame, the provision of bed linen and therefore of comfort was reasonably consistent, apart from the poorer section of the agricultural community where the provision was much lower, and in the case of the pillowbears for agricultural labourers virtually nonexistent. This suggests that lesser households not only enjoyed lower levels of material wealth but possibly also lower thresholds of domestic cleanliness, or 'ease'.

On top of the beds and sheets warmth was provided by blankets, rugs and quilts over which coverlets or coverings kept the bedding presentable and protected from the pervasive household dust. Of warm bedding[43] the 525 blankets were the most numerous, rugs numbering eighty-three and only ten quilts being listed. Blankets and rugs were in all probability sourced locally, readymade. Witney, some twenty-five miles distant in west Oxfordshire was already in the seventeenth century an important centre for the production of blankets and other broadcloth. The textile industry there had grown from the thirteenth century, being close to sources of wool, abundant water for washing and dyeing wool and powering fulling mills, and labour not entirely entailed to agriculture. By the sixteenth century cloth manufacture accounted for 40% of recorded occupations, and by the seventeenth century the town was, as noted by Robert Plot in his *Natural History of Oxfordshire*, specialising in blankets and other

---

[41] OHCA: MS. Wills Pec. 35/2/18
[42] See online Appendix 1, Table 5.14, 'Bed linen: frequency by occupational status category'
[43] See online Appendix 1, Table 5.9, 'Bedding and bed furniture: frequency'

broadcloths, much going to export.[44] In 1641 the Witney manufacturers petitioned the House of Lords specifically as 'blanket weavers', a marked example of a shift towards specialist commodity production. Blankets were made from the Cotswold coarse fell wool, both white and dyed. By this time the superior quality of yarn from sheep reared in harsher upland environments was being appreciated, with lowland flocks turning towards meat production, a shift which could in part explain the emergence in the later seventeenth century of Thame as a specialist supplier of fatstock for the London market.[45] The small number of quilts listed in the inventories may well have been assembled in the household, made of pre-manufactured cloth and combined, usually in three layers, to give greater warmth. (Later in the eighteenth century quilts were made of woollen or a worsted fabric, with a bottom layer of coarser woollen stuff, and a middle layer of soft carded wool). The stitching which held together these layers provided an opportunity for decorative work, in the seventeenth century frequently a 'Tree of Life' executed in woollen thread.[46] However, these were not, as might be expected, the furnishings of wealthier households. Although two were listed amongst the belongings of the gentleman John Striblehill in 1692, two were in the dwelling of the widow Anne Tipping in 1605 and one in that of William Poultney, a husbandman, in 1636, both of very modest means.[47] Whilst quilts with their decorative stitching may well have served as coverings of the bed as well as providing warmth, coverlets and coverings were designed primarily to keep the bedclothes presentable and clean. The 264 coverlets would have been principally covers overlying the bedding on the bedstead, possibly of wool or linen, or the combination of both, linsey woolsey, and the fifty-one coverings exclusively used as the top cover were probably of linen. The evidence does not indicate that these were on bedsteads of higher status; only ninety-nine, or 37%, of coverlets and coverings were found directly in association with bedsteads, and only forty, or 15%, in association with curtained bedsteads. A few were found on truckle beds. There is also no evidence of particular status associations; the incidence of coverlets and coverings was highest, between 93% and 75%, in the households of artisan-traders, widows, artisans and husbandmen, lowest in those of clerics (33%), gentlemen (20%) and agricultural labourers (also 20%), although the low figures for these high status categories may reflect the

---

[44] Robert Plot, *The Natural History of Oxfordshire* (Oxford, 1677), 2nd edn (London, 1705), pp. 283–5
[45] Simon Townley, ed., *A History of the County of Oxford: Volume 14, Bampton Hundred (Part Two)*, Victoria County History – Oxfordshire (London: Victoria County History, 2004), pp. 73–80; Kerridge, 'Wool Growing and Wool Textiles in Medieval and Early Modern Times', pp. 25–6
[46] H. Bevis and L. L. G. Ramsey, eds, *The Connoisseur Complete Encyclopaedia of Antiques* (London: The Connoisseur, 1975), pp. 632–9
[47] OHCA: MS. Wills Prob. 4 11085; MS. Wills Pec. 2/3/13; MS. Wills Pec. 48/2/35

Table 5.5 Curtained bedsteads: distribution by occupational status category

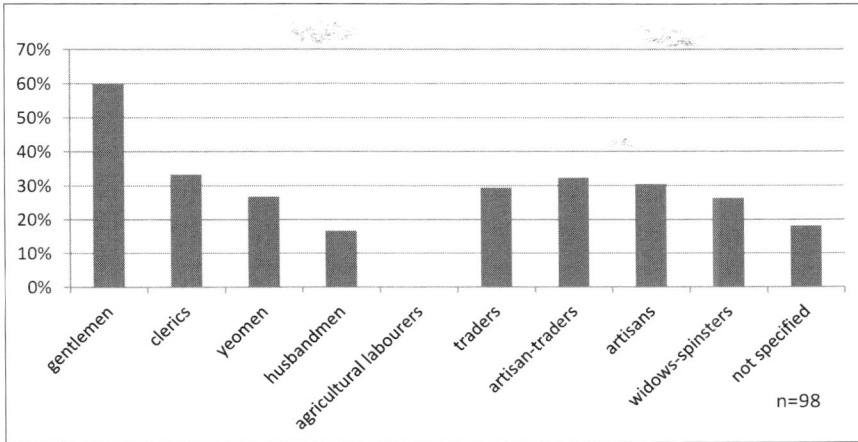

generic grouping of bedding in households with many other furnishings, as in the 'bed furniture'.

The textiles which furnished tester bedsteads[48] were frequently referred to as 'bed furniture' in the inventories: the curtains and the rods or wires from which they were suspended and the valance around the tester (Figure 5.2). The inventories listed 140 bedsteads and 26 'beds' with bed furnishings, consisting of 235 curtains in 65 households (of which 49 out of 84 listings were of unspecified multiples, given a value of 2). Where a numerical value is given it yields a mean frequency of 2.6 curtains per bedstead. There was little descriptive detail of the curtains, save that 15 were described as 'old', 6 as being green and 3 red. A total of fifty-seven valances were located in fifty-four households (fifteen as unspecified multiples). One valance was listed 'with worsted fringe'. Table 5.5 demonstrates that there was a clear correspondence of the ownership of a curtained bedstead to occupational status.[49] As we will see in the following chapter, it was not uncommon to find more than one bedstead in a chamber, implying that several people were sleeping in close proximity. To be secluded within curtains would therefore have carried particular connotations of personal space and 'comfort' in the contemporary affective sense. The highest occurrence of curtained bedsteads was 60% in gentlemen's households, considerably greater than that of the 25% to 30% in all other occupational status categories, 17%

[48] See online Appendix 1, Table 5.9, 'Bedding and bed furniture: frequency'
[49] See also Table 5.2, 'Curtained bedsteads: chronological occurrences by occupational status category'

of husbandmen's households and none in those of agricultural labourers. Similarly the mean frequency for such bedsteads in gentlemen's households was 2.5 and clerics 1.5, whereas in all other categories it ranged between 0.3 and 0.7, again with none for agricultural labourers.[50]

Warming Pans

Warming pans were enclosed containers, usually metallic, to hold hot coals, on long handles which could then be inserted between sheets under bedclothes. This may appear to indicate a desire for personal comfort, but was probably as much a device to keep bedclothes and linen dry and aired in chambers that were largely unheated and damp. Seventy-nine warming pans were listed during the entire study period, from all occupational status categories from the poorer to the wealthiest households. They are only absent from the inventories of gentlemen, again perhaps due to their being listing as relatively commonplace with generic brassware.

The Washing of Textiles

Textiles, especially bed linen, would have needed regular or periodic cleaning, as would the personal linen of the household, attendant with connotations of household propriety. As noted by Crowley, the contemporary term for personal physical amenity was 'ease', suggesting that this quality was as much about the avoidance of 'dis-ease' as bodily comfort in the present sense.[51] As a fabric which, unlike wool, could be easily and frequently washed, linen was employed close to the human body in both clothing and bedding. Routine household tasks do not manifest greatly in the inventories; for example, there were only two households where brushes were listed, those of Reynold Graunt, a yeoman, in 1619, and the widow Elizabeth Browne in 1625.[52] Presumably commonplace, others may have been amalgamated with anonymous 'lumber'. However, we do have some indication of the washing process from the seven bucking tubs listed in five households between 1603 and 1693. The process of bucking is defined as the operation of steeping or boiling of yarn, cloth or clothes in a lye of wood ashes; an old process of bleaching referred to as 'buck-washing'.[53] Figure 5.12 shows the processes of bleaching, beating with a paddle, and hanging the clothes on a rod. Three of the bucking tubs listed were in the inventory of a widow, Frances Minge, in 1622, suggesting perhaps the

50   Ibid.
51   Crowley, The Invention of Comfort, pp. 69–70
52   OHCA: MS. Wills Pec. 39/3/26; MS. Wills Pec. 32/5/16
53   OED

Figure 5.12 Washing linen

taking in of washing from other households as a source of income.[54] The others were found in the households of one gentleman and two artisans, a currier and a hemp dresser. Twenty-six smoothing irons were also listed in ten households between 1625 and 1694 – ranging in number from one to four, an average of 2.6 per household – of 3 widows and 1 spinster, 1 yeoman and 1 shepherd, 1 clerk, 1 blacksmith and 1 draper.[55] The ownership of smoothing irons does not thus apparently reflect large households or occupational requirements, apart possibly from those of the draper.

Conclusions on Furnishings of Rest

The furnishings for rest might appear, since in large part they were employed in a state of unconsciousness, to be relatively less important than more active household domains. In addition, rest took place in locations which seem to have been partially withdrawn from the heart of the dwelling. And yet we have seen that a very significant investment was made in these furnishings, implying that the objects of retirement and rest were considered important.

[54] OHCA: MS. Wills Pec. 46/1/42
[55] The occupation of one decedent was not stated

Like furnishings of commensality, they were objects which attended actions which brought people into socially potent proximity, and thus articulated the social dynamic. Bed chambers were places of private retirement, and therefore material differentiation expressed in the quality of bedsteads and their furnishings would have implications for the signification of the internal social dynamic. But in addition, as we shall see in Chapter 6, best chambers were places of select entertainment, and the quality of the bed-steads and furnishings therein would also have communicated householder and household status to the external peer group. Variations in the nature of the bedsteads, from the secluded, fully canopied and curtained, to the truckle bed or even the simple 'bed' on the floor, indicate that the provision of more comfortable and private accommodation for rest was desirable and linked with status. There were considerable variations in the nature of the bedding, ranging from down and feather to straw to fill the bed, bolster and pillow, and in the comfort afforded by various grades of bed linen. Rest was not, however, even in wealthier households, necessarily a solitary activity. There were the marital connotations of the bedstead, and in many cases the bed chamber was shared by members of the household of different ranks, with a servant or child on the truckle bed, so that who retired with whom to sleep would have formed an important part of the social relationships of the household, investing those objects and the spaces they occupied with affective and hierarchical significance.

Sanitation

Objects linked to personal sanitation were also listed in the inventories, reminding us that human waste is another aspect of domestic life, with its connotations of uncleanliness and pollution. Such contemporary concerns were articulated in complaints over the 'fylth, dunghills and other noise-some rubbage' deposited in the streets of Oxford in the mid-seventeenth century.[56] There were a variety of means available for personal evacuation: chamber pots, close stools and one 'house of office', recorded throughout the century. The most common were chamber pots (Figure 5.13), the name suggesting employment in the chamber when retired, but often listed in the kitchen along with cooking and eating vessels, where, presumably, after being emptied in a cess-pit they would have been cleaned and stored ready for night-time use. A total of ninety-seven pots were listed in thirty-eight households, averaging 2.6 pots per household. The highest frequency was in the households of urban dwellers – traders, artisan-traders, artisans and widows. Only the yeomen featured prominently amongst agriculturalists

---

[56] E. Cockayne, *Hubbub: Filth, Noise and Stench in England 1600–1770* (New Haven and London: Yale University Press, 2007), p. 69

Figure 5.13
Chamber pot,
1650–1700

with chamber pots, and strangely no gentlemen or clerics.[57] The material, pewter, is only given for thirteen chamber pots, perhaps explaining their apparent absence in these latter higher status households, where they may well have been listed generically with the other pewter. Other chamber pots were probably of pottery (Figure 5.13). Two close stools and one 'stool and pan' were listed – box-like constructions holding a removable receptacle for the waste which would have been located in the bed chamber and have afforded the user a degree of 'ease'.[58] These were listed in the households of Cornelius Carden, a locksmith, in 1617, blacksmith John Shreeve in 1682 and Thomas Middleton, a clerk, in 1694.[59] They were thus found not in households of the highest status, but in the centre of the town, where perhaps there were greater concerns over the disposal of human waste. However, the most permanent method of sanitation, a 'house of office' which would have been placed over a cess-pit, belonged to the shepherd William Symes in 1625.[60] If we see the household as a point of consumption, the presence of sanitary utensils reminds us of the need to deal with bodily waste, an often-concealed but challenging consequence of human subsistence. The fact that Cecilie Benson, a wealthy widow who owned a number of shops, bequeathed 'one Chamber pott' to Mary Wheeler in her will of 1626 suggests that this aspect of life was very much accepted and recognised.[61]

[57] See online Appendix 1, Table 5.15, 'Chamber pots: mean frequency by occupational status category'
[58] See above, Chapter 4, and Crowley, *The Invention of Comfort*, pp. 3–4, 69–70
[59] OHCA: MS. Wills Pec. 34/4/27; MS. Wills Pec. 51/4/15; MS. Wills Pec. 46/3/18
[60] OHCA: MS. Wills Pec. 51/1/43
[61] OHCA: MS. Wills Pec. 32/5/18

Order and Security: Storage Furniture

The probate inventories reflect an awareness of the value of objects and an ordering of the domestic domain. An important part of that ordering was the provision of storage furniture.[62] For general-purpose storage there was a near equal frequency of just over 300 coffers and chests, and a significant incidence of 138 boxes and 80 trunks. But other items of listed storage furniture were found in much smaller quantities. The thirty-eight presses, hanging and chest presses represented dedicated clothes storage, and the seven chests of drawers, whilst numerically insignificant, a novel and sophisticated type of storage furniture introduced into wealthier Thame households in the later seventeenth century. In Table 5.6 we see that the majority, 73%, of storage furniture was found in 83% of chambers. Smaller quantities of storage furniture were found in other parts of the dwelling: 9% in 23% of halls, 6% in 46% of parlours, 3% in 45% of lofts and 1% respectively in 7% of butteries and 6% of kitchens and service houses. The culture of domestic space as indicated by the association of objects will be examined in greater depth in Chapter 6, but if chambers suggested a degree of privacy then the preponderance of storage furniture there might imply their use for the storage of personal or valuable belongings. There is also evidence that they were used widely for the storage of bed linen; in the 'cheese chamber' of John Burton, a baker in 1643, 'iij Chestes ij boxes & a trunk' are listed 'with the bedding'.[63]

We can assume that since there were listings for significant numbers of both chests and coffers in the same domestic spaces, there was a distinction in contemporary minds between these two types of storage furniture, also observed by Chinnery.[64] Randle Holme distinguished the two types of storage furniture thus: 'If it have a straight, and flat cover, it is called a Chest; which in all other things represents the coffer, save the want of a circular lid, or cover'.[65] However, there is evidence that the two categories overlapped even in the contemporary mind; William Tipping, a shoemaker, bequeathed in his will of 1604 'two chestes one of them beinge myne owne coffer'.[66] The coffer was originally an item used for the conveyance of objects, and for this reason frequently covered in leather (Figure 5.14), with a distinct maker, the cofferer.[67] Chests, on the other hand, were rectangular in form, flat topped, and either of boarded construction like the coffer or joined, and unlike the coffer standing on feet (Figures 5.16 and

[62] See online Appendix 1, Table 5.16, 'Storage furniture: frequency'
[63] OHCA: MS. Wills Pec. 33/2/18
[64] Chinnery, *Oak Furniture*, pp.358-9
[65] Randle Holme, *The Academy of Armory; or, A Storehouse of Armory and Blazon* (1688), ed. I. H. Jeayes (London: Roxburghe Club, 1905), Book III, Chapter XIV, p. 14
[66] OHCA: MS. Wills Pec. 52/3/12
[67] Chinnery, *Oak Furniture*, pp. 358-9

Table 5.6 Storage furniture: spatial distribution

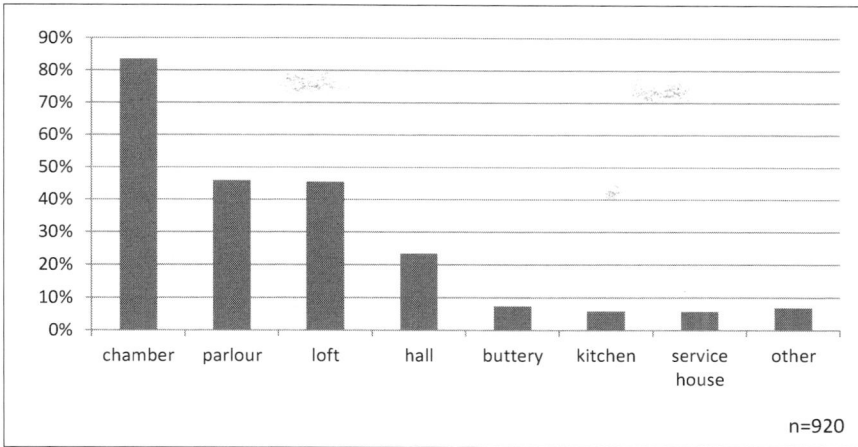

n=920

5.17). Twenty-eight, or 9%, of chests were described as joined, whereas no structural descriptions were given for coffers, which were probably of nailed construction. One chest was described as being constructed of elm, and two of cypress, a relatively rare timber effective in the deterrence of clothing moths due to its strong odour, and a reminder of the continual depredations of vermin in the early modern dwelling. Three chests were described as iron bound. Chests appear to have been of variable size, fourteen were described a 'great', whilst eight were 'small' or 'little'. The trunk, for which no structural details were given, seems to have been a smaller storage item sharing features of both the chest and coffer: flat topped but without feet and of simple boarded construction. It could have been that, apart from structural differences, these storage items were distinguished by customary function and location. One trunk, for example was described as being 'with the bedding'.[68] The distribution of storage furniture through the dwelling, however, indicates that the great majority of all types were found in chambers; of the coffer, chest and trunk, between 69% and 83% were found in chambers and only between 5% and 10% in the parlour, suggesting that the vast majority of storage might have been of textiles – bed linen and clothing in chambers – and little of other personal belongings, and that the distinctions between different types of storage furniture were simply structural and not due to any functional or conceptual qualities.

A significant number of boxes (Figure 5.17), 138 in seventy-five households, were listed in the inventories. There is very little indication as to what the boxes contained. Chinnery identifies them as containers of small

---

[68] OHCA: MS. Wills Pec. 33/2/18

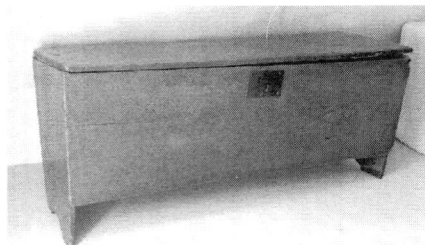

Figure 5.14 (*Top left*) Coffer, beech with Russian leather, late seventeenth century
Figure 5.15 (*Top right*) Boarded chest, chestnut, late seventeenth century
Figure 5.16 (*Left*) Joined oak chest, 1580–1630

goods, such as gloves, linen, lace, deeds, letters and books.[69] Certainly, smaller items of value, such as rings, gloves, lace and money feature in wills, especially those of widows. One box in the possession of William Bigge, a yeoman, in 1690 was described as being of iron, presumably a strong box.[70] Some books, of which we have seen a limited ownership, such as bibles might have been kept in boxes in wealthier households. The ownership of boxes broadly followed household occupational status, the highest mean frequency, 1.6, being found in the households of gentlemen, 1.0 in those of yeomen, and other categories falling between 0.4 and 0.9, apart from artisan-traders with 0.4, and husbandmen with none.[71] The figure of 0.3 for clerics appears to be anomalous for a category with presumably greater literacy and documentation.

Related to boxes were the eleven desks (Figure 5.18), of the same structure and size but provided with a sloping lid on which to write or read, and providing a further indication of literacy, in the households of 1 gentleman, 4 yeomen and 4 widows between 1619 and 1692. Of those listed, 5 were in chambers, 4 in halls and 1 in the study of John Striblehill, gentleman, in 1692.[72]

---

[69] Chinnery, *Oak Furniture*, p. 364
[70] OHCA: MS. Wills Pec. 33/4/27
[71] See online Appendix 1, Table 5.17, 'Boxes: mean frequency per household by occupational status category'
[72] OHCA: MS. Wills Prob. 4 11085

Figure 5.17 (*Left*) Boarded box, oak, mid seventeenth century
Figure 5.18 (*Right*) Desk box, oak, c. 1650

A type of storage furniture which served primarily for the storage of clothing was the press. This was a completely enclosed piece of furniture with doors, and generally provided with hanging pegs on the back interior (Figure 5.19).[73] In total thirty-three were listed in twenty-nine households; the majority, 26, in chambers, 1 in a loft, 3 in halls, 2 in a kitchen and 1 in a space not specified. The highest mean frequency, 0.8, was found gentlemen's households, presumably reflecting more convenient storage than chests for more clothing of greater worth, and much lower mean frequencies, between 0.1 and 0.3, in most other households, with none in the households of clerics or agricultural labourers.[74] There were also listings of four 'hanging' presses in four households, of a gentleman and three artisan-traders between 1644 and 1689. Chinnery suggests that this might refer to the hanging of clothes in the press but, given the absence of the adjective with the other presses, it seems probable that it refers to an item hanging on wall.[75]

The chest of drawers, of which seven were listed in the Thame inventories, was a chest fully fitted with drawers, offering greater sophistication and versatility in storage but also requiring considerably greater skill in the making. Being of recent invention, it would have been sourced in the lifetime of the decedent, in all probability from London but possibly also from the nearby city of Oxford. The evidence suggests that chests of drawers first appeared in this country around 1650.[76] Early chests of drawers were still constructed using a joined construction; a possible appearance is given in Figure 5.20. The first chest of drawers listed in a Thame inventory was in the hall chamber of John Shreeve, a blacksmith, in 1682, which may

[73] Chinnery, *Oak Furniture*, p. 329
[74] See online Appendix 1, Table 5.18, 'Presses: mean frequency per household by occupational status category'
[75] Chinnery, *Oak Furniture*, p. 329
[76] *Ibid.*, p. 369

Figure 5.19 Joined clothes press, oak, early seventeenth century

have been in the household for a period of time before his death. Although the parish records do not provide a record of the decedent's baptism or marriage, they do record the baptisms of two sons in 1679 and 1681, suggesting he was not of great age.[77] James Nixon, a victualler, possessed a chest of drawers in his best chamber in 1686.[78] Two chests of drawers were listed, one in the chamber and one in the study of the gentrified scion of a butcher family, Sir John Striblehill, in 1692, and two in the dwelling of Thomas Middleton, a clerk in 1694, one in his parlour chamber and one in his gallery.[79] A more sophisticated version of the chest of drawers, set on its own stand (Figure 5.21) was listed in parlour of Zachariah Hames in 1686, a merchant whose will indicates significant property and commercial interests in the region.[80] It is notable that all of these chests of drawers were displayed in the more prestigious domestic spaces such as best and hall chambers, a study and gallery. The acquisition of such pieces, although very limited in the context of Thame, is an indication of familiarity with metropolitan fashions, with a desire for a more sophisticated ordering of possessions and investment in 'comfort'.

[77] OHCA: MS. Wills Pec. 51/4/15
[78] OHCA: MS. Wills Prob. 11 382 22
[79] OHCA: MS. Wills Prob. 4 11085; MS. Wills Pec. 46/3/18
[80] OHCA: MS. Wills Prob. 4 15794

Figure 5.20 Joined chest of drawers, oak, c. 1680
Figure 5.21 Joined chest of drawers on stand, oak, 1680–1720

Conclusions on Storage Furnishings

The whole domestic domain in many ways represents the ordering of life.[81] Storage furniture signifies the affordance of the ordering of smaller domestic items – linen, clothing, books, correspondence and personal effects – keeping them accessible, safe and clean. In addition, most extant storage furniture from this period has locks of some sort on doors and lids (see Figures 5.15 to 5.21), which speaks eloquently not only of the fear of burglary from outside the dwelling, but also of pilfering and curiosity by servants, revealing some of the social tensions in the Thame household: the inclusiveness of the social 'household-family' challenged by the unequal control of material assets. The possession of the keys of the household also signalled the hierarchy of ownership. Above all, the presence of storage furniture, and in the shape of the chest of drawers its new sophistication, shows the growing number and importance of objects in domestic life.

---

[81] I. Hodder, *The Domestication of Europe* (Oxford: Blackwell, 1990)

Personal Adornment and Looking Glasses

The focus of this study is on the furnishings of the dwelling and their engagement by the members of the household, and considerable emphasis has been placed on human actions. The body was not, however, only an agent but also object, subject itself to affordance and agency. Much of the storage furniture discussed above was dedicated to the storage of apparel, listed in significant quantities in the inventories, generically grouped or individually itemised in wills. Other objects of personal adornment are listed: items such a bodkin for fixing a lady's hair, shaving equipment for men and items of personal jewellery. In addition, there are limited but significant listings in only ten households of twelve looking glasses and two mirrors, the former possibly a hand-held object, the latter wall hung. The metallic backing to glass was a Venetian invention of the early sixteenth century, first introduced in England by Sir Robert Mansell at his London glassworks early in the seventeenth century, but it was not until 1644 that the Worshipful Company of Glass-Sellers and Looking-Glass Makers was incorporated.[82] These, then, were expensive metropolitan luxuries. The first listing of a looking glass is in the inventory of the widow Elizabeth Browne in 1625,[83] but the majority were listed after 1683 in the possession of two gentlemen, a yeoman, a traders, an artisan trader and a spinster. The clerk Thomas Middleton possessed no fewer than three looking glasses in 1694.[84] These items could be seen as part of an evolving culture of 'comfort' and individualism, percolating from the modern metropolitan world into the localised and communal culture of Thame.

Summary of the Materiality, Affordance and Agency of Domestic Objects

We have thus looked in Chapters 3, 4 and 5 at the properties, affordance and agency of individual objects listed in the Thame inventories. Table 5.7 lays out the relationship between the *processes* which met household needs, involving *activities* with their *frequencies*, the *actions* associated with *objects* and their conceptual *significance*. The sheer quantity of over 27,000 objects listed, averaging some 143 per household (excluding those aggregated as 'lumber'), and the diversity of 685 distinct objects is a testament to the rich and complex material basis and commodification of early modern domestic life. Materials were resourced from the mineral, vegetable and animal environment and converted into objects to facilitate domestic processes. Some objects, such as

---

[82] R. Fastnedge, *English Furniture Styles from 1500 to 1830* (Harmondsworth: Penguin Books, 1955), p. 59; Gloag, *A Short Dictionary of Furniture*, p. 438
[83] OHCA: MS. Wills Pec. 32/5/16
[84] OHCA: MS. Wills Pec. 46/3/18

Table 5.7 The 'practice' of the Thame household: the interrelation of processes, activities, actions, objects and signification

Processes	Activities	Frequency	Actions	Objects	Signification
Foodstuff processing	Salting Dairying Boulting Baking Malting Brewing	Seasonal Daily Weekly? Weekly? Periodic Periodic	Cutting Milking Skimming Sieving Sifting Milling Pot tending Pouring Fire tending	Knives Troughs Tubs Barrels Bowls Churns Pots Bins Sieves Shovels	Nature to culture Sustenance Revenue Temporal ordering Routine Knowledge Gendered labour Spatial ordering Gendered space
Cooking	Foodstuff preparation Boiling Roasting Grilling Baking	Daily Daily Periodic Daily Weekly?	Chopping Grinding Mixing Sieving Holding Skimming Pot tending Turning Smelling Tasting Fire tending	Knives Boards Bowls Hearths Fire irons Chafers Pots Kettles Skillets Ladles Spits	Sustenance Temporal ordering Routine Knowledge Gendered labour Spatial ordering Gendered space
Consumption Conviviality	Eating Drinking Conversing	Frequent Frequent Frequent	Eating Drinking Sitting Conversing Fire tending	Eating vessels Drinking vessels Cutlery Salts Seating furniture Table furniture Cupboards Napkins Table/cupboard cloths	Sustenance Temporal ordering Spatial ordering Hierarchy Inclusion Status Hospitality Social differentiation
Housework	Cleaning Washing	Frequent Weekly?	Sweeping Wiping Filling Scrubbing Rubbing	Tubs Brushes Cloths	Cleanliness Order Probity
Rest	Retirement Sleeping	Frequent Nightly	Reclining Lying Sleeping	Bedsteads Truckle beds Beds Bolsters Pillows Linen Blankets Covers	Rest Security Privacy Comfort Status Social differentiation Intimacy Reproduction
Storage	Ordering Storage	Frequent Frequent	Sorting Placing Enclosing Securing Locking	Chest Coffers Trunks Boxes Presses Chests of drawers	Order Control Spatial ordering Security Possession Status

metalware and furniture, were robust and durable; others, pottery and textiles, more vulnerable and impermanent. At the most fundamental level it was the household itself which obtained raw materials (for example, foodstuffs and yarn) furnished largely by agriculture in the immediate environment and processed in the vicinity of the dwelling to provide for the household. Materials could also be sourced for processing from other suppliers, such as fuel and the grain for brewing and baking. Other durable objects within the household were provided by artisans in the locality using local materials: pottery vessels, wooden furniture and linen napery. Yet other objects were acquired from more distant materials and manufacture, such as the cooking irons and pots. All domestic objects would have been maintained through their lifetime by householders and local artisans.

Objects, or commodities within the household, had both use-value and exchange-value, and when produced for sale also monetary labour-value.[85] Their creation and consumption therefore had implications for the distribution of power within the household in terms of the allocation of resources material and human – as labour effort, time and skill – and the economic and social relationship of the household to its environment, and hence the wider economy and society. The apparent displacement of the familiar by the unfamiliar in terms of materials, techniques and producers – for example, the domestically woven wicker or straw seat for a chair manufactured at a distance, the chest by the chest of drawers and the acquisition of metropolitan artefacts such as looking glasses – could be seen as examples of the process of alienation,[86] distancing the production of commodities from their local social associations, and consumption from a significantly affective to a largely sensory experience – the emergence of a culture of 'comfort' and of social status more closely defined by personal material consumption.

Often inherited, household objects provided the template for traditional 'practice', the setting for normative ways of conducting domestic life. Objects were the focus of habitual actions and also of personal experience, in bodily motions and sensations.[87] The materiality of objects was experienced through their form, weight and tactile qualities: hard or easy to handle, with receptive or resistant textures. In terms of engagement, objects could be straightforward or difficult to employ, relying on bodily strength, acquired knowledge and skill; for example, the combustible qualities of wood for heat, the variable nature of vessels of metal and clay for foodstuff processing and consumption, and yarns spun for textiles. But engagement

[85] K. Marx, *Economic and Philosophic Manuscripts of 1844*, ed. D. J. Struik (London: Lawrence and Wishart, 1973), pp. 179–80

[86] *Ibid.*; D. J Struik, 'Introduction', in *ibid.*, pp. 46–7

[87] P. Bourdieu, *Outline of a Theory of Practice*, trans. R. Nice (Cambridge: Cambridge University Press, 1977); P. Bourdieu, *The Logic of Practice* (Cambridge: Polity Press, 1990); M. Heidegger, *Being and Time* (1927) (Oxford: Blackwell, 1962)

with objects was a part of human existence which was also potentially challenging – the smoking fire, the burnt food, the cracked vessel or the worn and dirty linen – and thus also implicit with social discord. Engagement with objects could generate positive or negative personal and collective emotions, a significant part of the experience of living. Within their affordance, objects therefore can be seen to be continually exerting agency on both the conduct and experience of human life.

Agency is to be found not only in single objects, but more frequently in associations of objects; the affordance of one complements and contrasts with that of another adjacent object. The association of objects therefore directs actions around objects, enmeshing social relationships and promoting social agency. Emotions generated by actions around objects, such as eating and drinking, become conceptualised as hospitality, with implications for the distribution of status and power. Indeed, it could be argued that the cognitive role of conceptualisation is to assimilate and condense these complex material and social associations. Probate inventories, primarily listing objects, do not generally provide (apart from a description of constructional materials) details of decorative embellishment and motifs which impart to functional objects important additional conceptual significance, signalling cultural affinities and social status. (See, for example, in Figure 5.1 the headboard of the ceiled bedstead featuring rounded Roman arches, and thus an association with elite humanist culture and values.)

We thus see the daily life organised around the activities of the household, in turn structuring relationships within the household. The frequency of actions ranging from the quotidian to the seasonal, and occasionally linked to the episodes in human life, were apparently still largely rooted in the rhythms of the natural world. However, as has been revealed in the previous chapters, the Thame household was also the site of gradual innovation. The economic and social intrusion of a wider world beyond the immediate environment – for example, in the greater supply of household provisions and furnishings from a greater distance, and a concomitant shift away from household provisioning to sale of commodities for the market – appears to have been eroding the close association of daily life to natural rhythms. Only three domestic clocks were listed in the Thame inventories late in the seventeenth century, novel and prestigious objects belonging to two gentlemen, John Striblehill and Anthony Price, and the wealthy merchant Zachariah Hames, between 1686 and 1692.[88] But their presence indicates the coming shift in the rhythm of life away from the natural, humane and localised to a more distanced and artificially regulated world. As we have noted, the significance of objects lies in their context, and two dimensions so far largely neglected are those of objects in place, and their use through time, to which we now turn.

---

[88] OHCA: MS. Wills Prob. 4 11085, MS. Wills Pec. 49/1/23, MS. Wills Prob. B4 15794

6

The 'Practice' and Domestic Culture of the Thame Household

In this chapter we shift the focus from individual objects to objects in association, and the dwelling itself as complex and multidimensional 'object'. Objects acquire meaning through context and association. One of the attractions of probate inventories as historical evidence lies in the way in which they list objects in association with one another, and frequently locate them in distinct settings within the dwelling. Notwithstanding the caveat that objects may not always have been listed in the locations in which they were customarily used, or that certain objects may have been removed prior to the appraisal process, this characteristic provides an opportunity to determine the habitual actions which occurred in specific spaces within the dwelling, and thence the way in which the dwelling was divided both spatially and conceptually – a manifestation of early modern 'practice' and its development through time.

The Differentiation of and Naming of Household Rooms:
Tradition, Concepts and Activities

It is through language and practice that undifferentiated 'space' is transformed into 'place'.[1] The probate inventories reveal the fact that dwellings in Thame were consistently divided into a limited number of distinctly named spaces, the frequencies of which are shown in Table 6.1. A number of terms (in bold in the table) – chamber, hall, parlour, kitchen, buttery, cellar, loft, 'room' and service houses of various descriptions (brew-, milk-, boulting- and slaughter house, for example) – occur with overwhelming frequency and will form the basis of this examination of the division of space and its definition. In Table 6.2a we see that these terms persist through the century, with a small diminution in the number of halls and butteries, and a small increase in the number of cellars, lofts and 'rooms'.

---

[1] M. P. Pearson and C. Richards, 'Ordering the World: Perceptions of Architecture, Space and Time', *Architecture and Order: Approaches to Social Space*, ed. M. P. Pearson, and C. Richards (London and New York: Routledge, 1994), p. 4

Table 6.1 Named domestic spaces: frequency

Space	Frequency	Mean frequency per household
chamber	382	2.04
hall	175	0.93
not specified	156	0.83
(service) house	107	0.57
kitchen	85	0.45
parlour	61	0.32
buttery	54	0.29
cellar	44	0.23
loft	33	0.18
'room'	29	0.15
garret	5	0.03
outhouse	4	0.02
workhouse	3	0.02
attic	3	0.02
study	3	0.02
entry	3	0.02
below stairs	1	0.01
staircase	1	0.01
pantry	1	0.01
'space'	1	0.01
gallery	1	0.01
larder	1	0.01

Sample: total spaces 1153; households 188

There are therefore a number of differentiated spaces within the dwelling, distinctions which are widespread and persistent. Do these terms indicate structural arrangements, tradition, distinct usages or a combination of all these factors? The architectural review of early modern houses in Thame in Chapter 2 revealed that construction was governed by a traditional concept of layout and subject to development with the introduction of chimney flues and the release of upper spaces for dwelling. The terminology applied to chambers – above the hall, parlour or kitchen – illustrates this structural development. Room nomenclature did have a historical precedence which we shall examine shortly, but since this is a study based primarily on the evidence of the seventeenth-century probate inventories we start by observing whether the assemblages of objects in these spaces reveal differentiation in their use and significance.

Table 6.3 shows overviews generated by the calculation of the mean frequency of objects listed within distinct domestic spaces, grouped around activities as, for example, eating vessels, bedding or seating furniture, in all dwellings over the entire study period. In this table the significance of the

Table 6.2a Named domestic spaces: distribution in inventoried Thame dwellings, mean frequency of rooms by quarter

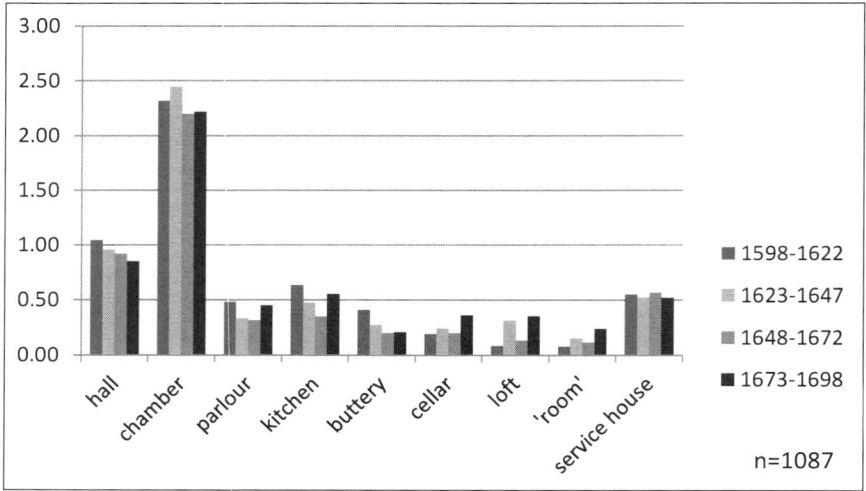

Table 6.2b Average number of dwelling rooms per household by quarter

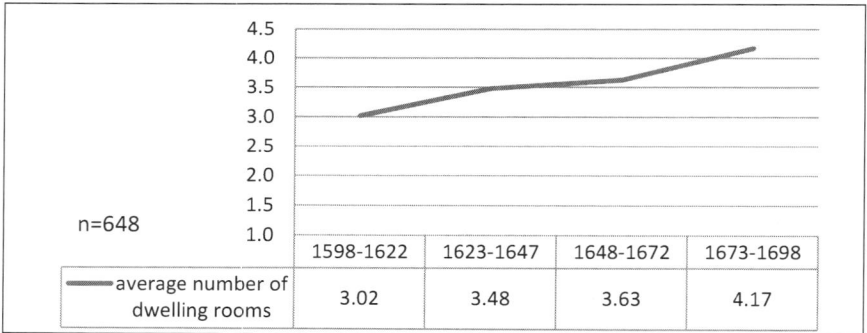

	1598-1622	1623-1647	1648-1672	1673-1698
average number of dwelling rooms	3.02	3.48	3.63	4.17

n=648

Table 6.2c Named domestic spaces: distribution in inventoried Thame dwellings, percentage of dwellings by size per quarter

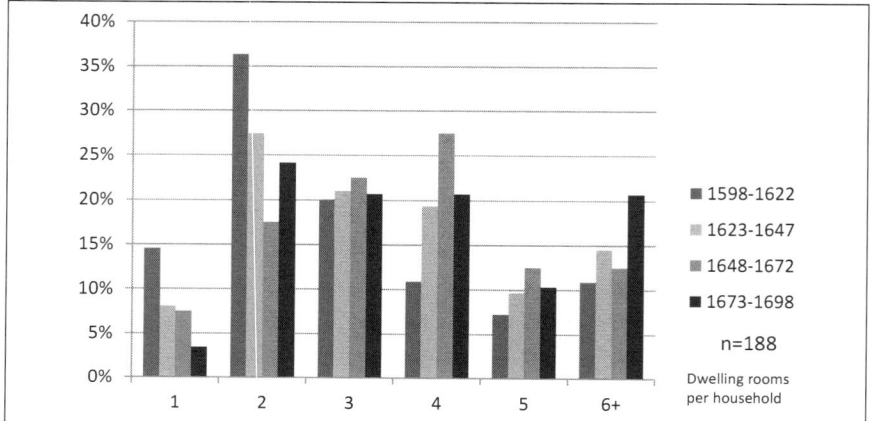

value of the mean frequency reflects the nature of an object; for example, 'table-cupboard linen' includes napkins which were listed by the dozen and thus yield a high numerical value, whereas one single piece of table furniture in a room would have had as great, or greater significance in terms of the use of that room. Seating furniture might consist of a single stool or chair, or a multiple-seating bench or form. In these tables only object groups that have a numerical mean frequency equal to or over a value of 0.5 are shown, on the basis that it is then as probable to find that object in that space as not. So, in the halls, the objects listed reveal an emphasis on food preparation, indicated by the presence of cooking utensils and hearth and cooking irons, and on commensality by eating and drinking vessels and cutlery, and seating (averaging six items) and an average of one table. In addition, cushions and items of lighting, in the form of a candlestick, indicate conviviality. The limited presence of table and cupboard linen, table cloths and napkins indicates a higher degree of table etiquette in some households. Display-storage furniture indicates the presence of a cupboard for eating and drinking vessels, again implying sociable consumption. The presence of bedding and bed linen in the hall may seem anomalous until we remember that in the smallest households consisting of the hall as the sole dwelling space, sleeping took place here also. (Those particular circumstances of hall use will be discussed in greater detail below.) The object groups listed in chambers show a clear use of these spaces for sleeping, with bedsteads, averaging one, and bedding and bed linen in clear evidence. Storage furniture was present too, apart from other articles possibly to store the linen listed there. There were also indications of commensality in the form of seating and eating vessels. Foodstuffs were present in small mean quantities, but these may well reflect the use of some chambers also for the storage of household foodstuffs, such as cheese, apples and cereals. Lofts displayed a wide range of object groups and potential actions, suggesting a multifunctional and adaptable space for both storage and sleeping: bedsteads (averaging one), bedding and bed linen, and, as in chambers, not only seating and drinking vessels but also storage furniture suitable for the bed, table and cupboard linen, with evidence of the storage of foodstuffs and components of yarn production. Parlours were again furnished with objects indicating a range of activities: seating (averaging four items) with cushions and a table, eating vessels and cupboards as display-storage furniture. In addition there is limited evidence of bedsteads, linen – both for the bed and for tables – and cupboards and storage furniture for the same. In the kitchens, unsurprisingly, we find a predominance of objects for the preparation of food: cooking utensils and cooking irons, as well as the storage of vessels for consumption, eating and drinking vessels, cutlery and lighting. There is limited evidence of seating, and of brewing utensils. The buttery also shows evidence of the storage of eating vessels, cooking utensils and lighting, and of brewing vessels, which in conjunction with cupboards and drinking vessels might indicate not only storage but drink consumption in this space. Cellars too show evidence of the storage or use of brewing and

Table 6.3 Grouped objects: frequency in household spaces

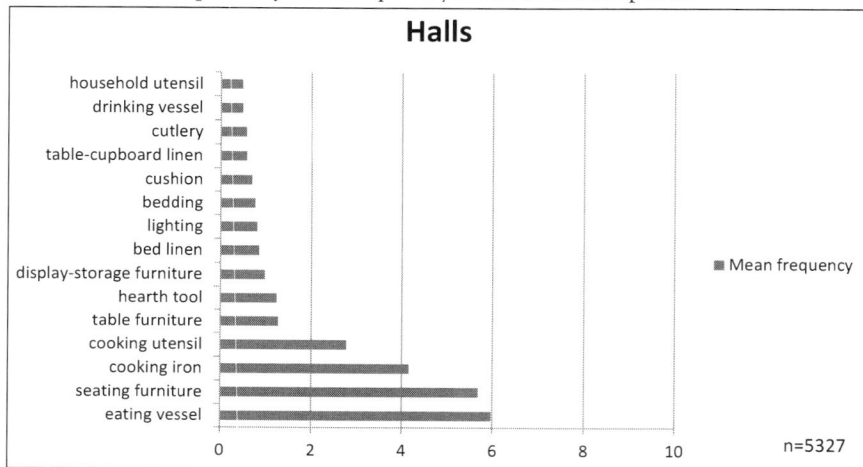

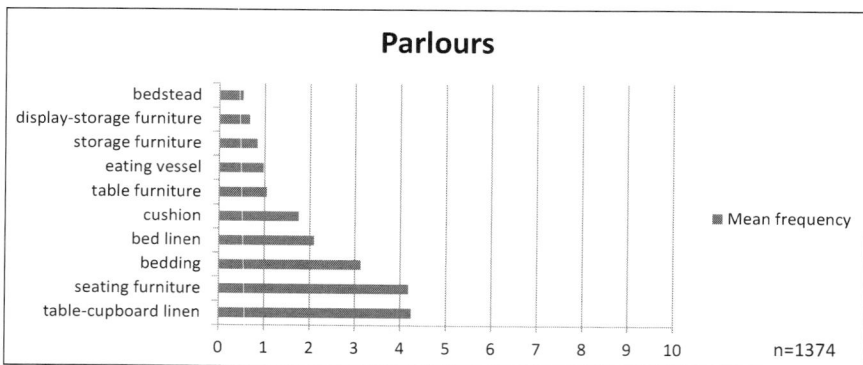

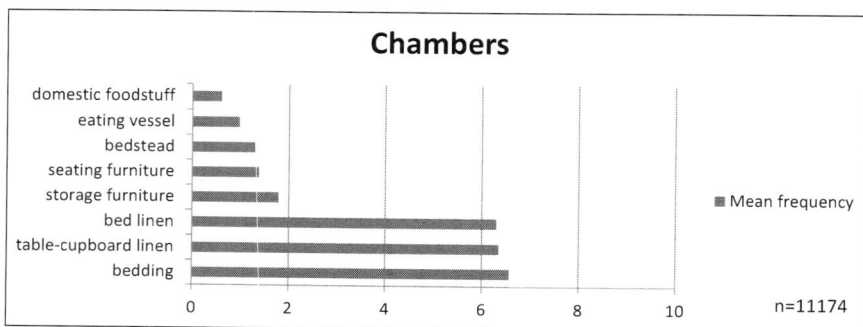

Halls

| household utensil |
| drinking vessel |
| cutlery |
| table-cupboard linen |
| cushion |
| bedding |
| lighting |
| bed linen |
| display-storage furniture |
| hearth tool |
| table furniture |
| cooking utensil |
| cooking iron |
| seating furniture |
| eating vessel |

■ Mean frequency

0　2　4　6　8　10　　n=5327

Parlours

| bedstead |
| display-storage furniture |
| storage furniture |
| eating vessel |
| table furniture |
| cushion |
| bed linen |
| bedding |
| seating furniture |
| table-cupboard linen |

■ Mean frequency

0　1　2　3　4　5　6　7　8　9　10　　n=1374

Chambers

| domestic foodstuff |
| eating vessel |
| bedstead |
| seating furniture |
| storage furniture |
| bed linen |
| table-cupboard linen |
| bedding |

■ Mean frequency

0　2　4　6　8　10　　n=11174

212

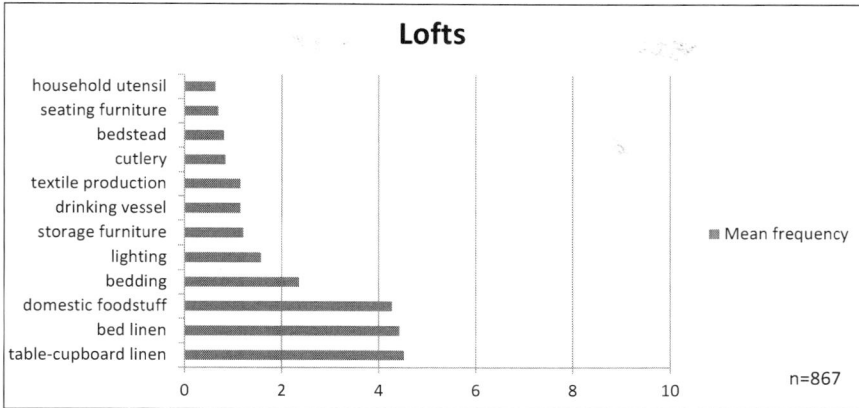

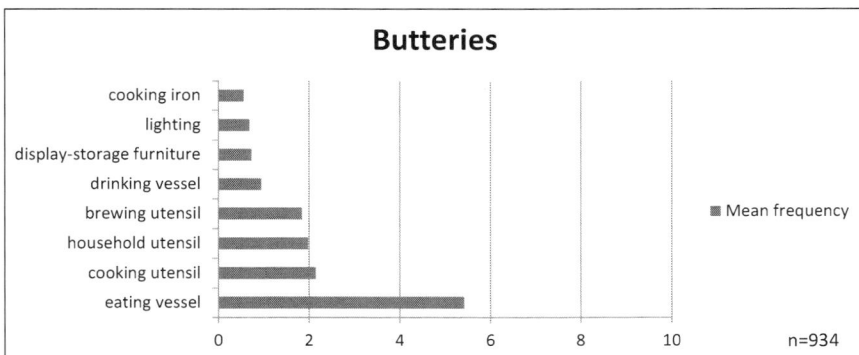

salting utensils. Finally the service houses had object groups related to the processing of various foodstuffs – dairying and brewing – and also vessels for the storage of beer and ale. Supplies of fuel, for food processing or for the household, were also recorded there.

The different spaces in the house therefore served the activities revealed in the previous chapters – the processing, cooking and consumption of food and drink, conviviality and the provision of rest and of ordering storage – in part divided into distinct spaces, but also with overlapping domains of actions. In the view of Pearson and Richards the rectilinear nature of Western dwellings has had the effect of constraining, compartmentalising and segregating the holism of human existence.[2] Figure 6.1 is designed to represent the manner in which actions were thus focussed on spaces but also overlapped the physical divisions. It is this ambiguity which undermines the structuralist view of the domestic domain as 'activity systems' in 'systems of settings',[3] although that analysis does acknowledge that mutable semi-fixed features may be better indicators of activities than built structures. Indeed, it is possible to see the changing architectural arrangements of the dwelling through the seventeenth century not only as a framework which altered the use and meaning of space, but also as a response to an earlier shift in object distribution and activities. Being relatively permanent, architecture is a powerful element in the continuity of *habitus*, predicating the organisation of activities in space, but may well have to be altered to accommodate intentional change in 'practice'.

Having established what the Thame inventories tell us of the objects in these named domestic spaces, to what extent were the actions which they evidence based on tradition? The use of the principal room names – hall, chamber and parlour – considerably precedes the seventeenth century. Sourcing these terms to their likely origin might reveal conventions of use and meaning, and notions of house form and organisation still prevalent in the early modern period.

The architectural and documentary evidence from the twelfth and thirteenth centuries suggests that the hall was the principal communal space for eating and living (not without internal social differentiation), complemented by a chamber for retirement. Both hall and chamber were used for socialisation, in elite houses the great chamber being an important and select commensal space. In the late Middle Ages elite houses were divided into the hall, chamber and service areas. Scant evidence from peasant housing, such as the early fourteenth-century Mill Farm Cottage at Mapledurham in Oxfordshire, suggests here also that the hall was complemented by a service area. In urban contexts the configuration of dwellings was adapted to the

[2] M. P. Pearson and C. Richards, 'Architecture and Order: Spatial Representation and Archaeology', *Architecture and Order*, ed. Pearson and Richards, pp. 59–60

[3] A. Rapoport, 'Systems of Activities and Systems of Settings', *Domestic Architecture and the Use of Space*, ed. S. Kent (Cambridge: Cambridge University Press, 1990), p. 12

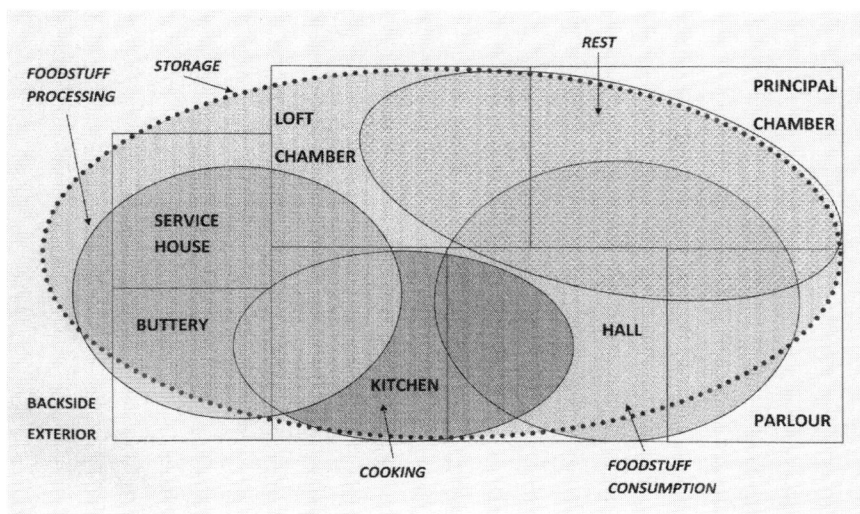

Figure 6.1 Schematic diagram of the distribution of domestic activities in relation to building structure

frequently more restricted conditions on narrow and elongated burgage plots, but was here also centred on the hall.[4] Contemporary commentators indicated a prescribed role for these spaces. The hall was for the preparation and consumption of food: 'In halle make fyre at yche a mele'.[5]

The parlour off the hall was seen as the place of private retirement for the lord of the house, and as early as the late fourteenth century the poet Langland complained that the lord and his lady preferred the privacy there away from the company in the hall: 'Now hath vche riche a reule to eten bi hym-selue In a pryue paloure'.[6] The parlour was also a place of retirement for the householder; Thomas Phelips in 1588 referred to the 'the parlour where I do customably rest and lie'.[7]

The chamber was seen as a place of retirement for the whole family although it could also be a place of private reception; 'In a chalmer preualy,

[4] J. Grenville, *Medieval Housing* (London and Washington: Leicester University Press, 1997), pp. 66, 86–9, 153–7

[5] *OED*; J. O. Halliwell-Phillipps, ed., *The Boke of Curtasye: An English Poem of the Fourteenth Century* (London: Printed for the Percy Society by C. Richards, 1841), p. 388

[6] *OED*; William Langland, *The Vision of William Concerning Piers the Plowman; Together with, Vita de Dowel, Dobet, et Dobest secundum Wit et Resoun*, ed. Walter W. Skeat (London: Trübner 1869), B. x. 97

[7] Quoted in M. Girouard, *Life in the English Country House* (New Haven and London: Yale University Press, 1978), p. 58

He held him and his cumpany'.[8] Barley suggests that chambers were found in association with the hall on the ground floor of the rural dwelling in the south-east of England from the thirteenth century, and would have been commonplace in Oxfordshire in the Tudor period.[9] However, from the early seventeenth century in Thame it is evident that chambers were more commonly found on the first floor of the dwelling, evidenced by the use of the description 'over' the hall, parlour, and other ground-floor rooms.[10] This may be a part of Hoskins' Great Rebuilding of vernacular buildings in the later sixteenth century; the insertion of chimney breasts and floors to create upstairs chambers permitted a marked expansion in the accommodation available.[11]

The kitchen was from the Middle Ages a space dedicated to the preparation and cooking of food. In non-elite dwellings in the early modern period there are strong indications that it was primarily a place for the storage of cooking utensils, and possibly also the preparation of food prior to cooking at the hall hearth. In 1656 Finett related the unsatisfactory arrangement of 'Giving him a lodging to lye in and no Kitching to dress his meate in'.[12] From the old French *bouteillerie* for a place to store bottles, the buttery was traditionally associated with the storage and distribution of drink: 'Take them to the Butterie, / And giue them friendly welcome euerie one'.[13] The cellar was a more general-purpose storage space. The term 'house' was used as a suffix to terms for various foodstuff processes we have already examined, such as the malt-, brew- and bakehouse. Yarranton was advising his readers in 1677: 'You must have a Bake-house and Brew-house of your own.'[14]

It therefore appears that in large part the named rooms in the Thame dwellings were continuing a traditional understanding of the spatial differentiation of domestic activities. As Rapoport observes, architecture cues social interaction.[15] The spatial divisions within the dwelling and their traditional nomenclature seem to have carried for contemporaries powerful significance. But in that activities overlapped the built divisions it appears that the functional differentiation was not clear cut. Rather

[8] OED; John Barbour, *The Bruce; or, The History of Robert I, King of Scotland* (c. 1375) (London: G. Nicol, 1790)

[9] M. W. Barley, *The English Farmhouse and Cottage* (London: Routledge & Kegan Paul, 1961), p. 44

[10] N. W. Alcock and C. R. J. Currie, 'Upstairs or Downstairs', *Vernacular Architecture* 20 (1989), 21–3, 21–3

[11] W. G. Hoskins, 'The Rebuilding of Rural England, 1570–1640', *Past and Present* 4 (1953), 44–59

[12] Sir John Finett, *Finetti Philoxenis* (London, 1656), p. 168

[13] William Shakespeare, *The Taming of the Shrew*, Induction, Scene i, *The Globe Illustrated Shakespeare: The Complete Works Annotated* (New York: Greenwich House, 1986)

[14] Andrew Yarranton, *England's Improvement by Sea and Land* (London, 1677), p. 163

[15] Rapoport, 'Systems of Activities and Systems of Settings', pp. 9, 16

than segregating activities, spatial differentiation may have been also a means of conveying through similar activities different social meanings. So the significance of food and drink consumption could have been altered by the spatial context, more select and discriminating in the chamber and the parlour than in the hall. If the functional and social use of the dwelling was governed by tradition, it was also open to variation and adaptation, as we shall examine below.

First, to what extent was the functional and social differentiation of domestic space a characteristic of all dwellings, and to what extent variable according to social and economic status and time? Table 6.4 illustrates the combination of different room types by dwelling size in the four quarters of the century from 1598 to 1698. The smallest dwellings of one and two rooms consisted largely (and in the case of one-roomed dwellings almost entirely) of a hall, and a chamber, with the occasional addition of a service house, parlour, kitchen or buttery in the second half of the century. In the middle-sized three- and four-roomed dwellings the hall was still nearly ubiquitous and the increased number of rooms were predominantly chambers, averaging around two per household. Parlours, butteries and especially kitchens were more frequent in this size of dwelling later in the century and the service house in the second half of the century. The largest households, with five or more dwelling rooms, still featured the hall but, as might be expected, the number of dwelling rooms was largely increased by additional chambers, averaging around 4.5 earlier in the century but declining to around 3.5 in the latter part. There was marked increase in the number of lofts in the last quarter. The parlour and kitchen

Table 6.4 Domestic spaces: mean frequencies by dwelling size and date

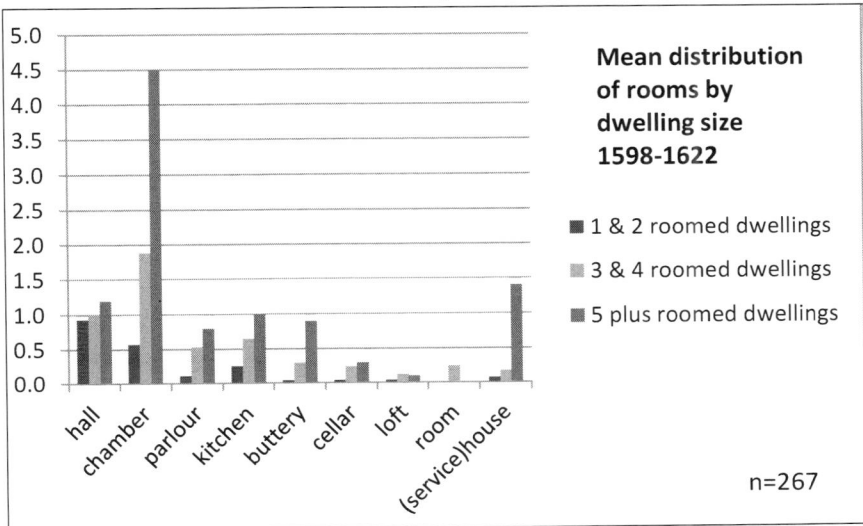

217

Table 6.4 (continued) Domestic spaces: mean frequencies by dwelling size and date

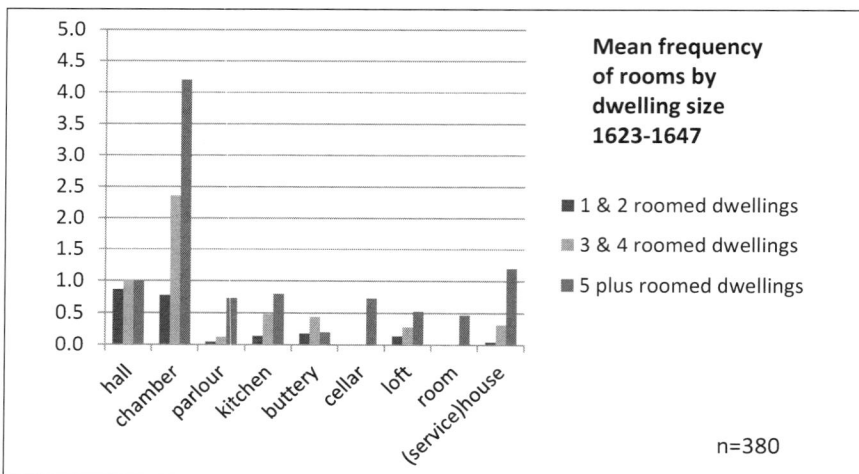

Mean frequency
of rooms by
dwelling size
1623-1647

■ 1 & 2 roomed dwellings

▨ 3 & 4 roomed dwellings

■ 5 plus roomed dwellings

n=380

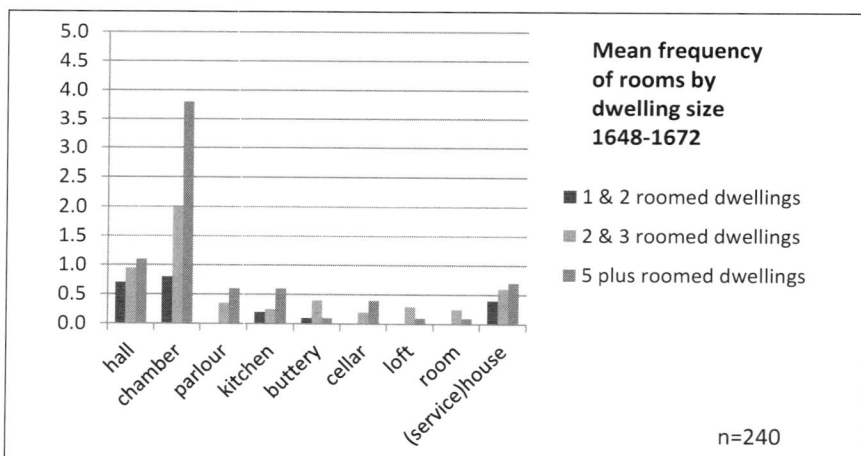

Mean frequency
of rooms by
dwelling size
1648-1672

■ 1 & 2 roomed dwellings

▨ 2 & 3 roomed dwellings

■ 5 plus roomed dwellings

n=240

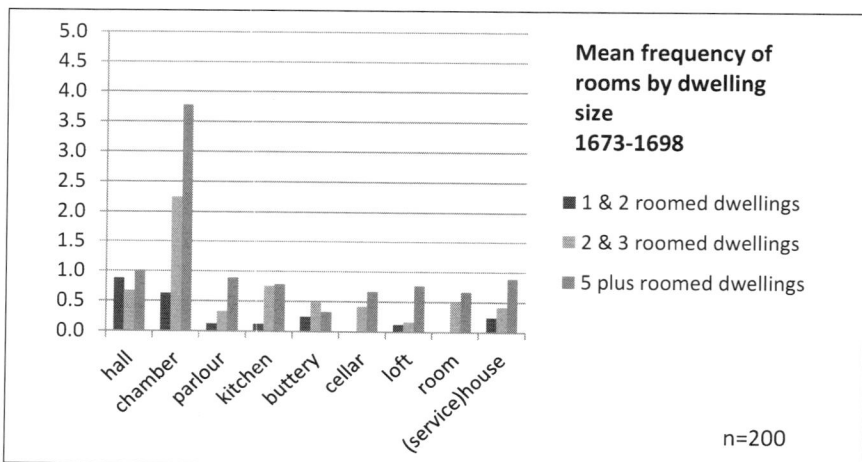

Mean frequency of
rooms by dwelling
size
1673-1698

■ 1 & 2 roomed dwellings

▨ 2 & 3 roomed dwellings

■ 5 plus roomed dwellings

n=200

also featured prominently in these households throughout the century. The incidence of butteries declined through the century, whilst that of cellars increased. In the early part of the century there was a marked preponderance of service houses (averaging one per household) in these larger dwellings, declining somewhat by the end of the century, whilst smaller dwellings were acquiring the same facilities. To summarise, all dwellings throughout the century were centred on the hall, with the number of dwelling rooms increased by chambers and to a lesser extent lofts – in larger dwellings supplemented by parlours – and kitchens, butteries, cellars and service houses. There was also a small but marked incidence and increase in the number of spaces which were described by the generic term 'room' in larger dwellings in the latter part of the century, the possible significance of which will be discussed below. If it is true that the additional named spaces offered some degree of social as well as functional differentiation, then their increased number in larger dwellings suggests more complex organisation and internal hierarchies. The mean number of dwelling rooms per household increased by 38% between the first and last quarter of the century, as illustrated in Table 6.2b. In Table 6.2c we see that the number of dwellings with one room decreased by 80%, and two-roomed dwellings by 33% whilst the percentage of those with three rooms stayed approximately static, increasing by only 5%. Dwellings with four rooms increased over the century by 90%, those with five rooms by 42% and those with six or more rooms by 90%. The century therefore sees a shift towards dwellings with more rooms, with implications for the way in which household life was organised, providing opportunities for the separation of activities and greater social distinctions. We will therefore now examine in detail the way in which the objects and associated actions within domestic spaces varied with the passage of time and according to the size of the dwelling, and by implication social status.

Halls

Examining the mean frequency of object groups in halls,[16] over all four quarters there was a predominance of eating vessels (diminishing from a mean frequency of around seven items to five over the century), cooking irons and cooking utensils, suggesting the presence of a hearth. Seating was also listed in the hall throughout the century, initially at an average of around six items (which were a combination of both single and multiple forms of seating and therefore representing seating for a company of around ten), and dropping later in the century to around four items, (or seating for around six) and cushions in first two quarters, and an average of one table.

[16] See online Appendix 1, Table 6.10, 'Halls: mean frequency of grouped objects by date', at http://boybrew.co/9781783270415

An average of one cupboard (as display-storage furniture) occurred in the first three quarters, and drinking vessels appeared in the last quarter. The most striking diachronic variation is the larger number of object groups in the hall in the first quarter, including bedding and bed linen. This is explained by the fact that the first quarter was the period when the most dwellings of one room only, almost always the hall with sleeping furniture, occurred (see Table 6.2c). This would also explain the presence in this quarter of linen of various descriptions and furniture for storage. So, apart from the first quarter, when the existence of the hall as the only dwelling room manifests itself in the object groups, the hall was consistently through the century a place, with perhaps the principal hearth of the household, of cooking and commensality, but it appears that the company diminished and dined here with less conviviality (with the disappearance of cushions and the cupboard) over the passage of the century.

By assessing the number of object groups – that is, the number of different activities – within the hall, it is possible to deduce the degree of specialisation and differentiation of space within the dwelling.[17] The largest number of such object groups is found in halls in the smallest dwellings of one and two rooms (due to the inclusion of single-roomed dwellings consisting only of the hall and therefore used for a wide range of domestic purposes), and the smallest number in the largest dwellings. The increase in the number of rooms in the household therefore resulted in a specialised use of space and the shifting of activities away from a communal core to other space. In the halls of the smallest dwellings we find sleeping furniture, bedding, bed linen and storage furniture for the latter. In the halls of dwellings of all sizes there was a predominance of cooking utensils and irons (indicating the presence of a hearth), eating vessels and cutlery. The seating furniture in the hall averaged around four items in the smallest dwellings and was unsurprisingly more numerous in the larger, averaging over six items and reflecting the greater number to seat and feed. There were also cushions in the medium and larger dwellings, suggesting more comfort. The mean frequency of tables rose from one in the smallest dwellings towards two in the largest, again accommodating a larger company. In all dwellings there was a cupboard for display and storage of consumption vessels in the hall. So, apart from single-roomed dwellings – where it was also used as sleeping accommodation and storage – in different sized dwellings the hall appeared to be employed for the same activities, the preparation and collective consumption of food and drink, in larger dwellings indicating larger household numbers.

As already mentioned, the hall was not always part of an assemblage of rooms, but could stand alone as the sole living space. Whilst it true that

---

[17] See online Appendix 1, Table 6.11, 'Halls: mean frequency of grouped objects by dwelling size'

the listing of one room only in an inventory is not conclusive proof that that was the full extent of the decedent's dwelling, in the case of Thomas Clerke whose inventory was dated 1602,[18] a shepherd of the hamlet of Moreton outside Thame, his hall contained all that was necessary for a simple way of life: seating, cooking vessels, eating and drinking vessels, a flockbed and bedding, coffers, his apparel and the milk bowls and buckets of his occupation, in a form of hall dwelling still extant in modified form in the hamlet. The single hall dwelling was an arrangement which belonged to the beginning of the period under review; of the ten inventories which fall into this category nine were dated between 1603 and 1627, and just one in 1665. In percentage terms single-roomed dwellings made up 13% of inventoried households in first quartile, 3% in second quartile and only 1% in third quartile. These would appear to have been the poorest households, with an average total furnishings value of £8.25, less than a third of the average value for all households in the study of £28.19. The occupations of these decedents were generally at the lower end of the economic scale represented in the inventories: 1 shepherd, 2 labourers (one described as a 'yeoman labourer'), 1 yeoman and 3 widows. A glover and carpenter both inventoried in 1627 with a single-roomed households had higher average contents value of £14.93 (the occupation of the decedent in 1665 was unspecified). The mean frequency of objects found in halls as the sole dwelling space[19] displays a wide range of fifteen object types: cooking vessels and cooking irons, hearth tools, seating (averaging three items) and a table, sometimes a cupboard, lighting, a bedstead, bedding, linen and storage furniture, and apparel. Such dwellings provide us with a useful insight into the probable nature of the living conditions for the large portion of the population which fell below the economic level of inventoried households.

Chambers

As noted above, the increase in the number of dwelling rooms came first from the addition of chambers to the hall. In the broad survey looking at the general range of object groups found in each room (Table 6.3), the chamber appears to have been dedicated primarily to sleeping and to the storage of household goods. If we take the value of furnishings as being indicative of the status of a domestic space, then chambers and the furnishings of sleep were of considerable importance, perhaps a reflection of the high relative cost of fabrics, but also the emphasis placed on 'comfort'. An average investment of £5.70 was made in furnishing chambers, greater by some 62% than

[18] OHCA: MS. Wills Pec. 34/3/24
[19] See online Appendix 1, Table 6.12, 'Halls as sole dwelling room: mean frequency of grouped objects'

that of the £3.55 in all other dwelling rooms. Unlike halls, parlours and kitchens, of which there were ordinarily only one per dwelling, chambers could range in number from one to seven. This allowed for a degree of variation in the nature and value of the furnishing of different chambers in a dwelling, with implications not only for their use but also for their status. This differentiation was reflected in the nomenclature of chambers. Five chambers were described as 'great' between 1607 and 1665 in dwellings of six to nine rooms belonging to 3 yeomen, 1 baker and 1 widow, and sixteen chambers were described as the 'best' between 1636 and 1692 in the dwellings of 2 gentlemen, 4 yeomen, 3 victuallers, a malster, milliner, dyer, ploughwright, barber, scrivener and a widow, representing some of the more prosperous households. There was a considerable difference between the furnishing value of the principal chamber and that of secondary chambers.[20] Making a comparison of these values between the first and last quarters of the seventeenth century reveals that principal chambers in the smaller dwellings consumed some 60% of the expenditure on all chamber furnishings, rising to around 75% later in the century, whilst even in larger dwellings, obviously with more chambers to furnish, the percentage both at the start and end of the century was over 50%. Examining the relationship of the second chamber to the principal, again in terms of furnishing value, shows that at the start of the century it was approximately half the furnishing value in dwellings of all sizes, the differential later in the century slightly diminishing.[21]

As to the range of furnishing values of chambers in the same dwelling (where range values are adjusted against the mean furnishing value of *all* chambers per household),[22] at the start of the century the range was relatively insignificant in smaller dwellings, but some 2.5 times as much in larger dwellings, whilst later in the century the range in larger dwellings had diminished to that of the smaller. In other words, the distinction between the better and lesser chambers – marked at the beginning of the century – had later reduced in all dwellings. This may be due to the fact that larger households only featured servants' chambers in the first half of the century, reflecting possibly changing living arrangements and relationships with servants. Six households with between two and four chambers in total and belonging to 2 yeomen, 2 butchers, 1 cordwainer and 1 widow were listed with servants' chambers between 1598 and 1637; four households of between two and four chambers in total and belonging to a butcher, milliner, vicar and widow were listed with maids' chambers between 1598 and 1679; not the largest dwellings but predominantly urban. The butcher Rich-

---

[20] See online Appendix 1, Tables 6.13a), b) and c), 'Relationship of principal chambers to secondary chambers by furnishing values 1598–1622'; Tables 6.13 d), e) and f), 'Relationship of principal chambers to secondary chambers by furnishing values 1673–1698',

[21] Online Appendix 1, Tables 6.13b) and e)

[22] Online Appendix 1, Tables 6.13 c) and f)

ard Striblehill in 1598 had in his dwelling a chamber for both servants and maids.[23] In summary, the principal chamber enjoyed a marked differential in terms of furnishing value at the start of the century, especially in larger dwellings, but by the end of the century that had diminished, whilst in smaller dwellings the principal chamber was conversely becoming slightly more differentiated from other chambers. We could see this as a dual process: the differentiation of the principal chamber, with its significance of social distinction, diminishing whilst the level of comfort expressed in chamber furnishings increased in lesser dwellings.

We turn now to the object groups which featured in the principal and secondary chambers in the first and last quarters of the century.[24] In the first quarter bedsteads were present, around one in the principal and two in secondary chambers, and a more generous allowance of bedding (approximately six items to the bedstead) in the principal chamber, as opposed to approximately three in the secondary chambers. Significant amounts of linen were listed in both primary and secondary chambers, with approximately two items of storage furniture. In both also were seating – approximately two items evenly divided between single seating, chairs and stools, and multiple benches and forms – and a table. The evidence therefore suggests in the earlier part of the century that the principal bed-chamber was a more privileged and comfortable place of retreat furnished for a limited degree of sociability. In the latter part of the century the frequency of bedsteads had fallen slightly in both primary and secondary chambers, pointing to a lower density of chamber occupation, but the degree of comfort in terms of bedding had risen to approximately nine items on the principal and six on the secondary bedsteads, suggesting that the increase in chamber numbers later in the century was due to a desire for comfort and privacy, rather than pressure of population. Again there is ample evidence of linen of all sorts and approximately two storage items in all chambers. In both primary and secondary chambers were one table and an increased number – approximately three items – of seating, divided primarily between single seating of chairs and stools. Significantly, there is evidence of a court cupboard for the display of eating and drinking vessels, and a hearth possibly using the same flue as the hall below, and curtains on the windows.[25] Such was the arrangement in the house in the High Street in Thame analysed by Airs and Rhodes and discussed in Chapter 2.[26] This

---

[23] OHCA: MS. Wills Pec. 50/5/20

[24] See Online Appendix 1, Table 6.14 a) and b), 'Principal and secondary chambers 1598–1622: mean frequency of grouped objects'; Table 6.14 c) and d), 'Principal and secondary chambers 1673–1698: mean frequency of grouped objects'

[25] The social implications of having a space distinct from the hall for select entertainment are discussed below.

[26] M. Airs and J. Rhodes, 'Wall-Paintings from a House in Upper High Street, Thame', *Oxoniensia* 45 (1980), 235–59

suggests the greater use of the principal chamber later in the century for select consumption and conviviality.

In conclusion, chambers were clearly spaces dedicated to sleeping and storage, but in larger dwellings there existed a differentiation in terms of the value of furnishings in a principal chamber. This surplus was mainly expressed in additional textiles, hangings, bedding and linen. The principal chamber appears also to have been the domain, especially in the later part of the century, of some form of socialising. Given that the hall with its furnishings of commensality also existed in these dwellings at this period, this suggests that the principal chamber provided the householder with the opportunity for discriminating sociability and hospitality removed from the main household. This may have been a delayed emulation of the role of the great chamber in the elite house in the later sixteenth century, a place of select entertainment in the form of eating, drinking, conversing and dancing away from the servants in the hall.[27] It would also have represented a significant break with the inclusive commensality of the hall. In the lower gentry, yeoman and tradesman's dwelling the extent of the accommodation may have permitted a partial imitation of this social differentiation, reflected in the nomenclature of the principal chamber, allowing the householder to express social aspirations beyond the household.

Lofts

Although only thirty-three lofts are recorded, their frequency increased during the study period (see Table 6.4). The broad overview of spatially defined activities in Table 6.3 indicates that they performed a similar function to that of chambers, as places of retirement and rest, but object groups indicate that, perhaps as a complement to the notion of distinct spaces facilitating the ordering of domestic life, lofts might have served as repositories for miscellanea. The mean frequency of object groups in lofts by date and by dwelling size (admittedly with small sample sizes due to the limited incidence of lofts)[28] indicates that rest remained an important function, with furnishings for sleeping, bedsteads, bedding and bed linen, in the first, third and fourth quarters of the study period, and with storage for all types of linen in the first and third quarters, and apparently storage of cooking utensils and irons too. This also sometimes appears to have been a place of some sort of social association, having a table and two or three items of seating in the first and fourth quarters. But in addition the loft served as a repository for a wide and varying range of objects. Brewing utensils were recorded in the first quarter and domestic foodstuffs in

[27] Girouard, *Life in the English Country House*, p. 88
[28] See online Appendix 1, Table 6.15, 'Lofts: mean frequency of grouped objects by date'

the second and third quarters, ranging from apples and bacon to cereals, maslin and wheat, and the 130 cheeses of the yeoman Edward Kent in 1658.[29] The loft, then, served in all quarters as an additional sleeping space, but also for the storage, diminishing towards the end of the study period, of a considerable miscellany other household objects. Analysed by dwelling size,[30] lofts in the smallest dwellings again served mainly for sleeping, with an average of one bedstead, bedding and bed linen, and storage for linen. The presence of cooking irons and cutlery was also recorded, and the provision of a table and seating. In approximately half of these smallest dwellings the loft was the second room (the hall being the other room), and could thus have served for some kind of sociable retreat. In 1638 Margaret Greene bequeathed to her son William 'the table & forme in ye lofte'.[31] In the medium-sized dwellings again there is incidence of sleeping furniture, a bedstead, bedding and linen, with storage furniture for the same, and the storage of cooking utensils, and eating and drinking vessels. There is, however, no table or seating, presumably provided elsewhere. The storage of yarn provides evidence of textile production. In the larger dwellings the loft contained fewer object groups. Stored there were textile yarn and brewing utensils, and it still retained its role as a sleeping place, with bedstead and bedding. In summary, the loft appears to have provided in all instances sleeping accommodation and storage for the miscellany of domestic life, but in smaller dwellings also additional social space.

Parlours

As we have already seen in Table 6.3, parlours manifested a variety of functions through the objects found there: sleeping accommodation in the form of a bedstead, bedding and bed linen, storage furniture, and also multiple seating, a table and cupboard. It therefore appears to have been a more private multifunctional space situated off the hall, available to the head of the household for personal retirement and for more select conference or socialising; in the collective household it was a place of privacy or discriminating association. There was no marked variation in the frequency of parlours during the study period; in the first quarter parlours were found in 36% of inventoried households, in the second quarter in 24%, in the third quarter in 32% and in the fourth quarter in 41%. But there was a clear association of parlours with larger dwellings, being found in only 7% of one- and two-roomed dwellings, 31% of three- and four-roomed dwellings and 72% of dwellings with five or more rooms. During the century

---

[29] OHCA: MS. Wills Pec. 44/4/9
[30] See online Appendix 1, Table 6.16, 'Lofts: mean frequency of grouped objects by dwelling size'
[31] OHCA: MS. Wills Pec. 39/4/26

there were approximately the same numbers of object groups found in the parlour in each quarter, so there was no perceptible diachronic change in the volume of activity.[32] In the first quarter there is evidence of sleeping, with the limited presence of a bedstead with bedding and bed linen, a continuation of sixteenth-century practice. The storage furniture listed may have served for the security of the valuable possessions of the head of the household, as well as the linen found there. There was in this period limited seating (averaging two items) with cushions and one table, which with the eating vessels and cupboard (display-storage furniture) may have served for more select socialising than that in the collective hall. Much the same pattern is revealed in the second quarter, with the mean frequency of seating items rising to three. In the third quarter there was a rise in both the number of object groups, including greater evidence of a hearth, and in the mean frequency of seating items to seven with cushions, still around one table, which now appears to have been furnished with a carpet. The picture is one of a comfortable sociable retreat furnished for a moderate company. Again in the fourth quarter seating remained numerous at a mean frequency of six items, and although bedding and linen was present with storage furniture, a bedstead was absent; instead books and pictures appeared for the first time. On this evidence the parlour, therefore, appears to have been at the start of the century a private retreat, a secure storage location and space for discreet socialising by the head of the household, tending towards the end of the century to the comfortable entertainment of a larger company, possibly an alternative space to the principal chamber for discriminating peer entertainment away from the household.

Examining parlours in relation to the size of the dwelling shows a consistent number of object groups in households of all sizes, with essentially the same object-activities represented but in varying frequencies.[33] In one- and two-roomed dwellings we find evidence of furnishing for rest; bedding, bed linen and a bedstead. Storage furniture is evident, with an average of three items. Seating was also present but limited to two items with one table. A cupboard (display-storage furniture) indicates vessels used for consumption of food and drink, and the cooking vessels found here may have been simply stored, or used with a chafer. In the parlours of three- and four-roomed dwellings a bedstead, bedding and bed linen were recorded, with storage furniture (averaging two items), presumably for table and cupboard linen which appeared here as well. Seating had increased in frequency to a mean of three items with cushions and one table. In the larger households with five or more dwelling rooms the bedstead was absent, but bedding and bed linen were still in evidence.[34]

---

[32] See online Appendix 1, Table 6.17, 'Parlours: mean frequency of grouped objects by date'
[33] See online Appendix 1, Table 6.18, 'Parlours: mean frequency of grouped objects by dwelling size'
[34] Being more numerous, items such as bed linen may still appear at a mean frequency

Storage items had fallen to a mean frequency of one item, whilst that of seating had risen to five items with cushions and one table. Fire irons suggest the presence of a fire. In summary, as dwellings increased in size the parlour shifted from a place primarily of retreat to one of more extensive and comfortable, if discerning, sociability. Both as dwellings increased in size, and as the century passed, this trend becomes evident, indicating an evolution in the manner in which space was being used to conduct social relationships both within and quite possibly beyond the household.

Dressing Domestic Space: Painted Cloths, Wainscot Panelling, Portals, Window Curtains and Carpets

It has been noted that the tenor of social engagement is suggested not only by object-related activities, but by the associations or agency of objects. And the same applies to the embellishment of the domestic environment, such as the painted cloths and wainscot panelling listed in the Thame dwellings. Ayres notes that painted cloths with narrative or naturalistic designs were popular in Tudor houses.[35] Harrison stated: 'the walls of our houses in the inner sides ... be hanged with tapestry, arras work, or painted cloths, wherein either divers histories, or herbs, beasts, knots, and suchlike are stained'.[36] The ninety-eight instances of painted cloths in thirty-eight Thame households all occurred between 1598 and 1643, apart from two in 1692 and 1694 respectively in the great chamber of John Striblehill, gent, and the parlour chamber of Thomas Middleton, clerk.[37] Their purpose was not only decorative but made timber-framed dwellings less draughty, the distribution within dwellings being largely divided between halls (48%) and chambers (41%), with most of the remainder (8%) in parlours. Painted cloths were found in low frequencies across all occupational status, but more frequently in the households of gentlemen and clerics, and in those of husbandmen, agricultural labourers, artisan-traders and widows-spinsters.[38] Similarly they were found in dwellings of all sizes, in greater frequency in larger dwellings but also in the smallest. They were then a form of interior embellishment, perhaps already in decline but found across the range of inventoried households.

above 0.5 per parlour when the frequency of the occasional bedstead has fallen below 0.5

[35] James Ayres, *Domestic Interiors : The British Tradition 1500–1850* (New Haven and London: Yale University Press, 2003), pp. 131–2

[36] William Harrison, *The Description of England* (1587), ed. G. Edelen (Washington and New York: Folger Shakespeare Library, Dover Books, 1994), p. 197

[37] OHCA: MS. Wills Prob. 4: 11085; MS. Wills Pec. 46/3/18

[38] See online Appendix 1, Tables 6.19a) and b), 'Painted cloths: distribution by occupational status and dwelling size'

Wooden panelling, constructed in essentially the same framed form as joined furniture (Figure 4.3), also provided greater comfort and could have been embellished with decorative mouldings. The descriptive term used, 'wainscot', indicates the source of some of the material used; to quote Harrison 'the walls ... are ceiled with oak of our own or wainscot brought thither out of the East [Baltic] countries, whereby the rooms are not a little commended, made warm, and much more close than otherwise they would be'.[39] Of the fifty-eight wainscoted rooms in thirty-seven households, thirty-one (84%) were listed in the first half of the century, between 1603 and 1643, and only six (16%) between 1662 and 1690. Most wainscot panelling (67%) was in halls, with the remainder (22%) in chambers (of which half were great, best or hall chambers) and parlours (11%). The distribution of wainscot panelling by occupational status has certain anomalies.[40] Although yeomen's, traders', artisan-traders' and widows-spinsters' dwellings are well represented, there is a curious absence of gentry households. This (and the preponderance of listing in the earlier part of the century) may be explained by the fact that inventories were designed to record moveable assets. As we saw earlier, improvements in dwellings such as new floors were initially regarded as moveable assets. It may be that, having been installed in gentry houses for a longer time, the panelling was already regarded as part of the structure. Even so, wainscot panelling was markedly more frequent in larger dwellings.[41] A further significant element of interior embellishment was the portal, a wooden structure surrounding an interior doorway, creating a cer-emonial entrance. These were features in elite houses and it is interesting to note that in the Thame inventories they are listed in the principal rooms of wealthy tradesmen, earlier in the century between 1603 and 1638: the halls of Philip Pytman, shopkeeper, William Tipping, shoemaker, and his widow Anne, and in the chamber over the hall of Robert Coke, brewer.[42] The interior dressing of domestic space thus manifests a desire to emulate elite culture, and provided connotations of discriminating hospitality.

In twenty-one households throughout the century (between 1598 and 1693) window furnishings are also listed, indicating a further degree of comfort or 'ease' imparted to that space. There are fifteen listings of window curtains (nine with the rods on which they were hung) and two of shutters, predominantly divided between halls and principal chambers, found representatively in the dwellings of gentlemen, traders, artisan trad-ers, yeomen and widows-spinsters, but excluding those of artisans and agricultural labourers.

---

[39] Harrison, *The Description of England*, p. 197
[40] See online Appendix 1, Tables 6.20a) and b), 'Wainscot panelling: distribution by occu-pational status and dwelling size'
[41] See online Appendix , Table 6.20b)
[42] OHCA: MS. Wills Pec. 48/1/16; MS. Wills Pec. 52/3/12–13; MS. Wills Pec. 35/1/10

Forty-eight carpets were listed in thirty-three households spanning the entire century: those of gentlemen, clerics, yeomen, traders, artisan-traders and widows. As valuable commodities imported from a considerable distance – even the Near East – these were not to recorded in the houses of artisans and agricultural labourers, and were listed in chambers and parlours, employed customarily as table coverings rather than spread on the floor.

Kitchens

We have observed objects and attendant activities in dwelling spaces: halls, chambers and parlours. We turn now to those parts of the house that might be referred to as the service areas – the kitchen, buttery, cellar and various service houses – although the spatial division between dwelling and service activities was not always clear cut. The initial broad survey in Table 6.3 indicated a space primarily dedicated to the preparation of food for cooking, and the storage of cooking irons and utensils and eating vessels. Looking at the development of the kitchen during this study period, we see from the evidence of object groups in the first quarter that it was a space not only for the preparation of food (evidenced by cooking utensils) and possibly the occasional presence of a hearth and cooking of food (by the slight presence of hearth tools and cooking irons) but also for the storage of a wide range of objects: eating and drinking vessels, lighting in the form of candlesticks, bedding and both bed and cupboard and table linen.[43] In addition, there were husbandry implements in the four kitchens of a yeoman, shoemaker, glover and widow: axes, saws, hatchets, mattocks, handbills and a spade and utensils for brewing and for salting meat.[44] In the second quarter there is again strong evidence of the preparation of food in cooking utensils and cooking irons, and the slightly greater presence of hearth tools. Assuming that food was consumed in the hall, eating vessels, cutlery and lighting were also in the kitchen for storage. In this period a limited amount of seating furniture, around one item, appeared. Dairy utensils were also in evidence. In the third quarter we still find food preparation well in evidence with cooking utensils and irons, and possibly cooking with hearth tools. There was also the continuing storage of eating vessels and lighting, display-storage furniture in the form of a cupboard, and brewing and dairy utensils. The provision of seating furniture had grown to nearly two items. In the final quarter food preparation was again in evidence with cooking utensils and irons, and the storage of eating and drinking vessels, and cutlery. However, the processing of foodstuffs had disappeared and we now find a number of seats, nearly four items, and a table. Throughout the century the kitchen therefore appears to have been a

---

[43] See online Appendix 1, Table 6.21, 'Kitchens: mean frequency of grouped objects by date'
[44] OHCA: MS. Wills Pec.52/3/12; MS. Wills Pec.52/3/13; MS. Wills Pec.54/3/30; MS. Wills Pec.34/4/40

place for the preparation and sometimes the cooking of food, with at least the storage of processing utensils. The evidence for the presence of a cooking hearth in the kitchen is ambiguous from the inventories, since the cooking irons (averaging four items in all quarters) could be stored here for use in the hall, and hearth tools are not evident in the last quarter. The mean frequency of cooking irons in halls diminished through the study period from around four items in the first quarter to only two in the last quarter, pointing towards a shift of cooking away from the hall hearth. By the end of the century there is evidence of more seating for a company with a table, suggesting that by this time the kitchen was not only a functional space for the preparation of food but possibly also for social association (of domestics) and also for some forms of commensality.

Analysed in relation to the size of dwelling,[45] in the smallest dwellings of one and two rooms the kitchen manifests its role in the preparation of food and the storage of cooking utensils and irons, but apparently without a hearth, presumably employing the hearth in the adjacent hall. It was also the locus for the storage of eating and drinking vessels and cutlery. But in addition it contained on average one table and four items of seating, enough for a reasonable company. Brewing utensils were also recorded here, indicating that activity, even in smaller households. In the medium-sized dwellings of three and four rooms the objects listed were predominantly again for the preparation and cooking of food, but with the evidence of hearth tools suggesting the possible presence of a hearth. Eating and drinking vessels were in evidence, with cutlery, and lighting in the form of candlesticks. There was also evidence of food processing with the presence of dairy and brewing utensils. There was less seating furniture (averaging around two items) and a mean of approximately one table. In the largest dwellings we have again evidence of the preparation and cooking of food, and the possibility of a hearth, and the storage of eating and drinking vessels. However, the only processing evidenced was brewing – other processing utensils being in larger households possibly in dedicated service houses – and seating had diminished to an average of one item with no table. In relation to the size of the household, then, we gain the impression of a room which had a greater diversity of use in smaller dwellings, with food preparation only – rather than food processing – in the absence of a hearth, storage of consumption vessels and the utensils of various foodstuff processes. There was seating and table furniture sufficient for a company, but whether for commensal purposes or for use in food preparation, or both, is difficult to ascertain from the inventoried objects alone. In the larger dwellings the evidence suggests the preparation and also the cooking of food and the storage of consumption vessels. The kitchen had for long

[45] See online Appendix 1, Table 6.22, 'Kitchens: mean frequency of grouped objects by dwelling size'

served the purpose of storing cooking utensils away from the hearth in the hall, and acting as a space for the preparation of food. However, the creation of a hearth within the kitchen had the potential to change the whole dynamic of the household, shifting cooking, predominantly women's work, away from the heart of the house at the hall hearth to a more specialised but also peripheral location.

Butteries and Cellars

Butteries and cellars were both spaces dedicated to the storage of items connected with consumption. As noted in Table 6.3, butteries contained more items involved with cooking, eating and drinking, whilst cellars, holding fewer object groups, were used for foodstuff processing, brewing and salting utensils. Butteries are initially noted most in larger houses, but through the century become an element in medium-sized houses, with a slightly increased presence in smaller houses. The incidence of cellars grew through the century in medium and larger houses, possibly a reflection of the growth in size and complexity of dwellings (see Table 6.4). Butteries occurred in 29% and cellars in 23% of inventoried households. Buttery and cellar together were found in only eight (or 4%) of dwellings. The overview in Table 6.3 indicates that the functions in many ways overlapped – the storage of eating and drinking vessels, cooking utensils and irons, household utensils and some processing utensils, especially those for brewing. There are indications, through the presence of drinking vessels and cupboards, that the buttery was sometimes used as a place for sociable drinking. In terms of variation through time the number of object groups in butteries through the study period diminished from nine to five.[46] At the start of the century there was ample evidence of storage, of eating vessels (averaging twelve items) and drinking vessels (and a cupboard perhaps indicating drinking here also), cutlery, cooking utensils and lighting. The number of eating and cooking utensils diminished in the third quarter, with a mean frequency of only two eating vessels, and cooking utensils diminishing from four to two items. At the same time the frequency of foodstuff processing utensils increased: those for brewing from the second to the fourth quarters from a mean of under two to nearly four items. Dairying and salting utensils were also stored or used in a space possibly for those households that did not have dedicated service houses. The categories and volumes of objects in butteries do not show much variation according to dwelling size.[47] In all sizes of dwelling there was storage of eating vessels, ranging from a mean of

---

[46] See online Appendix 1, Table 6.23, 'Butteries: mean frequency of grouped objects by date'

[47] See online Appendix 1, Table 6.24, 'Butteries: mean frequency of grouped objects by dwelling size'

around four to seven items, drinking vessels, lighting, cooking utensils and irons. Brewing utensils were consistently listed in the butteries of dwellings of all sizes, and the household utensils consisted of barrels, tubs, troughs and stands. In medium and larger dwellings cupboards were also present and there is evidence of textile production, flax yarn, in the largest dwellings. In summary, the buttery can be seen as part of the ordering of the apparatus of the household, a space in addition to the kitchen to store commensal vessels and cooking utensils, a depository of beverage processing utensils and also possibly occasionally used in the consumption of drink.

Since cellars were predominantly a feature of larger dwellings we examine their variation through time only.[48] Unsurprisingly, brewing utensils featured in all quarters but were prominently in the second and third quarter, and the household utensils featuring in the fourth quarter included barrels, tubs and stands, such as the 'three barrells of beare six barrells one hogshed two stands' and 'one upstand' belonging to the barber James Cowden in 1691.[49] Drinking vessels also featured in the first and second quarters, reinforcing the connection with the home consumption of brewed drink. In the second quarter we also find other foodstuff processing utensils for the salting of meat.

Service Houses

The addition of service houses to dwellings for the processing of various foodstuffs not only presumably facilitated a more efficient processing of materials in larger quantities but may also have been in part the deliberate creation of a greater separation of the mundane from the social within the household. Service houses appeared more frequently in larger dwellings, predominantly those of yeomen and widows, suggesting that they were still significantly self-provisioning up to end of the century or processing foodstuffs for economic benefit. As already noted above, Yarranton in 1677 was advising his readers to create for themselves bake- and brew-houses.[50] As the century progressed, service houses occurred increasingly in medium-sized and smaller dwellings (see Table 6.4). Table 6.5 shows the chronological spread of service houses by occupational status, first evident in the households of yeomen, traders, artisan-traders and widows-spinsters, and in those of husbandmen and artisans by the second quarter of the century. There is none in the dwellings of agricultural labourers, who were possibly unable to afford the investment, and curiously none recorded in those of gentlemen, who may have considered such mundane tasks in proximity to their dwellings demeaning.

---

[48] See online Appendix 1, Table 6.25, 'Cellars: mean frequency of grouped objects by date'
[49] OHCA: MS. Wills Pec. 35/3/35
[50] Yarranton, *England's Improvement by Sea and Land*, p. 163

Table 6.5 Service houses: chronological distribution by occupational status category

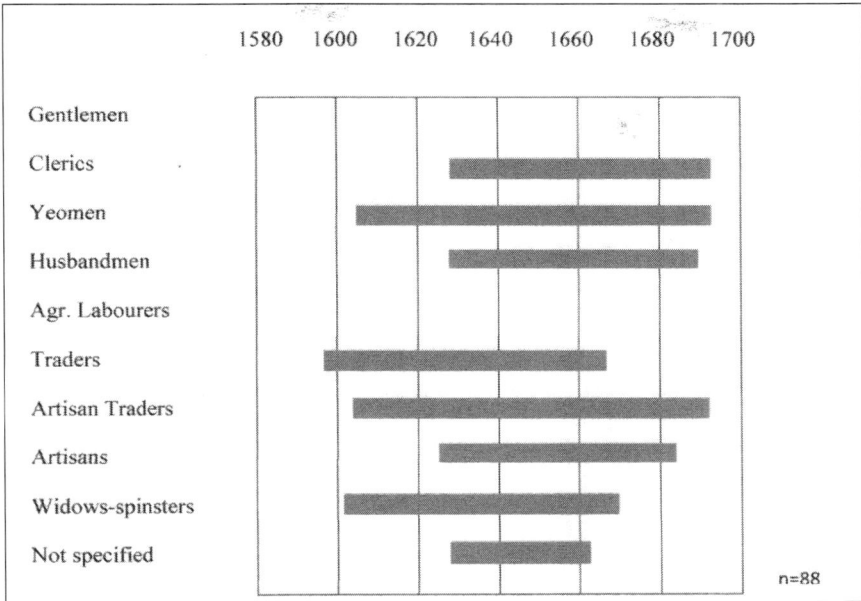

Table 6.6 Service houses: distribution in relation to dwelling size and date

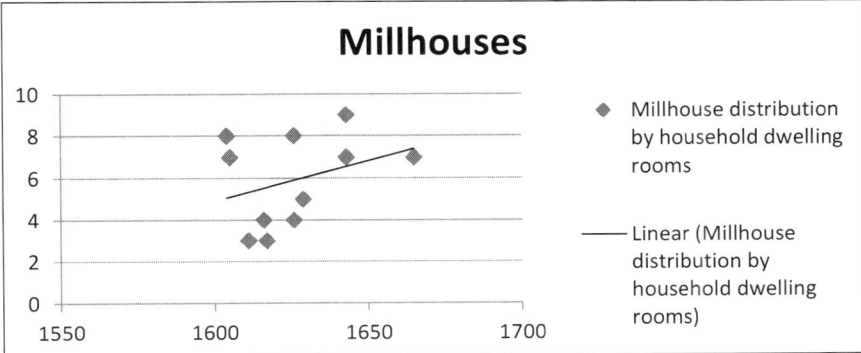

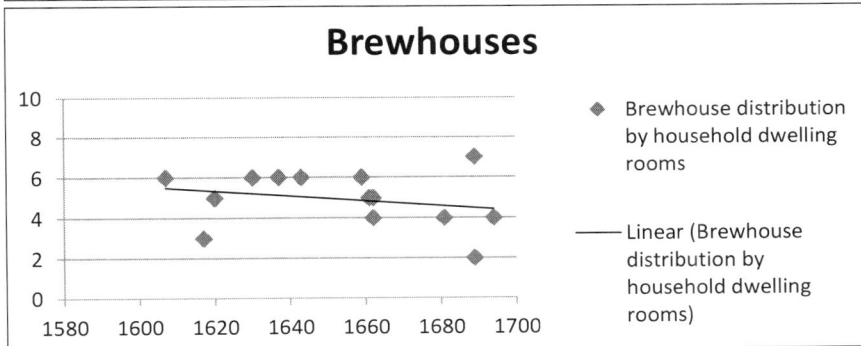

Table 6.6 (continued) Service houses: distribution in relation to dwelling size and date

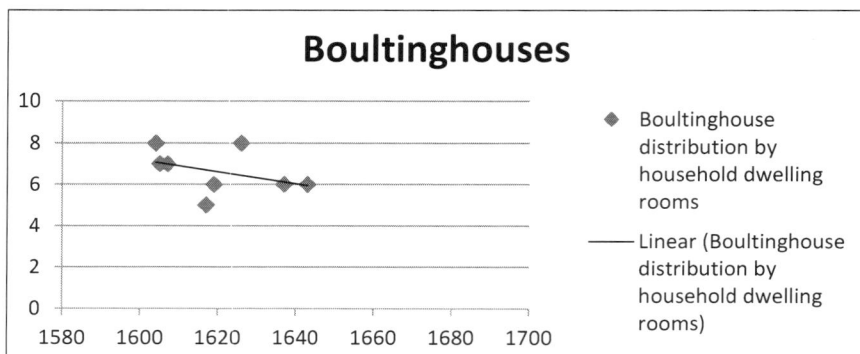

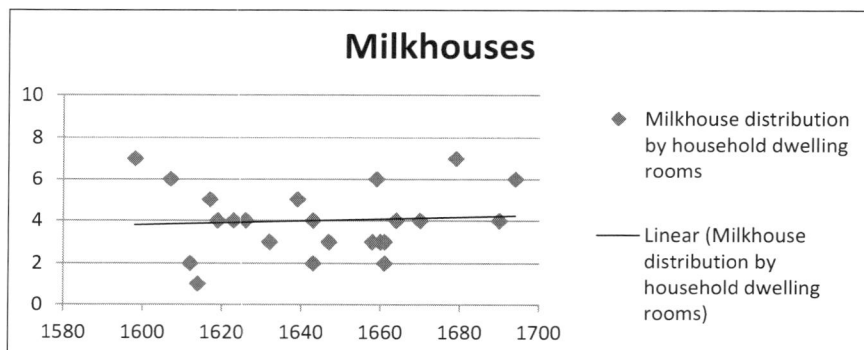

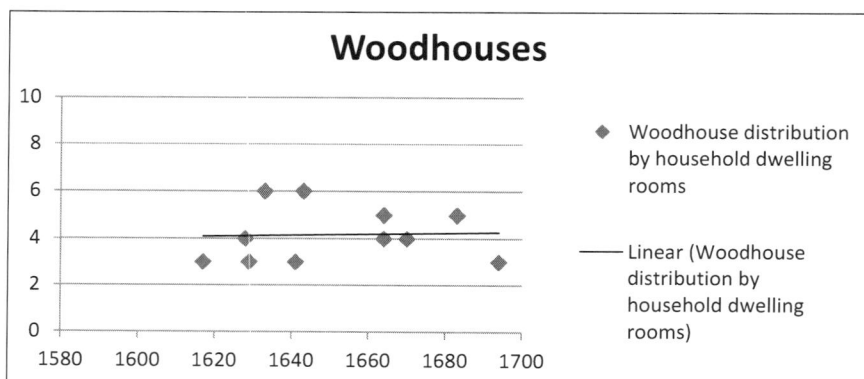

A distinction is also found in the type of foodstuff processing and the average size of the dwelling; boulting houses, for the sifting of meal, were most common in the largest dwellings averaging seven dwelling rooms, mill houses for the grinding of malt in six-roomed households, brew houses in five-roomed houses, milk houses for dairying and woodhouses for the storage of fuel both averaging four-roomed dwellings. This suggests that self-provisioning in meal and malt was the preserve of wealthier households, whilst dairying was also the occupation of smaller households. However, Table 6.6 shows that whilst brewing and dairying were processes that continued in the household throughout the century, the milling of malt and boulting of meal were activities which had disappeared from the domestic domain by the second half of the century, suggesting that these had now become commercial activities – the possible erosion of domestic production of some commodities by external commerce. Unsurprisingly, the mean frequencies of objects most commonly listed in service houses reflect the processes for which they were named.[51] In mill houses malt mills were listed amongst other brewing utensils. Other contents included chests and a shovel,[52] possibly for the storage of the malt, and tubs. In brew houses brewing utensils included coppers for boiling the mash, coolers, furnaces (along with a supply of fuel) and a mash vat, and barrels and tubs. Also found in the brewhouse of Thomas Middleton, a clerk, in 1694 were no fewer than sixty bottles, possibly for the bottling of ale or beer.[53] In boulting houses were found objects for the production of meal – boulting mills and boulting wyches and troughs – as well as the tubs and sacks of meal. The items listed in milk houses reflected the variety of products to which milk could be turned: churns for the production of butter, cheese vats, cheese presses, as well as cheese racks and shelves. In woodhouses were stored billets and firewood, and also other processing utensils for brewing. The incidence of service houses in larger households from the start of the study period, and their growing incidence in smaller households during the century, may have not only reflected increased economic activity, but also a greater internal organisation and differentiation of tasks, with implications for social and gender relationships within the household.

Rooms

The descriptor 'room' is used for only twenty-nine domestic spaces, but with increasing frequency; twelve, or 41%, of instances occurred in the last quarter of the study period. Examples of its use are the 'outward drinking

[51] See online Appendix 1, Table 6.26, 'Service houses: mean frequency of grouped objects'
[52] Listed as household utensils in online Appendix 1, Table 6.26
[53] OHCA: MS. Wills Pec. 46/3/18

room' of the baker John Burton (senior) in 1643, and the 'dining room' and 'writing room' of the gentleman John Striblehill in 1692.[54] This could be seen as a small but significant shift towards the naming of rooms in functional rather than conceptual terms, which in part displaces the traditional terms in the following century – a change in the perception of domestic space from being primarily conceptual and social to one holding commodities and defining functions.

Shops

In the discussion of the provisioning of the household it was recognised that, especially in the dwellings of agriculturalists, the processing of foodstuffs was also an economic activity. Reference has been made to the fact that the social household was as much a productive partnership as a reproductive one, and thirty-eight dwellings, those of traders, artisan-traders and artisans (as well as small number of widows and yeomen), incorporated shops for the production and sale of goods, the term being applied both to retailing and manufacturing premises. For example, John Totnall, deceased in 1631, was carrying on his trade as a mercer retailing a range of textiles; Vincent Hester, cordwainer (1605), was making and selling shoes; Thomas Shriefe, blacksmith (1664), was forging ironwares; and James Cowden, barber (1691), was grooming and possibly performing minor surgical procedures on the townsmen.[55] The inventories provide a rich vein of information on objects employed and produced in the practice of trades. However, as this study is focussed on the domestic arrangements of the household we only observe here that the operation of trades was frequently part of the daily life of the household, its social composition and relationships with the inclusion of apprentices and servants, and a significant way in which the external world crossed the threshold of the domestic domain.[56] As observed above, it seems probable from the distribution of dedicated drinking spaces in dwellings that conviviality overlapped commerce. As can be seen in Table 6.7, showing the mean frequency of shops in relation to *all* inventoried households, apart from a dip in the third quarter of the century which may be a reflection of economic disruption in the aftermath of the Civil War, there was a growing incidence of shops in dwellings throughout the study period, reinforcing the notion of the household as an economically productive unit and the picture of Thame as a thriving centre of commerce.

[54] OHCA: MS. Wills Pec. 33/2/18; MS. Wills Prob. 4 11085
[55] OHCA: MS. Wills Pec. 52/4/9; MS. Wills Pec. 41/1/38; MS. Wills Pec. 51/3/12; MS. Wills Pec.35/3/35
[56] C. King, '"Closure" and the Urban Great Rebuilding in Early Modern Norwich', *Post-Medieval Archaeology* 44:1 (2010), 54–80, 72

Table 6.7 Shops: mean frequency by date and dwelling size

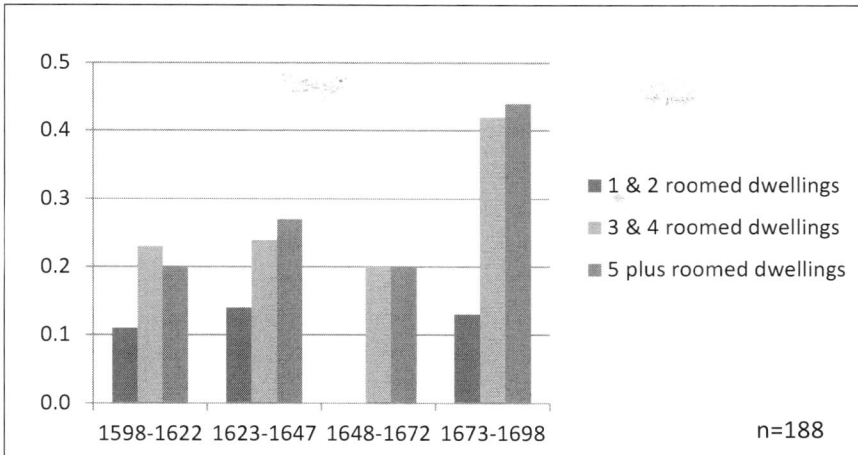

The Interrelationship of Domestic Activities and Spaces

In previous chapters we explored the activities represented by the objects listed in the Thame inventories and in this chapter those which were particularly associated with the distinct spaces in the dwelling. We saw that the traditional names given to those spaces incorporated expectations of their use and significance. No action or space exists in isolation, and as has been argued before it is the context and relationship with other actions and spaces which in large part produce meaning. The distribution of habitual actions could be seen as an early modern expression of Bourdieu's 'practice', but although the Kabyle house undoubtedly involved considerable conceptual complexity there was in the operation of *habitus* an expectation of regularity and continuity. The Thame household presents a more complex picture. The inventoried dwellings ranged considerably in size, from one to sixteen rooms. This variation in domestic space provided a range of possibilities for the distribution of activities and the resultant social dynamic. The idea of conceptually 'weighted' space provides a useful perspective with which to view the attribution of meaning to different parts of the dwelling.[57] Where the hall was the only dwelling room it accommodated all the principal activities of the household: the processing, cooking (on the household hearth) and collective consumption of foodstuffs, and the provision of rest and storage, the latter activities displaced to the chamber when that was added to the hall. The development of accommodation on an upper floor within the dwelling added another vertical spatial dimen-

---

[57] Pearson and Richards, 'Ordering the World', pp. 1–2

sion to the social dynamic. A small dwelling might also have incorporated a kitchen, at the start of the century principally a space for the storage of cooking utensils and the preparation of foodstuffs for cooking on the hall hearth, segregating some of the mundane household tasks and leaving the hall as a more distinctly social space. A parlour provided the householder with a place of retirement, and possibly discreet socialising, thus diminishing the inclusive social culture of the hall and household. The distinction of a principal chamber furnished not only for rest but for reception also provided the householder and spouse with a space for discriminating (and exclusive) hospitality. And finally the addition of service houses for various foodstuff processes further distanced the mundane and emphasised the social domains and possibly gendered role distinctions of the household.

Thus, activities were not always restricted to specific spaces but were sometimes found simultaneously in different parts of the dwelling, hence differentiating the significance and social dynamic of actions. And also, the culture of the Thame household did not remain static during the century, but underwent considerable change. The hall remained important as the centre of the household on a conceptual level but in larger dwellings diminished in its functional and social centrality. This was partly due to the shift of the cooking of food to the kitchen, which with the increased incidence of service houses led to a greater separation of the mundane from the social noted above. The parlour was altering from a private retreat for the head of household and what might be termed discreet association, to a space for discriminating association of larger companies, apparently dining there rather than in the hall. If it was used for the entertainment of outsiders, the parlour increasingly expressed *external* associations *within* the dwelling. In tandem with the development of the parlour, the role of the principal chamber also evolved as a discriminating social space. This narrative reflects, in a world of increasing commercial tempo and requirements of economic credit, the necessity of good relationships with the peer group, and with neighbours in particular.[58] The increased expenditure on furnishings in all chambers suggests both a desire to express personal and household status and a growing emphasis on the individual gratification of comfort, in a physical and conceptual sense – motivations which perhaps ultimately lie at the base of mercantile endeavour.

As a final example of the role of objects in articulating actions and the social significance of space, Tables 6.8 and 6.9 show the shifting distribution of one significant object group – seating furniture – in halls, principal chambers and parlours in the first and last quarters of the study period. In Table 6.8

---

[58] J. Boulton, *Neighbourhood and Society: A London Suburb in the Seventeenth Century* (Cambridge and New York: Cambridge University Press, 1987); Craig Muldrew, *The Economy of Obligation : The Culture of Credit and Social Relations in Early Modern England* (Basingstoke: Macmillan, 1998), pp. 125–30

Table 6.8 Frequency of all items of seating in halls, principal chambers and parlours in the first and last quarters of the seventeenth century

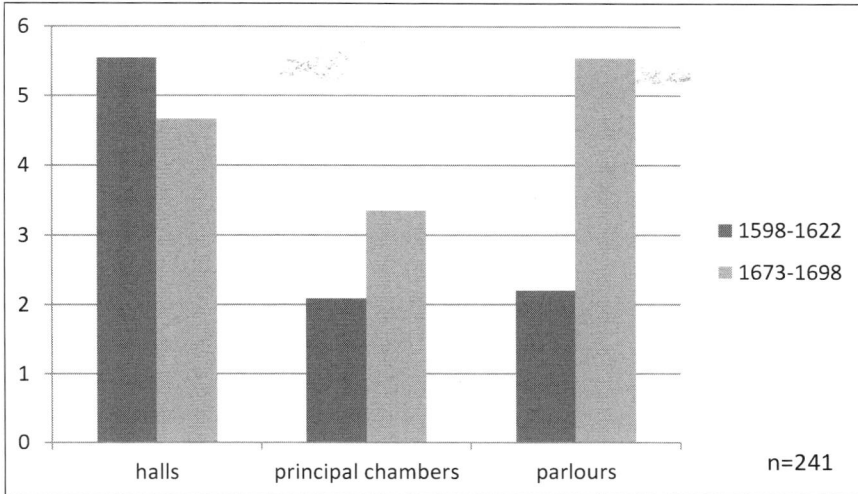

we see that the number of seating items had fallen slightly in halls, but had risen significantly in principal chambers, and more than doubled in parlours. Breaking this down into different sorts of seating – higher-status chairs, singular-seat stools and multiple-seat benches and forms – we see in Table 6.9 that in halls the frequency of chairs had approximately doubled from a low base of one, whilst those of stools and multiple benches and forms had fallen significantly. In principal chambers the number of chairs quadrupled during the period, whilst those of stools and benches and forms, in lower numbers, fell slightly. But it was in parlours that the most dramatic transformation occurred, with the number of chairs multiplying approximately tenfold, whilst stools virtually disappeared, and multiple-seat benches and forms remained low and diminished in frequency. This redistribution tells the story of a changing social dynamic in the household: of the introduction of a moveable form of seating which privileged the individual, and a shift away from communal to selective social engagement. An attempt to present this complex and shifting picture in the whole dwelling in a simplified and schematic form is given in Figure 6.2, which illustrates the manner in which increased internal compartmentalisation in the form of more rooms, within which assemblages of objects cued diverse actions varying according to status and time, facilitated the distancing of the mundane from the social – in the development of the kitchen into a cooking space and in the creation of distinct foodstuff processing areas – and permitted in the principal chamber and parlour more discriminating commensality than that of the collective hall. The implications of such changes are discussed further in the final

Table 6.9 Comparison of mean frequencies of seating types in halls, principal chambers and parlours in the first and last quarters of the seventeeth century

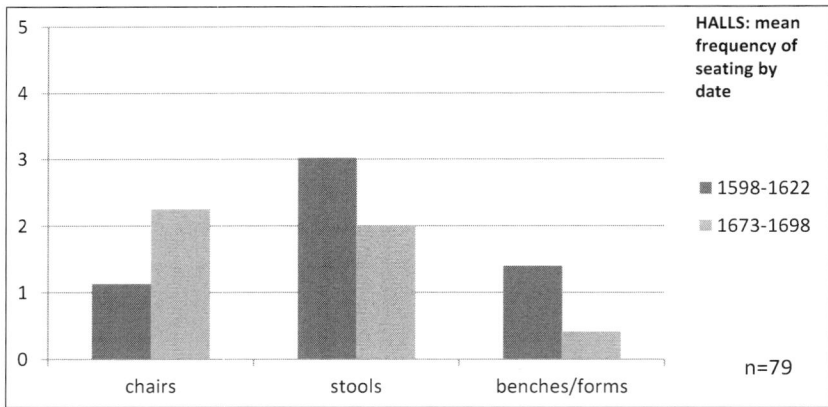

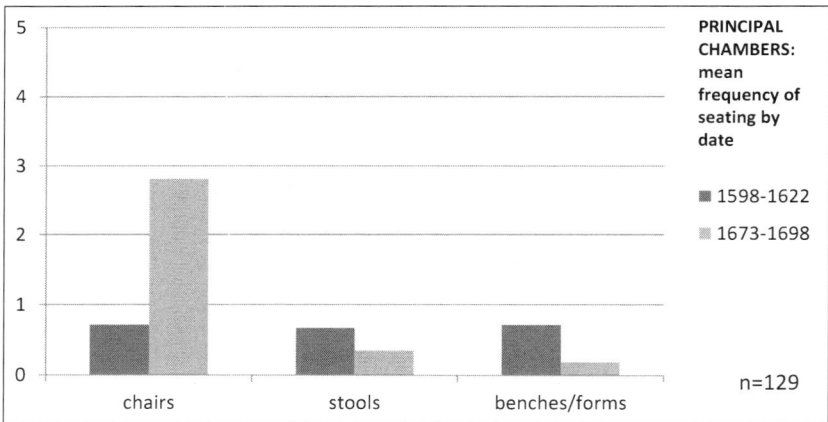

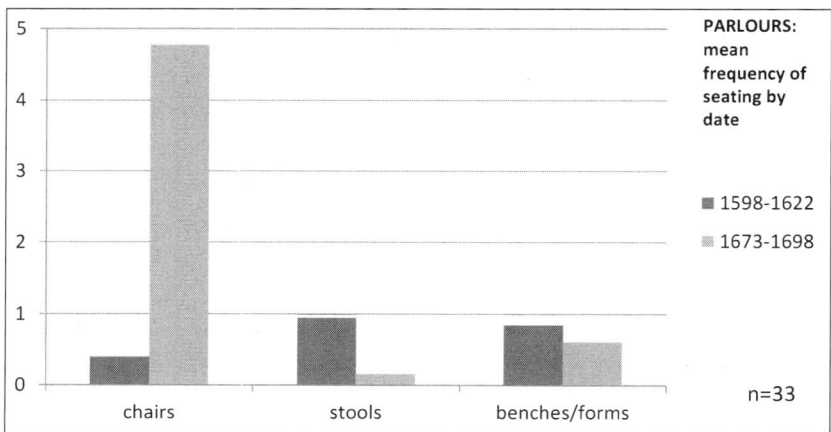

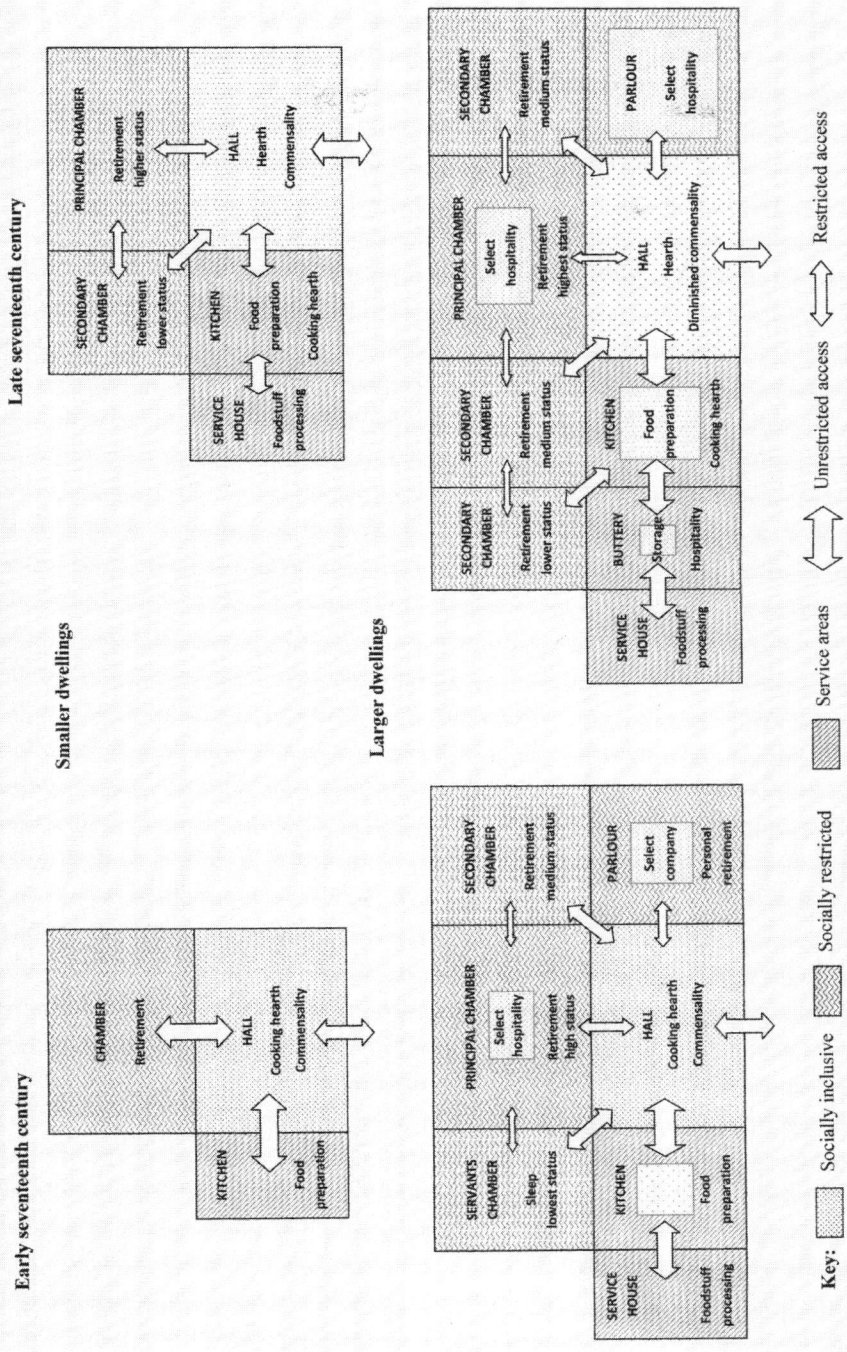

Early seventeenth century

Smaller dwellings

Late seventeenth century

Larger dwellings

Figure 6.2 Schematic representation of the spatial social dynamic within Thame households

chapter. The arrows which indicate the relative 'social flow' between spaces are a reminder of the fact that the culture of the dwelling does not consist of insulated activities but of differentiation between them. The manner in which human activity is channelled and held in the built structure of the dwelling in large part directs the social dynamic, but not without the possibility of reinterpretation.[59] In the words of Hillier and Hanson: 'The ordering of space in buildings is really about the ordering of relations between people. Because this is so, society enters into the very nature and form of buildings.'[60]

How then can we best comprehend the early modern household, and explain its internal dynamic? From the outside it appeared as a delimited, autonomous and ordered institution, as building, social group and concept, providing for the biological and cultural reproduction, sustenance, security and conviviality of its members; in effect, a society in miniature, a view articulated by contemporary commentators. However, as we have observed, the Thame household contained internal hierarchies and conflicts of loyalties and agendas. Inevitably it was an expression of the status and interests of some members of the household, notably the householder and spouse, more than others. The internal differentiation of space and activities can thus be seen as a way of ordering power and exercising control, a *habitus* of architecture and objects structuring actions and values. But in an increasingly complex society, the associations, ideologies and allegiances *beyond* the household created tensions around relationships *within*, leading to a reconfiguration of actions and the objects associated with them, ultimately reflected in an altered spatial configuration. The changes in the ordering of the Thame household in the seventeenth century suggest that the householder in part no longer wished or indeed needed to see him- or herself primarily identified with their household, but increasingly through association with peers in the wider community. Whilst select socialising with guests might be seen as a way of enhancing the social and economic standing of the household, it also involved the householder turning away from his or her household, and the invasion of the household, physically and socially, by external allegiances. The communal was being challenged and diluted by individual agendas, the invasion and fragmentation of apparent domestic homogeny by the economic and social dynamic of the world beyond. The focus of this study therefore ultimately returns to the environment in which the household was set, dependent on agriculture and trade for its subsistence, as a context for its physical entity and social associations, and – both in its establishment and in its internal dynamics – subject to a wider culture.

---

[59] F. E. Brown, 'Continuity and Change in the Urban House: Developments in Domestic Space Organisation in 17th-Century London', *Comparative Studies in Society and History* 28 (1986), 558–90, 567; B. Hillier and J. Hanson, *The Social Logic of Space* (Cambridge: Cambridge University Press, 1984), pp. 144–6; King, '"Closure" and the Urban Great Rebuilding in Early Modern Norwich', 73

[60] Hillier and Hanson, *The Social Logic of Space*, p. 2

7

Thame Households

This chapter is intended to 'flesh out' the data, which has been treated largely in a descriptive and statistical fashion in hitherto. The decision to aggregate inventory data is based on the desire to iron out anomalies of life cycle and circumstance in individual households. And yet each household does have its own special circumstances of condition and composition, frozen at the moment of the death of the householder. Wills provide valuable additional data which reveals a little of the social matrix and affections of the householder and household. These can in turn be related to other records such as parish registers, and of civil life of Thame in this period, frankpledge and quarter session records. The distribution of assets, of property and of personal belongings can reveal a little more of the world experienced by the inhabitants of Thame in the seventeenth century.[1] In this chapter nine households have been selected as approximately representative of different occupational and status groups: the yeoman, husbandman, labourer, artisan, trading artisan, trader, cleric, gentleman and widow. The line drawings for each decedent are intended only to suggest the possible spatial layout of the dwelling and its principal furnishings from the evidence of probate inventory and will. The ratio of the room furnishing value to the total furnishing expenditure is shown after each room. The exact appearance of the furniture is also conjectural, based on extant examples.

---

[1] A full prosopographic survey of the elite social networks of Thame in the seventeenth century would be possible given the extent of the available data. For an outline of methodology see Bonnie H.Erickson, 'Social Networks and History: A Review Essay', *Historical Methods: A Journal of Quantitative and Interdisciplinary History* 30:3 (1997), 149–57. As this chapter selects only nine examples of different occupational and status profiles for comparison, a circumscribed picture of such networks emerges.

Agriculturalists

John Corner, Yeoman

Yeomen were traditionally owner-occupiers of land to the value of at least forty shillings, but in practice were those agriculturalists, whatever the manner of land holding, who could produce a significant marketable surplus over domestic requirements, usually with the help of hired labour.[2] In a market community set in its fertile valley, we commence with a portrait of those households in Thame which were primarily agricultural by occupation and identity. In his will John Corner,[3] a yeoman who died in early July 1619, commended his 'soule to Allmightie God and my bodie to be buried in the Church yard of Thame'. He left a wife, Elizabeth and a son Robert, still a minor.[4] His inventory reveals his agricultural activities:[5] cultivating crops, '2 acres & a half of wheate and beanes' 'in the [common] fields', a bushel of wheat and quantities of maslin and rye near the dwelling, and raising livestock: 2 beasts, 2 bullocks, 2 hogs, 1 sow and 4 pigs. Farming life also permeated his dwelling place, with the 'backside' of his house comprising cow racks, watering and hog troughs. He also owned two horses with their harnesses, and in a long cart the means to convey crops and a dung cart manure back to the fields. The beasts' sustenance and bedding was provided by 'one parcell of hay' and 'one p[ar]cell of white straw'. The inventory also indicates the processing and consumption of the produce foodstuffs in the dwelling: the milk house with its seven 'milke bowles', a cheese press, a quantity (£4 4s)[6] of malt and a malt mill, and for brewing barrels in the cellar. For the processing of grain there were a 'wynnowinge sheete', and a boulting wych. A 'poudringe trough' would have served to salt slaughtered livestock, including the 'one flitch & a half of bacon'.

From the rooms listed in the inventory, his dwelling consisted of a hall, two chambers, kitchen, cellar and milk house (Figure 7.1). The hall was furnished for the collective consumption of food with 'one longe table and one frame' and seating of 'seven high stooles' and 'two turned chaires' with 'five greene cushions', and 'one standinge presse cup board'. Hospitality – or at least dining with a degree of status – is also suggested by three table cloths and eight napkins, and by the added decoration and comfort of 'the painted cloth about the hall'. Cooking also took place at a hearth in the

---

[2] Keith Wrightson, *Earthly Necessities: Economic Lives in Early Modern Britain 1470–1750* (London: Penguin Books, 2000/2002), p. 34

[3] OHCA: MS. Wills Pec. 34/4/32. The value of household effects in John Corner's dwelling were £26.89, against a mean for all inventoried yeomen of £35.57

[4] Under twenty-one years of age.

[5] Value of agricultural assets £20.93

[6] Where values in this chapter are quoted directly from the documentary evidence they are in pounds, shillings and pence, not their decimal equivalent

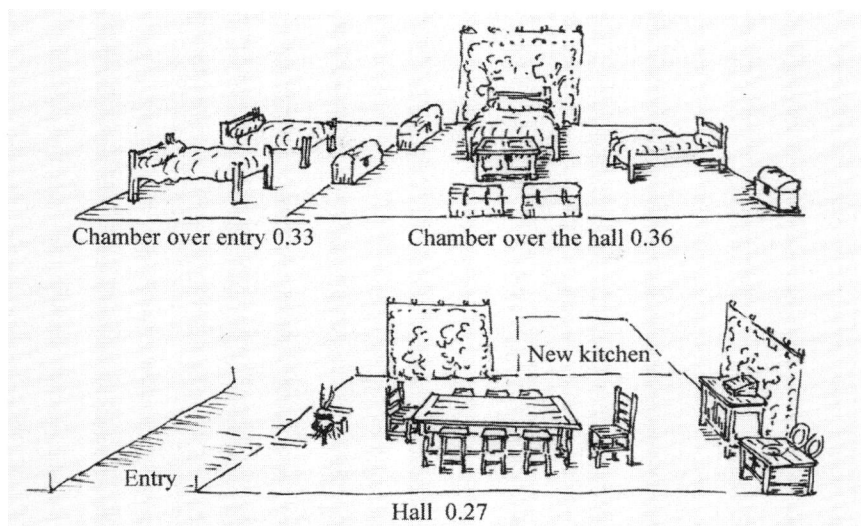

Figure 7.1 Dwelling and furnishings of John Corner, yeoman, 1619

hall, indicated by 'one paire of little [fire] doggs' on' two pott hangers' and 'one paire of great [spit] racks'. But cooking utensils were listed in another (possibly adjacent) space, the milk house. (There was also a 'new kitchen' listed, but without significant contents).[7] Three chambers are noted. The 'chamber over the hall' was frequently the principal chamber, being over the largest ground-floor space. This room represented the greatest expense in furnishing,[8] largely due to the value of £3 of the ' one standinge bedsteede' with its comfortable furnishings of 'one fetherbed' (over one flockbed and one straw bed), ' fetherbolster', 'coverlett ' and two 'blancketts'. Another bedstead and bedclothes in the room was of lesser value (£1 10s) but featured a painted cloth canopy, and for household storage no fewer than five coffers and one joined chest. A second chamber was recorded as the 'chamber ov[er] the entrye'.[9] Furniture of lesser value was listed as old; '2 old bedsteds [and one] old coverlett'. A third 'chamber ov[er] dormans shopp' had only agricultural implements and dry foodstuffs and could have

---

[7] These vagaries remind us that furnishings might well have been shifted during the upheaval following the death of the head of the household

[8] £5.50 out of a household total of £26.89. The principal bedstead and its bedclothes represent over 10% of total household furnishing value

[9] The entry was in all probability a wagon way into the backyard, as found in the house in Thame High Street recorded by M. Airs and J. Rhodes, 'Wall-Paintings from a House in Upper High Street, Thame', *Oxoniensia* 45 (1980), 235–59, noted in Chapter 2, see Figure 2.4

served as servant's quarters or – as is found frequently in chambers – for storage. Ten pairs of linen sheets are noted.[10]

John Corner's will, signed with a mark, suggests both a desire to leave a dignified legacy and also concern for his dependants, his wife Elizabeth and especially his (apparently only) son Robert. He seems to have been a man of some status in the community, appointed tithingman in 1616 for the east quarter of the town at the frankpledge court,[11] a standing confirmed by charitable donations in his will – to the parish church 10s, to the Almsmen of Thame 6d apiece, and to the poor of the parish 3s 4d. He had evidently incurred debts necessitating a mortgaging of 'certain Lands and houses' to a Michael Saunders. After discharge of this debt remaining goods were to be divided between his widow Elizabeth and his son Robert at the discretion of Michael Saunders, and his 'saide wife shall have the government of my saide sonne and the use of the stock and of my Lands and houses remaining during his minorytie'. But if she chose to remarry she was to retain only a third portion and the goods which she had brought to the marriage, and Michael Saunders, described as 'my saide trusty & Loving frend and neighbo[u]r', was to take charge of the upbringing and security of his son Robert: 'the educacon of my sayde sonne and the ordering of that stock and house and Lands for the best behoofe of my sonne'. If his son should die without issue then his share of the estate was to pass to the niece and nephew, the offspring of John Corner's two sisters, and to his sister-in-law. There is here a sense of familial responsibility and affection, and we glimpse the operation of the culture of neighbourly interdependence and obligation.[12] Michael Saunders was both a significant creditor to John Corner, presumably having assisted at a time of financial difficulty, and also a trusted friend and neighbour tasked with the equitable discharge of his estate and the ultimate care of his son and heir. Other neighbours Mr Hester and Mr Burt – the latter also serving as an appraiser – were requested to oversee the distribution of his estate, and yet others, male and female,

---

[10]   Given that John Corner died whilst his son was in his minority we might deduce that this was a household at the peak of its operation, and the indications in hall seating and linen suggest a household of perhaps half a dozen. This would indicate possibly some servants in addition to the family

[11]   The tithingman was the spokesperson for the group of (nominally ten) households joined together by a traditional system of joint surety for good conduct termed frankpledge (from the Old Saxon word 'peace-pledge'). After the termination of the Bishop of Lincoln's Thame manor in 1559, frankpledge courts and manorial courts continued to be held by the bishop's successors to the manor through the first half of the seventeenth century. The court appointed tithingmen and jurors, and regulated market activities through the appointment of inspectors of meat, flesh and ale tasters, leather sealers and scavengers. Offences tried commonly consisted of misselling foodstuffs and goods, or failing to clear waste from the street. The frankpledge system thus represents the legal significance of relationships between neighbours and households. Archer M. White, *Outlines of Legal History* (London: S. Sonnenschein, 1895), pp. 52–3; VCH

[12]   The gift to a sister-in-law is also a reminder of the importance of trusted marital liaisons

served as witnesses to an affidavit to the will. John Corner was not only a debtor to Michael Saunders but also a creditor to widow Gabrielle (to the sum of 25s) and goodwife Shrowe (10s), and Edward Grout owed him £3 2s 8d for '14 q[uar]ters of chaff' and a quantity of malt. Death, especially apparently premature, exposed the web of interdependence, both financial and affective, which provided personal and household security and comprised a significant part of the social fabric of the community.[13]

John Simons, Husbandman

Husbandmen were farmers on a smaller scale than the yeoman, able to support a family and produce a modest surplus, predominantly with family labour.[14] John Simons,[15] a husbandman, made his will in mid-June 1605, dying shortly thereafter and buried in early July. His domicile was the outlying neighbourhood of Luddesden (Ludsden; see Figure 1.3), adjacent to New Thame. He left his widow Elizabeth, one son, John, of age and four other children all minors, Elizabeth, Walter, Margaret and Henry. His inventory gives an indication of his agricultural occupation and assets. There is no record of crops in the field, but in his barn – presumably adjacent to his dwelling – he had quantities of wheat, rye, barley and pulses, and a load of hay. He also owned two beasts and a bullock, three sutes (bloodhounds), and poultry.[16]

The only rooms listed in John Simons dwelling were a hall and a chamber (Figure 7.2). The hall, dressed with painted cloths, was furnished for the preparation and consumption of food. A limited amount of seating around the 'table with the frame' was provided by three chairs and a form, offering differentiation of degree in seating. One chair, possibly for a child, is described as 'little'. The table was well furnished with 2 salt cellars, 2 table cloths, 6 table napkins and the household with 2 pewter and 3 brass candlesticks. In addition there were a cupboard 'of Wayscott' (panelled construction and possibly also oak)[17] and 'one safe of Tinne', possibly for

---

[13] As Muldrew notes: 'In early modern discourse about the market, economic trust was interpreted in terms as emotive as other forms of human interaction such as neighbourliness, friendship and marriage, while, conversely, interest and contract, which now might be thought of as purely pragmatic economic relations, were concepts applied to a much broader spectrum of social interaction'. Craig Muldrew, *The Economy of Obligation: The Culture of Credit and Social Relations in Early Modern England* (Basingstoke: Macmillan, 1998), p. 125

[14] Wrightson, *Earthly Necessities*, p. 34

[15] OHCA: MS. Wills Pec. 50/5/30. The value of household effects in John Simons' dwelling was given at £9.08, the mean for inventoried husbandmen was £11.13

[16] Total value of agricultural assets £31.85

[17] See William Harrison, *The Description of England* (1587), ed. G. Edelen (Washington and New York: Folger Shakespeare Library, Dover Books, 1994), p. 197

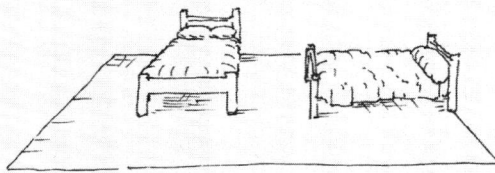

Figure 7.2 Dwelling and furnishings of John Simons, husbandman, 1605

Chamber 0.66

Hall 0.34

the storage of foodstuffs. The hearth is indicated by 'a pair of Cobyrons', a ' fyre shovell' and a 'payre of tongues [and] a pair of Bellowes', cooking in the hearth by two spits and dripping pans, 'two potthooks & one potthanger'. For cooking are 3 brass pots, 3 kettles, 3 pans, a frying pan and 2 posnets, and the table is furnished with six 'great platters' and six 'middle dishes', 'four fruit dishes, foure porringers & six sawcers', and two tasters. This may be a modest household in terms of wealth, and yet it appears well furnished for the preparation and consumption of food. The single listed chamber contained two bedsteads 'of koords' – presumably low structures with a cord base – with 2 featherbeds, 2 coverlets and a pair of blankets. Nine pairs of sheets are listed. If this was the extent of the sleeping accommodation it suggests multiple occupations of beds, especially by children.

The brief will asks for £3 to be distributed to each of the minors on their coming of age at twenty-one years, and to his (presumably eldest) son John 'one wainscot Cubbord standing in the house' which 'he shall not have ... till my wife his mother dyeth', 'my bowe and arrowes'[18] and 'my spice morter', the latter not infrequently featuring in wills as a prized personal possession. The balance of his estate was to go to his widow and executrix Elizabeth. One of the overseers of his estate was his neighbour John Striblehill, who with the vicar John Trinder, a signatory to the will, were also both appraisers of the inventory.[19]

---

[18] In combination with the hounds, the bow and arrow may have been implements of the hunt
[19] Possibly John Striblehill, a wealthy tanner who died in 1618, with no fewer than four servants remembered in his will. OHCA: MS. Wills Prob. 11 131 29

Hall 1.0

Figure 7.3 Dwelling and furnishings of Thomas Francklin, labourer, 1611

Thomas Francklin, Labourer

The lowest level of occupation in income and status that appears in the inventories is that of labourer. Labourers were those in the community with rights to a few acres of cultivable land and pasturage, keeping a beast or two but relying on the hire of their labour for their existence.[20] The fact that the estate of Thomas Franklin[21] was subject to formal probate indicates that he was indeed relatively prosperous. He made his will 'sick of bodie but of good and p[er]fit memory thanks be to god' in late September of 1611 shortly before his death. His agricultural assets were simply listed as a small quantity of beans, and some tubs, and his dwelling as one hall (Figure 7.3). The furnishings were equally sparse: a simple trestle table – without mention of seating – with '13 peeces of pewter great and small', 2 candlesticks and a saltcellar, an 'old' cupboard, 3 'sorry' kettles, a pot, a skillet (the term 'sorry' is commonly applied to household artefacts in very poor condition). There is no mention either of a bedstead,[22] but 1 featherbed, 1 bolster, 1 coverlet and 1 blanket, 5 pairs of sheets and 3 coffers.

The reason why the estate of Thomas Francklin was subject to probate may have been his financial credit, distributing significant sums in his will. His bequests to his grandchildren – 20s each to the (unnamed) offspring of his son Thomas and 10s each to those of his son William – indicate that he had reached what in the seventeenth century would be regarded as a good age at time of death. He also bequeathed 5s each to his sons Thomas and William, and to John Aclee. He bequeathed 20s each to the children of Thomas Aclee, John, Jane Mary and Margery, and to Richard and Blanche the children of Robert Aclee. He therefore evidently has a close affective relationship with the Aclee family.[23] All of these monetary bequests were to

---

[20] Wrightson, *Earthly Necessities*, p. 35
[21] OHCA: MS. Wills Pec. 38/3/16. The value of household effects in Thomas Francklin's dwelling was given at £3.53, the mean for inventoried labourers was £5.34
[22] But this could have been excluded, deemed property of the widow
[23] Who could possibly have been in-laws

be paid from a considerable debt of £17 6s 8d recovered from his brother, also named as Thomas Francklin. Francklin named his widow Alice his wife and executrix 'to this my last Will Testa[men]t to see my debts [and] Legacies paid [and] my bodie brought to earth', granting her the residue of the estate. His 'good neighbour Mr John Hester [and] brother Richard Wheeler' were granted 12d each to oversee the will. The paucity of Thomas Francklin's dwelling gives some indication of the quality of accommodation of the large percentage of the population which fell below the probate threshold, but the relative assets of these three agriculturalists indicate that individual fortune varied within the parameters of ascribed status.[24]

Artisans, Artisan-Traders and Traders

John Greene, Artisan, Carpenter

We pass now to those in Thame who exercised crafts and made and traded in commodities. There appears in the early seventeenth century to have been no necessary distinction between those who primarily cultivated the land and raised livestock, and those in other occupations. The carpenter John Greene,[25] who died in the spring of 1627, cultivated five portions of land in the Thame field including five acres of corn, and possessed 3 cows, 2 calves, 2 pigs, 1 sheep, 4 hens and 1 cock. Trade activities must therefore have been integrated into the agricultural year. He left his widow Margaret, sons John and William and married daughter Elizabeth (Calcott) and (apparently unmarried) daughters Eleanor and Joan. Only a hall is listed for his Thame dwelling in his inventory, although his will does also mention at least one 'lowe' chamber and a loft (Figure 7.4).[26] The hall was furnished with a joined table with its frame, seating of 2 stools and 2 forms and a cupboard with pewter candlesticks. The reference also to the 'wainscott' suggests that the hall was panelled,[27] and four tablecloths and

[24] In his will of 1624 Anthony Nore described himself as a yeoman. Following his death in 1627/8 his appraisers described him as a labourer. The value of his household effects was £13.65. OHCA: MS. Wills Pec. 47/1/77

[25] OHCA: MS. Wills Pec. 39/3/37. The value of household effects in John Greene's dwelling was given at £23.55, the mean for inventoried artisans was £18.29

[26] This again is an instance and a reminder of the partial and potentially unreliable nature of inventories as quantitative evidence. The 'lowe' chamber could be a reference to a low-ceilinged chamber, but also to an increasingly uncommon incidence of a chamber on the ground floor at the start of the seventeenth century. See M. W. Barley, *The English Farmhouse and Cottage* (London: Routledge & Kegan Paul, 1961), p. 44 and Chapter 6 above. The diagram assumes the latter, but the furnishing content remains the same.

[27] The listing of wainscot panelling in the inventories suggests that this improvement was still regarded as a temporary moveable element. Was it because of his occupation that John Greene was able to invest in a domestic improvement which was at that time something of a luxury?

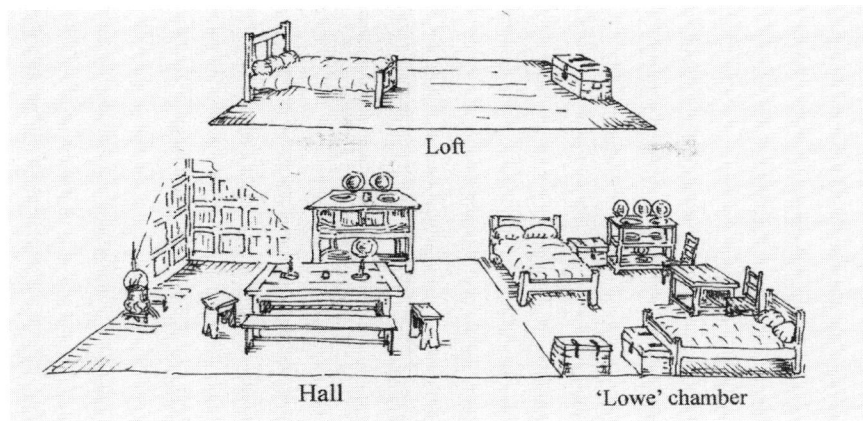

Figure 7.4 Dwelling and furnishings of John Greene, carpenter, 1627. (Relative furnishing values not supplied as some furnishings mentioned, unvalued, in the will.)

a dozen napkins imply a degree of hospitable dining with status. A hall hearth is indicated by fire dogs, 'the Bellowes, fire shovell and tongs', and cooking by pothangers, 3 kettles, 2 pots and a chafer. These cooking irons and implements suggest a diet of boiled food – pulses and limited meat – rather than roasted meats. The reference in the will to 'my bedsteed in ye chamber belowe' suggest inventoried 'bedsteds' with 'a feather bedd' and '2 flockbeds', 4 bolsters, 3 pillows and a pair of pillowbears, 3 coverlets and 5 blankets. Eight pairs of sheets were listed. Possibly also in the chamber were the 'little Table and two chaires' and 'a court cubbard', providing a degree of discreet sociability even in this modest dwelling. A box may have provided storage for papers and miscellanea, and four chests for the linen and also for his apparel, 'Linnen and Woollen'.

In his will – signed with his mark – John Greene appears to own timber on land which he wished to pass on to his eldest son John: 'if there be any maner trees that by Lawe [and] maybe removed my will is that they shall not be cutt down rooted upp or any maner of way willfullie defaced but to remayne to him entirely'. To his son John he also bequeathed 'my bedsteed in ye chamber belowe' and in the loft 'my great chest', 'ye benches [and] wainscott'. Indicating the relative novelty and impermanence of upper floors to dwellings in the early seventeenth century he also desired that 'ye bordes in ye floore should not be removed but remaine to him'.[28] To his younger son William and his heirs he bequeathed 'all my five landes

---

[28] In some cases new floors were still considered to be moveable items. See Chapter 2 above for the changing distinction between the moveable and permanent parts of the dwelling structure.

in Thame field', in want of issue to pass to his youngest daughter Joan and her heirs, or ultimately return to the eldest son John or next of blood after the decease of their mother. The anxiety over legal title is emphasised by the repeated requirement that the heirs be of his or her body 'lawfully begotten'.[29] To his married daughter, Elizabeth, John Greene bequeathed 5s 'of good [and] lawful monie of England', as also to his (apparently unmarried) daughter Eleanor, who was also bequeathed the cupboard 'in ye lowe Chamber' and the joined bedstead 'in ye loft' after her mother's decease. His daughter Joan was bequeathed 6s together with the table, stools, forms and cupboard in the hall after his widow's decease.[30] John Greene also bequeathed 12d to each of his unspecified godchildren, a sum also given to each of the overseers of his will, his brother-in-law Thomas Springall, and 'my good neighbour' Richard Pinder. His wife Margaret was appointed his executrix, 'to see my debts and legacies paid and my funerall expenses executed' and inheritor of the residue of his goods. John Greene's will then seeks to establish his two sons in his carpentry trade and as a farmer respectively, with modest bequests in money to his daughters, and furnishings only when his wife no longer has any need of them. His respected status in the community is perhaps indicated by an appointment to the role of juror on the frankpledge court in 1611.[31]

Robert Stone, Artisan-Trader, Chandler,

The inventory evidence suggests that many artisans who processed materials – foodstuffs, textile yarn, iron and wood – were also engaged in the sale of the commodities that they produced, working as both artisans and traders. Robert Stone, a chandler,[32] engaged in the production of candles, was one of these. He was buried in early September 1641, possibly having been critically unwell for some time previously, as his will was nuncupative (given verbally before witnesses whose testament was later recorded). 'On or aboute the seaventeenthe daye of August' Robert Stone made his will, 'haveinge a full mynde purpose and meaninge to make and declare

---

[29] An Elizabeth Greene married a John Calcott in 1614, and a John Greene married an Elizabeth Calcott in 1620, suggesting the possibility of a close inter-family relationship bonded by marriage.

[30] Whilst Joan was bequeathed one more shilling than her sister Eleanor, the bedstead that the latter inherited had a value worth considerably more than the table and seating inherited by Joan. The married daughter Elizabeth received only a monetary bequest. The usual clause allowing the widow the use of the household furniture during her lifetime could have resulted in a significant rearrangement of furnishings in the existing households of offspring at a later date

[31] OHCA: Thame Frankpledge Court Rolls

[32] OHCA: MS. Wills Pec. 51/2/40. The value of household effects in Robert Stone's dwelling was given at £28.25, the mean for inventoried artisan traders was £30.29

his Last Will and Testament' before Steven Cousens, Thomas Crewes and William Roper, who swore: 'All such words and speeches or to the named effect and purpose he the said Robert Stone declared spake and uttered'. He left his widow Joan but no recorded children.[33] His inventory, for which Stephen Cousen was also an appraiser, with Thomas Aclee[34] and Humfrey Jemot, provides clear evidence of the operation of his trade adjacent to his dwelling; as well as a hall and chamber there were a chandle house and a shop within the building. Within the chandle house implements of the trade were listed – a furnace, a press, a mould and weights and scales, valued at the not inconsiderable sum of £6. But considerably more investment was in materials of his trade, wick yarn (£2 10s) and tallow (£53), valued together at £55 10s. The shop held 'smale ware & some fewe goods' valued at £14, and a woodhouse a load of billet valued at £1. Artisan traders therefore required considerable assets or access to credit in order to conduct their trade.

The hall of Robert Stone was furnished with a table, two joined stools and a chair described a 'turned', and a cupboard (Figure 7.5). The eating vessels consisted of unspecified pewter worth £2. He also possessed 3 table cloths and 18 napkins, enough for sociable consumption of food and drink. A hall hearth is evidenced by various fire irons, and the 'other iron worke' may have constituted a pothanger for the 'brasse pott' and 'Two Kettles'. The chamber over the shop – indicating the proximity of work to dwelling space – was furnished with 'one standinge Bedsteed', with 2 feather beds, 2 flock beds, 2 feather bolsters, 1 flock bolster and 2 feather pillows. There were 8 pairs of sheets, and 6 pillowbears, possibly kept in the 'great Cheste' (with two other 'littel Chestes') and 1 coverlet and 2 blankets. A warming pan was also noted. This was evidently a chamber furnished for comfort. But there are indications of a social function too. The furniture of the chamber also included a court cupboard, 'one table [and] frame' and two joined forms, suggesting neighbourly if not extravagant hospitality. In the cellar were six runlets, drink containers of a fair size which may indicate the brewing of beer on the premises. A cockloft was furnished with a 'halfe headed bedstead' with two straw beds, and a rug, possibly accommodation for a servant.

---

[33] A Robert Stone was baptised in Thame on 26 January 1606/7. Until 1752 in England, where the Julian calendar was employed, the year commenced on 25 March. Adopting the Gregorian calendar the Calendar (New Style) Act 1750 altered the start of the year to 1 January. The year dates given here therefore indicate those deriving from both Julian and Gregorian calendars.

Robert Stone married Joan Inet in Thame, presumably of the parish, in February 1634/5. If this was the same man he would have been aged thirty-four at the time of his death, and twenty-seven at the time of his marriage. No offspring to a Robert Stone are recorded in the Thame baptismal records

[34] Possibly the Thomas Acclee baptised in 1612, son of Robert Acclee. A Robert Acclee was mentioned in the will of the labourer Thomas Franklin in 1611, above.

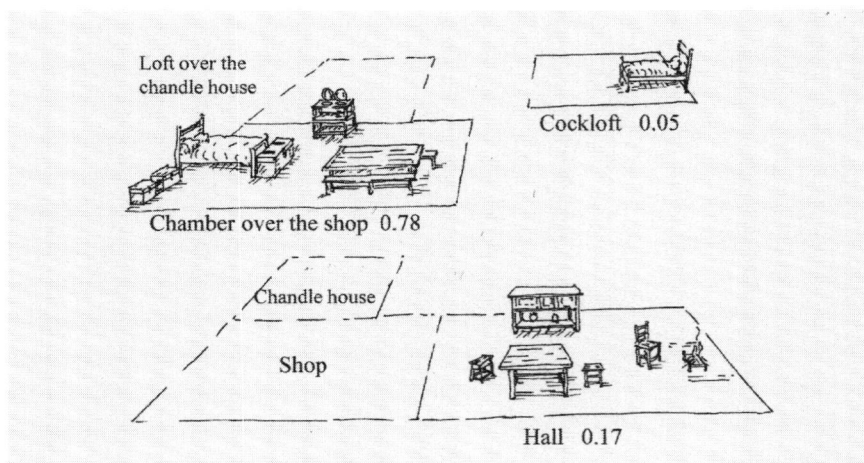

Figure 7.5 Dwelling and furnishings of Robert Stone, chandler, 1641

Being apparently childless, Robert Stone's bequests were to neighbours and their offspring. To Edward Adkins he bequeathed his wearing apparel and one load of billet (firewood), and to Edward's daughter Margaret 20s, whilst 10s was bequeathed to Ellen, the daughter of Thomas Stone, presumably a close relative.[35] The monetary bequests to two unmarried women or girls could be an indication, *in extremis*, of affection. To Robert Crewe, the son of Thomas Crewe, presumably the same as the witness to his will, he bequeathed his Bible, the sole article mentioned and perhaps an indication of Robert Stone's strong religious inclinations. Finally he appointed his wife Joan the rest of his goods and appointed her executrix. Notably he did not disperse his trade goods, and it was not uncommon for widows to continue to manage their deceased husband's trades. On the threshold of the Civil War a picture emerges of a pious artisan and shopkeeper at his craft, childless but with close and affectionate relationships with family and neighbours.

Richard Striblehill, Trader, Butcher

Amongst the most prosperous traders of Thame, a prominent livestock market in a fertile valley, were the butchers. Although Richard Stribble-hill[36] died in the summer of 1607, at the start of our seventeenth-century

---

[35] An Elenor Stone, daughter of Thomas Stone, was baptised on 6 October 1630, making her at the time of Robert Stone's death eleven years of age. A Thomas Stone was baptised in Thame on 27 August 1601

[36] OHCA: MS. Wills Pec. 50/5/36. The value of household effects in Richard Stribblehill's

study period, the wealth and size of his domicile was representative of other traders through the century. He left his wife Jane and two daughters, the married Mary Carter and Elizabeth, still a minor. The inventory gives an indication of his trade; possibly adjacent to the house were a slaughter house and stable. In the slaughter house were a cow and a calf, two sheep and a lamb, possibly awaiting slaughter. However, like the other townsmen, Striblehill was also engaged in agriculture. He possessed at time of death 'Corne on the grounde' and also livestock – nine pigs and 'two beaste'. In the stable were racks, a manger and a quantity of hay. His dwelling also comprised a dairy house, with dairying bowls and shelves with no fewer than fifty-seven cheeses, a commercial rather than domestic production. He also employed servants: three men, John Burton, Marmaduke Dakes and Charlie Persie, quite possibly outdoor servants, and one woman Mary White, who may have worked in the house, or in the dairy.

Striblehill's dwelling comprised a hall, a kitchen, a parlour and five chambers (Figure 7.6). The hall was furnished with a table and frame, 6 joined stools[37] and 3 chairs. A company of nine could therefore sit down to eat, and plate and napery suggests some style: 3 dozen platters, a dozen fruit dishes and a dozen saucers, 9 salt cellars and 6 dozen napkins. The dozen towels could serve with the 'bason [and] a ewer', the mark of ceremonial dining. And a dozen table cloths were complemented by six dozen napkins, either indicating large companies or the desire to dine regularly with clean linen. Drinking vessels included 2 cups, 2 tasters, a quart and a pint pot. However, although no fewer than six cupboards were noted in the house none was listed in the hall. The hall was panelled with wainscot and there was a hearth, indicated by fire irons – a pair of fire dogs, bellows, tongs and a fire shovel – providing warmth but possibly not for cooking. The kitchen appears to have been not only the room, as customary, for the storage of cooking utensils and the preparation of foodstuffs, but also a very well-equipped and dedicated cooking space. A significant hearth is indicated by 2 pothooks and 2 pothangers, and boiled dishes by 6 brass pots, 8 kettles and 3 postnets, a skimmer and 4 ladles. A diet rich in meat is also indicated by 3 spits and a pair of racks, 2 dripping pans and a frying pan, and also the mustard mill. The significant preparation of food within the dwelling was complemented by the boulting house with its tubs, troughs and quarter of meal to produce flour, and the moulding board and troughs in the kitchen to make bread. A furnace, a malt mill and 'the brewing vessells' evidence the production of beer, and a still, possibly of medicinal distillations or liquor. This was a household which was equipped to produce significant and varied quantities of food, whether for the internal consumption of a

---

dwelling was given at £54.81, the mean for inventoried traders was £30.80

[37] There are indications that commensal furnishings were reckoned by the dozen: half a dozen stools, and eating vessels by the dozen. Napkins are always numbered by the dozen

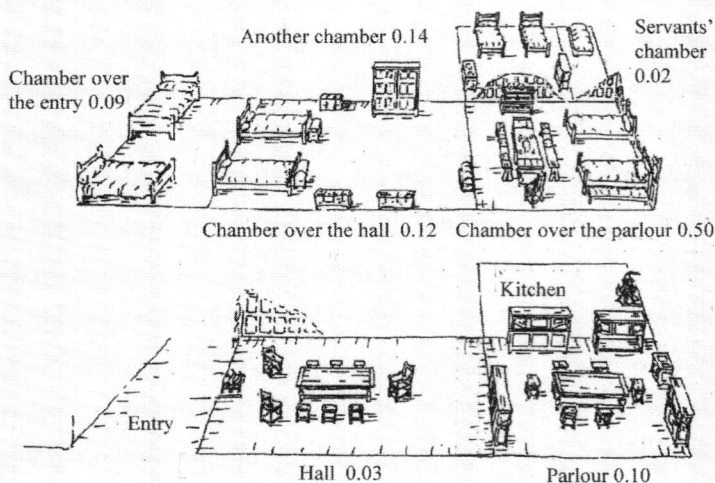

Figure 7.6 Dwelling and furnishings of Richard Striblehill, butcher, 1607

large household or – suggested by furnishings of the parlour and principal chamber – for entertainment.

Probably adjacent to the hall was the parlour, furnished with a table, six stools and no fewer than four cupboards, possibly as a place of more select entertainment or commercial transaction. It also contained a chest, coverlet and blankets. The most expensively furnished room in the house was the chamber over the parlour.[38] The listed furnishing comprised 2 joined bedsteads, with 2 feather beds. There was also a truckle bed with a flock bed, possibly for a servant or a child. For bedclothes were 9 pillows, 5 bolsters, 4 coverlets and a quilt. In addition there were a joined table and frame, a 'little chair' and a form and benches with six cushions, providing accommodation for a significant company, and three carpets (probably for dressing the furniture), and a court cupboard denoting hospitality. The room was also wainscot panelled. This, then, was a place for comfortable retirement – a warming pan was included in the inventory – but also for considerable entertainment. Four other chambers were listed, with fewer and less valuable furnishings. 'Another chamber' contained 2 bedsteads with a feather bed and 2 flock beds and 2 coverlets. This chamber also contained a court cupboard – but no table or seating – and significant storage, four coffers and a chest. The chamber over the hall also contained two bedsteads with flock beds, bolsters, blankets and coverlets, and again ample

[38] The chamber over the parlour had a furnishing value of £15 out of a total of a total of £29.79 for all dwelling rooms

storage in six coffers and a press. The chamber over the entry contained '2 little bedsteds' – possibly for children – a feather bed, bolsters, coverlet and blanket. Finally the servants' bedchamber indicates the accommodation of servants within the dwelling, and was furnished with a bedstead with a flock bed, a bolster, blanket and coverlet. The value of furnishings in this chamber was 10s, some thirtieth that of the principal chamber.[39] The household was provided with 27 pairs of sheets, 8 pairs of pillowbears, for lighting after dark 5 pewter and 4 brass candlesticks and for convenience 4 chamber pots. As well as the wainscot panelling in various rooms, it was a well-dressed dwelling with 'painted cloths throughout the house'.

Richard Stribblehill's will, signed with his mark, commenced – after the preamble commending his 'soule to allmightie God' and his 'bodie to be buryed in the Church yeard of Thame' – with charitable bequests to the poor of the parish of 20s, 'to be distributed at the day of my buryall', reinforcing his community standing. Next he concerned himself with the care of his daughters. To his married daughter Mary Carter he bequeathed £5 to be paid within three years of his decease, but to his unmarried daughter Elizabeth he left the considerable sum of £40 to be given to her 'when she shall accomplish the age of one [and] twentie years', ensuring her ability to make a secure match.[40] To each of his servants he bequeathed 2s 7d, and appointed his wife Jane sole executrix and bequeathed her the remainder of his property. Although bereaved, she would now enjoy the status of a wealthy widow. Richard Striblehill's inventory and will therefore present the picture of prosperous trading household, although a limited family an extended household with a number of servants, with extensive accommodation, comfortable furnishings and the capacity to entertain on a significant scale. His rise to this standing may have been uneven; a Richard Striblehill was fined in the frankpledge court for the selling of bad mutton in 1595 and presented for blocking a watercourse at the pump, but by 1605 had been appointed a juror to the court.[41]

Clerics

John Trinder, Cleric, Vicar

Although many of the decedents signed their wills with a mark, as did appraisers and witnesses, as has already been noted Thame was proud of its grammar school and possessed an educated and literate non-gentry class

---

[39] 'Another chamber had furnishings valued at £4.50, the chamber over the hall £3.50, the chamber over the entry £2.00

[40] It is probable that Striblehill would already have settled a similar sum on his daughter Mary when she married

[41] OHCA: Thame Frankpledge Court Rolls

who might be termed clerics. John Trinder,[42] the vicar of St Mary's church from 1589 to 1629, described himself as a clerk (in holy orders) in his will dated 2 November 1629. His name appears frequently in the period of his incumbency as an appraiser and witness, possibly regularly tasked, in addition to his spiritual duties, with making a written record of significant legal events in the life of his community. In so doing he might have been intimately acquainted with the day-to-day interactions of his parishioners. In the words of George Herbert: 'The priest ... doth stand between God and the people, ready press'd in the behalf of both to do his best'.[43] Like his fellow townsmen Trinder also engaged in agriculture, leaving corn in his barn and 'in the field'. His dwelling appears to have been simple, comprising a hall, a kitchen and a buttery, a chamber over the hall and a maid's chamber. Outside was a woodhouse for the storage of firewood.[44]

John Trinder's hall was wainscott panelled, and dressed with painted cloths (Figure 7.7). It was furnished with 2 tables, 3 chairs, 6 joined stools and 2 low stools with 4 cushions, enough seating to entertain a significant company. With the pewter dishes, 3 table cloths, over 3 dozen napkins and a 'little drinking Cloth of diaper', this would have been entertainment with status. There is no record of fire irons in the hall, so it is not clear whether cooking took place there or in the kitchen. Cooking irons are recorded in the kitchen, but no pothangers or hooks: 3 spits, and a pair of (spit) racks, 2 dripping pans, a gridiron, a frying pan and trivet, along with a 'little' furnace – suggesting a diet rich in meat – and brass pots and kettles. In the buttery were a powdering trough, for the salting of meat, and a beer stand for storage of the drink (but not necessarily its production) and two stills for distillations of some sort. The principal chamber over the hall contained a joined curtained bedstead with a feather bed, 2 feather bolsters, 2 down, 3 other pillows and a rug, and the household was provided with 8 pairs of sheets. In addition, the room was furnished with a court cupboard and two joined chests. This was a comfortably furnished chamber but without table and seating, suggesting a private space of retirement.[45] The maid's chamber was furnished with a bedstead with a flock bed and a 'healing', a form of cover.[46] This then was an apparently small household – seemingly

---

[42] OHCA: MS. Wills Pec. 52/4/5. The value of household effects in John Trinder's dwelling was given at £17.88; the mean for inventoried clerics with wills was £19.00

[43] George Herbert, *The Temple: Sacred Poems and Private Ejaculations* (1633) (London: Pickering, 1838), p. 310

[44] One of the appraisers of his inventory was another member of the prominent Striblehill family, Augustine

[45] At £3.50 the value of furnishing of this principal chamber was over three times that of the hall

[46] 'Healing' or 'heling' was defined by John Ray in *A Collection of English Words, Not Generally Used* (London, 1674) as 'A Bed-Healing (Derb.), a coverlet: it is also called absolutely a Hylling in many places'. The use of the term here and its placement with the bedstead could indicate some sort of fabric canopy

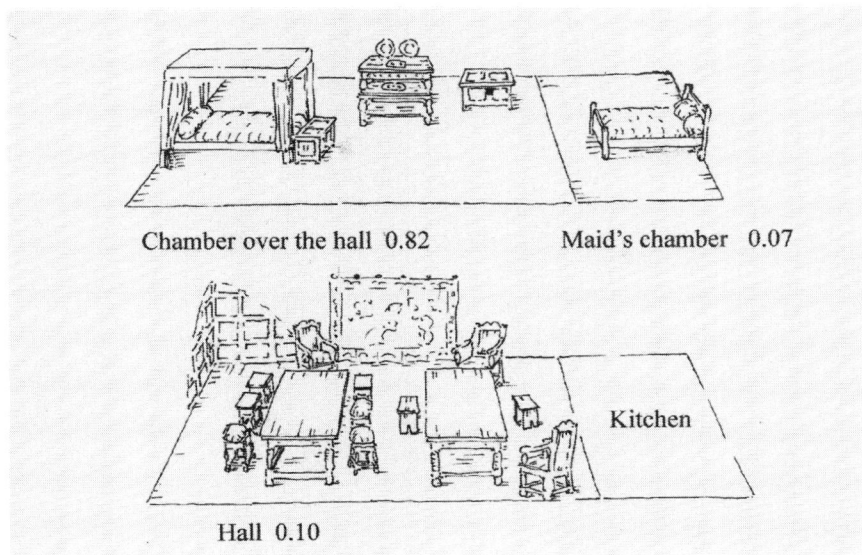

Figure 7.7 Dwelling and furnishings of John Trinder, vicar, 1629

consisting of husband, wife and maid – furnished in modest comfort and equipped for a fair degree of hospitality.

In his brief will John Trinder bequeaths his' soule to god' and his body for burial in the chancel of the church, a prerogative of the clergy and an aspiration of the elite of the community. After the payment of unspecified debts, he bequeathed to his wife Margaret all his goods 'to maintain her during her naturell life', and wills that she bestows their worldly wealth at her discretion at her departure from this life.

Gentlemen

Richard Somers, Gentleman

Although this study has deliberately attempted to focus as largely as possible – given the financially advantaged status of inventoried decedents – on non-elite culture, lesser gentry were an important part of the local community. Some, like the Lords Norris of Rycote House, were established at a distance from the town. Others appear to have been more proximate physically and socially to the community. Some seem to have risen out of the town elite, like Thomas Striblehill of Old Thame (died 1680), of the family of prosperous butchers, who appointed as his overseers of his will a draper of New Thame, George Burrowes, and another gentleman, Thomas Dorrell the younger of Old Thame, both described as his 'loveing friend'. Another such gentleman was Richard Somers,[47] noted as living in Priestend at the north-western extremity of the small market town. His inventory – of whom another Striblehill, John, was an appraiser – made after his death late in 1665, firstly indicates that Somers was, as befitted his gentry status, a man of property. At the time of his death he was owed £145 upon specialty,[48] £100 in leases and £10 in other debts. However, in some capacity Somers was also engaged in agriculture. His inventory notes three cows, and cow racks which may have been adjacent to his dwelling, fodder and bedding in a quantity of hay and straw, and harvested crops, quarters of wheat and barley. In addition, £1 worth of cheese was in the dwelling house.

It appears from his will, made some four years prior to his death, that Richard Somers was childless at that point, leaving only his wife Joan.[49] His dwelling consisted of a hall, a kitchen, a parlour and a chambers over each of these spaces (Figure 7.8). The hall was furnished with a table and frame, and seating comprising 2 leather chairs and 2 joined chairs, a joined stool and a joined form. Table cloths and napkins are noted but not itemised. There appears to have been a hall hearth; as well as fire irons, 3 pothangers, 2 spits and jack to turn the spit were noted.[50] In addition, two iron pots were listed in the hall, and brass cooking and pewter eating and drinking vessels elsewhere, including seven silver spoons and a silver tankard which were highly valued at £8. A kitchen is identified by the chamber which lay over it, but without contents. This could, however, be where the 'breweinge vessell', processing barley into drink, was employed. The parlour was comfortably furnished with a number and variety of seating: a 'Great Chare', 2 upholstered (fether'd) chairs – possibly early examples of luxurious urban furnishing – 2 'Chares of Turkie worke', a leather stool and no fewer than 19 cushions. There was a joined cupboard, 6 cupboard cloths and 3 carpets, which might by this time have been found not only over furniture – as had been the custom – but on the floor. A picture is also noted, and it might be that his 'bookes' were also here. The furnishing implies an emphasis on display of comfort in this space of householder sociability. The chamber over the hall had furniture of status, comprising bed furniture of curtains and valance, feather bed and feather bolster, 4 feather pillows, a red rug, 3 blankets, valued at £9 or a tenth of the value of the total household furnishings.[51] The chamber also contained a table and frame, a 'side' cupboard,

---

[47] OHCA: MS. Wills Pec. 51/3/18. The value of household effects in Richard Somers' dwelling was given at £92.70; the mean for inventoried gentlemen was £88.23

[48] A 'specialty' is a sealed document that has been given as security for the payment of a specifically indicated debt

[49] There are no records of children by the name of Somers in the parish baptismal registry

[50] A Richard Somers appears in the 1665 Hearth Tax returns paying for three hearths

[51] A bedstead itself is not noted. Given the value of the bed furniture and the presence of curtains and valance, it seems likely that one was present and its omission an error or that the actual bedstead was deliberately excluded

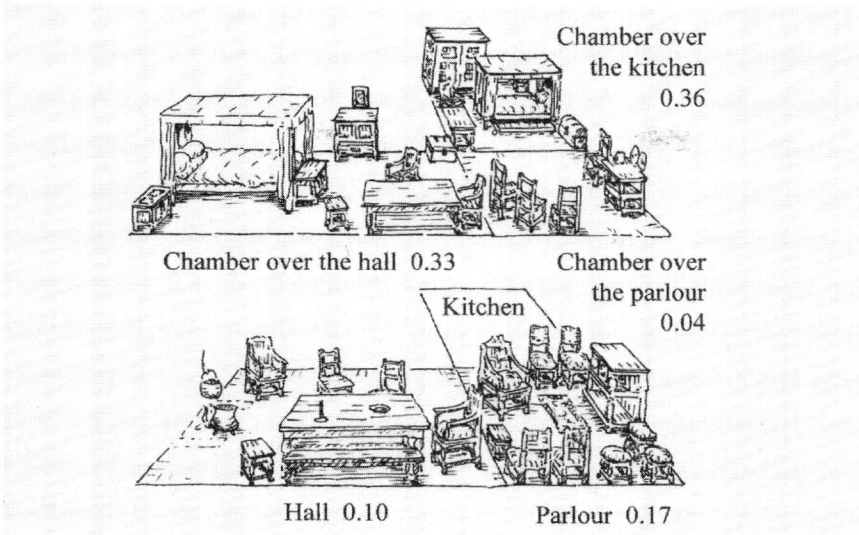

Figure 7.8 Dwelling and furnishings of Richard Somers, gentleman, 1665

two chairs and a stool. For storage were two joined chests and a trunk. A looking glass is also listed, a luxury commodity (valued at £1 10s) and relative novelty at the time and certainly acquired from a distance, quite possibly London. The chamber over the kitchen was also unusually equally well furnished. The bedstead noted here also had curtains and valence, a feather bed and feather bolster, a feather pillow, a rug and pair of blankets. Another set of curtains and valence, feather bed and bolster was also noted, with blankets and a worsted rug. In this chamber there was a trundle bed (given Somers' age possibly for servants). There was a table and frame with limited seating of a chair, and storage provided by a joined press, a coffer and a trunk. The chamber over the parlour was sparsely furnished with a court cupboard and four chairs, a reminder that households were inventoried at different times in the life cycle when spaces might vary in intensity and nature of use.[52] The household was provided with fourteen pairs of sheets. Compared to that of Thomas Francklin the labourer, earlier in the century, this was a dwelling of wealth and sophistication.

In his will Richard Somers leaves very modest sums of money to his siblings, reinforcing the impression that this was a childless couple; to his brother John, his sisters Margaret (Browne) and Eleanor (Browne) 12d apiece. To his 'Lovinge wife'[53] Joan he bequeathed the rest of his goods and chattels, and

---

[52] This is also a sound reason for the aggregation of probate inventory data where possible, in order to iron out anomalies
[53] A relatively rare mark of personal affection

appointed her executrix. We have here then the portrait of one of the lesser gentry, quite aged in years, a man of some property but engaged in some form of agriculture, educated and living in comfort but not ostentation.

Widows

Elizabeth Francklin, Widow

Finally we turn to a widow of Thame. Aptly last perhaps, because the evidence suggests that after a marriage lasting on average approximately twenty years widows outlived their husbands by approximately ten years and represent some 20% of the inventoried decedents of this study. Due to their independence, and sometimes the accumulation of assets in property and cash, they could enjoy a considerable degree of personal status and financial leverage in the community. In her study of the economic status of widows in Thame and Woodstock in the seventeenth century, Mary Hodges identified them as major sources of finance for family and neighbours.[54] Elizabeth Francklin[55] passed away on 29 September 1622, the widow of Gabriel Francklin,[56] a yeoman who had died in May 1606. At the time of his death five children were mentioned: Edward, Henry, Margaret, Mary and Elizabeth, the latter two still being minors. In Elizabeth's will there is mention of all of her offspring. She had therefore been widowed for sixteen years, but had prospered in that time. Her husband's estate was valued at £20 14s, hers at £60 4s (allowing for inflation during her widowhood equivalent to £54 3s 6d). She therefore left a valuable estate, and had evidently also lent money, being owed £8 by bond. Indications of some continuing agriculture are found in the mention of the backside to the dwelling, hogs and hurdles, but predominantly widow Francklin gives an impression of a woman of property.

Her extensive dwelling was noted as consisting of a hall, kitchen, buttery, parlour and two chambers (Figure 7.9). Her wainscot-panelled hall contained a table and frame, a chair, eight stools (two of which are listed as 'low'), benches and a cupboard with cupboard cloth. To furnish the table were 30 trenchers, 2 dozen platters, 7 fruit dishes, 6 saucers and 5 salts, and the status of the company would have been expressed by Elizabeth Francklin's ten silver spoons. The table linen comprised 8 table cloths,

[54] M. Hodges, 'Widows of the Middling Sort and their Assets in Two Seventeenth-Century Towns', *When Death Do Us Part: Understanding and Interpreting the Probate Inventory Records of Early Modern England*, ed. T. Arkell, N. Evans and N. Goose (Oxford: Leopard's Head Press, 2000), p. 308
[55] OHCA: MS. Wills Pec. 38/4/7. The value of household effects in Elizabeth Francklin's dwelling was given at £42.10; the mean for inventoried widows and spinsters was £22.46
[56] OHCA: MS. Wills Pec. 38/3/11. Gabriel Francklin, making otherwise only monetary bequests, had left 'All the resydue of my goods unbequeathed' to his wife and executrix Elizabeth

over 2 dozen napkins and 4 towels. Drinking vessels were a quart pot and six 'drinkinge tunnes', and she also possessed a relative novelty, a glass cupboard, which could have housed the luxury commodity of drinking glasses. The room also contained a chest, some books, and it appears that the windows were curtained with 'A curteine [and] curteine rods'. Two safes may have been wall hung, ventilated receptacles for dry foodstuffs.[57] There was also a capacious hall hearth, evidenced by various fire irons and implements, four pairs of (pot)hangers and pair of racks. This, then, was a comfortable hall furnished for the entertainment, if wished, of a significant company. The kitchen appears still to be primarily a place for the preparation of foodstuffs: meat (a powdering trough and tub), bread (a hair sieve and moulding board), and drink (an ale vat, and seven barrels). The buttery in this household seems to have performed as a place for food preparation and for the storage of cooking implements, with a table and a form. For food preparation 1 chopping and 2 shredding boards are listed, a mincing knife and a chopping knife, and a mortar and pestle. Cooking vessels comprised 5 kettles, 5 brass pots with 2 skimmers, 5 posnets, 3 spits with 2 dripping pans and a basting spoon and a frying pan. The dining trenchers were stored here along with a chafing dish and a brass basin, and the room was furnished with 7 shelves and 3 stands for storage. The house was therefore well equipped for the preparation of a varied diet and for the entertainment of a considerable company. Her 'little' parlour was modestly furnished with two tables – table and frame, and 'one litle standinge Tabell' – with benches and joined stool. It was wainscot panelled and dressed with painted cloths.

The principal and most lavishly furnished chamber was that over the buttery.[58] It was furnished for comfortable rest with 'one standinge bedd with hangings', a feather bed, bolster and pillow, coverlet and blankets . But in addition it was equipped for hospitality, with a table and frame (and a carpet possibly for the table), a chair, six stools with cushions, a form and 'benches [and] backe of wainscote' providing seating for a plentiful company. There was also a court cupboard with a cupboard cloth, and a painted cloth. Well furnished but for private retreat was the chamber over the hall, the bedstead with 2 feather beds, 2 pillows, blanket and 2 coverlets. Possibly a small table was listed with a single chair, but there also seems to be status on display with a court cupboard and a quantity of plate. Personal storage of small valuables and textiles could be provided by the box and chest. There appears to have been a fire in this chamber, sharing a flue with the hearth in the hall below,[59] evidenced by a pair of andirons and providing a

---

[57] See Chapter 4 above
[58] The furnishings were valued at £9, nearly a quarter of the value of all furnishings
[59] See Chapter 1 above; M. Airs and J. Rhodes, 'Wall-Paintings from a House in Upper High Street, Thame, *Oxoniensia* 45 (1980), 235-59 describes a similar arrangement in an extant house in Thame High Street

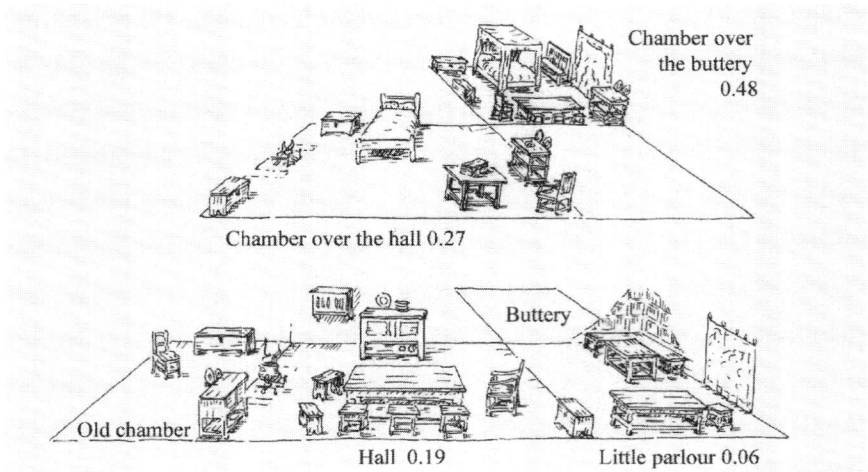

Figure 7.9 Dwelling and furnishings of Elizabeth Francklin, widow, 1622

further degree of private personal comfort. The 'old chamber' was sparsely furnished with assorted pieces of furniture, and may have been a chamber located on the ground floor (as was found prior to the insertion of flooring and the creation of upper-floor accomodation). The household was equipped with 8 pairs of sheets and 6 pillow bears. Lighting was provided by 5 pewter and 3 brass candlesticks, and bodily convenience by 3 chamber pots. The chamber accommodation therefore implies a combination of physical comfort, retirement but also on occasion significant hospitality.

Elizabeth Francklin had made her will some two years before her demise, witnessed by the vicar John Trinder[60] and Augustine Striblehill. Like many widows' wills it concerns itself with not only the dispersal of property but also careful disposal of personal belongings. After the preamble committing her soul to God and her body to be buried the churchyard at Thame, she commences the disposal of the assets with charitable bequests to the community; 10s to the church and 20s to the poor of the parish, which like the bequest of the butcher Richard Striblehill were to be 'distributed at the day of my buriall'. To her servant Margaret Eeles she bequeathed various items which might help to furnish other accommodation – a pair of sheets, a coarse table cloth, half a dozen napkins, 2 great platters, 2 'lesser' candlesticks – and items of clothing, an 'olde saveguard'[61] and 'my old hat'. One feels here a degree of generosity and thought limited by a sense of quality of goods proper to station. To Benjamin – possibly an outdoor servant – she bequeathed 'fortie

---

[60] Given 10s for his pains
[61] OED: A safeguard: an outer skirt or petticoat worn by women to protect their clothing

shillinges'. The rest of the bequests were to her children. To her son Edward she bequeathed 40s a year during the remainder of the lease of her dwelling, to her (presumably married) daughter Margaret Adkins better and more personal furnishings and clothing than that bequeathed to the servant Margaret: her 'little gold ringe', 'my brasse pott [that] I use every day', 'one of my best table clothes and one dozen of napkins', 'a paire of new canvas sheets', 'my best gowne' and 'one of my smockes'. To each of Margaret's children (her grandchildren) she bequeathed 40s. To her (presumably married) daughter Mary Hester she bequeathed £5 and to Mary's daughters (her grandchildren) 20s and a little brass pot. And to the unmarried Elizabeth Francklin a quantity of clothing: 'my best hatt and my best petticote' 'my best aprone and the rest of my wearing L[ine]nne and all the rest of my clothes and a newe gowne [that] I never wore', and 'my Great brasse pott' and a considerable sum of money, £20. There is a clear distinction made in the quantity and composition of bequests to her daughters, implying different conditions of life and affections. The residue of her estate, the 'rest of my goodes whatsoever unbequeathed', she left to 'my sonne Henry Fran[c]klin whom I make executor to this my last will and testament to see my debts and legacies paide and funerall expences executed and discharged'. But if he should fail in his duty then the overseers were instructed to 'take my house and goodes into their hands' and discharge her last wishes, the remainder apportioned to her son Henry. To the last, Elizabeth Francklin was a woman in control of her affairs. The gift of 10s to each of the overseers, Mr Butcher, Mr Ballowe and Mr Kendall, all 'friend [and] neighbour' is a reminder of the custom of the distribution of beer at the 'forth-coming' of the corpse to the burial service and interment.[62]

In this chapter we have taken a closer view of specific households, and of the various livelihoods, familial and neighbourly relationships and affections of a variety of individuals of Thame, embracing those engaged in agriculture at various levels, the affluent controllers of land and producers of surplus, those selling their labour (providing an indication of the significant element of the population that lay below the probate threshold), the producers and the traders who processed the production of the landscape and provided for the needs of households. We have also looked at the more educated elite and the affluent widow – her status a reminder of the creation and dissolution of households through the natural cycle of life. The furnishings of the dwellings indicate the provision made in upper echelons of Thame society – primarily mercantile, clerical and gentry – for social entertainment within the house. And whilst probate inventories provide a picture of the material circumstances of households, wills can provide a richer narrative of the personal and neighbourly relationships which linked and underpinned household and communal life.

[62] See Chapter 3 above

Conclusion

This study commenced with three aims. The first was to gain an insight into the experience of non-elite domestic life in the past, specifically in the early modern period. The second aim was to understand the way in which this culture might have been related to a wider early modern economic and social culture. The third aim was to create a conceptual framework within which the domestic culture could be theorised, interpreted and comprehended.

The inquiry was based primarily on the evidence of probate inventories, not simply for want of better but on the theoretical assertion that human life is founded in material existence, and that it is not only a functional engagement, but one in which actions around objects articulate social relationships and carry conceptual meanings, in turn investing objects and actions with wider significance. An understanding of the objects themselves involved an investigation of the way in which they afford certain possibilities to their users, having been created with certain affordances in mind. But objects are not only acted on by humans, they also assert agency on humans. Following Heidegger and Bourdieu, associations are all important in the creation of meaning, and so an effective reading of the material evidence must be contextual or hermeneutic, observing how objects are situated in relation to other objects in place, and how actions operate through time.[1] The scale of the study is important here, through a detailed reading of a dense body of data allowing the complex interrelation of the many elements in domestic life to be revealed. This approach provides an interpretive framework, applicable not only to this work but to the operation of domestic life in general, addressing the third aim of this study: a concept of domestic culture, comprehending the network of relationships linking the elements of domestic life – material, social and conceptual – in place and through time. If it has proved possible to create an informed picture of early modern domestic life in Thame, not just in its

---

[1] M. Heidegger, *Being and Time* (1927) (Oxford: Blackwell, 1962); P. Bourdieu, *Outline of a Theory of Practice*, trans. R. Nice (Cambridge: Cambridge University Press, 1977); P. Bourdieu, *The Logic of Practice* (Cambridge: Polity Press, 1990)

material but also in its social and conceptual dimensions primarily through a contextual reading of the material evidence, then this should provide justification for the theoretical propositions underlying this study and the concept of a 'domestic culture'.

The Experience of Domestic Life in Seventeenth-Century Thame

To what extent has the foregoing interpretation of the evidence of the Thame probate inventories, enriched with other contemporary sources, yielded an insight into the experience of domestic life in the households of the more affluent members of a rural and market community in the seventeenth century? Firstly, the household did not come into being or exist in a vacuum. We saw in Chapter 1 that the settlement of Thame was based on the properties of the environment in which it was situated, making possible certain forms of agriculture, in turn leading to the establishment of a centre of exchange and commerce. The environment also comprised a social and ethical climate, regulating the conduct of relationships both without and within the dwelling in which the domestic group was housed. The wider society prescribed the manner of the formation of the household through marriage, and as we saw in Chapter 2 the early modern household was regarded as largely autonomous, as much an economic as a reproductive unit. The conjugal relationship, although nominally set within an ideology of patriarchy, was akin to a working partnership in which the male and female roles were well defined, but nevertheless continually open to the discourse and negotiation noted by contemporary commentators. As an economic unit the household also included domestic servants, both male and female, assisting in its business and in the domestic work. The existence of the inventories makes us aware of the transitory nature of the household, passing through the reproductive phase into dispersal and eventual dissolution. The Thame household therefore existed in the wider context of its immediate neighbourhood and culture, engaged with it and subject to influence emanating from without and change.

The objects listed in probate inventories represent an estimation of the importance of materiality in personal identity. As we have seen in the previous chapters, the Thame household existed on a rich material base, averaging some 144 listed objects per household (apart from others aggregated as 'lumber'), providing for a range of activities. This material base, both inherited (as evidenced by bequests in wills) and acquired, consisted of perishable objects of little worth, and those of durability and value, some created by local artisans from local materials and using relatively simple techniques, and others sophisticated and distanced technologies and materials. At the heart of the Thame household was the provision of sustenance. Indeed, in an agricultural community there were few not involved in some way in the cultivation of foodstuffs, partly for sale in the market and beyond, but also for subsistence.

In a very real sense, then, the immediate environment and more distanced world were essential to and permeated the daily existence of the household. As part of its economic identity much of the processing, consisting of the preservation of perishable foodstuffs, was carried out in the household. Such tasks needed a considerable degree of acquired knowledge and organisation of labour, structuring the daily life of the dwelling. Work in the fields was considered largely the responsibility of the man of the house, whilst the processing of foodstuffs that of women and domestics, distinctions which helped to establish status and gender divisions, further emphasised where domestic accommodation allowed for the housing of foodstuff processes in dedicated spaces, distancing the mundane from the social and creating domains of gendered control. The food brought into the house, either through cultivation or purchase, was then cooked for consumption. At the start of the century most food appears to have been cooked on a hall hearth, and then consumed by the entire household in the same room around a rectangular table. Differentials in social standing could be expressed by the nature of seating and the position at the table. Commensality was thus an expression of an integrated social body but also an acknowledged internal hierarchy. The hall and its hearth, and the consumption of the produce of joint labour made a daily statement of the social and affective integrity of the household.

Commensality also provided an opportunity for outsiders to be brought into the dwelling in a process of reciprocal entertainment, establishing and confirming neighbourly status, especially at moments of seasonal or ritual significance. Sometimes this hospitality took place in parts of the dwelling, the best chamber and the parlour, which signalled an internal distinction in social status between the householder, his wife and guests, and the rest of his household, as demonstrated in Figure 6.2. In engaging thus with outside guests he or she distanced themselves socially from their own 'family', potentially creating a tension between internal and external allegiances. Chambers also provided the members of the household with a place of retirement. This was not only seclusion; considerable sums were spent on the furnishings, bedding and bedsteads, indicating a desire for display as well as for comfort. In fact, the quality of fabrics was one area of materiality which provided opportunities for sensory discrimination, and thus statements of status. Chambers also provided important space for the storage of the increasing number of personal and household goods, not only securing but also ordering the domestic world. The domestic world revealed here is one which was in many ways alien from the present day, where reproduction, subsistence, economic labour and commensality all occurred within one dwelling, housing not only the nuclear family but also sundry associates, servants and possibly relatives – in Laslett's expression, a 'world we have lost'.[2]

---

[2] Peter Laslett, *The World we Have Lost: Further Explored*, 3rd edn (Abingdon: Routledge,

CONCLUSION

The 'practice' of the early modern Thame household took place in a web of space and time on varying scales. Spatially, it occurred in the wider world beyond the horizon, and in the local landscape and community, within the dwelling, with its internal divisions and inhabitants, down to engagement with assemblages, and even the single object and individual. Temporally, it embraced the single brief action, the diurnal tasks in housework, husbandry and trade, to the weekly and seasonal occasions, and so to the span of the life of the household and its inhabitants with its occasional rites of passage, and beyond individual lives into the continuation and variability of the community and its culture. In so far as it catered for the biological reproduction, sustenance, security and personal identity, the early modern household could be said to correspond to the archetypal domestic group outlined in Chapter 2, a manifestation of the control and manipulation of resources. And to the extent that it articulated these functions, it could be seen as a version of Bourdieu's *habitus*, transmitting cultural values through the meanings attached to habitual actions. However, as we have seen above, the Thame household was not a standardised institution, but manifested considerable variation according to status, in space and through time. In this respect it demonstrated the scope of agent intentionality in the re-enactment of inherited culture.[3] As the number of rooms and the spatial options increased, so it appears did distinctions between the mundane and the social, and discrimination within the social sphere. The messy, odorous and mundane processes which supported the subsistence of the household were distanced, thereby also detaching the women and domestics from the hall, the traditional heart of the dwelling, and its social body. The addition of a parlour or chambers provided opportunities for retirement and social distinction within the household. The elaboration of internal physical divisions thus fostered social differentiation, people ordering and being ordered by their material environment. Seventeenth-century Thame domestic life was in this sense a house society, the building expressing the culture and identity of the social group.[4] The architectural framework and the terminology of spaces in the Thame dwelling, as well as the objects associated within them, provided conceptual clues to the actions and relationships to be articulated there. But, as we have seen, notwithstanding the continuation of the nomenclature of the rooms, assemblages of objects changed through time, appearing, shifting in their context and associations, and disappearing from the record, subtly changing the way in which spaces were used and relations conducted, altering the social geography of the house.

1983)
[3] Bourdieu, *Outline of a Theory of Practice*; A. Giddens, *The Constitution of Society* (Cambridge: Polity, 1984)
[4] C. Lévi-Strauss, *Anthropology and Myth: Lectures, 1951–1982*, trans. R. Willis (Oxford: Basil Blackwell, 1987)

The wider environment (including other households) in which it was set therefore acted on the household, providing a template for its external situation and internal physical configuration, the site of habitual actions, the source of materials both for production and consumption. But households, singly and collectively, were also a fundamental component of that environment,[5] and variations in the domestic culture – for example, changing social relationships within the dwelling and altered preferences for and emphasis on certain commodities – conversely permeated outwards to modify the economic, social and ideological context in which they were set.

On an experiential and personal level, then, life was circumscribed by the natural environment, a sense of well-being very much dependent on its potential and limitations, and hazards such as the vagaries of the weather. The exploitation of the immediate landscape was nominally set in a web of tradition in terms of modes of husbandry and labour, as an asset for the benefit of the whole community, but in actuality with an awareness of its unequal distribution. Rhythms were imposed by agriculture and the trades of its produce, all the other occupations of the market town and the running of the household governed day-to-day life, a life mainly of physical labour interspersed with periods of repose. These habitual actions were centred on a wide range of objects, a rich material culture, often engaged unconsciously but nevertheless, in their materiality and affordances forming the sensory experience of life. Social relationships were structured within these activities, the hierarchies of the community and of each household, and for each individual a sense of acknowledged *and* contested status. Here also behaviour was decreed by tradition, with religion ultimately providing authority for the ordering of and the sense of being in the world. And, given the widespread incidence of domestic service, the daily 'practice' of the household provided a template for domestic culture not only for the kin group but also for their servants. This was not a fixed and dependable world. The circumstances of life were subject to the alteration of birth and death, and the vagaries of injury and sickness. The wider world, which provided an outlet for some of the produce of the locality, also increasingly invaded it with its larger economic, political and cultural impulses, creating new opportunities and greater wealth for some, but fear of destitution for others. Modes of production were moving away from subsistence and towards specialisation, the resultant profit purchasing for some additional personal space, new commodities and levels of material comfort. The organisation of the household was changing, and with it the sentiments expressed between its members, with perhaps greater distance between master and servant, and a changed dynamic between the houseman, the housewife and their offspring, and between the householders and their servants. The collective sense of the community and of the household was gradually being eroded

---

[5] I. Hodder, *The Domestication of Europe* (Oxford: Blackwell, 1990), pp. 33–9.

by the more restricted interests of the occupational group. And changed behaviour was reflected in a debate of moral conduct and in the emergence of new modes of religious expression. The most dramatic experience of this changing world was the Civil War sweeping through the town in the middle of the century.

The Thame Household in the Early Modern Narrative

The account given above reveals a complex and shifting set of relationships between the elements of domestic culture – material, social and conceptual – only made evident by restricting the study to limited spatial and temporal dimensions. Does this mean that the picture it reveals is only of parochial interest? The conduct of the study within a defined theoretical and methodological framework is intended to offer the potential of a wider interpretation. Geertz, promoting the virtues of a dense reading of the evidence, maintains that a microstudy such as this need not be theoretically void.[6] In addition, Braudel asserts that the social structures visible in the past were constructed on the myriad of events which constituted daily life, an understanding of which becomes essential to a true reading of that historical totality.[7] A broad agreement exists that the early modern period saw significant changes in many aspects of English life in terms of moral values, social relations and the production and consumption of goods; indeed, the designation 'modern' rests on the premise of this alteration. It was the deliberate intention of this study *not* to employ in advance this narrative as a context for the research but rather to let the evidence of the probate inventories speak for itself. However, the evidence that has emerged in this study suggests that there was both a strong thread of continuity and also change occurring in the domestic culture of Thame in the seventeenth century.

To what extent is the evidence from one rural market town still under manorial sway and largely employing a traditional system of land management really useful in an analysis and understanding of a changing society? Arguably it is this unremarkable nature which makes it a fit and representative subject for study. But the town was also developing an artisan and service economy during the period in growing contact with a wider and metropolitan market, and it included in its social and moral culture a wide range of status and contemporary ideologies. It can therefore also be argued that it is the very complexity and ambiguity of Thame, its representation of many other small agricultural communities in a country where such a way of life had been commonplace for generations but where local custom

[6] C. Geertz, *The Interpretation of Cultures* (New York, Basic Books, 1973), p. 27
[7] F. Braudel, *Civilization and Capitalism 15th to 18th Century: Volume 1, The Structures of Everyday Life: The Limits of the Possible* (London, Collins, 1979/1981), p. 29

was coming under the influence of new national cultures, that make it a relevant example.

The evidence derived from probate inventories suggests a culture which was developing a rich material base, with status increasingly defined by material possessions and their benefits. This culture was one not only of accumulation but also of changing preferences in the disposal of wealth – consumption based less on subsistence and increasingly on choice. The volume and varied quality of linen, for example, provided distinctions of comfort which were evidently appreciated and, given the additional expenditure involved, significant. As previously noted, in the early modern period the term 'comfort' was more closely associated with social inclusion than physical amenity, and within the social dynamic cleanliness carried powerful connotations of respect of and to the person and to the group.[8] Fabrics, and especially washable linen, therefore represented an evident and convenient way in which such respect could be manifested. Personal physical amenity was indicated by the term 'ease' (with its corollary of personal discomfort through 'dis-ease'), a quality which was found, along with personal differentiation, in the backed single chair as opposed to the stool or bench. The changing nature and consumption of commodities can therefore be taken to indicate overlapping inclusive and exclusive tendencies, with a gradual shift away from social affection towards an emphasis on personal gratification.[9] Household goods thus not only afforded greater comfort, but were also intimately connected with notions of status, often articulating social distinctions in increasingly differentiated spaces within the dwelling. And there is evidence; for example, later in the century – in the furnishings of secondary chambers in the larger, and chambers in the smaller households – of a downward spread of the consumption of 'comfort'. This emerging culture of consumption – in which Thame as an economic entity was participating, switching part of its cultivation to fodder crops and husbandry to livestock for the metropolitan market[10] – manifests itself in the inventories in the increasing appearance of commodities which did not have a local source: metal cooking, eating and drinking wares, textiles, furniture and books, for example. The material culture of the Thame dwelling, thus, whilst placing a greater emphasis on physical comfort and fetishisation of objects, would also have created an alienation from local producers and affinities, eroding the autonomy of the local community and drawing

---

[8] J. E. Crowley, *The Invention of Comfort: Sensibilities and Design in Early Modern Britain and Early America*, (Baltimore and London: Johns Hopkins University Press, 2001), pp. 3–6
[9] The mid-eighteenth-century culture of sensibility could be seen as an attempted corrective to this tendency
[10] Richard Blome, *Britannia; or, A Geographical Description of the Kingdoms of England, Scotland, and Ireland, with the Isles and Territories Thereto Belonging* (London, 1677), p. 189; M. A. Havinden, *Household and Farm Inventories in Oxfordshire 1550–90* (Oxfordshire Record Society, London: HMSO, 1965), pp.73–8

it yet further into a wider world. As Daniel Defoe noted of the English dwelling in *The Complete English Tradesman* early in the next century: 'Come next to the furniture of their house. It is scarce credible, to how many counties of England, and how remote, the furniture of but a mean house must send them, and how many people are every where employed about it.'[11] He also noted the sourcing of specific furnishing items by this later date and possibly at an earlier date also: fabrics from various counties in the west and north of England, 'the blankets from Witney in Oxfordshire', cooking metalware from the Midlands, and that 'the chairs, if of cane, are made at London; the ordinary matted chairs perhaps in the place where they live. Tables, chests of drawers etc made at London; as also looking-glass.' The apparently active participation of Thame in this process in the seventeenth century, albeit stimulated by proximity to larger urban centres, corresponds with the conclusions of Weatherill on the localised stimulation of a commodified culture of consumption in the next century.[12]

So, does the diversification of dwelling space (illustrated in Figure 6.2) and its differentiated furnishing point to a growing desire for privacy, as suggested by Hoskins in his assessment of the Great Rebuilding?[13] In part, yes, as the principal figures sought to restrict their social engagement with the rest of their household, the increasing differentiation of space providing for retirement. Such a development has been identified from contemporary literary sources by Orlin,[14] and argued by Stone: 'in the seventeenth and eighteenth centuries the housing of all classes to that of yeoman and tradesman became more varied, more subdivided and more specialized in function, and this afforded greater privacy'.[15] But there is also strong evidence, in the reinterpretation of the parlour as a space of select commensality and entertainment, of a social reorientation away from the collective household towards greater association with external peer groups, neighbours and economic associates: 'privacy' not so much as seclusion but as choice of association. Also those daily tasks on which the subsistence of the household was founded, and the female members of the household and servants who performed them, were simultaneously being shifted away from the hall at the heart of the dwelling towards the periphery in kitchens, butteries and service houses. These developments may correspond with the emergence, postulated by Glassie and Johnson and referred to in Chapter 2, of a self-interested entrepreneurial and

[11] Daniel Defoe, *The Complete English Tradesman* (1726) (Gloucester: Alan Sutton, 1987), pp. 230–31

[12] L. Weatherill, *Consumer Behaviour and Material Culture in Britain 1660–1760* (London: Routledge, 1988)

[13] W. G. Hoskins, 'The Rebuilding of Rural England, 1570–1640', *Past and Present* 4 (1953), 44–59

[14] L. C. Orlin, *Private Matters and Public Culture in Post-Reformation England* (Ithaca and London: Cornell University Press, 1995)

[15] L. Stone, *Family, Sex and Marriage in England 1500–1800* (London: Weidenfeld and Nicolson, 1977), p. 78

individualistic culture, leading to enclosure not only of the rural landscape but also of the previously inclusive household and dwelling.[16]

As we saw in Chapter 1, Thame in the seventeenth century was set in a world of significant economic, political and social change. Under the influence of this new culture and with the increasing segmentation of the dwelling the householder and associates could withdraw physically and affectively from the rest of the household. If commensality in the hall had expressed communality, albeit with an internal hierarchy, the new arrangement meant a segregation of consumption and of occupational 'classes' within the dwelling.[17] It is argued that the householder was becoming increasingly managerial in attitude toward his or her household, with the social focus at least partially reorientated to external and self-interested association. Muldrew's study of commerce in the early modern period identifies the importance of social association as a foundation for trust and financial credit.[18] Much of this would take place in the market place and shop, but the spatial and furnishing differentiation of the early modern house suggests that some significant peer association took place in the domicile. And this reading is supported by the aspirational furnishings evidenced in mercantile houses, such as court cupboards and portals, in part in imitation of elite interiors but also with an apparent emphasis on shared 'comfort' in socially discriminating space, in contrast possibly to a fading culture of undiscriminating 'largesse' in the dwellings of yeomen. We could go further and suggest that the merchant desired the material trappings which he (or she) associated with elite social status, but within a culture less predicated on the link between privilege and social responsibility, although other evidence such as the Enslow Hill rebellion of 1596 suggests that for some of the local population, despite the veneer of 'honour' culture, the local elite had already shown themselves to be largely self-interested.[19] And, as we have seen in Chapter 1, contemporary comment now defined gentry status in terms of an ability 'to live without manual labour' whilst affording the right presentation to the world.[20] In an exploration of the significant focus on 'politeness' in early modern culture, Green argues that 'acts of building need to be understood in terms of social relationships as "self-and-other-aware"'.[21]

---

[16] H. H. Glassie, *Folk Housing in Middle Virginia: A Structural Analysis of Historic Artifacts* (Tennessee: University of Tennessee Press, 1975); M. Johnson, *Housing Culture: Traditional Architecture in an English Landscape* (London: UCL Press, 1993); M. Johnson, *An Archaeology of Capitalism* (Oxford: Blackwell, 1996), p. 155

[17] Johnson, *An Archaeology of Capitalism*, p. 175

[18] Craig Muldrew, *The Economy of Obligation: The Culture of Credit and Social Relations in Early Modern England* (Basingstoke: Macmillan, 1998), pp. 95–119

[19] R. B. Manning, *Village Revolts; Social Protest and Popular Disturbances in England, 1509–1640* (Oxford: Clarendon Press, 1988), pp. 220–52

[20] William Harrison, *The Description of England* (1587), ed. G. Edelen (Washington and New York: Folger Shakespeare Library, Dover Books, 1994), pp. 113–14

[21] A. Green, 'The Polite Threshold in Seventeenth- and Eighteenth-Century Britain', *Ver-*

CONCLUSION

Changing sentiment towards others was first articulated in the spatial rearrangement of objects and actions, and then given built expression. Whilst architectural configuration traditionally provided the template for differentiation of activities and association, objects played a more versatile mnemonic role moving beyond and between physical thresholds – a shift from architectural to artefactual meanings.[22] Habitual actions were no longer locked into traditional architectural configuration but were now open to a greater variety of interpretation, a Foucauldian contestation of the signification of space. The increasing commodification of the early modern dwelling provided an expression of new ways of acting. Surplus expenditure no longer went primarily towards corporate identities but self-aggrandisement, a manifestation of the emergence of raw 'materialism'.[23] New consumer objects such as chairs were both individualistic and versatile, not 'standing' as in the old order but with a capacity to move around the room, creating a varied, selective and non-hierarchical social dynamic. The house was a stage for the redefinition not just of relationships but of people themselves. The medieval household, in contemporary theory and largely in practice, consisted of a community united in enterprise and accommodating an internal hierarchy; the early modern period saw new forms of external enterprise which facilitated the breakdown of this internal interdependence.[24] The shift away from the collective heart of the house, the hall, to the discriminating service areas and to the parlour can be seen as redefining the household into more distinct occupational groups, the householder enacting a desire to redefine himself more closely and self-interestedly with his social and economic peers. It is perhaps not surprising that the domestic domain was a significant arena in this social and economic reconfiguration, still being for most the centre of their material and social existence, and where social differences were most acute because most proximate; in the words of King, 'the domestic context became an increasingly important locale for the expression and negotiation of middling social relationships and identities'.[25] This process has been seen as a rise of individualism,[26] and the greater physical comfort imparted by commodities could certainly be seen as a mark of self-indulgence, but can also be seen as the manifestation of a new awareness of shared class interest and identity of the 'middling ranks'. It mirrors the external withdrawal of the middling ranks from community ownership (expressed in the process

nacular Architecture 41 (2010), 1–9, 1

[22] Johnson, *An Archaeology of Capitalism*, pp. 171–3

[23] *Ibid.*, p. 171; C. Mukerji, *From Graven Images: Patterns of Modern Materialism* (New York: Columbia University Press, 1983), p. 8

[24] Johnson, *Housing Culture*, p. 137

[25] C. King, '"Closure" and the Urban Great Rebuilding in Early Modern Norwich', *Post-Medieval Archaeology* 44:1 (2010), 54–80, 73

[26] Johnson, *Housing Culture*, p. 171; Johnson, *An Archaeology of Capitalism*, p. 157; A. Macfarlane, *The Origins of English Individualism* (Oxford: Blackwell, 1978)

of land enclosure) and local popular culture, and embracing rather local peer and ultimately national forms of enterprise and culture.[27] It has been noted that knowledge of practice is gathered not only in actions but in the direction of movement around an environment.[28] In the domestic culture of the early modern period we see one form of practice being weakened and substituted by redirected actions. In the words of Johnson: 'Architecture and material culture formed a critical area of social and cultural transformation and a key arena in the emergence of modern social relations'.[29]

Johnson and Leone link the new mentality to changing religious ideology.[30] It is perhaps significant that Thame saw an upswell of Puritan activity and affiliation during the first half of the seventeenth century.[31] Max Weber's celebrated argument for the central influence of Protestant ideology on the rise of a capitalist economy has been criticised as lacking an evidential foundation; it has nevertheless suggested a plausible conjunction of religious and commercial innovation.[32] Weber argued against institutional determinants for change in the economic life of Europe in the modern period, suggesting rather individualistic capitalist enterprise, and Hill argues that Puritanism – representing more extreme anti-institutional sentiments of Protestantism – in the early seventeenth century was as much a political as spiritual movement, with strong economic connotations.[33] Religious virtue was no longer segregated from but became integrated into mundane activity, resolving the medieval distinction and tension between economic and ideological life. Indeed, within Calvinist ideology material success became a mark of divine favour: 'the good man of the house, by planting godliness in his family, doth not a little advance and set forth his private profit and own commodity'.[34] Central to this mentality was a drive for greater order. It has been argued that it was Puritans who successfully addressed, through their own spirit of enterprise, the problems of the country's economic and labour organisation.[35] If idleness was an opportunity for the devil to make mischief, then self-discipline and application to work represented virtue, and the benefits of work virtue's reward. As the Puritan

[27] A. Fletcher and J. Stevenson, eds, *Order and Disorder in Early Modern England* (Cambridge : Cambridge University Press, 1985), pp. 1–41; C. Hill, *Society and Puritanism in Pre Revolutionary England* (London: Mercury Press, 1966), p. 418

[28] T. Ingold, *Being Alive* (London and New York: Routledge, 2011), p. 160

[29] Johnson, *An Archaeology of Capitalism*, p. 157

[30] *Ibid.*, pp. 170–6; Leone, *The Archaeology of Liberty*

[31] VCH, pp. 211–12

[32] M. Weber, *The Protestant Ethic and the 'Spirit' of Capitalism and Other Writings* (1905) (New York: Penguin Books, 2002)

[33] Hill, *Society and Puritanism in Pre-Revolutionary England*, p. 7

[34] Henry Bullinger, *The Decades of Henry Bullinger: The First and Second Decades* (1587), trans. H. I., ed. Thomas Harding (Cambridge: Cambridge University Press, 1849), p. 258

[35] Weber, *The Protestant Ethic and the 'Spirit' of Capitalism*, pp. 152–5; M. Douglas and B. Isherwood, *The World of Goods: Towards an Anthropology of Consumption* (London: Allen Lane, 1979), pp. 27–30; Hill, *Society and Puritanism in Pre-Revolutionary England*, pp. 389, 418–20

sought to develop a personal and blessed relationship with God, so within his dwelling the householder was held to be fount of moral authority, tasked with the instruction and direction of his wife, children and servants to a purer life, and thus eternal salvation, his domestic subjects exhorted to be obedient and dutiful. These sentiments were expressed in numerous contemporary spiritual texts such as Cleaver's *A Godly Forme of Household Government*.[36] The distancing of the mundane – foodstuff processing and cooking – from the social has been seen as a misogynistic Puritan move to keep women at home away from the evils of the world.[37] In John Bunyan's *Pilgrim's Progress* (1678) it was the 'House Beautiful' that represented virtuous Christian society, and in Puritan households the virtuous wife was not infrequently held up as the symbol of probity and a moral guide.[38] For some, the religious and domestic life therefore became synonymous, effectively 'a church in his house'.[39] The economic and social tensions of the early modern period were thus manifested within the household: 'The economic tension of the community in the process of breaking up is focussed on the household, in transition from a patriarchal unit of communal production to a capitalist firm.'[40] As argued in Chapter 2, the relative strength of domestic and social relationships shifts with the increasing complexity of a society, and affective links tend to diminish as material assets increase.[41] The householder became a moral and occupational manager rather than a patriarch to his household, often preferring to associate for personal advancement with his or her peer group, the cohesion of the 'middling ranks' being expressed more in domestic hospitality than in the local church.[42] Ultimately the efficacy of this pursuit of self and class interest would become established in the eighteenth-century philosophies of Adam Smith (1776) and Jeremy Bentham (1789).[43]

So, as has been argued in this study, domestic culture is a fusion of material, social and conceptual or ideological elements, seen in the changing identities and actions in the Thame early modern household. The spatial configuration of the dwelling tended towards an occupational and social

---

[36] Robert Cleaver, *A Godlie Forme of Householde Gouernment for the Ordering of Priuate Families, According to the Direction of God's Word* (London, 1598); Hill, *Society and Puritanism in Pre-Revolutionary England*, pp. 101, 105, 112, 330–1

[37] C. Shammas, *The Industrial Pre-Consumer in England and America* (Oxford: Clarendon Press, 1990), pp. 186–8

[38] B. S. Capp, *When Gossips Meet: Women, Family and Neighbourhood in Early Modern England* (Oxford: Oxford University Press, 2003), p. 18

[39] Cleaver, *A Godlie Forme of Householde Gouernment for the Ordering of Priuate Families*, A4; Johnson, *An Archaeology of Capitalism*, pp. 134, 172–3

[40] Hill, *Society and Puritanism in Pre-Revolutionary England*, p. 422

[41] M. Fortes, 'Introduction', *The Developmental Cycle in Domestic Groups*, ed. J. Goody (Cambridge: Cambridge University Press, 1958), pp. 3, 8; M. Douglas, *Man in Society: Patterns of Human Organisation*, (London: Macdonald & Co., 1964), pp. 100, 102

[42] Hill, *Society and Puritanism in Pre-Revolutionary England*, p. 422

[43] B. Russell, *History of Western Philosophy* (London: Allen and Unwin, 1961), pp. 740–4

segregation, and a growing emphasis on the 'profit' and 'comfort' provided by commodities, both in their production and in their consumption, resulting in an affective distance within the household. It is argued that this reorientation of domestic culture has its roots in the desire by the middling ranks to redefine their relationships with the outside world and with the members of their households, underpinned by growing commercial specialisation and religious ideology. This forms a plausible conjunction of materiality, activities and intent. This study has argued that life was largely lived in the domestic domain, and that actions carried social, conceptual and ideological significance; it is therefore credible that ideology would permeate and influence such an important area of human engagement. However, this hypothesis needs to be approached with caution. In the words of Charles Parker, the contrast between modern individualism and medieval communalism may have become an 'overdrawn dichotomy'.[44] It should not be assumed, for example, from the above that there was a simple correspondence of commercial activity and nonconformist ideology to changes in the reorganisation of domestic life and relationships. As has emerged from this study, even a relatively insignificant community in seventeenth-century England was a complex blend of tradition and innovation, and numerous and variable individual and household agendas.

The evidence employed in this study shows no absolute attribution of change to one occupational group of householders in Thame, and it can be argued that the seventeenth-century yeoman and husbandman were potentially as entrepreneurial in their commercial attitude as the tradesman and artisan.[45] Rather, the picture gained is of a whole community in the process of gradual change, with considerable variations between households, syn- and dia-chronically, although – as the evidence of this study suggests and Wrightson notes – the agriculturalists appear generally to have been slower in their acquisition of new domestic consumables, retaining the apparatus of largesse such as the table cloth and commensal washing vessel.[46] Thomas Fuller also characterised the yeoman as traditionally having been 'bountifull both to strangers and poore people', keeping a generous table, but a custom that by mid-century was rapidly disappearing.[47] It is also interesting to note that, whereas agriculturalists – yeomen and husbandmen – were, like gentry, invested with a group identity through their occupational designation, tradesmen and artisans were identified by their individual trades and crafts, and may therefore have felt more impelled to establish new allegiances and a new

---

[44] C. Parker, 'Introduction; Individual and Community in the Early Modern World', *Between the Middle Ages and Modernity: Individual and Community in the Early Modern World*, ed. C. H. Parker and J. H. Bentley (Lanham: Rowman and Littlefield, 2007), p. 3

[45] K. Wrightson, *Earthly Necessities: Economic Lives in Early Modern Britain 1470–1750* (London: Penguin Books, 2000/2002), p. 137

[46] *Ibid.*, p.298

[47] Thomas Fuller, *The Holy State and the Profane State* (Cambridge, 1642), p. 117

shared class identity. Thame was being drawn into a new commercial world, increasing in population and trade through the seventeenth century, and into the economic hinterland of the metropolis. But it still retained its parish institutions and its open field system with links to the community values of the past. And in the dwellings the hall, with its connotations of the integrated household, still sat beside the newly discriminating parlour. Johnson acknowledges the playing out through this period of centrifugal against centripetal forces within the household.[48] The imprecise spatial differentiation of activities within dwellings suggests no hard and fast template of material and social engagement, and the evidence hints at divergences of practice within individual households. We cannot be certain, for example, whether women were becoming marginalised in their domestic work[49] or esteemed as skilled practitioners and managers of domestic activities[50] and co-hosts in household entertainment.[51] The historical evidence therefore presents a complex and not infrequently ambiguous picture of the domestic culture of Thame, with individuals in each dwelling pursuing varying agendas, a mix of tradition and innovation. In the words of Vere Gordon Childe: 'men gradually discover by experiment how things and persons can be arranged spatially'.[52]Change in the domestic domain is usually a subtle process of shifting associations of objects, actions and concepts emerging gradually over time out of a context of tradition. Nevertheless, we could postulate that in the households of early modern Thame we are seeing a conjunction of changes in commodification – of the nature and sourcing of objects and their 'consumption' – and of shifting social allegiances, underpinned by ideology; all part of the broader reconfiguration of early modern society.

Domestic Culture:
An Interpretive Framework and Theoretical Perspective

To come, then, to the conclusion of this study. Limited in scale but dense in detail, it has attempted to embrace the very many interrelated elements of domestic life: the natural, economic, social, conceptual and moral environment in which the Thame household was posited, the prescribed form of the social unit and dwelling space, the furnishing of the household with a wide range of objects affording acts of subsistence, commensality,

---

[48] Johnson, *Housing Culture*, p. 137
[49] N. Cox, '"A Flesh Pott, or a Brasse Pott or a Pott to Boile in": Changes in Metal and Fuel Technology in the Early Modern Period and the Implications for Cooking', *Gender and Material Culture in Historical Perspective*, ed. M. Donald, and L. Hurcombe, Studies in Gender and Material Culture 3 (London: Macmillan, 2000), pp. 143, 148
[50] S. Pennell, 'The Material Culture of Food in Early Modern England, circa 1650-1750' D.Phil. thesis (University of Oxford, 1997), pp. 203, 217, 240-2, 283-4
[51] F. Heal, *Hospitality in Early Modern England* (Oxford: Clarendon Press, 1990), pp. 179-83
[52] V. G. Childe, *Society and Knowledge* (Westport: Greenwood, 1956), p. 298

conviviality and rest, and their spatial ordering and use though time. All of these elements combined to constitute the domestic culture, a complex and shifting matrix. An interpretive framework has been proposed and employed in order to attempt a comprehension of this complexity in the case of this study of seventeenth-century domestic life in Thame. Underpinned as it is by theoretical perspectives, it is to be hoped that such an approach could be more widely applicable to the study of all domestic life. At its root lies an assertion of the fundamental place of the material in human existence, engagement with the environment giving rise to actions which articulate relationships and convey meanings. Arguably, domestic life is based on identifiable structures, through the operation of the 'practice' of habitual actions communicating norms of behaviour and shared values, cued by the configuration of buildings, their internal divisions and assemblages of objects. However, although such 'structures' appear to have a determinable entity, their interrelationship and relative significance in the composition of domestic life is frequently hard to determine. A more productive approach is to focus on the relationship between these elements themselves, tracing interlinked networks of materiality, actions and significance. But relationships are by their nature transitory and fugitive, especially those of a social and conceptual nature, and, being in the past, fade from sight. For this reason this study has focussed on the evidence derived in the main from the assemblages of objects presented in the probate inventories, their location and association with humans operating in social space and time, enriched where appropriate by other contemporary sources. And if it has succeeded in deriving from quantitative analysis indications of the affective nature of social relationships and their consequences in terms of the organisation of the material world, then it will have substantiated the phenomenological theoretical assertion that *all* human existence is grounded in engagement with the material world. Other studies of historical domestic culture will derive evidence from sources of a different nature, communicating diverse aspects of human experience, but I would argue that the conceptual needs always, as far as is possible, to be related to its physical context, and vice versa. As in life, bodily experience and thought are in a continual dialogue. 'Domestic culture' is therefore presented here as a structuring and structured network of relationships, incorporating the material, social and conceptual elements of domestic life, and also as a theoretical perspective and as an interpretive framework, sufficiently comprehensive and flexible to accommodate this complexity. And in focussing on the domestic domain this study asserts the centrality of domestication in human development, identity and experience.

Bibliography

Contemporary Printed Sources

Where I have consulted a modern reprint, the details of that edition are included

Barbour, John, *The Bruce : or, The History of Robert I. King of Scotland* (c. 1375) (London, 1790)

Blome, Richard, *Britannia: or, A Geographical Description of the Kingdoms of England, Scotland, and Ireland, with the Isles and Territories Thereto Belonging* (London, 1677)

Bodleian Library Broadside Ballad Collection

Bullinger, Henry, *The Decades of Henry Bullinger: The First and Second Decades* (1587), trans. H.I., ed. Thomas Harding (Cambridge, 1849)

Bunyan, John, *Pilgrim's Progress* (London, 1678)

Cleaver, Robert, *A Godlie Forme of Householde Gouernment for the Ordering of Priuate Families, According to the Direction of God's Word* (London, 1598)

Comenius, Johann Amos, *Orbis Sensualium Pictus*, 3rd London edn (London, 1672)

Cotgrave, Randle, *A Dictionarie of the French and English Tongues* (1611) (Menston, 1968)

Defoe, Daniel, *A Tour through the Whole Island of Great Britain, Vol. 1* (1725), Everyman Library (London, 1962)

Defoe, Daniel, *The Complete English Tradesman* (1726) (Gloucester, 1987)

Drayton, Michael, *The Complete Works of Michael Drayton* (1622), introduction and notes by R. Hooper (London, 1876)

Ellwood, Thomas, *The History of Thomas Ellwood ... Written in his Own Hand*, 4th edn (London, 1791)

Filmer, Sir Robert, *Patriarcha and Other Works of Sir Robert Filmer* (London, 1680)

Finett, Sir John, *Finetti Philoxenis* (London, 1656)

Fuller, Thomas, *The Holy State and the Profane State* (Cambridge, 1642)

Gataker, Thomas, 'Marriage Duties Briefly Couched Together', *Certaine Sermons* (London, 1637)

Greene, Robert, *Defence of Conny Catching* (London, 1592)

Griffith, Matthew, *Bethel: or, A Forme for Families* (London, 1634)

Halliwell-Phillipps J. O., ed., *The Boke of Curtasye: An English Poem of the Fourteenth Century* (London, 1841)

Harrison, William, *The Description of England* (1587), ed. G. Edelen (Washington, 1994)

Herbert, George, *A Priest to the Temple* (1652), ed. H. C. Beeching (Oxford, 1908)

Herbert, George, *The Temple: Sacred Poems and Private Ejaculations* (1633) (Chiswick, 1838)

Holme, Randle, *The Academy of Armory; or, A Storehouse of Armory and Blazon* (1688), ed. I. H. Jeayes (London, 1905)

Hindley, C., ed., *The Roxburghe Ballads* (London, 1874)

Huloet, Richard, *Abcedarium Anglico Latinum* (London, 1552)

Jewel, John, *The Second Tome Book of Homilies* (London, 1571)

Josselin, Ralph, *The Diary of Ralph Josselin 1616–1683*, ed. A. Macfarlane, British Academy Records of Economic and Social History, n.s. 3 (London, 1976)

King, Gregory, 'Natural and Political Observations and Conclusions upon the State and Condition of England' and'Of the Naval Trade of England A' 1688 and the National Profit then Arising Thereby' (1688), ed. with an introduction George E. Barnett (Baltimore, 1936)

Langland, W., *The Vision of William Concerning Piers the Plowman; Together with, Vita de Dowel, Dobet, et Dobest secundum Wit et Resoun*, ed. W. W. Skeat (London, 1869)

Locke, J., *An Essay Concerning Human Understanding in Four Books*, 4th edn (London, 1700)

Markham, Gervase, *The English Housewife* (1615), ed. M. R. Best (Kingston and Montreal, 1986)

Markham, Gervase, *Markham's Farewell to Husbandry* (London, 1620)

Markham, Gervase, *A Way to Get Wealth by Approved Rules of Practice in Good Husbandry and Huswiferie* (London, 1625)

Mayo, Richard, *A Present for Servants, from their Ministers, Masters, or Other Friends* (London, 1693)

Milton, John, 'L'Allegro' (1631), in John Milton, *The Poetical Works of John Milton*, ed. H. C. Beeching (Oxford, 1900)

Minsheu, John, *The Guide into Tongues etc.* (London, 1617 and 1627)

Misson, Henri, *M. Misson's Memoirs and Observations in his Travels over England* (London, 1719)

Morris, Robert, *The Book of Pottage and Broth 1580–1660* (Bristol, 2006)

Nourse, Timothy, *Campania Foelix: or, A Discourse of the Benefits and Improvements of Husbandry* (London, 1700)

Philips, Edward, *The New World of English Words: or, A General Dictionary* (London, 1658), ed. J. Kersey, 6th edn (Menston, 1969)

Plot, Robert, *The Natural History of Oxfordshire* (Oxford, 1677), 2nd edn (London, 1705)

Ray, John, *A Collection of English Words, Not Generally Used* (London, 1674)

Shakespeare, William, *The Globe Illustrated Shakespeare: The Complete Works Annotated* (New York, 1986)

Smith, Sir Thomas, *The Common-wealth of England and the Maner of Gouernement Thereof* (London, 1609)

Stukeley, William, *Itinerarium Curiosum: or, An Account of the Antiquities, and Remarkable Curiosities in Nature or Art* (London, 1776)

BIBLIOGRAPHY

Walton, Izaak, *The Compleat Angler* (London, 1653)
Wood, Anthony, *The Life of Anthony Wood in his Own Words*, ed. N. K. Kiessling (Oxford, 2009)
Yarranton, Andrew, *England's Improvement by Sea and Land* (London, 1677)

Secondary Sources

Abbott, Mary, *Family Ties: English Families 1540–1920* (London, 1993)
Airs, M. and J. Rhodes, 'Wall-Paintings from a House in Upper High Street, Thame', *Oxoniensia* 45 (1980), 235–59
Alcock N. W., 'The Great Rebuilding and its Later Stages', *Vernacular Architecture* 14:1 (1983), 45–8
Alcock, N. W., *People at Home: Living in a Warwickshire Village 1500–1800* (Chichester, 1993)
Alcock, N. W. and C. R. J. Currie, 'Upstairs or Downstairs', *Vernacular Architecture* 20 (1989), 21–3
Allison, Penelope M., ed., *The Archaeology of Household Activities* (New York, 1999)
Amussen, S. D., *An Ordered Society: Gender and Class In Early Modern England* (Oxford, 1993)
Appadurai, A., 'Introduction: Commodities and the Politics of Value', *The Social Life of Things: Commodities in Cultural Perspective*, ed. A. Appadurai (Cambridge, 1986)
Arkell, T., 'Interpreting Probate Inventories', *When Death Do Us Part: Understanding and Interpreting the Probate Records of Early Modern England*, ed. T. Arkell, N. Evans and N. Goose (Oxford, 2000)
Arkell, T., 'The Probate Process', *When Death Do Us Part: Understanding and Interpreting the Probate Records of Early Modern England*, ed. T. Arkell, N. Evans and N. Goose, (Oxford, 2000)
Ayres, James, *Domestic Interiors: The British Tradition 1500–1850* (New Haven and London, 2003)
Axel, B., 'Introduction: Historical Anthropology and its Vicissitudes', *From the Margins: Historical Anthropology and its Futures*, ed. B. Axel, (Durham, 2002)
Baines, P., *Spinning Wheels: Spinners and Spinning* (London, 1977)
Bakhtin, M. M., *The Dialogic Imagination: Four Essays* (Austin, 1981)
Bapty, I. and Yates, T., eds, *Archaeology after Structuralism* (London, 1990)
Barley M. W., *The English Farmhouse and Cottage* (London, 1961)
Barth, F., 'Towards Greater Naturalism in Conceptualizing Societies', *Conceptualizing Society*, ed. A. Kuper (London, 1992)
Bauman, Z., 'Hermeneutics and Social Science', *Theory, Culture and Society* 1:3 (1978), 32–43
Bell, J., 'The Mortality Crisis in Thame and East Oxfordshire 1643', *Oxfordshire Local History* 3:4 (1990), 137–52
Bentham, J., *A Fragment on Government; and, An Introduction to the Principles of Morals and Legislation* (1789) (Oxford, 1948)
Benveniste, E., *Indo-European Language and Society* (London, 1973)

283

Best, M.R., ed., 'Introduction', *Gervase Markham; The English Housewife*, ed. M. R. Best (Kingston and Montreal, 1986)

Bestall, J. M., *History of Chesterfield* (Chesterfield, 1974)

Bevis, H. and L. L. G. Ramsey, eds, *The Connoisseur Complete Encyclopaedia of Antiques* (London, 1975)

Binford, L. *New Perspectives in Archaeology* (Chicago, 1968)

Blunt, A. and R. Dowling, *Home* (London, 2006)

Boulton, J., *Neighbourhood and Society: A London Suburb in the Seventeenth Century* (Cambridge and New York, 1987)

Bourdieu, P., *Outline of a Theory of Practice*, trans. R. Nice (Cambridge, 1977)

Bourdieu, P., *Distinction: A Social Critique of the Judgment of Taste*, trans. R. Nice (London 1984)

Bourdieu, P., *The Logic of Practice* (Cambridge, 1990)

Braudel, F. *Civilization and Capitalism 15th to 18th Century, Volume 1, The Structures of Everyday Life: The Limits of the Possible* (London, 1979/1981)

Braudel, F., *Civilization and Capitalism 15th to 18th Century, Volume 2, The Wheels of Commerce* (London, 1983)

British Geological Survey, *Geology of the Country around Thame* (London, 1995)

Brown, F. E., 'Continuity and Change in the Urban House: Developments in Domestic Space Organisation in 17th-Century London', *Comparative Studies in Society and History* 28 (1986), 558–90

Brunskill, R. W., *Houses and Cottages of Britain: Origins and Development of Traditional Domestic Design* (London, 1997)

Buchli, V., 'Architecture and the Domestic Sphere', *The Material Culture Reader*, ed. V. Buchli (Oxford, 2002)

Buettner-Janusch, J., *Origins of Man; Physical Anthropology* (New York, 1966)

Burges, E. W. and H. J. Locke, *The Family, from Institution to Companionship* (New York, 1945)

Burke, P., 'Overture: The New History: Its Past and its Future', *New Perspectives on Historical Writing*, ed. P. Burke (Cambridge, 2001)

Butler, J., *Bodies that Matter* (New York and London, 1993)

Buxton, A., 'Domestic Culture in Early Seventeenth-Century Thame', *Oxoniensia* 67 (2002), 76–115

Canter, D., *The Psychology of Place* (New York, 1977)

Capp, B. S., *When Gossips Meet: Women, Family and Neighbourhood in Early Modern England* (Oxford, 2003)

Carsten, J. and S. Hugh-Jones, eds, *About the House: Levi-Strauss and Beyond* (Cambridge: Cambridge University Press, 1995)

Carsten, J. and S. Hugh-Jones, 'Introduction', *About the House: Levi-Strauss and Beyond*, ed. J. Carsten and S. (Cambridge, 1995)

Chafe, W. L., *The Meaning and Structure of Language* (Chicago and London, 1970)

Childe, V. G., *Society and Knowledge* (Westport, 1956)

Chinnery, V., *Oak Furniture: The British Tradition* (Woodbridge, 1979)

Cieraad, Irene, ed., *At Home: An Anthropology of Domestic Space* (Syracuse, 2006)

Clark, D. R., *Oxfordshire Buildings Record Report No. 90* (2010)

Clark, P. and P. Slack, *English Towns in Transition 1550–1700* (Oxford, 1976)

Clarke, G., *The Book of Thame* (Buckingham, 1978)

Cochran, M. D. and M. C. Beaudry, 'Material Culture Studies and Historical Archaeology', *The Cambridge Companion to Historical Archaeology*, ed. D. Hicks and M. C. Beaudry (Cambridge, 2006)

Cockayne, E., *Hubbub: Filth, Noise and Stench in England 1600–1770* (New Haven and London, 2007)

Comaroff, J. and J. Comaroff, *Ethnicity and the Historical Imagination* (Boulder and Oxford, 1992)

Counihan, C. and P. Van Esterick, 'Introduction', *Food and Culture: a Reader*, ed. C. Counihan, and P. Van Esterick, (London, 1997)

Cox, N., '"A Flesh Pott, or a Brasse Pott or a Pott to Boile in": Changes in Metal and Fuel Technology in the Early Modern Period and the Implications for Cooking', *Gender and Material Culture in Historical Perspective*, ed. M. Donald and L. Hurcombe, Studies in Gender and Material Culture 3 (London, 2000)

Cox, J. and N. Cox, 'Probate 1500–1800: A System in Transition', *When Death Do Us Part: Understanding and Interpreting the Probate Records of Early Modern England*, ed. T. Arkell, N. Evans and N. Goose (Oxford, 2000)

Crowley, J. E., *The Invention of Comfort: Sensibilities and Design in Early Modern Britain and Early America* (Baltimore and London, 2001)

Currie, C. R. J., 'Time and Chance: Modelling the Attrition of Old Houses', *Vernacular Architecture* 19 (1988), 1–9

Csikszentmihalyi, M. and E. Rochberg-Halton, *The Meaning of Things: Domestic Symbols and the Self* (New York, 1981)

Davies, K., 'Continuity and Change in Literary Advice on Marriage', *Marriage and Society*, ed. R. B. Outhwaite (London, 1981)

Deetz, J., *In Small Things Forgotten: An Archaeology of Early American Life* (New York, 1977)

Deetz, J. and P. S. Deetz, *The Times of their Lives* (New York, 2000)

Department of the Environment, *List of Buildings of Special Architectural or Historical Interest; District of South Oxfordshire; Town of Thame* (London, 1988)

Derrida, J., *Of Grammatology*, trans. Gayatri Spivak (Baltimore and London, 1977)

Dils, J. and D. Schwartz, *Tudor and Stuart Shrivenham* (Reading, 2004)

Dilthey, Wilhelm, *Hermeneutics and the Study of History*, ed. Rudolf A. Makkreel and Frithjof Rodi (Princeton, 1996)

Dobres, M. and J. E. Robb, eds, *Agency in Archaeology* (London, 2000)

Donley-Reid, L. W., 'A Structuring Structure: The Swahili House', *Domestic Architecture and the Use of Space*, ed. S. Kent (Cambridge, 1990)

Douglas, M., *Man in Society: Patterns of Human Organisation* (London, 1964)

Douglas, M. and B. Isherwood, *The World of Goods: Towards an Anthropology of Consumption* (London, 1979)

Durkheim, É. and M. Marcel, *Primitive Classification* (1902) trans. and ed. with intro. R. Needham (Chicago, 1963)

Durant, D. N., *Bess of Hardwick: Portrait of an Elizabethan Dynast*, rev. edn (London, 1999)

Dyer, A., 'Small Market Towns 1540–1700', *The Cambridge Urban History of Britain, Volume 2: 1540–1840*, ed. P. Clark (Cambridge, 2000)

Earle, P., *The Making of the English Middle Class: Business, Society and Family Life in London, 1660–1730* (London, 1989)

Edwards, R., *The Shorter Dictionary of English Furniture* (1964) (Twickenham, 1987)

Engels, F., *The Origin of the Family, Private Property and the State* (1884) (New York, 1972)

Erickson, Bonnie H., 'Social Networks and History: A Review Essay', *Historical Methods: A Journal of Quantitative and Interdisciplinary History* 30:3 (1997), 149–57

Evans, I. H., ed., *Brewer's Dictionary of Phrase and Fable* (1870) (London, 1981)

Evans-Pritchard E. E., *Anthropology and History* (Manchester, 1961)

Everleigh, D., *Brass and Brassware* (Princes Risborough, 1995)

Farley, M., 'Pottery and Pottery Kilns of the Post-Medieval Period at Brill, Buckinghamshire', *Post-Medieval Archaeology* 13 (1979), 127–52

Fastnedge, R., *English Furniture Styles from 1500 to 1830* (Harmondsworth, 1955)

Fearn, J., *Cast Iron* (Princes Risborough, 1990)

Flather, A., *Gender and Space in Early Modern England* (Woodbridge, 2007)

Fletcher, A. and J. Stevenson, eds, *Order and Disorder in Early Modern England* (Cambridge, 1985)

Fletcher, M. and G. R. Lock, *Digging Numbers: Elementary Statistics for Archaeologists* (Oxford, 1991)

Fortes, M., 'Introduction', *The Developmental Cycle in Domestic Groups*, ed. J. Goody (Cambridge, 1958)

Foucault, M., *The Archaeology of Knowledge* (London, 1972)

Foucault, M., *Discipline and Punish: The Birth of the Prison* (Harmondsworth, 1979)

Fussell G. E., 'Robert Loder's Farm Accounts, 1610–20', *Camden Society*, Third Series, 53 (1936)

Garlick, J., 'Farming Activities at Thame and Woodstock in the Early Seventeenth Century: The Evidence of Probate Inventories', *Oxfordshire Local History* 3:7 (Autumn 1991), 291–317

Geertz, C., *The Interpretation of Cultures* (New York, 1973)

Gell, A., *Art and Agency* (Oxford, 1998)

Gentle, R. and R. Feild, *Domestic Metalwork Dates 1640-1820* (1975), rev. and enlarged B. Gentle (Woodbridge, 1994)

Gentilecore, David, 'The Ethnography of Everyday Life', *Early Modern Italy, 1550–1796*, ed. John Marino (Oxford, 2002)

Gentilecore, David, 'Anthropological Approaches', *Writing Early Modern History*, ed. Garthine Walker (London, 2005)

Gibson, J. J., 'The Theory of Affordances', *Perceiving, Acting and Knowing*, ed. R. Shaw and J. Bransford (New York, 1977)

Gibson, J. J., *The Ecological Approach to Visual Perception* (New York, 1986)

Giddens, A., *Central Problems in Social Theory: Action, Structure and Contradiction in Social Analysis* (Basingstoke, 1979)

Giddens, A., *The Constitution of Society* (Cambridge, 1984)

Gilbert, C., *English Vernacular Furniture 1750–1900* (New Haven and London, 1991)

Gillespie, Susan D., 'Beyond Kinship: an Introduction', *Beyond Kinship: Social and Material Reproduction in House Societies*, ed. R. A. Joyce and S. D. Gillespie (Philadelphia, 2000)

Gillespie, Susan D., 'Levi-Strauss: *Maison* and *Societé à Maisons*', *Beyond Kinship:*

Social and Material Reproduction in House Societies, ed. R. A. Joyce and S. D. Gillespie (Philadelphia, 2000)

Girouard, Mark, *Life in the English Country House* (New Haven and London, 1978)

Girouard, Mark, *Hardwick Hall* (London, 1989)

Glassie, H. H., *Folk Housing in Middle Virginia: A Structural Analysis of Historic Artifacts* (Tennessee, 1975)

Glennie, P. and I. Whyte, 'Towns in an Agrarian Economy 1540–1700', *The Cambridge Urban History of Britain*, ed. D. M. Palliser, P. Clark and M. J. Daunton (Cambridge, 2000)

Gloag, J., *A Short Dictionary of Furniture* (London, 1977)

Goldstone, Jack A., 'Urbanization and Inflation: Lessons from the English Price Revolution of the Sixteenth and Seventeenth Centuries', *American Journal of Sociology* 89:5 (March 1984), 1122–60

Goody, J., 'The Evolution of the Family' *Household and Family in Past Time*, ed. P. Laslett and R. Wall (Cambridge, 1972)

Gosden, C., *Social Being and Time* (Oxford, 1994)

Gosden, C., 'Introduction', *The Prehistory of Food: Appetites for Change*, ed. C. Gosden and J. Hather (London, 1999)

Gray, H. L., *English Field Systems* (London, 1969)

Green, A., 'The Polite Threshold in Seventeenth- and Eighteenth-Century Britain', *Vernacular Architecture* 41 (2010), 1–9

Greenstein, D. I., *A Historian's Guide to Computing* (Oxford, 1994)

Grenville J., *Medieval Housing* (London and Washington, 1997)

Halliwell-Phillipps, J. O., *A Dictionary of Archaic and Provincial Words: Obsolete Phrases, Proverbs and Ancient Customs, from the Fourteenth Century* (London, 1901)

Hamilton, H., *The English Brass and Copper Industries to 1800* (London, 1967)

Harvey, C. and J. Press, *Databases in Historical Research* (Basingstoke, 1996)

Harris, Roy, *Reading Saussure: A Critical Commentary on the Cours de Linguistique Générale* (London, 1987)

Havinden, M. A., 'Agricultural Progress in Open-field Oxfordshire', *Agricultural History Review* 9:2 (1961), 73–83

Havinden, M. A., *Household and Farm Inventories in Oxfordshire 1550–90* (London, 1965)

Heal, F., *Hospitality in Early Modern England* (Oxford, 1990)

Heidegger, M., *Being and Time* (1927) (Oxford, 1962)

Hicks, D., 'From "Questions that Count" to Stories that "Matter" in Historical Archaeology', *Antiquity* 78 (2004), 934–9

Hicks, D. and M. C. Beaudry, eds, *The Cambridge Companion to Historical Archaeology* (Cambridge, 2006)

Hicks, D., L. MacAtackeny and G. Fairclough, eds, *Envisioning Landscape: Situations and Standpoints in Archaeology and Heritage* (Walnut Creek, 2007)

Hill, C., *Society and Puritanism in Pre Revolutionary England* (London, 1996)

Hillier, B. and J. Hanson, *The Social Logic of Space* (Cambridge, 1984)

Hodder, I., ed., *Symbolic and Structural Archaeology* (Cambridge, 1982)

Hodder, I., *Reading the Past* (Cambridge, 1986)

Hodder, I., *The Domestication of Europe* (Oxford, 1990)

Hodder, I., *Reading the Past: Current Approaches to Interpretation in Archaeology*, 3rd edn (Cambridge, 2003)

Hodges, M., 'Widows of the Middling Sort and their Assets in Two Seventeenth-Century Towns', *When Death Do us Part: Understanding and Interpreting the Probate Inventory Records of Early Modern England*, ed. T. Arkell, N. Evans and N. Goose (Oxford, 2000)

Hopkins, B. C., *The Philosophy of Husserl* (Durham, 2011)

Hopkins, S. V., 'Seven Centuries of Building Wages, *Economica* 22:87 (1955), 195–206

Hoskins, W. G., 'The Rebuilding of Rural England, 1570–1640', *Past and Present* 4 (1953), 44–59

Hoskins, W. G. 'Harvest Fluctuations and English Economic History, 1480–1619', *Agricultural History Review* 12:1 (1964), 28–46

Hoskins, W. G., 'Harvest Fluctuations and English Economic History, 1620–1759', *Agricultural History Review* 16 (1968), 15–31

Hoskins, W. G., *The Making of the English Landscape* (London, 2006)

Houlbrooke, Ralph A., *Church Courts and the People during the English Reformation, 1520–1570* (Oxford, 1979)

Houlbrooke, Ralph A., *The English Family 1450–1700* (London, 1984)

Houlbrooke, Ralph A., *English Family Life, 1576–1716: An Anthology from Diaries* (Oxford, 1988)

Hudson, P., *History by Numbers: An Introduction to Quantitative Approaches* (London, 2000)

Huizinga, Johan, *The Waning of the Middle Ages* (London, 1924)

Ingold, Tim, 'The Temporality of Landscape', *World Archaeology* 25:2 (October 1993), 152–74

Ingold, Tim, *Being Alive* (London and New York, 2011)

Ingram, M., 'The Reform of Popular Culture? Sex and Marriage in Early Modern England', *Popular Culture in Seventeenth Century England*, ed. B. Reay (London, 1985)

Ingram, M., 'Ridings, Rough Music and Mocking Rhymes in Early Modern England', *Popular Culture in Seventeenth Century England*, ed. B. Reay (London, 1985)

Ingram, M., 'Juridical Folklore in England Illustrated by Rough Music', *Communities and Courts in Britain, 1150–1900*, ed. C. W. Brooks and M. Lobban (London, 1997)

Insoll, T., *Archaeology, the Conceptual Challenge* (London, 2007)

Inwood, M., *Heidegger: A Very Short Introduction* (Oxford, 2000)

Jeckyll, G., *Old English Household Life: Some Account of Cottage Objects and Country Folk* (1925) (London and Sydney, 1975)

Johnson, M., *Housing Culture: Traditional Architecture in an English Landscape* (London, 1993)

Johnson, M., 'Rethinking the Great Rebuilding', *Oxford Journal of Archaeology*, 12:1 (1993), 117–25

Johnson, M., *An Archaeology of Capitalism* (Oxford, 1996)

Johnson, M., *Ideas of Landscape* (Oxford, 2006)

BIBLIOGRAPHY

Joyce, R., 'Writing Historical Archaeology', *The Cambridge Companion to Historical Archaeology*, ed. D. Hicks and M. C. Beaudry (Cambridge, 2006)

Kent, Joan R., *The English Village Constable 1580–1642* (Oxford, 1986)

Kerridge, E., 'Wool Growing and Wool Textiles in Medieval and Early Modern Times', *The Wool Textile Industry in Great Britain*, ed. J. J. Gerraint (London, 1972)

King, C., '"Closure" and the Urban Great Rebuilding in Early Modern Norwich', *Post-Medieval Archaeology* 44:1 (2010), 54–80

King, J., 'Historical Archaeology, Identities and Biographies', *The Cambridge Companion to Historical Archaeology*, ed. D. Hicks and M. C. Beaudry (Cambridge, 2006)

King, S., 'Chance Encounters? Paths to Household Formation in Early Modern England', *International Review of Social History* 44 (1999), 23–46

Knappett, C. and L. Malafouris, eds, *Material Agency: Towards a Non-Anthropocentric Approach* (New York and London, 2008)

Kopytoff, I., 'The Cultural Biography of Things: Commoditisation as Process', *The Social Life of Things: Commodities in Cultural Perspective*, ed. A. Appadurai, (Cambridge, 1986)

Kropotkin, P., *The Conquest of Bread* (1892) (London, 1972)

Kussmaul, A., *Servants in Husbandry in Early Modern England* (Cambridge, 1981)

Laslett, P., 'Introduction: The History of the Family', *Household and Family in Past Time*, ed. P. Laslett and R. Wall (Cambridge, 1972)

Laslett, P., 'Family and Household as Work and Kin Groups', *Family Forms in Historic Europe*, ed. D. M. Palliser, R. Wall, J. Robin and P. Laslett (Cambridge, 1983)

Laslett, Peter, *The World we Have Lost: Further Explored*, 3rd edn (Abingdon, 1983)

Laslett, P. and R. Wall, eds, *Household and Family in Past Time* (Cambridge, 1972)

Latour, B., *Reassembling the Social: an Introduction to Actor-Network Theory* (Oxford, 2005)

Law, J., *Organizing Modernity* (Oxford, 1994)

Lawrence R. J., 'Interpretation of Vernacular Architecture', *Vernacular Architecture* 14 (1983), 19–28

Layder, D., *Understanding Social Theory* (Thousand Oaks, 1994)

Leach, R., *Culture and Communication: The Logic by which Symbols are Connected* (Cambridge, 1976)

Leone, M., *The Archaeology of Liberty in an American Capital: Excavations in Annapolis* (Berkeley, 2005)

Levi, G., 'On Microhistory', *New Perspectives on Historical Writing*, ed. Peter Burke (Cambridge, 2001)

Lévi-Strauss, C., *The Raw and the Cooked* (London, 1969)

Lévi-Strauss, C., *Anthropology and Myth: Lectures, 1951–1982*, trans. R. Willis (Oxford, 1987)

Lobel, Mary, ed., *A History of the County of Oxford, Volume 7: Dorchester and Thame Hundreds*, Victoria County History (London, 1962)

Lock, G. and B. L. Molyneaux, 'Introduction: Confronting Scale', *Confronting Scale in Archaeology: Issues and Theory of Practice*, ed. G. Lock and B. L. Molyneaux (New York, 2006)

Locke, John, *An Essay Concerning Human Understanding in Four Books*, 4th edn (London, 1700)

Lorenz, C., *Studies in Animal and Human Behaviour* (London, 1971)

Lupton, H., *Extracts from the Accounts of the Proctors and Stewards of the Prebendal Church of the Blessed Virgin in Thame, Commencing in the Year 1529 and Ending in the Year 1641, and of the Churchwardens of Thame Beginning in the Year 1542* (Thame: Henry Bradford, 1852)

Macfarlane, A., *The Family Life of Ralph Josselin: An Essay in Historical Anthropology* (Cambridge, 1970)

Macfarlane, A., *The Origins of English Individualism* (Oxford, 1978)

Machin, R., 'The Great Rebuilding: A Reassessment', *Past and Present* 77 (November 1977), 33–56

Manning, R. B., *Village Revolts: Social Protest and Popular Disturbances in England, 1509–1640* (Oxford, 1988)

Marx, K., *Comments on James Mill* (1844), at www.marxists.org/archive/marx/works/1844/james-mill/index.htm (accessed 13 July 2015)

Marx, K., *Capital: A Critique of Political Economy* (1867), trans. B. Fowkes (Harmondsworth, 1976)

Marx, K., *Economic and Philosophic Manuscripts of 1844*, ed. D. J. Struik (London, 1973)

Maslow, A. H., 'A Theory of Human Motivation', *Psychological Review* 50:4 (1943), 370–96

Masse, H. J. L. J., *Chats on Old Pewter* (New York, 1971)

Mathieu, J. R. and R. E. Scott, 'Introduction: Exploring the Role of Analytical Scale in Archaeological Interpretation', *Exploring the Role of Analytical Scale in Archaeological Interpretation*, ed. J. R. Mathieu and R. E. Scott, BAR International Series 1261 (Oxford, 2004)

Mauss, M., *The Gift: Forms and Functions of Exchange in Archaic Societies* (1925), trans. I. Cunnison (London, 1969)

Mennell, S., A. Murcott and A. H. van Otterloo, *The Sociology of Food: Eating, Diet and Culture* (London, 1992)

Michaelis, F. R., *Antique Pewter of the British Isles* (London, 1955)

Michaelis, F. R., *British Pewter* (London, 1969)

Miller, D., *Material Cultures: Why Some Things Matter* (London, 1988)

Miller, D., *Home Possessions: Material Culture Behind Closed Doors* (Oxford, 2001)

Milward, R., *A Glossary of Household, Farming and Trade Terms from Probate Inventories*, Derbyshire Record Society Occasional Paper 1 (Chesterfield, 1977)

Motla, P., 'The Occupational Structure of Thame c. 1600–1700', *Oxfordshire Local History* 4:2 (1993), 62–77

Muir, R., *The New Reading the Landscape: Fieldwork in Landscape History* (Exeter, 2000)

Mukerji, C., *From Graven Images: Patterns of Modern Materialism* (New York, 1983)

Muldrew, Craig, *The Economy of Obligation: The Culture of Credit and Social Relations in Early Modern England* (Basingstoke, 1998)

Murdock G. P., *Social Structure* (New York, 1949)

Musson, Jeremy, Roy Strong and Paul Barker, *English Country House Interiors* (New Haven and London, 1978)

Norman, D., *The Design of Everyday Things* (London, 1998)

Orlin, L. C., *Private Matters and Public Culture in Post-Reformation England* (Ithaca and London, 1995)

Orlin, L. C., 'Boundary Disputes in Early Modern London', *Material London, ca. 1600*, ed. L. C. Orlin (Philadelphia, 2000)

Osborne, H., ed., *The Oxford Companion to the Decorative Arts* (Oxford, 1975)

Overton, M., 'Computer Analysis of an Inconsistent Data Source: The Case of Probate Inventories', *Journal of Historical Geography* 3 (1977), 317-26

Overton, M., 'Computer Analysis of Probate Inventories: From Portable Micro to Mainframe', *History and Computing*, ed. D. Hopkins and P. Denley (Manchester, 1987)

Overton. M., 'A Computer Management System for Probate Inventories', *History and Computing* 7 (1995), 135-42

Overton, M., 'Prices from Probate Inventories', *When Death Do Us Part: Understanding and Interpreting the Probate Records of Early Modern England*, ed. T. Arkell, N. Evans and N. Goose (Oxford, 2000)

Overton, M., J. Whittle, D. Dean and A. Hann, *Production and Consumption in English Households, 1600-1750* (London, 2004)

Oxfordshire County Council Record Office, *A Handlist of Inclosure Acts and Awards Relating to the County of Oxford*, Oxfordshire County Council Record Publication 2, 2nd edn (Oxford, c. 1975)

Pantin, W. A., 'The Development of Domestic Architecture in Oxford', *Antiquaries Journal* 27 (1947), 120-50

Parker, C., 'Introduction: Individual and Community in the Early Modern World', *Between the Middle Ages and Modernity: Individual and Community in the Early Modern World*, ed. C. H. Parker and J. H. Bentley (Lanham, 2007)

Parsons, Talcott, *Social Systems and the Evolution of Action Theory* (New York: Free Press; London: Collier Macmillan, 1977)

Pearson, M. P. and C. Richards, 'Architecture and Order: Spatial Representation and Archaeology', *Architecture and Order: Approaches to Social Space*, ed. M. P. Pearson and C. Richards (London and New York, 1994)

Pearson, M. P. and C. Richards, 'Ordering the World: Perceptions of Architecture, Space and Time', *Architecture and Order: Approaches to Social Space*, ed. M. P. Pearson and C. Richards (London and New York, 1994)

Pennell, S., 'The Material Culture of Food in Early Modern England, circa 1650-1750', D.Phil thesis (University of Oxford, 1997)

Piaget, J., *The Construction of Reality in the Child* (London, 1955)

Plumb, J. H. *The Death of the Past* (London, 1969)

Pollock, L., *Forgotten Children: Parent-Child Relations from 1500 to 1900* (Cambridge, 1983)

Porzig, W., 'Das Wunder der Sprache', *Probleme, Methoden und Ergebnisse der Modernen Sprachwissenschaft*, Vol. 71 (Munich and Bern, 1950)

Powell, C. L., *English Domestic Relations 1487-1653: A Study of Matrimony and Family Life in Theory and Practice as Revealed by the Literature, Law, and History of the Period* (1917) (New York, 1972)

Priestly, U., P. J. Corfield and H. Sutermeister, 'Rooms and Room Use in Norwich Housing, 1580-1730', *Post-Medieval Archaeology* 16 (1982), 93-123

Rapoport, A., 'Systems of Activities and Systems of Settings', *Domestic Architecture and the Use of Space*, ed. S. Kent (Cambridge, 1990)

Richardson, C. and T. Hamling, eds, *Everyday Objects: Medieval and Early Modern Material Culture and its Meanings* (Aldershot, 2010)

Robin, C. and N. A. Rothschild, 'Archaeological Ethnographies: Social Dynamics of Outdoor Space', *Journal of Social Archaeology* 2:2 (2002), 159–72

Roden, D., 'Woodland and its Management in the Medieval Chilterns', *Forestry* 41:1 (1968), 59–71

Russell, B., *History of Western Philosophy* (London, 1961)

Salmond, A., 'Theoretical Landscapes: On a Cross-Cultural Conception of Knowledge', *Semantic Anthropology*, ed. D. Parkin (London, 1982)

Sanders, D., 'Behavioural Conventions and Archaeology: Methods for the Analysis of Ancient Architecture', *Domestic Architecture and the Use of Space*, ed. S. Kent (Cambridge, 1990)

Savile, Anthony, 'Historicity and the Hermeneutic Circle', *New Literary History*, 10: 1 (Literary Hermeneutics) (Autumn 1978), 49–70

Schapera, Isaac, 'Should Anthropologists be Historians?', *Journal of the Royal Anthropological Institute of Great Britain and Ireland* 92 (1962), 143–56

Schumer, B., *Wychwood: The Evolution of a Wooded Landscape* (Charlbury, 1999)

Scott J. C., *Domination and the Arts of Resistance. Hidden Transcripts* (New Haven, 1990)

Shammas, C., *The Industrial Pre-Consumer in England and America* (Oxford, 1990)

Shanks, M. and C. Y. Tilley, *Re-Constructing Archaeology: Theory and Practice* (Cambridge, 1987)

Smith, Adam, *An Inquiry into the Nature and Causes of the Wealth of Nations* (1776), intro. E. R. A. Seligman (London, 1910)

Smith, Toulmin, *The Parish: Its Powers and Obligations at Law* (London, 1857)

Smyth, A., 'Introduction', *A Pleasing Sinne: Drink and Conviviality in Seventeenth Century England*, ed. A. Smyth (Cambridge, 2004)

Spencer, H., *The Principles of Sociology*, 3rd edn (London, 1898–1900)

Spufford, M., 'The Limitations of the Probate Inventory', *English Rural Society 1500–1800: Essays in Honour of Joan Thirsk*, ed. J. Chartres and D. Hey (Cambridge, 1990)

Steer, F. W., *Farm and Cottage Inventories of Mid-Essex 1635–1749* (London and Chichester, 1969)

Stobart. J. and A. Owens, eds, *Urban Fortunes: Property and Inheritance in the Town, 1700–1900* (Aldershot, 2000)

Stone, L., *Family, Sex and Marriage in England 1500–1800* (London, 1977)

Stone, L. and J. C. Fawtier, *An Open Elite? England, 1540–1880* (Oxford, 1995)

Struik, D. J., 'Introduction', in Karl Marx, *Economic and Philosophic Manuscripts of 1844* (1932), ed. D. J. Struik (London, 1973)

Tadmoor, N., 'The Concept of Household-Family in Eighteenth Century England', *Past and Present* 151 (May 1996), 111–40

Tarlow, S. and S. West, *The Familiar Past: Archaeologies of Later Historical Britain* (London and New York, 1999)

Thomas, J., *Time, Culture and Identity: An Interpretive Archaeology* (London, 1996)

Thomas, Keith, 'History and Anthropology', *Past and Present* 24 (1963), 3–24

Thomas, Keith, *Religion and the Decline of Magic* (London, 1971)

Tosh, J., *The Pursuit of History*, 3rd edn (Harlow, 2002)

Townley, Simon, ed., *A History of the County of Oxford: Volume 14, Bampton Hundred (Part Two)*, Victoria County History – Oxfordshire (London, 2004)

Trevelyan, G. M., *English Social History* (1944) (London, 1978)

Trigger, B., *A History of Archaeological Thought* (New York, 1989)

Underdown, D., 'The Taming of the Scold: The Enforcement of Patriarchal Authority in Early Modern England', *Order and Disorder in Early Modern England*, ed. A. Fletcher and J. Stevenson (Cambridge, 1985)

Veblen, T., *The Theory of the Leisure Class* (1899) (New York, 1953)

Vickery, Amanda, *Early Modern Things: Objects and Their Histories, 1500–1800* (London, 2012)

Wall, R., 'Beyond the Household: Marriage, Household Formation and the Role of Kin and Neighbours', *International Review of Social History* 44 (1999), 55–67

Wall, R., P. Laslett and J. Robin, *Family Forms in Historic Europe* (Cambridge, 1983)

Weatherill, L., 'Using "Dataretrieve" to Analyse Data from a Sample of Probate Inventories', *History and Computing*, ed. D. Hopkins and P. Denley (Manchester, 1987)

Weatherill, L., *Consumer Behaviour and Material Culture in Britain 1660–1760* (London, 1988)

Weber, M., *The Protestant Ethic and the 'Spirit' of Capitalism and Other Writings* (1905) (New York, 2002)

White, Archer M., *Outlines of Legal History* (London, 1895)

White, L. A., *The Evolution of Culture* (New York, 1959)

Whittle, J., 'The House as a Place of Work in Early Modern Rural England', *Home Cultures* 8:2 (July 2011), 133–50

Wilk, R. R., 'The Built Environment and Consumer Decisions', *Domestic Architecture and the Use of Space*, ed. S. Kent (Cambridge, 1990)

Wilkie, L. A., 'Documentary Archaeology', *The Cambridge Companion to Historical Archaeology*, ed. D. Hicks and M. C. Beaudry (Cambridge, 2006)

Wilson, P. J., *The Domestication of the Human Species* (New Haven and New York, 1988)

Wordie, J. R., 'The South: Oxfordshire, Buckinghamshire, Berkshire, Wiltshire, and Hampshire', *The Agrarian History of England and Wales, Volume 5(i): 1640–1750*, ed. J. Thirsk (Cambridge, 1984)

Wrightson, Keith, 'The Social Order of Early Modern England', *The World we Have Gained: Histories of Population and Social Structure*, ed. L. Bonfield, R. Smith and K. Wrightson (Oxford, 1986)

Wrightson, Keith, *Earthly Necessities: Economic Lives in Early Modern Britain 1470–1750* (London, 2000/2002)

Wrightson, Keith, *English Society 1580–1680* (Abingdon, 2003)

Wrightson, Keith and David Levine, *Poverty and Piety in an English Village: Terling 1525–1700* (New York, 1979)

Yentch, A. E., *A Chesapeake Family and their Slaves: A Study in Historical Archaeology* (Cambridge, 1994)

Index

Domestic commodities, spaces and activities are largely grouped, in order to aid cross referencing. Significant primary and secondary theoretical textual sources are listed. Decedents with *multiple* references are grouped by occupation category. Images are listed in italics. Bold indicates the main discussion of an item or concept. n = note reference

STUDIES IN EARLY MODERN CULTURAL,
POLITICAL AND SOCIAL HISTORY